Britain, Egypt, and Iraq during World War II

Britain, Egypt, and Iraq during World War II

The Decline of Imperial Power in the Middle East

Stefanie Wichhart

I.B. TAURIS
LONDON • NEW YORK • OXFORD • NEW DELHI • SYDNEY

I.B. TAURIS
Bloomsbury Publishing Plc
50 Bedford Square, London, WC1B 3DP, UK
1385 Broadway, New York, NY 10018, USA
29 Earlsfort Terrace, Dublin 2, Ireland

BLOOMSBURY, I.B. TAURIS and the I.B. Tauris logo are trademarks of Bloomsbury Publishing Plc

First published in Great Britain 2022

Series design by Adriana Brioso
Cover image: British troops in Baghdad, 11 June 1941.
(© Imperial War Museum [E 3464])

A catalogue record for this book is available from the British Library.

A catalog record for this book is available from the Library of Congress.

ISBN: HB: 978-0-7556-3452-1
PB: 978-0-7556-4419-3
ePDF: 978-0-7556-3453-8
eBook: 978-0-7556-3454-5

Typeset by Integra Software Services Pvt. Ltd.

To find out more about our authors and books visit www.bloomsbury.com and sign up for our newsletters.

Contents

List of Illustrations		vi
List of Maps		vii
Acknowledgements		viii
Note on Names and Transliteration		ix
Introduction		1
1	The Shadows of War, September 1938–August 1939	9
2	"We Have Nothing to Do with That War," September 1939–April 1940	21
3	Calling Britain's Bluff in the Middle East, May 1940–January 1941	35
4	Iraq and the Rashid 'Ali Coup, January 1941–May 1941	47
5	Getting the "Muddle out of 'Muddle East,'" June 1941–December 1941	61
6	Abdin Palace and "British Bayonets," January 1942–October 1942	75
7	"The Cause of the United Nations Is the Cause of the Arab Nation," November 1942–June 1943	91
8	"Let Us Stand by Our Friends," March 1943–December 1943	107
9	Democracy and Development, January 1944–September 1944	121
10	Fighting the New Protectorate and the New Mandate, September 1944–May 1945	135
11	War's End, May 1945–September 1945	149
12	The Postwar "Bill of Reckoning" and the Decline of Imperial Power, 1945–6	161
Notes		173
Bibliography		216
Index		223

Illustrations

Cover Image: Original caption: "British troops looking at the old city of Baghdad from a balcony." June 11, 1941. Imperial War Museum (E 3464)

1 British Ambassador Sir Miles Lampson, Oriental Counsellor Sir Walter Smart, and Crown Prince Muhammad 'Ali at an embassy party in Cairo, April 1942. Imperial War Museum (E11060) 81
2 Egyptian air raid wardens in Cairo during the Flap, July 1942. Imperial War Museum (E15054) 86
3 Publicity for the elite: A film viewing in Baghdad, December 1941. Imperial War Museum (K1364) 99
4 Publicity for the masses: The river steamer *Showboat* hosts viewings of British publicity films along the Euphrates River, July 1944. Imperial War Museum (K7174) 99
5 Wendell Willkie at a British embassy luncheon in Baghdad, 1942. Imperial War Museum (K3578) 103

Maps

Map 1	Egypt	x
Map 2	Iraq	xi

Acknowledgements

"Slow and steady wins the race" has always been my theme as a researcher, and this project has indeed been an extended enterprise. I remain grateful for the support and encouragement I received in the early stages of my research as a graduate student at the University of Texas at Austin. Wm. Roger Louis supervised the dissertation from which this current work has evolved and instilled in me, as for so many other historians, an appreciation of the joys of archival research and the historian's craft. Foreign Language and Area Studies (FLAS) funding from the Center for Middle Eastern Studies supported my Arabic language training and research funding from the Department of History provided me with the luxury of a year delving into the archives in the UK. The archivists and librarians at the National Archives in Kew, the Asian and African Studies Reading Room of the British Library, and the Middle East Centre Archive, St. Antony's College, Oxford, all provided most welcome assistance.

I had the great pleasure of participating in the 2008 International Research Seminar on Decolonization sponsored by the National History Center, which allowed me to explore where my work fits in the broader history of decolonization. The camaraderie and delightful intellectual debate of the seminar, balanced with research time at the National Archives and Records Administration (College Park, MD) and the Library of Congress, were a wonderful gift. I am honored to be part of the circle of historians in the field of decolonization studies whose scholarship was shaped by these workshops.

I have explored the themes of Arab internationalism, British propaganda, and Britain's Kurdish policy in greater depth in previously published journal articles and chapters in edited collections. Portions of those texts are included here by permission of the original publishers and are listed in the endnotes and the bibliography. I thank the Imperial War Museum for permission to reproduce the historical photographs included in this work.

As a historian I have found a welcome home in the Department of History at Niagara University in western New York. My colleagues have helped me navigate the challenge of balancing teaching and research and I have benefitted from the cross-pollination of ideas that occurs in a small and collegial department. The Niagara University Research Council has provided generous funding for archival research trips, and the librarians and staff of the Niagara University library have offered world-class research assistance in tracking down sources. Kristi Barnwell, a friend from graduate school, supplied some much-needed accountability in the later stages of this project.

While historical research is usually a solitary endeavor, it does not take place in a vacuum. I am deeply grateful for the lifelong encouragement of my parents Wright and Jeannine Ellis who instilled in me a curiosity about the world and offered a welcome home base and logistical support through all of my travels. I dedicate this book to my husband, Ryan, who saw it through from beginning to end, and to Ben, Sam, and Sarah, who joined us along the way.

Note on Names and Transliteration

This work spans the fields of British imperial history and Middle Eastern history, and my hope is that it might contribute to the ongoing dialogue between them. However, this raises the challenging issue of transliteration of Arabic names and titles as the system used by British officials in the archival sources differs from that in current usage. While I have retained the original spellings in all direct quotes, in the rest of the text I have followed a simplified version of the *International Journal of Middle East Studies* guidelines without diacritics and with the substitution of ' for ' *ayn* and ' for *hamza*. For some prominent leaders I have used a more widely recognized spelling (e.g., King Farouk). In cases where the spelling of a name used in the British archival sources may not be readily apparent from the transliteration, I have added an explanatory endnote.

Maps

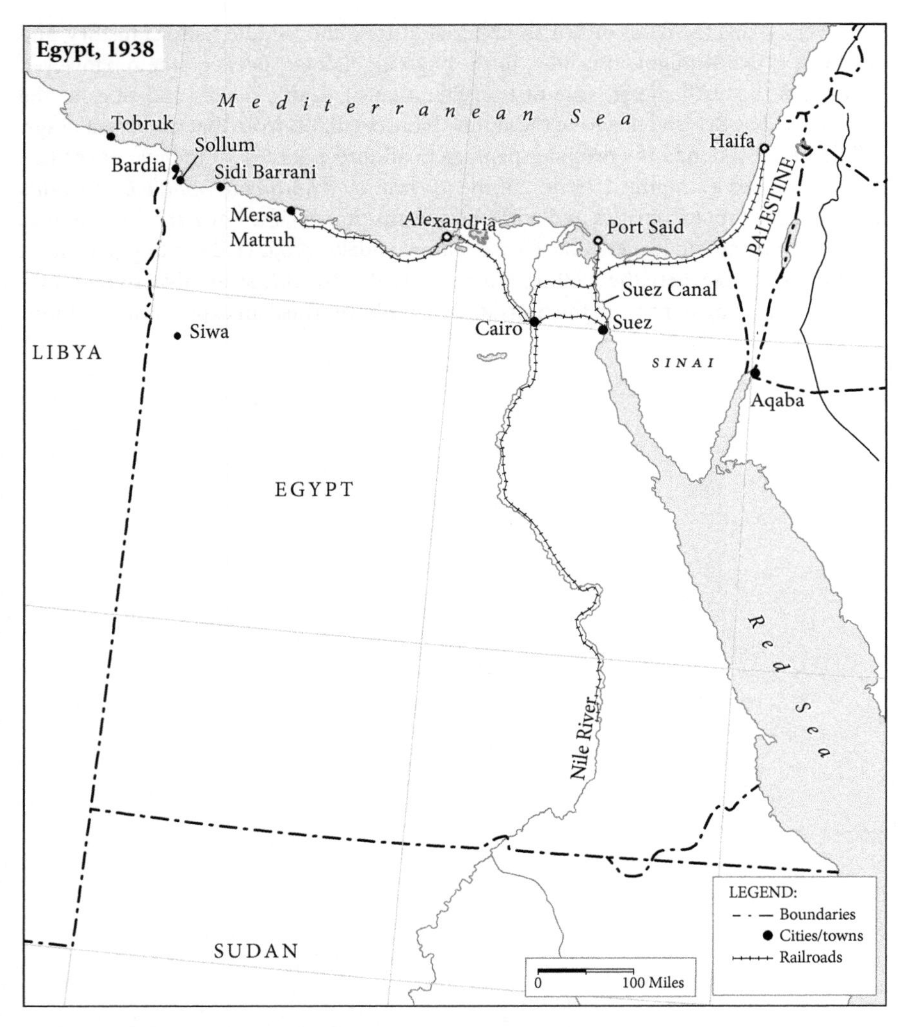

Map 1 Egypt 1938: The map indicates the status of the railroad lines on the eve of the war, linking Cairo, Alexandria, and the Suez Canal Zone with Upper Egypt in the south and Palestine to the east, and terminating at Mersa Matruh in the Western Desert.

Adapted from: "Sketch Map of the Middle East," 1938, published by the War Office, MPI 1/464/5, The National Archives, UK.

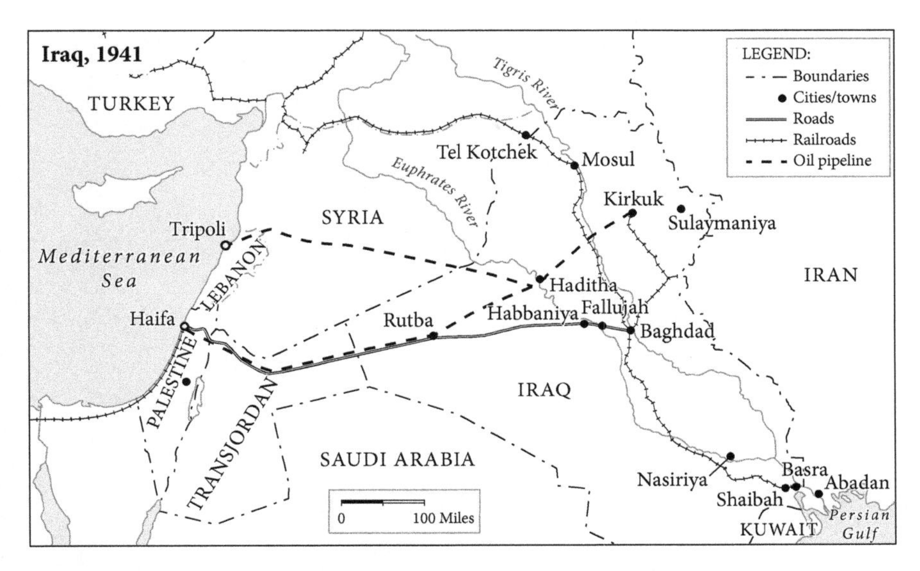

May 2 Iraq 1941: The Haifa-Baghdad road connected the railroad from Basra to Baghdad with that from Haifa to the Suez Canal Zone, forming the basis of Britain's projected overland route for troop reinforcements. Habforce followed the portion of the road from Transjordan to Habbaniya in its relief operation during the Rashid Ali coup in 1941 (see Chapter 4).

Adapted from: "Sketch Map of the Middle East," 1938, published at the War Office, MPI 1/464/5, The National Archives, UK; "Syria and Iraq Mid 1941" (Map 17) in I.S.O. Playfair, *The Mediterranean and Middle East*, vol. 2 (London: Her Majesty's Stationery Office, 1956); and Daniel Silverfarb, *Britain's Informal Empire in the Middle East* (NY: Oxford University Press, 1986), 2.

Introduction

Elizabeth Monroe, in her classic account of British policy in the Middle East, noted that "British paramountcy endured until the end of the Second World War, and for longer in Middle Eastern imaginations; the shadow of power is long, and remains after the substance has gone."[1] Monroe observed this process firsthand, having served as director of the Middle East Division of the Ministry of Information in London during the war, responsible for molding the vision of Britain to be projected to the Middle East at a time when Britain's fortunes were at their lowest. The military history of the region during the war has been well told: the spectacular North African campaign, with desert territory switching hands over three years, the 1941 military operations in Iraq, Syria, and Iran to remove Axis influence, and the opening of the Persian Corridor to funnel Allied supplies to the Soviet Union. From the perspective of the prosecution of the war and the immediate objective of victory over fascism, Britain's policies were ultimately successful. The lines of communication to India did not fall to the Axis, Rommel did not march down the streets of Cairo, Middle East oil supplies remained safe, and with the exception of the tumultuous events of 1941 the region remained generally quiet for the duration. Yet by 1945 it was evident that the war had not resulted in a resurgent imperial presence but rather the decline of British power, a development fostered partly by the growing influence of other outside actors in the region, the United States and the Soviet Union, as well as by Britain's own wartime policies.

The Second World War in the Middle East is most frequently examined as either the postscript to the interwar period debates about British strategy in the Mediterranean or the prelude to the Cold War and era of decolonization. This work highlights the way in which the events, institutions, and rhetoric of the war were woven into the fabric of Anglo-Iraqi and Anglo-Egyptian relations at the local level over the complete arc of the conflict, from the debates about appeasement during the Munich crisis of September 1938 through the immediate postwar period. British officials on the spot were well aware of the potential long-term consequences of policies adopted to meet the exigencies of wartime but these considerations were secondary to the immediate war effort, especially in the difficult early years of 1940–2. The spring and summer of 1943 served as the critical pivot point not just for the Second World War but also for

Britain's relationship with the Arab states. It is the decisions made during this second act of the war in the Middle East, after the Axis threat largely receded, that hastened the transition from substance to shadow, shaped postwar relations, and solidified the tensions surrounding British motives and influence that lingered long after the British troops had departed.

The wartime experience of Egypt and Iraq provides a valuable lens for exploring this region-wide phenomenon. Egypt and Iraq were of vital strategic importance to Britain but its ability to secure its objectives in these states was complicated by the fact that they were not under direct British administrative control. Both were independent states within the heavily circumscribed parameters outlined in the 1930 Anglo-Iraqi Treaty, which came into effect in 1932, and the 1936 Anglo-Egyptian Treaty. The Second World War proved to be the greatest test case of the "empire by treaty" system of informal empire through bilateral treaties, which will be examined in more depth below.[2]

Military power remained an important component of empire by treaty and the treaties carefully delineated not only how many British troops could be stationed in each country, but where they could be located. During the war these numbers swelled, and the treaty institutions designed to set clear parameters on British influence were stretched to form a vast umbrella that sheltered a whole host of new military, intelligence, and propaganda organizations operating in both countries in order to meet wartime requirements. The "Middle East" from the British military perspective was not a geographic term but a reference to the expansive Middle East Command, which encompassed operations stretching from Libya to Iraq and from Greece to East Africa. In November 1941 Middle East Command "had 750,000 troops between Libya and Iraq, with over 14,000 in and around Cairo itself," and by the end of the war, the Suez Canal Zone Base was the largest military installation in the world.[3] Iraq was passed back and forth between the Middle East Command, India Command, and the various structures that ultimately became the independent Persia and Iraq Command (PAIC) with headquarters in Baghdad, a reflection of its liminal position between multiple strategically important spheres of influence.

While British officials readily admitted that this expanded wartime troop presence played a crucial role in discouraging local unrest, they also believed that British prestige was vital to securing local compliance in their wartime requirements. As a Foreign Office official noted in the difficult days of 1940: "Prestige is a hateful word, but nevertheless it is the one thing which holds our position in the Middle East together and must continue to do so until we are militarily much stronger there than we are at present."[4] Prestige is admittedly a vague term, but to British officials during the war it came to mean many things: convincing local populations of their ability and will to protect them, tackling challenges created by the war and the massive military presence in cooperation with local governments, and living up to the Allied publicity messages and the vision they conveyed about what the Allies were fighting for, not as defined in London but as interpreted and appropriated in the local context. At the same time, all of these messages led to public debates about what it meant to be an independent state in treaty relations with Britain in the transformed world emerging from the war, a debate that would shape postwar treaty negotiations. Editorials, political cartoons, petitions, and party manifestos reveal the way in which this wartime rhetoric was incorporated into critiques of the war's impact as well as longstanding domestic political rivalries and debates.

Tracing the wartime transition from substance to shadow in Egypt and Iraq requires looking behind the front lines to the decisions made by the British officials, diplomats, advisers, and publicity staff charged with keeping the Middle East quiet in the midst of these military operations. The outbreak of war in September 1939 found British officials scrambling to breathe new life into ossified institutions of British influence and prestige that had been allowed to wither in the interwar period. During wartime the embassies took on additional functions as the heart of what the American legation in Baghdad described as the "British control apparatus," which included networks of publicity and political intelligence organizations.[5] The buildup of these organizations did not escape the notice of the local population and shaped the form of the postwar British shadow by reinforcing local suspicions of British intervention, what one official described as its role as the "silent, omnipotent power."[6] Monroe's comment alludes to the long-term legacy of this development.

Intervention through the mechanism of the treaties proved to be insufficient to meet British demands in the critical years 1941–2, leading to the 1941 British military operations in Iraq after the Rashid ʿAli coup and the 1942 Abdin Palace incident in Egypt. In facing these internal crises, military and civilian officials debated: was the moment militarily opportune, as well as politically opportune for British intervention, and was the threat so severe that it was worth the sacrifice on other fronts? As a result of these two events, hostile leaders were replaced with pro-British governments led by Mustafa al-Nahhas in Egypt and Nuri al-Saʿid in Iraq. This facilitated greater cooperation in the interest of the war effort through the critical period of 1942, but it came at a price. Both governments faced repeated charges of corruption and inefficiency and were regarded by local citizens and the British themselves as conservative and reactionary forces. The methods by which these leaders came to power, by "British bayonets" as Egyptian critics frequently described it, weakened their nationalist credentials and the British were viewed as complicit in their failures.

As the immediate threat of the war receded in 1943, the treaty argument in support of Britain's expanded presence wore thin with Arab nationalists. For the Allies, the Arab states still had a vital role to play in the economic realm as a source of grain and oil, as a base for the launching of operations in the Mediterranean, and for the transport of supplies to the Soviet Union. These requirements led to greater economic controls and increased intervention in the internal affairs of Egypt and Iraq, undermining the façade of independence.

In 1943, British and Arab leaders began turning their attention to their desiderata for the postwar Middle East. Arab nationalists saw the approaching end of hostilities as a chance to push for British evacuation and harness the internationalist rhetoric of Allied declarations, in particular the Atlantic Charter and United Nations Declaration, to support their calls for independence. The Arab unity movement, which culminated in the formation of the Arab League in 1945, was envisioned as a way to address the future of Palestine, Syria, and Lebanon and also, for Egypt and Iraq, a tactical move to internationalize their calls for treaty revision with Britain. It was the expectation of postwar conferences where the Arab states might present their demands that drove both countries to declare war, Iraq in 1943 and Egypt in 1945. War's end saw increased pressure for the opening of negotiations on treaty revision, forcing Britain to reassess the means by which it could ensure that its Arab allies remain within the British orbit. The changing realities of the postwar environment called for new forms of British influence using technical advisers and development projects, although financial limitations and the suspicions generated by the wartime control apparatus undermined their efficacy.

A comparative study that unfolds against the backdrop of the complex local, regional, imperial, and global events of the Second World War creates special challenges in balancing depth and breadth. The chapters below examine key episodes that highlight the many ways in which the war transformed the Anglo-Egyptian and Anglo-Iraqi relationships, laying the foundation for decolonization in the postwar period. Space does not allow for a full recounting of the wide-ranging debates over British strategic planning or the operational history of the Second World War in the Middle East.[7] Nonetheless, it is important to keep in mind that events on the front lines, whether in the Western Desert or Greece or further afield in the Soviet Union or the Pacific theater, shaped the decisions of British military and civilian officials and their Arab counterparts. One embassy official recalled of wartime Cairo: "War rumbled beneath the dance-floor," and the broader wartime narrative and the heavy reality of conflict rumbled beneath the more localized events and debates presented here.[8]

Empire by Treaty

A frequent wartime British refrain was the demand that Egypt and Iraq observe both the "letter and the spirit" of the treaties of alliance, exposing the inherent tension between Britain's expansive interpretation of treaty obligations and Egypt and Iraq's minimalist interpretation.[9] In light of the central role the treaties played in British wartime policy-making toward Egypt and Iraq and in the response of local leaders, it is helpful to examine their genesis in greater depth. British officials hailed the 1930 Anglo-Iraqi Treaty and the 1936 Anglo-Egyptian Treaty as the culmination of a steady march toward self-government, in Iraq's case dating to the granting of the mandate, and in Egypt's case going back to the 1882 occupation.[10] Yet as a Commonwealth observer admitted, in fact Britain was "endeavouring to give to Egypt as small a present as possible, wrapped up in as large a parcel as possible."[11] Egyptian nationalists were under no illusions as to the size of the gift; Huda Sha'rawi compared the treaty "to a Christian marriage for which the bride pays the expenses and yet is bound to her husband for ever, even if she has to lead a miserable life."[12]

The concept of "empire by treaty" had a long history in the British Empire but was back in vogue in the interwar period. In Egypt and Iraq, treaties allowed Britain to transfer the façade of sovereignty to local rulers while ensuring British control of key military bases and access to critical local infrastructure in times of conflict.[13] Both the Suez Canal and the air lines of communication through Iraq were described as arteries of the empire, a reminder of the way in which Britain's strategic interests crossed national boundaries (see maps 1 and 2).[14] The Egyptian port of Alexandria was vital for the defense of the eastern Mediterranean and served as the base of the Mediterranean Fleet during the war. Iraq was an important imperial crossroads with rail links, Imperial Airways routes, and the oil pipelines which transported the oil of Kirkuk to the Mediterranean ports of Haifa and Tripoli. The overland route for troop reinforcements to the Canal Zone passed through Iraq via Basra and it held strategic importance as a potential base from which to protect the vast oil refinery at Abadan in neighboring Iran.[15]

The Anglo-Egyptian and Anglo-Iraqi Treaties shared many key provisions, but they tied Britain to two very different countries. Iraq was, by all accounts, a young state, created in the aftermath of the First World War from three Ottoman provinces of Basra, Baghdad, and Mosul and granted to Great Britain as a mandate under the League of Nations. Britain aimed to foster the ideal of a united Iraqi nation with loyalties over and above those of religion, ethnicity, region, and class, centralizing authority in Baghdad under the new Iraqi Hashemite monarchy. Yet in practice many of its mandate-era policies exacerbated existing divisions.[16] Iraq was the first of the mandates to receive independence, and its status as a sovereign state with representation at the League of Nations rankled the Egyptians, whose support for treaty negotiations in 1936 was partly driven by their desire, in High Commissioner Sir Miles Lampson's words, to have "the stigma of being treated worse than Iraq removed."[17]

Egypt was the giant of the Arab world, with a long history of centralized government emanating from Cairo. The British first occupied Egypt in 1882, a temporary measure formalized during the First World War when Britain declared a protectorate in the country. After the war, amidst widespread protests against British control, the protectorate was replaced with a treaty in 1922, but it suffered from a number of fatal flaws. It was imposed on Egypt unilaterally and the Four Reserved Points, which provided for Egypt's defense, administration of the Sudan, protection of foreigners and minorities, and British lines of communication in Egypt, angered nationalists by limiting Egyptian sovereignty. The British made numerous attempts at formalizing their post-protectorate status in Egypt, but all failed due to a combination of internal Egyptian political gridlock and Britain's unwillingness to make the military concessions demanded by the Egyptians.

Only six years separated the drafting of the Anglo-Iraqi and Anglo-Egyptian Treaties, and yet in the interim the international environment had changed dramatically. In 1935 Italy invaded Abyssinia, occupying it the following year. This event, added to Italian encroachment in Libya, unrest in Palestine, and the emergence of a united political front in Egypt, paved the way for the successful negotiation of a new treaty of alliance in 1936.[18]

The 1930 Anglo-Iraqi Treaty and 1936 Anglo-Egyptian Treaty reflect the delicate balancing act between Britain's priority of protecting its strategic interests and the Egyptian and Iraqi priorities of protecting their independence. If either Britain or its Arab ally found itself at war, the other agreed to "immediately come to his aid in the capacity of an ally."[19] Annexes set clear parameters on the number of British troops that could remain in country. Britain's military presence in Iraq was limited to two RAF air bases at Shaibah and Habbaniya, protected by the Iraqi levies.[20] In Egypt

Britain was limited to 10,000 troops and 400 pilots and support personnel to be placed in clearly defined locations to defend the Suez Canal, although in practice Britain exceeded this number. In an attempt to ease local concerns, both treaties stated that the presence of British troops did not imply an occupation, but rather the protection of British interests and the independence of Egypt and Iraq. Despite the similarities in the treaties, the military terms of the Anglo-Egyptian Treaty lay a heavier burden on Egypt than the treaty with Iraq. This gap was partly a reflection of geopolitical realities and the relative importance of Egypt and Iraq to Britain's strategic requirements, but also a product of the different contexts in which the treaties were drafted. As a Foreign Office official observed, "The post-treaty position in Egypt has been over-shadowed by the growing international menace, whereas Iraq gained her freedom in comparatively spacious times."[21]

A well-equipped modern army was the hallmark of an independent state and had been a priority of both the Egyptian and Iraqi monarchies in the interwar period. British military authorities realized that implementing the treaties would require building efficient local forces to take over some of the duties previously held by British troops, but at the same time they viewed strong local armies as a potential threat to imperial power.[22] Treaty annexes stipulated that Britain would provide military instruction and up-to-date military equipment. A British Military Mission to each country would serve as a liaison with local forces and oversee training. In return, both governments agreed to hire any needed military instructors from Britain and to use the same military equipment as the British forces to aid the alliance. These conditions became a recurring source of friction, as Arab officers often viewed the military missions as deliberately obstructing their modernization and hindering their effectiveness, especially when military supplies were in short supply during the war.[23]

If British interests were safeguarded by the military provisions of the treaties, Egyptian and Iraqi independence was fostered by their recognition of sovereignty. Although the buildings in which they operated remained the same, the high commissions now became embassies, and the high commissioners held the new title of ambassadors, signaling Egypt and Iraq's altered status. After signing the treaties, both states were granted the golden ticket of sovereignty, admission to the League of Nations, Iraq in 1932 and Egypt in 1937. Egyptian Prime Minister Mustafa al-Nahhas acknowledged this quid pro quo in a speech he gave in London at the signing of the Anglo-Egyptian Treaty, noting that the negotiations required them "to base our relations both on respect for *our* independence and on the safeguarding of *your* interests."[24]

Yet the treaties were far from equal, and sovereignty was granted on British terms. Even the change in diplomatic relations was in many ways symbolic and superficial. More than just buildings that housed diplomatic outposts, the British embassies in Egypt and Iraq retained many of the old functions of the high commissions and were also strong visual symbols of British prestige and influence. The British found creative ways to preserve this influence, folding some of the intelligence and advisory functions that British officials employed by the local governments had fulfilled back into the embassy structure. The decision to retain Sir Miles Lampson, who as high commissioner had negotiated the treaty on behalf of Great Britain, as Britain's first ambassador to Egypt, sent a clear message of continuity. A seasoned diplomat, Lampson's dominating personality ensured that the embassy weathered the transition to life under the treaty with British prestige and influence intact.[25] The new embassy in Baghdad did not enjoy the same kind of stability of leadership, and by the late 1930s Britain's footprint in Iraq had been dramatically reduced.

Shaped by the preoccupations of the interwar period, the Anglo-Iraqi and Anglo-Egyptian Treaties were designed to anticipate future conflicts. As Britain faced the growing German and Italian threat in the late 1930s and found its defense budget stretched thin, the treaties would prove their worth, with profound implications for Britain's execution of the war in the Middle East. British officials wondered if the treaties were sufficient to ensure that Egypt and Iraq cooperated on the war effort while Egyptian and Iraqi leaders expressed concern that these same treaties were being used to drag them into a conflict that did not concern them. The war was the exact contingency for which the treaties were designed and put their provisions to the test.

1

The Shadows of War, September 1938–August 1939

The September 1938 Munich crisis brought home for both Arab and British leaders the ways in which events in Europe would reverberate in the Middle East. In light of the Italian presence in Libya, Britain informed the Egyptian government that this was an "apprehended international emergency" and invoked its treaty rights. All three services reinforced their positions and British troops were sent to Mersa Matruh, with plans to send additional reinforcements from India. Britain found Prime Minister Muhammad Mahmoud's government to be extremely helpful in facilitating these measures, and took its response as proof of the value of the Anglo-Egyptian Treaty.[1]

Yet the crisis also raised questions about Britain's ability to protect small states and damaged its prestige in the Middle East. Both Egypt and Iraq were in treaty relations with Britain that were designed to provide for their defense and they had just witnessed the dismantlement of Czechoslovakia, a country that had a military treaty with France. Would their treaties be enough to protect them, or would the obligations they entailed undermine their sovereignty and put them in harm's way? Takla Pasha, proprietor of the Egyptian newspaper *al-Ahram*, told an embassy official that Egypt needed a strong ally and the clear lesson from Munich was that "England had given way to a show of force … Egyptians were seriously asking themselves whether the Anglo-Egyptian Alliance was really worth the candle."[2] Britain faced a real public relations challenge in Egypt; as one British official noted, "The moral of the recent crisis, as far as Egypt is concerned, seems to be that Egyptian policy in the event of war or rumours of war will depend partly on how much Egypt fears Italy, but even more on how much she respects our armed strength."[3]

The December 1938 Speech from the Throne to the Egyptian Parliament addressed the shadow of Munich, leading to a debate among Egypt's political elite as to the country's treaty obligations. Under Article 7 Egypt was committed to offer "all the facilities and assistance in his power, including the use of his ports, aerodromes and means of communication," but did this mean that Egypt would be required to declare war?[4] In the ensuing debate former Prime Minister Isma'il Sidqi concluded that it did not but warned that the requirements of Article 7 would make Egypt a belligerent party by default. The country would pay a high price for cooperating with Britain in war and the treaty needed to permit Egypt to place its own interests first and act freely in decisions affecting its defense. As he later stated in defending his position: "In the light of the crisis of September … is not an Egyptian justified when he asks that Egypt and her inhabitants, to whom the Sudeten question is of very secondary importance to Egypt, shall not be dragged into a possible future conflict arising from this or from a similar cause?"[5]

Sidqi's speech caused an uproar and sparked an extended discussion in both Egyptian and British official circles as to Egypt's obligations to Britain should war break out in Europe. Saʿdist Party leader Ahmad Mahir argued that Egypt should declare war when the time came and Prime Minister Muhammad Mahmoud reaffirmed the government's commitment to fulfill all of the terms of the treaty. He privately approached British Ambassador Sir Miles Lampson and suggested that an article in the *Times* responding to Sidqi's speech would be a useful warning. The article, which highlighted the fact that Sidqi was undermining the 1936 treaty which he had himself signed, had the desired result. It was widely quoted in the Egyptian press and Lampson was particularly amused by an Egyptian cartoon that showed Britannia, representing the *Times*, spanking Sidqi while the world looked on.[6] Yet the damage had been done, and Lampson reflected that "the evil seed sown during the September crisis, of the idea of Egyptian neutrality in the event of war began to bear poisonous flowers" in the following months.[7]

The Egyptian debate over Munich was part of a broader exchange in the local press about the rise of fascism, the health of Egypt's parliamentary system, and the merits of the Anglo-Egyptian Treaty. While many of these voices were quick to point out the threat that aggressive Italian and German expansionism posed to Egypt, these developments had troubling implications for Britain on the verge of war, exposing alternative visions for Egypt's future.[8] British officials had long described Egyptian politics using the analogy of the three-legged stool. According to this model the palace, the nationalist Wafd Party, and the British were the three pillars of stability, with power circulating among them in an orderly pattern that could, in the estimation of many British officials, predict future political developments.[9] By 1939 it was clear to the embassy that the other two legs of the Egyptian stool might prove obstructive to wartime preparations.

Sidqi's speech in support of Egyptian neutrality and sympathy for the fascist model was particularly troubling given his close ties to the palace and King Farouk. A long-time advocate of authoritarian government, Sidqi placed Egypt's response to the crisis within the larger global debate over the merits and weaknesses of fascism compared to Western liberalism. He called on the Egyptian people to follow Germany's example "to sacrifice individual interest for the good of the collective, in order to make Egypt a strong nation."[10] King Farouk, in a meeting with embassy officials in August 1939, echoed this argument, observing that given the serious international climate "it was surely advisable for Egypt to discard such aspects of democratic procedure as had proved useless or inapplicable and supplant them by something more calculated to 'get a move on.'"[11]

Lampson attributed these developments to the influence of Italian propaganda as "both the Italians and Germans were exploiting the idea that Egypt might be dragged by the Anglo-Egyptian Alliance into a war which was not directly her concern, and that her path of safety lay in re-insurance with Great Britain's probable adversaries."[12] Egypt had a sizeable Italian community and the Egyptian monarchy had long-standing ties to Italy, where Farouk's father had lived in exile. The palace had many Italian courtiers, from the king's hairdresser to his masseur to his mistress, all of whom were perfect mediums for the Italian legation to spread its message among Egypt's elite.[13]

The other leg of the stool, the Wafd Party, endorsed the fulfillment of Egypt's treaty obligations in the midst of the Munich crisis, but it weighed in on the broader debate over democracy versus fascism from a different perspective. The Wafd had its origins in the events surrounding the 1919 Egyptian Revolution and party leader Mustafa al-Nahhas had served as the main Egyptian negotiator of the 1936 Anglo-Egyptian Treaty during his tenure as prime minister. The Wafd prized its role as the nationalist and democratic voice in Egypt and argued that the problem was not liberal democracy itself but rather the way in which Britain had interfered with its smooth functioning by sins of both omission and commission. When the Wafd fell from power in 1937 Nahhas blamed Britain for failing to protect his administration from attacks by the palace and refusing to intervene in the 1938 parliamentary election in which, as the embassy admitted, "every form of pressure was applied to voters to support the Government candidates and to prevent them from voting for the Wafd."[14] In a spring 1939 anti-British press campaign the Wafdist press publicized examples of British intervention in internal Egyptian affairs that overstepped the parameters of the treaty. Lampson reported that the Wafd were now "encouraging non co-operation with us in any war on the grounds that the Egyptian people deprived of their democratic liberties, have no interest in fighting for democracies and that Egyptians should not be sent to be killed for British interests."[15] Nahhas informed a British official that, if allowed to enjoy a truly democratic political system, free of British interference, Egypt would gladly fight to defend freedom.[16]

In light of these challenges, in February 1939 Lampson undertook a detailed examination of the status of democracy in Egypt but reached a different conclusion. Democracy in Egypt was flawed not due to British intervention but due to internal factors, particularly the way in which it threatened the ruling class, who undermined it at every step. Experience had, in Lampson's opinion, proven that the constitutional model was unsuitable for Egypt and created the difficult situation where the king and court "must obviously dislike this democratic virus with which we have inoculated the Egyptian people." British intervention had not stifled democracy, and in fact those who yearned for a viable constitutional system in Egypt "turn naturally to England as the legendary Deus ex Machina, who, in spite of treaty fictions, is still confidently believed to be able to exercise decisive influence in these directions." Yet this very intervention further undermined Britain's ability to sell itself as a democratic power, a tension that lay at the heart of the three-legged stool model of Egyptian politics.[17]

How, then, could the British effectively respond to these threats and the trend toward Egyptian neutrality? In a statement that would define Lampson's doctrine for relations with the palace throughout the war, he wrote: "A youthful and headstrong Oriental potentate can in the end only be swayed by considerations of force. It lies with us so to strengthen our position in the Eastern Mediterranean that neither

King Farouk nor his entourage can have any doubt of our power to defend Egypt, and, if necessary, to force her rulers to comply with our wishes."[18] This sentiment reveals the rationale behind Lampson's relentless requests for troop reinforcements for Egypt, to the great frustration of the military authorities, but also provides insight into Lampson's notoriously strained relationship with King Farouk. The ambassador repeatedly vacillated between a strongly held conviction that Farouk must go, and a hope that "the boy may yet make good."[19]

The three-legged stool provided a convenient model for evaluating and predicting Egyptian politics, but it obscured a number of forces that were becoming increasingly important in the interwar period. The Wafd supported a paramilitary organization called the Blue Shirts while *Misr al-Fatat* (Young Egypt), an ultra-nationalist group led by Ahmad Husayn, organized the rival Green Shirts movement. Both provided the impetus for street protests and violence until the Mahmoud government banned paramilitary groups in 1938. *Al Ikhwan al-Muslimun* (the Muslim Brotherhood), established in 1928 by Hassan al–Banna, provided another focal point of opposition to the political status quo. Islamic movements in Egypt were emboldened by the palace's 1938–9 campaign to position Farouk as Caliph, with visions of leadership of the Islamic world. While the palace's effort ultimately failed, it added a religious dimension to Egyptian advocacy of the Palestinian Arab cause in the midst of the Arab revolt of 1936–9. The Muslim Brotherhood was particularly active in organizing protests and raising funds and in autumn 1938 Cairo hosted the World Inter-Parliamentary Congress of Arab and Muslim Countries for the Defence of Palestine.[20]

The status of Palestine became a lightning rod for growing anti-British rhetoric in Egypt in the late 1930s. The spring 1939 Wafdist anti-British press campaign, examined above, included attacks on Britain's Palestine policy sparked by the St. James Conference on Palestine held in London in February and March. In addition to the Zionist and Palestinian Arab delegations, the Arab states of Transjordan, Saudi Arabia, Iraq, and Egypt were invited to send representatives. When the conference ended in March without a resolution Ambassador Lampson was instructed to continue discussions with the Arab representatives in Cairo. The May 1939 White Paper, drafted with the changing international context and the looming conflict in mind, was designed to assuage Arab concerns. It set limits on Jewish immigration and land purchases and established a framework for a unified state in treaty relations with Britain.[21] These developments presented multiple problems for the British. Writing in May 1939, Lampson reflected on the events of 1938:

> The situation in Palestine was, indeed, a matter of the utmost concern on strategical grounds throughout the whole year. It placed the Egyptian Government in a very awkward position and complicated their day to day relations with the Embassy; it tended to detract from the mutual confidence which was essential for the implementation of the treaty; it was a happy hunting ground for the anti-British propagandist who did not shrink from endeavouring to enlist the sympathies of powerful Moslem divines in Egypt and elsewhere; and finally it denuded Egypt of much needed British troops just at a moment when their presence at their normal stations was most necessary.[22]

Preparing for War in Egypt

Britain praised Egypt's cooperation during the September crisis, which served as a "valuable rehearsal" for war, but it also exposed some worrying vulnerabilities in British defense plans for Egypt.[23] In February 1939 Sir Thomas Russell Pasha, the British head of the Egyptian police, bewailed the lack of preparedness for the impending conflict: "Never have things been more unsatisfactory out here … A complete lack of direction either from the Government or from the Embassy … 'Make believe' rules the country." As for intelligence, "no such thing exists. We know nothing of what … the Germans are doing inside the country."[24] Russell Pasha's comments reflect a sense of unease common among British officials in the Middle East in the early months of 1939. Given its strategic significance and geopolitical location, Cairo saw an expansion of the British presence on the eve of the war to address military, intelligence, and propaganda needs. Wartime organizations-in-waiting were placed under the umbrella of either the embassy or the military mission, in keeping with the terms of the Anglo-Egyptian Treaty.

Egypt's most immediate threat came from the Italian presence in neighboring Libya and East Africa, as the Italian garrison in Libya slowly expanded to a total of 215,000 men by August 1939.[25] The disparity in British and Italian air power in the region was a particular point of concern for the Egyptian prime minister, who requested that Britain send additional reinforcements.[26] The threat of an Italian air attack loomed large in the minds of both British planners and the Egyptian public. Air defenses were vital to protect key strategic assets such as Alexandria harbor and the Suez Canal. A British anti-aircraft brigade arrived in Egypt in 1938 and trained local troops, and even at a time when there were great demands for anti-aircraft equipment around the empire and at home Britain sent additional guns to Egypt in 1939.[27] The decision was both strategic and political, as Axis propaganda capitalized on the threat bombing posed and the Foreign Office identified the fear of air raids as a root cause of the push for Egyptian neutrality.[28]

As Lampson alluded to, the Arab revolt in Palestine further complicated defense planning for Egypt. The Middle East Reserve Brigade, formed in 1938 to supplement the troops stationed in Egypt under the terms of the treaty, was transferred back and forth between Egypt and Palestine multiple times in 1938–9 in response to the ebb and flow of the revolt. One such transfer of troops to Palestine right before the Munich crisis was particularly problematic and further undermined Egyptian faith in Britain's ability to protect it. The arrival of reinforcements from India and three additional RAF squadrons helped to alleviate some of these concerns but British authorities in Egypt would repeatedly request more troops and equipment to prepare to face a potential Italian threat and reassure the public.[29]

Britain's strategic priorities in Egypt centered around four key zones, each with their own defense challenges. The Suez Canal Zone was vulnerable to air attacks and the potential for deliberate blockage of the canal by a scuttled ship remained a perpetual concern. Cairo served as the headquarters of British forces while the city of Alexandria was Egypt's key commercial port, the new base of the British Mediterranean Fleet, and the location of key fuel and supply reserves. The fourth key zone was the Western Desert on the border with Libya, with the port of Mersa Matruh as a particularly important outpost at the end of the railway line. As part of the 1936 treaty negotiations Britain had agreed to move British forces out of Cairo and Alexandria and concentrate them within the Suez Canal Zone. In return Egypt agreed to undertake a hefty list of infrastructure projects to facilitate communication, including expanded road networks and railway lines and the construction of new barracks in the Canal Zone at Egyptian expense. Subsequent discussions led to an Egyptian agreement to undertake significant improvements to the port of Alexandria.[30]

The international crises of 1938–9 made all of these projects even more vital and yet work had stalled as the full financial implications of these commitments became clear. The barracks issue was particularly sensitive for the Egyptian government because the removal of the British troops from the cities had been a critical nationalist demand in the treaty negotiations, and yet the public was balking at the cost at a time when Egypt's economy was struggling. Young Egypt argued that the money should instead be spent on improving Egypt's own nascent army and building Egypt's capacity to defend itself; other critics called for investment in domestic initiatives. In the end Britain agreed to cover half of the cost, but the construction of the barracks was effectively shelved and British troops remained in Cairo and Alexandria through the war.[31] This suited both the British and the Egyptians for the moment. As the official British history noted, "It was easy to sympathize with those Egyptians who felt that for the present there could hardly be too many British troops at hand, but who, on a longer view, looked forward to a happy condition in which there would be none."[32]

Britain's official policy toward the Egyptian army was "that they shall be developed into efficient modern forces capable of co-operating with the British Forces in the defence of Egypt."[33] The British Military Mission was charged with training the Egyptian army under the terms of the 1936 treaty. In the period after the signing of the treaty, the Egyptian army saw a rapid expansion, more than doubling its size in two years, with the opening of the officer corps to men from more modest backgrounds. This decision had significant long-term consequences, as it also contributed to the increasing politicization of the Egyptian army as these new officers were incorporated into existing patronage networks.[34] Among those who began their officer training as a result of this initiative were many of the future leaders of the Free Officers Movement behind the 1952 Egyptian revolution.[35]

An ongoing source of tension between the Egyptian army and the British Military Mission was the supply of equipment. Ambassador Lampson and the first head of the British Military Mission, General James Marshall-Cornwall, pushed for both troop reinforcements and equipment, with the latter going to creative lengths to create at least the appearance of meeting Egyptian demands.[36] In preparing for conflict Britain faced the challenging task of bolstering Egypt's defenses without provoking a nationalist response. The Wafd Party, for example, cited the work of the British Military Mission as evidence of Britain's determination to undermine Egyptian sovereignty, hampering the Egyptian prime minister's ability to cooperate on defense plans. The mission found its efforts at times obstructed by the Egyptian Ministry of War, which, as the embassy reported in 1938, had adopted a five-year plan for improvement but "successive Ministers had lacked the courage to carry through."[37] In August 1939 Egyptian army officers traveled to Turkey to consult on training methods but the venture was organized without consulting the British Military Mission. In response, Britain protested "this failure to fulfil the spirit of Anglo-Egyptian military co-operation."[38]

Summer saw additional reorganization of the military leadership in the Middle East. General Sir Henry Maitland Wilson arrived in Cairo in June 1939 to serve as the new general officer commanding-in-chief, British Troops in Egypt (BTE). In July General Sir Archibald Wavell was appointed to the newly created position of general officer commanding-in-chief, Middle East. Wavell, along with Air Chief Marshal Sir William Mitchell, the air officer commanding-in-chief, Middle East and Admiral Sir Andrew Cunningham, the commander-in-chief of the Mediterranean Fleet, all based in Egypt, would form the new High Command established in August "responsible for co-ordinating the defence policy in the Middle East."[39] MEIC, the Middle East Intelligence Centre (short title of the Combined Middle East Intelligence Centre), was formed to coordinate intelligence in the region, keep track of enemy propaganda, and offer suggestions on countering this propaganda to the Joint Intelligence Committee, to which it answered. These objectives would frequently put it in conflict with not only the British embassy in Cairo, but diplomatic posts throughout the region.[40]

By late August all three services in Egypt were prepared for approaching war. Wavell moved troops into the Western Desert and Wilson initiated nightly meetings with Egyptian Minister of Defence Saleh Harb Pasha and the new head of the British Military Mission, General Macready, to coordinate Egypt's defense arrangements. Troop reinforcements arrived from Palestine and India over the summer and on the eve of the war Britain had 36,000 troops in Egypt.[41]

Testing the Treaty in Iraq

The Munich crisis created fears of war in Iraq as well, leading to hoarding and a drastic increase in the price of imported food in autumn 1938. As in Egypt, the Iraqi government assured Britain of its intention to fulfill its treaty obligations but Iraqi observers drew their own lessons from the events. The embassy in Baghdad reported that, while generally positive about Chamberlain's settlement as a means of restoring peace, Iraqi newspapers contrasted "the success which has attended Germany's firm stand for the rights of the Germans in Czechoslovakia with the failure of the efforts made by the Arab countries to help the Arabs of Palestine and the moral is drawn that only those people who are strong enough to command respect can expect just treatment from others in this wicked world."[42] As the first of the mandated Arab territories to gain independence Iraq claimed for itself a special role as protector of the interests of those Arabs still under European control, a mission that complemented the Arab nationalist vision of a united Greater Syria.

Iraq in the late 1930s was still wrestling with the legacy of the mandate and Iraqi politics had spiraled into a cycle of coups and intrigues far removed from the representative government promised in the Constitution. King Ghazi, who took the throne on King Faysal's death in 1933, was initially quite popular with the Iraqi people, but lacked his father's political experience and the Iraqi monarchy proved ill-equipped to serve as a break on competing political forces. The monarchy and parliament failed to ensure smooth transitions between governments, leading the various factions to resort to other means. The 1936 coup was a watershed moment in Iraqi history and subsequent governments only held office with the support of the increasingly politicized Iraqi army dominated by the ex-Sharifian officers, Ottoman officers who had fought with Faysal in the Arab Revolt during the First World War.[43]

It was yet another coup in this endless cycle that returned Prime Minister Nuri al-Sa'id to power in December 1938. One of Britain's most stalwart allies in Iraq, Nuri posed a number of dilemmas for the British. He was widely regarded as the politician most likely to ensure that Iraq fulfilled the terms of the Anglo-Iraqi Treaty in case of war, but his public support for Britain, and the general sense that he was a tool of the British, led many Iraqis to oppose his return to power.[44] These public perceptions of Nuri's allegiances hid a more complex agenda. Cooperation with the British was a means of achieving his dream of Arab unity, but this goal often put him at odds with the British over Palestine and Syria.

The international crises of the late 1930s brought home for the British the importance of resolving these issues to win Arab support in any future conflict. Groups in Iraq had raised funds and supplied arms to support the Arab revolt in Palestine and Nuri had represented Iraq at the St. James Conference on Palestine in London.[45] In March 1939, in the midst of these negotiations, the Government of Iraq presented the embassy with the findings of a study they had commissioned on Iraq's responsibilities under the treaty in time of war. It noted that the treaty brought obligations but "at the same time Iraq also has obligations, of a nature not less important than those devolving upon her under the said treaty, towards neighbouring Arab countries who are still awaiting the attainment of the independence promised them long ago by Mandatory Powers."[46] In keeping with this study Nuri outlined a dual-track foreign policy, committed to both Britain via the treaty and to the Arab states.[47]

Britain, however, had grave doubts as to Iraq's ability to fulfill its treaty obligations while also championing the Arab nationalist cause. These fears were reinforced when, later that month, Baghdad was the site of a large-scale anti-French protest. This March 31st demonstration was particularly noteworthy as it had government sanction and was far better organized than the usual spontaneous outbursts. British intelligence reports noted that "there were banners, loud-speaker vans, corner-boys with revolvers and daggers, coached in their responses to party cries with the painstaking accuracy of choir-boys to a litany, and all the elements of a carefully planned organization that belied any suggestion of spontaneity." While ostensibly aimed at French policy in Syria, Britain was tainted by association, with some of the slogans of the protest including "Down with the Colonisers and long live Arab Unity" and "England and France are our Shoes."[48]

Iraqi support of Syria went beyond demonstrations to include finances and arms. As Franco-Syrian treaty negotiations stalled, members of the Syrian Nationalist Party fled to Iraq. RAF Intelligence noted in April 1939 that the Syrian issue aroused even more anger in Iraq than the status of Palestine and the presence of Syrian teachers infused pan-Arab, anti-British sentiment into the Iraqi school system.[49] Even more troubling to British officials, anti-British and pan-Arab sentiment made

Iraq vulnerable to German influence. It was an ideal base for German propaganda to the Arab world as its independence meant less Anglo-French surveillance and it hosted large numbers of Arab nationalists in exile from both Palestine and Syria. The Muthanna Club, established by the Shawkat family in Baghdad as a literary society, became the focal point of extreme pan-Arabism, attracting not only young Iraqis but youth from around the region. Dr. Amin Ruwayha, a prominent member of the club, was in close touch with the German legation, and the club's headquarters also hosted the Palestine Defence Society (PDS), which had official sanction and counted Minister of Defence Taha al-Hashimi among its former presidents.[50] All government officials were pressured to contribute a portion of their salary to the work of the society, and the reach of the PDS extended beyond political circles in Baghdad, as they circulated pamphlets in the Iraqi provinces.[51]

The limitations on Britain's military presence in Iraq and the weakness of its diplomatic presence hampered Britain's ability to respond to these crises. The staff of the embassy was far smaller than that of the high commission that it replaced and suffered from frequent turnover in leadership.[52] When Sir Basil Newton arrived in Baghdad in May 1939, he was the fourth ambassador in five years and it was his first post in the Middle East. The Oriental Secretariat at the embassy in Baghdad did not exert the same influence over Iraqi affairs as its counterpart in Egypt, and while they could still rely on a network of British advisers within the Government of Iraq, their numbers had been greatly reduced under the Anglo-Iraqi Treaty. Among those who remained was C. J. Edmonds, adviser to the Ministry of the Interior.[53] Edmonds had a long history of service in Iraq and was valued by both Iraqi and British officials as an expert on tribal affairs. His position within the Iraqi government allowed him to keep a close watch on Iraqi politics and gave him a different perspective on events from that of the embassy staff.

The treaty also transformed Britain's presence in the provinces and officials frequently lamented the lack of information on developments outside Baghdad. Under the mandate the British had maintained an extensive surveillance apparatus in the Iraqi provinces that was largely dismantled after 1932. The British Military Mission was charged with liaison with the Iraqi army but found it difficult to exert its influence and gather information and, as with its counterpart in Egypt, its inability to provide the requested military supplies further undermined its effectiveness.[54] Britain maintained consulates in Mosul and Basra, but for knowledge of developments in the more remote areas of the country, the embassy relied on the reports of RAF area liaison officers (ALOs). A relic of the mandate period, the ALOs were hampered by local suspicions of their motives, and by the late 1930s they found it increasingly difficult to gather useful intelligence from Iraqi officials.[55]

The Iraqi government in Baghdad had limited control over outlying areas and tension in the provinces centered on conscription and land settlement issues. As the embassy reported on the situation in the Middle Euphrates in early 1940: "Taxes have not been collected, conscripts have not been sent in, the police have been unable to make arrests of wanted men several hundreds of whom are at large. If there has been outward calm it is because officials have seldom attempted to enforce the authority of government."[56] The weakness of the central government concerned the British as Iraqi politicians mobilized tribal support and fomented unrest to circumvent the constitutional system.[57] By 1939 tensions in Europe added a new dimension to this threat as there was growing evidence that Germany was distributing funds and propaganda in the Middle Euphrates to turn the Shi'i tribes against the government and planned to incite rebellions with the goal of disrupting British troop movements in time of war.[58]

The British frequently commented on how important individual relationships and personalities were to diplomacy in the Arab world, and yet this was an area where the Germans had a distinct advantage. The German legation included on its staff a number of officials fluent in Arabic who had extensive experience in the region. Dr. Fritz Grobba, a Middle East specialist, built up an extensive local network during his seven-year tenure as German minister to Iraq.[59] Grobba was assisted by Dr. Jordan, who had worked in the Iraqi Department of Antiquities and then been attached to the German legation as an archaeologist attaché, a position which served as thin cover for his role as Nazi Party representative in Iraq.[60] The Germans built social contacts with a wide range of Iraqis, many of whom fell outside the social sphere of the British embassy. While the British community in Iraq was frequently criticized for its insularity, the entire German community in Iraq was enlisted for the legation's propaganda efforts.[61]

The embassy viewed the combination of Arab nationalism and growing fascist influence as a particularly dangerous development. The anti-British sentiment that it fostered was not limited to the elite but permeated Iraqi society through the secondary school system and the Futuwwa movement.[62] This state-sanctioned youth organization was led by Dr. Sami Shawkat, the director-general of education and an ardent pan-Arab nationalist, who, in the words of the British ambassador, was "convinced that the amazing success of Nazism is a lesson to the Arabs in the way in which the regeneration and reunion of the Arab world could be achieved."[63] Shawkat viewed military training as the best way to inculcate Iraqi youth with the ideals of "manliness and chivalry" and revive the virtues that had been lost through years of occupation and imperial control. Participation in this military training was obligatory for all boys in the intermediate and secondary schools, while younger boys participated in a related scouting movement. Shawkat estimated that there were 100,000 boys in the Iraqi school system who would participate in the movement, and if each boy had contact with ten other Iraqis then "Through the one hundred thousand school boys the same spirit and qualities will be imparted to one million of the population of the country, and this one million constitutes no less than one-fifth of the whole population."[64]

The British were also troubled by German penetration into Iraqi markets and their use of commercial activity as a form of propaganda. German firms established in Iraq in the late 1930s sold cheap, highly subsidized German goods and placed advertisements in local newspapers to buy support. At a time when Britain was struggling to fulfill its military contracts with Iraq these investments sent a powerful message. These firms helped to finance German propaganda activities, provided a vehicle for getting foreign currency into Iraq, and gave cover to German intelligence operations. Herr Stocks, the commercial secretary at the German legation, would accompany engineers out to rural areas to help install German equipment. Fluent in Arabic, he built ties with local leaders and spread the message of the economic benefits of the Nazi system, arguing that National Socialism was what allowed them to provide these goods more cheaply than other countries.[65]

One of the more creative German plans was to offer 200–300 rams as well as German sheep breeding experts to improve Iraq's sheep stock. In return Germany would purchase the wool from the resulting sheep. The British embassy was concerned that this would not only tie Iraq's wool production to Germany, but also give free rein to "so-called German shepherds to wander all over the country, spying, making propaganda and preparing to make trouble in the event of an emergency."[66] There was little chance of success, as all European sheep stock introduced into Iraq in the past had died of malaria, but it provided useful cover for German reconnaissance in rural areas.

Britain was well-placed to coordinate a strong propaganda campaign in Egypt from the embassy given the extensive contacts staff already had with the local press and within the government. By contrast, British influence in Iraq was far more tenuous, weakened by a shrinking British presence and deliberate relationship building on the part of German representatives. One embassy official warned of comparing the situation in Iraq to that in Egypt, noting "here, they are at least ten years ahead of Egypt in independence."[67] The Foreign Office concluded that a strong pro-British campaign in Iraq would be ineffective if not impossible.[68] Instead, the embassy in Baghdad focused on cultural and educational initiatives to counteract the anti-British sentiment in the school system and Axis influence among youth.

On April 4, 1939, King Ghazi died after hitting an electric light pole while driving his car, igniting a series of crises that reinforced the precarious nature of Britain's influence in Iraq. The king's death raised the issue of royal succession, as his son was only a child. The British viewed the new regent, Amir 'Abd al-Ilah, as weak but friendly, further destabilizing the Iraqi monarchy as a political force and providing even greater scope for intervention on the part of the Iraqi military.[69] The accident led to widespread speculation about British complicity and a murder plot as it came at a particularly sensitive moment, just weeks after a thwarted assassination attempt against the king and at a time when tensions were high over developments in Syria and Palestine. German newspapers perpetuated the rumors of British involvement and long after the war it remained widely believed that the British, assisted by Nuri, were behind the king's death.[70] Pan-Arab sentiment was further fanned at the ceremonies observing the final day of mourning. Representatives from across the Arab world attended the event and it became a platform for speeches in support of Arab unity. Palestinian representative Akram Zuaitar called on Arabs to take advantage of the opportunity provided by the world crisis to push for the fulfillment of Arab aspirations in Palestine.[71]

Public mourning in Mosul soon turned violent. Rumor of Britain's complicity in the death of the king circulated around the city and a crowd marched on the consulate. When the British Consul Monck-Mason approached the crowd he was attacked and the consulate was burned. The murder of Monck-Mason shocked the British in Iraq and brought home the strength of anti-British sentiment.[72] Authorities concluded the attack was not premeditated but that "latent xenophobia had, however, been aggravated by the action of the authorities in allowing the dissemination of anti-British and anti-French propaganda through the medium of broadcasts, the press, demonstrations, and subversive lectures and discussions amongst the students in the secondary schools" creating "a potentially dangerous situation."[73] British investigators cited the influence of Mosul's Syrian teachers, who used their classes as a platform to spread anti-British and anti-French messages through their teaching of modern history, as a root cause of the attack.[74]

The Projection of Power, the Projection of Ideals[75]

As the British surveyed the political situation in the Middle East on the eve of the war, there was much that caused them disquiet. The events of 1939 demonstrated that in the Middle East British policy itself was a roadblock to efforts to win Arab support and ensure that Egypt and Iraq would fulfill their treaty obligations. British officials believed that if Britain could resolve the situation in Palestine and address Arab grievances most of the anti-British sentiment would disappear, not just in the Middle East but among Indian Muslims as well.[76] While not responsible for French policy in Syria and Lebanon, Britain was found guilty by association, and the cession of Syrian Alexandretta to Turkey in June 1939 only reinforced Arab frustrations with the policies of the Western powers. The Egyptian newspaper *al-Mokattam* noted, "The English Press ... reproaches the countries of the Near East for their relationship with the Axis Powers, but how can they expect the Arabs to profess sentiments of loyalty and friendship in return for the broken promises of the democracies?"[77]

The Egyptian response to the Munich Agreement and the anti-British protests after King Ghazi's death demonstrated that Britain would face two serious propaganda challenges in winning Arab support for the war effort. The first challenge was to convince Arab audiences that they had the will and the ability to win the war and protect Egypt and Iraq in keeping with the terms of the treaties. Projecting power requires having force to back it up, and Britain in 1939 faced the dilemma of needing to convince Arabs of their ability to defend them at a time when they were facing serious overextension of military resources.

Secondly, the ideological cause for which the British were fighting: democracy and freedom, in stark contrast to the slavery and oppression of fascism, should be the Arabs' cause as well. The projection of ideals was complicated by the uncomfortable question of continued British meddling in internal affairs and Egyptian and Iraqi sensitivities to any infringement of their national sovereignty. As a result, the rhetoric surrounding the struggle between fascism and liberal democracy and the events of the late 1930s were enfolded into existing debates about Britain's imperial presence. For many local observers, the events of 1938–9 provided a warning of the real dangers posed by fascist expansionism and reinforced their commitment to liberal democracy. To others the authoritarian model seemed to provide the antidote to what ailed both Egypt and Iraq: poorly functioning constitutional systems and weakness resulting from years of British control and intervention. Winning Arab support for the impending war would require both the projection of British power and the projection of British ideals, but officials found that these campaigns ran up against the stark reality of military limitations and regional policy.

2

"We Have Nothing to Do with That War," September 1939–April 1940

When Britain declared war on Germany the expectation was that her allies, including Egypt and Iraq, would follow suit and declare war simultaneously in a show of solidarity. The British did not expect the Arab states to make a substantial material contribution to the war effort, but they believed a declaration would rally local populations to the Allied cause, provide Britain with greater freedom to operate in the region, and reinforce the Anglo-Iraqi and Anglo-Egyptian Treaties. There was also great symbolic importance in getting Egypt and Iraq to declare war and this act came to be viewed as a litmus test of Egypt and Iraq's loyalty and their intention to carry out their treaty obligations in spirit as well as in letter.

Egyptians and Iraqis viewed the situation in a different light, perhaps best exemplified by the shaykh of al-Azhar, Mustafa al-Maraghi, who declared on behalf of Egyptians: "We have nothing to do with that war."[1] Despite Britain's prewar publicity campaigns, they had still failed to convince Arab leaders that this new conflict would not be another imperialist war. The early months of the war saw a series of extended debates in both Egypt and Iraq over what exactly their obligations were under their treaties with Britain, highlighting the complex negotiations around the notion of sovereignty in wartime. Neither state was convinced that the treaties demanded an outright declaration of war and doing so might open the door to greater British intervention, threatening their already fragile independence.

At the same time, the war also provided opportunities to press for concessions from Britain in return for cooperation. These sentiments alarmed British officials, who soon realized that a declaration of war by either country would be accompanied by expectations of a quid pro quo. By the end of 1939 future postwar desiderata were beginning to crystalize as the basis of wartime cooperation: for Egypt it would involve British evacuation and Iraq demanded concessions on Palestine and Syria.

There was another deeper cause for their hesitation to declare war, and that was the looming shadow of the Arab world's experience in the First World War. The biggest lesson the Arabs took from the earlier conflict was the heavy price to be paid for backing the losing side and a determination not to be left out of the settlement of their own destiny by the great powers. This drive led Arab leaders to make decisions that, to the British at the time engaged in a struggle for survival, smacked of ingratitude and naiveté. For the Arab states it was a different kind of war for survival, namely, the preservation of hard-won sovereignty.

Preserving the Status Quo

Egypt's response to the outbreak of war in Europe was complicated by the fact that internal politics were in a period of transition. Prime Minister Muhammad Mahmud, an able administrator well-liked by the British, resigned from office in August 1939 citing ill health. The king chose ʿAli Mahir, the chief of the Royal Diwan, as his replacement. The new prime minister issued strong statements of support to Britain, promising full cooperation and the fulfillment of all of the requirements of the treaty. Egypt implemented emergency measures such as an *état de siège*, the breaking off of diplomatic relations and commercial ties with Germany, and the institution of press censorship, and the Egyptian army took up pre-assigned posts in the Western Desert.[2]

The Iraqi government also implemented the emergency measures that had been planned in advance. Iraq broke off diplomatic relations with Germany; deported, interned, or turned over to Britain Germans residing in the country; and imposed censorship. The government declared a state of emergency, granting the minister of the interior special powers to deal with foreigners, and issuing a decree giving the government greater economic control.[3]

Despite this early action, both states stopped short of declaring war. ʿAli Mahir used a number of delaying tactics to deflect British pressure. He told Lampson that the real reason for the delay was that the Germans were holding Egyptians in Germany until they had confirmation that the Germans in Egypt had been allowed to leave. Given the gravity of the decision, he suggested that the Egyptian Parliament needed to be convened to declare war and, while he had the majority of the Cabinet behind a declaration, he wanted to wait until he had unanimous support.[4] Iraq's pro-British prime minister, Nuri al-Saʿid, pressed for an Iraqi declaration, but it soon became clear that the rest of the Cabinet and the army officers who helped to put him in power in 1938 did not support this decision.[5]

The British saw Egyptian and Iraqi declarations as closely linked, and hoped that if Egypt took the lead that Iraq would follow as a matter of prestige. Officials tried to keep each state in the dark as to the progress of negotiations with the other.[6] As deliberations continued through the month of September, it became increasingly clear that both Egypt and Iraq expected concessions in return for such a declaration, and the basis of these demands began to crystalize. ʿAbd al-Rahman ʿAzzam, one of the key opponents to a declaration in the Egyptian Cabinet, told an embassy official that the problem was that Britain expected Egypt to sacrifice and declare war on Germany without remuneration. Egypt wanted a declaration of Britain's intent to completely evacuate the country at the end of the war, pay all wartime expenses, support Egypt's claims in the Sudan, and also offer support for Arab unity.[7]

Iraqi leaders had their own demands, and on September 6 the Iraqi Cabinet issued a list of five assurances they requested from Britain before making a final decision. The first three related to the treaty; Iraq wanted assurance that declaring war would not involve additional obligations, that Britain would defend Iraq if attacked, and that Britain would provide financial assistance for military expenditures. The other two points reflect Iraq's postwar desiderata, including Minister of Defence Taha al-Hashimi's demand for representation at any postwar peace conferences, and also that Britain and France "will duly consider 'rights' of Arab states to whom the two Powers previously guaranteed liberty and independence especially since they have both now in war espoused the cause of liberty and independence of the nation."[8]

As the scope of Arab demands became clear, British officials began to question whether declarations of war were indeed necessary. Lampson and his staff concluded that other issues, such as local stability, were more important. As the ambassador reflected in his diary, 'Ali Mahir's government was "thoroughly bad" and in peacetime would have been replaced, but war called for a different response. There had been many rumors of 'Ali Mahir's anti-British feelings, and he had not come through on the declaration of war, but with that exception "Ali Maher has so far done everything we have asked him to do and done it extremely well and expeditiously." While he would be happy to see a change of government (as well as a change on the throne if need be), he doubted whether London would really follow through with the threat.[9]

The Foreign Office came to agree and on September 13 it instructed the embassies in both Cairo and Baghdad that they no longer needed to press for declarations of war. Newton informed the Iraqi government that if they did declare war Britain confirmed that they would be represented at postwar peace talks and that Britain intended to "carry out their undertakings to the Arab States." At the same time, Britain would not press for an actual declaration "if the Iraqi Government for their part are satisfied that they can in fact, without such a declaration, fulfill their obligations under the Treaty of Alliance."[10]

Once the initial window of opportunity had passed, Britain decided that it was better to be able to use the lack of a declaration as a means of quieting any calls for treaty revision after the war. As one Foreign Office official explained, "I always had a feeling that we might muddle through quite effectively without the declaration and have the compensation of having a grievance ourselves instead of having given the Egyptians one."[11] As for Iraq, the Foreign Office acknowledged that "conduct such as toleration of British forces on Iraqi territory in time of war, to say nothing of further measures taken by Iraqi Government such as interning and deporting German nationals ... is of so unneutral a character as to mean that for all practical purposes a state of war between Iraq and Germany must and does exist." The declaration was desirable "more for its moral than its practical results," and as long as the Iraqi government took the necessary measures the lack of a declaration would not prevent the British from making use of Iraqi territory as needed for the war effort.[12]

As the declaration of war debate died down, both Egypt and Iraq returned to business as usual. When war appeared immanent in August, the main question on the minds of Egyptians, as one observer noted, had been whether or not Italy would declare war. Italy's decision to declare a state of non-belligerence led to relief in Egypt.

This announcement removed the immediate threat and gave the British military a window of opportunity to pursue the infrastructure projects necessary to prepare for an eventual conflict in the Western Desert and a greatly expanded British troop presence in Egypt.[13]

The war was most evident in its impact on the local economies, exacerbating prewar financial challenges. Egypt's financial problems had a myriad of causes, from population growth, to the strain of defense costs on the national budget, to inefficiencies in the tax system. The outbreak of war led to an increase in the price of goods in Egypt as well as the loss of German markets for Egyptian cotton. Britain agreed to supplement the purchase of the cotton crop to replace lost German sales, but Lampson pressed London to provide more economic aid: "It is not a question of the economic rights of the Egyptian claim for this assistance from us. It is a question of political expediency."[14]

By October 1939 RAF intelligence noted that the war was not a pressing matter in Iraq either. The Anglo-Turkish and Anglo-French pacts alleviated Iraqi concerns about the security of the northern border and while it had disrupted trade and Iraq's oil revenue, in general "the War had dwindled in perspective" and "was now a convenient 'bargain counter' at which pan-Arabists could chaffer over the price to be paid for Arab loyalty to the Allied Cause. This feeling is not necessarily anti-British, but it is opportunist and, as such, devoid of sentiment, affection, or gratitude for past services."[15]

The war set in motion a series of unsettling developments including an influx of returning Iraqi students who had been studying in Germany and Iraqi politicians who had been summering in Lebanon. More troubling was the arrival of over 200 Syrian and Palestinian teachers who had been hired by the Department of Education and a number of Palestinian political refugees who had been living in Syria but, with the outbreak of war and the imposition of French wartime controls, felt it expedient to leave. The most notorious of these Palestinian exiles, the Mufti of Jerusalem al-Hajj Amin al-Husayni and his entourage, arrived in mid-October.[16] The Germans in Iraq had been expelled at the outbreak of the war but had now been replaced by a virulently anti-British, Arab nationalist contingent from Palestine and Syria.

British officials were well aware of the dangers posed by these developments. In November 1939 the War Office sent an alarmed message to the Foreign Office that raised a number of concerns with Iraq's actions, pointing to the threat posed by the mufti's presence in Iraq, the failure to declare war, and the dissemination of anti-British propaganda in the schools. Lacy Baggallay of the Foreign Office took a fairly pragmatic view that reflects the status quo policy that Britain would pursue during the early months of the war, namely to avoid stirring up trouble that might require more active British intervention. All of those charges were indeed "reprehensible" but in the end, the Iraqis were cooperating on most issues related to the war, and "allies are rarely entirely satisfactory." As far as the war effort went, "it is presumably in our interest that we should have as quiet a time as possible in Iraq and the other countries of the Middle East." In spite of the troubling activities of Syrian and Palestinian nationalists in Iraq, Nuri was carrying out the alliance and meeting British requirements on all major issues. If this was no longer the case they would have to act, but this would require troops.[17]

The Politics of Wartime Patronage[18]

While the status quo policy served Britain's wartime needs, it conflicted with another widely held goal: that of preserving British prestige and projecting British power. British officials believed that perceptions of British weakness in the war effort and Allied losses on the battlefield were more damaging than German propaganda. Local populations must be convinced that Britain still mattered and would ultimately win the war.[19] Lampson frequently echoed this refrain in his telegrams to the Foreign Office, and this became a real source of tension, as the ambassador at times took decisions that threatened to provoke an Egyptian response that would upset the status quo policy.

'Ali Mahir's prevarication on declaring war reinforced British suspicions of his motives. The treaty required Britain to consult with Egypt in case of conflict, but Lampson did not feel comfortable sharing confidential intelligence with the new prime minister, as he had with his predecessor, because he was convinced that the information would get to Germany.[20] 'Ali Mahir's new Cabinet was, in the words of one British official, a "brain trust" of experienced ministers, but the embassy questioned the loyalties of some of them, in particular 'Aziz al-Masri and 'Abd al-Rahman 'Azzam. Upon taking office 'Ali Mahir had promised swift administrative reform to force the Egyptian government out of its bureaucratic stupor, and one of his first acts was to purge the government of ineffective ministers in the name of efficiency.[21] The British detected more nefarious motives behind this action, as some of those dismissed were also well-known British allies. Lampson admitted some of them were not terribly effective administrators, but took these dismissals as a real affront to British prestige. G. H. Thompson, commenting on Lampson's concerns at the Foreign Office, agreed: "If the impression gets abroad that any Egyptian whose friendliness towards us is evident incurs a real danger of losing his appointment, we will be denied the collaboration we need, and friction will increase to the point of danger."[22]

Most troubling was 'Ali Mahir's dismissal of Amin 'Uthman, an Oxford-educated Egyptian under secretary of state for finance widely regarded as one of Britain's staunchest supporters. Amin 'Uthman served as secretary-general of the Egyptian delegation during the 1936 treaty negotiations and later acted as the Wafd's intermediary with the British embassy while Nahhas was in power from 1936 to 1937 and again from 1942 to 1944.[23] His working relationship with the British was widely known and was even the subject of political cartoons in the Egyptian humor weeklies in the summer of 1939.[24] The Foreign Office warned of the danger in Amin 'Uthman's dismissal, as it might lead to the view that "helpfulness to the British Government constituted a reason for Royal displeasure and possible discharge. This is very serious, as our influence in Egypt is very largely based on each individual's expectation of favours or penalties to come and on the deep-seated tradition that in the last resort we are the masters."[25]

Political clients are vulnerable to the ebb and flow of their patron's power, and Britain's relationship with 'Ali Mahir highlights some of the key tensions inherent in British influence in Egypt under the treaty, with its reliance on patronage and intermediaries. Tensions over these dismissals erupted again in the new year when Cairo's satirical weeklies published a series of articles and cartoons that exposed the embassy's patronage networks. Lampson and his staff were experts at "dinner party diplomacy" and the ambassador's diary gives great detail about the numerous luncheon and dinner parties held, the guests invited, the topics of discussion, and any useful tidbits of information or gossip provided by those who stayed behind afterwards for private talks. The embassy invited leading opposition figures to a series of social events in January 1940 but *al-Misri Effendi,* critical of the embassy's use of dinner party diplomacy, noted: "Ministerial circles do not attach importance to this. A certain minister stated that the time was past when a party at the Embassy might cause a change of Government, since Egypt had now become an Independent State." The cartoons that accompanied the article offended Lampson and he created a diplomatic row when he sent a heated letter of protest to ʻAli Mahir, who he considered to be behind the press campaign.[26]

While working to dismantle the embassy patronage networks, ʻAli Mahir was also invested in developing his own, especially by building influence in the Egyptian army. ʻAziz al-Masri's appointment as chief of the general staff was one of many politically motivated appointments in the army.[27] The embassy grew increasingly concerned with reports "that the army was being tampered with in order to gain its support for the present Ministry, that the influence of the British Military Mission was being undermined, and that, under cover of territorial forces and sporting clubs, quasi-military formations were being organised to serve political ends in the future." ʻAziz al-Masri was identified as the source of these attitudes as well as growing pro-German sentiment in the army.[28] The embassy pressed for his removal from office and ʻAli Mahir agreed, but then delayed implementing the order and publicized it as evidence of British intervention in Egyptian affairs. ʻAziz al-Masri was ultimately placed on sick leave. Young Egypt and the young military officers in his circle of influence protested his removal and attributed this action to British pressure.[29]

The British had a different kind of patronage problem in Iraq. British officials firmly believed that Iraqi politics were "a matter of personalities rather than policy," and Prime Minister Nuri al-Saʻid exemplified this sentiment.[30] Nuri was a master of political patronage, using the distribution of political offices to maintain power, but his pro-British views weakened his legitimacy in the eyes of many Iraqis and could backfire against British interests. For example, the embassy received reports that some Cabinet members refused to endorse a declaration of war primarily because doing so would have bolstered the prime minister. Nuri was in power not because he had widespread support, but because there seemed to be no workable alternative.[31] As in Egypt the Iraqi military was involved in patronage networks, which played a role in their growing politicization in the late 1930s.[32] Given these concerns and the strength of local intrigues against Nuri from the beginning, the British were faced with a dilemma: how far should they go to support a government that was pro-British or at least cooperative in the war effort when it was not popular locally?

This issue became more urgent after the minister of finance, Rustam Haydar, was killed in January 1940. Nuri quickly arrested two former Cabinet ministers for complicity in the murder, and British officials feared he would take the opportunity to seek revenge on his political opponents. There were real benefits to keeping Nuri in power but "if we allow him to get rid of all his opponents by dubious means, we run the serious risk of being regarded as his partner in oppression, or even in crime."[33] This had the potential to add fuel to the anti-British fire in Iraq, and the Foreign Office concluded that given Nuri's close ties to the British they were justified in intervening in this case, even though it was an internal Iraqi affair.[34] Nuri's government finally fell in March 1940 due to divisions within his Cabinet. While not happy with the outcome, the British did not object to the change. As one Foreign Office official reflected, while the embassy was often criticized for not taking a stronger line in Iraq, "there is such a thing as conserving influence and on the whole we do get what we want out of Iraq in major matters."[35]

The new prime minister, Rashid 'Ali al-Kaylani, was the chief of the Royal Diwan at the palace and an experienced politician, having served as prime minister in the 1930s. As a result of complex political negotiations aimed at addressing endemic factionalism and military intervention in Iraqi politics, Rashid 'Ali's new Cabinet included four former prime ministers, with Nuri taking the position of minister of foreign affairs. However, the symbiotic relationship between the Iraqi army and politicians was so firmly ingrained in the political system that this effort to limit their influence proved a failure.

Britain's response to the challenges posed by both Nuri's fall and 'Ali Mahir's attack on patronage networks reflects the status quo policy of the early war years. Beyond the fact that Egypt was technically independent, Thompson at the Foreign Office pointed out that they could not take a more interventionist approach and declare a protectorate as they did during the First World War for the very practical reason that they did not have the manpower in place to administer Egypt. He noted:

> It is a fact that however much we might wish to control the country physically, we cannot do it for the lack of the odd four thousand British officials scattered about in every branch of the administration whose assistance would be vital and upon whom we could once count. Since effective Egyptian cooperation in the war is a necessity, it seems desirable, if we possibly can, to avoid political crises and disputes. What we want to do is to work amicably with an Egyptian Administration that is sufficiently efficient to get things done.[36]

These comments reflect the heart of British policy in the Middle East in the early years of the war: nonintervention as far as possible unless the local situation could disrupt the larger war effort, even if it meant turning a blind eye to questionable practices on the part of local governments.

British Propaganda Organizations in the Middle East[37]

Britain's declaration of war in September 1939 put in place a whole host of organizations that had been waiting in the wings. This transformation was particularly pronounced in Cairo due to its strategic position as the center of Britain's presence in the Middle East. In the words of one Foreign Office official, British military authorities and intelligence officers were "descending upon Egypt like the locusts of old" to set up office.[38]

At the outbreak of war Britain had over 20,000 troops in Egypt and was planning to send an additional brigade from Palestine and reinforcements from India. The presence of these troops had an important psychological effect, as Lampson noted: "The more impressive our forces in Egypt the better politically."[39] They provided a powerful visual reminder of Britain's commitment to defend Egypt, but they also brought a new challenge to the prestige and power of the British embassy in Cairo, which had long been the unquestioned British voice in Egypt, and revived old civilian-military tensions. Lampson complained about the rapid expansion of GHQ ME, which, as he noted, even some of its own staff had taken to calling "Muddle East."[40] While highly complementary of General Wilson, the general officer commanding-in-chief, BTE, Lampson and General Wavell, the commander-in-chief, Middle East, clashed immediately and were frequently at odds over what Lampson considered to be the military's attempts to influence policy and civilian matters that were under the authority of the embassy and the Foreign Office.[41]

The Axis powers were already on a war footing in terms of propaganda, but Britain was following a policy of avoiding any action that might provoke an Italian response which limited the scope of its prewar publicity. As a result, in the months leading up to the war British propaganda officials took a two-pronged approach in the Middle East, emphasizing "antidote" material to respond to Axis anti-British propaganda and the production of "good, positive, pro-British material."[42] Upon the outbreak of war propaganda campaigns could now be implemented with full force. The message disseminated through the rapidly expanding wartime propaganda apparatus was crafted by the Ministry of Information in London. Laurence Rushbrook Williams, who had worked on publicity in Palestine for the Colonial Office, was the Ministry of Information official charged with developing propaganda for the Arab world.

Stories of Nazi atrocities and the heroism of Allied civilians and troops could be used to rally support in the West, but in the Middle East it was feared that these messages would have the opposite effect, convincing Arab audiences of German strength and the disastrous consequences of participating in the war. The Ministry of Information was first and foremost committed to convincing the Arabs that Britain would emerge victorious and that it was in their interest to support this cause. They would publicize Allied military strength but also "the idealism of the Allied cause," the way in which these ideals aligned with Islam, and "Britain as the protector of small nations." Nazi paganism and hostility to religion were to be emphasized, as well as its racial prejudices.[43] The Ministry of Information relied on its local representatives to tailor these propaganda lines to fit specific local environments. Ernest Main, who was in charge of publicity in Iraq, noted that "I find many differences of demand, even in Middle East, e.g. I have to tone down the scurrilities which Egypt finds successful, and our stuff is rather too respectable for Egypt, although Aden, Jerusalem and Damascus like it."[44]

Cairo was the behemoth of Britain's propaganda and intelligence efforts during the Second World War, a fact that was both recognized and resented by the other posts. The expansion of the embassy's Publicity Section (Pubsec), days before the declaration of war, reflected the importance of the Egyptian press as one of the most useful vehicles for overt propaganda, not just in Egypt but throughout the Arab world. An Egyptian journalist was hired to write local news items and Reginald Davies, a member of the Sudan Civil Service and the assistant director general of the Alexandria Municipality, was appointed its director.[45]

Press work in the Arab world had an important commercial dimension, something the Germans and Italians had capitalized on before the war. As one Egyptian journalist told Williamson-Napier, the press officer at the embassy, "There can be no honey without money."[46] Williamson-Napier negotiated advertising contracts which provided financial incentives for papers to maintain a pro-British tone in editorials and publish embassy materials. To avoid the appearance of direct British intervention the embassy paid an independent organization called the Travel Association to place ads in leading Egyptian papers, yet these subtler forms of influence could backfire.[47] The editor of *al-Ahram*, Tekla Pasha, realized that his paper had received payments for two months without having received any ads to place, and the Young Egypt newspaper *Misr al-Fatat* published an exposé highlighting this tactic of influencing the press.[48]

Pubsec answered to the Ministry of Information in London but was also considered to be "an integral part of the Embassy" and fell under Lampson's supervision. This arrangement facilitated propaganda coordination with the work of the Oriental Secretariat. Led by the Oriental Counsellor Sir Walter Smart, this office lay at the heart of Britain's prewar publicity and political intelligence networks in Egypt and was the main source of local knowledge at the embassy. For counter-espionage operations, the British were able to draw on this office's already existing relationships with local officials and informants, and this coordination allowed Pubsec to tap into the special funds Lampson had for "black" propaganda.[49] The Oriental Secretariat financed and supervised the publication of a weekly Arabic magazine, *Zahrat al-Sharq* and directed the editorial policy of the *Journal d'Egypte* and through that influenced the other French- and English-language newspapers in Egypt run by the same organization.[50]

One of the most important challenges that any embassy faces is how to maintain contact with the local population. The British embassy in Cairo during Lampson's tenure as ambassador was a bustling social hub, but in Iraq the current of anti-British feeling limited these social interactions. Major General D. G. Bromilow, the head of the British Military Mission in Iraq, noted that in the prewar years the Germans had "genuine social intercourse" with the Iraqis and were "'good mixers,' in marked contrast to the British insularity and aloofness." The Germans also delivered on supplies and commercial contracts, while the British made long-term promises.[51] Ambassador Newton made it a priority to repair these social relationships and C. J. Edmonds, adviser to the Ministry of the Interior, noted approvingly that "He has taken up strongly the harm hitherto done by the 'isolationist' policy of the Embassy and is being very good over giving parties and establishing contacts."[52]

The British publicity organization in Iraq was also expanded with the outbreak of war. Iraq provides a useful case study of how Britain's propaganda machinery functioned in areas on the periphery of the war effort in the Middle East, where a more modest military presence limited the ability to enforce compliance. The British Council sent a representative in November 1939 to establish a British Institute in Baghdad, and Ernest Main was given a joint appointment as press attaché and Ministry of Information representative at the embassy. While on a much smaller scale than in Cairo, the embassy in Baghdad also focused on increasing its influence over the Iraqi press, providing the Iraqi Arabic newspapers with free translations of Reuters wireless news service into Arabic in order to facilitate sympathetic coverage of the war and make the local press dependent on these British sources.[53] Political articles were closely censored and, with the exception of the newspaper *al-Istiqlal*, the Iraqi press was projecting a fairly neutral tone in the early months of the war.[54] Main optimistically reported in November 1939 that he was able to get 80 percent of his material published in the Iraqi press.[55]

As in Egypt, publicity work extended beyond influence to financial incentives, but British officials in Iraq were far more hesitant to use press subsidies and other payments. The Foreign Office and Ministry of Information frequently expressed frustration at what Rushbrook Williams described as Newton's "prewar" sensibilities when it came to propaganda.[56] The Germans were known to have expended great sums of money in prewar Iraq and British officials estimated that Grobba dispensed £3,000 a month in bribes before he was expelled from the country. Brigadier Iltyd Clayton, at the time Wavell's publicity liaison officer, suggested to Ernest Main that he should pick up some of these payments and he was allocated £50 a month as a start. This arrangement alarmed the Foreign Office, which believed that "the actual control of propaganda was so much tied up with political considerations that it should not be taken out of the hands of His Majesty's Representative in the Middle East." This was not a question of press subsidies, but "downright bribery," and it was being organized without consulting the ambassador.[57]

While Britain had some success in regulating the wartime messages in the Arab newspapers in the early months of the war, they were less successful in controlling the airwaves. Radio broadcasts were a way to reach the masses outside of the educated urban populations who were reading the local newspapers, and yet this was an arena where the British were at a disadvantage. The BBC Arabic broadcasts came under frequent fire for their formal Arabic and dull materials that did not compare well with their more sensationalistic Axis competitors. The British consul in Mosul described BBC Arabic broadcasts as "insipid," with no appeal to the masses whom they were trying to reach: "I cannot see how we are going to do it with talks on Andalusian art and favourite English dishes, to quote from recent Arabic programmes, at a time when we are fighting for our existence, and Yunis Bahri is talking about marching victoriously down Rashid Street." In the view of the men on the spot, Britain was losing the broadcast war.[58]

The publicity sections took on a wide range of new wartime duties. Traveling cinema units showed educational films to Egyptian schoolchildren on topics such as hygiene with propaganda messages worked in, reaching 18,000 Egyptians a month in 1939. To reach audiences outside of Cairo Pubsec hired the traveling vans of the International Tea Bureau, the Ministry of Health, Chilean Nitrates Ltd., and the People's Dispensary for Sick Animals and equipped them with photographic displays and films, boasting by the end of 1940 that "the vans of the I.T.B. carried our publicity to more than a million people in over a thousand villages." Punch and Judy-style traveling shows accompanied an exhibit of a captured Italian airplane that was displayed in the poorer neighborhoods of Cairo.[59]

Ambassador Newton supported the expansion of these programs to Iraq, suggesting that short documentary films "showing, on the one hand, the strength of Britain's armed forces, and on the other hand the ordered and progressive character of Britain's social and economic organisation, even in time of war, would be those best calculated to make the desired impression upon the local mind."[60] Britain retained a monopoly on the supply of newsreels to Iraqi cinemas, and these proved popular and were the ideal forum for the projection of power campaign with images of British military might.[61] Descriptions of British naval power in the press, for example, had little impact in Iraq, where few people had experience with ships larger than river craft. The Foreign Office worked to remedy this by arranging for Baghdad showings of a film titled "Battle Fleets of Britain," noting "the more naval films they show there the better."[62]

"Publicity without Victory"[63]

In spring 1940 Rushbrook Williams undertook a fact-finding mission to evaluate the status of British propaganda in the Middle East that included a meeting in Cairo that he later identified as the turning point in Britain's propaganda efforts.[64] The Ministry of Information had invested heavily in overt, "white" propaganda which either took the form of antidote material, responding to Axis propaganda attacks, or the building up of pro-British sentiment. By the summer of 1940, however, it became increasingly clear that this white propaganda was failing to appeal to local audiences, and propaganda officials began investigating the potential for "black" propaganda in the Arab world, by definition propaganda that appeared to come from non-British sources.[65] Edmonds, writing from his vantage point as an adviser to the Iraqi government, argued that the Germans and Italians in Iraq had been more effective in exploiting what he described as "the normal working of the bazaar mind which, with a misty but ingenious logic, deduces the possibilities or the probabilities from any known set of circumstances and then reports them as facts."[66] A successful response to this challenge required more than carefully tailored BBC broadcasts and well-placed newspaper articles. Propaganda organizations needed to engage local agents and British Arabic experts who purportedly knew how this mind worked and could generate rumors and whispers that would appeal to its sensibilities while hiding the British source.

The Ministry of Information machinery housed in the British embassy in Cairo was not highly respected in the early years of the war.[67] Laurence Grafftey-Smith, a member of the Levant Consular Service, recalled that when he was informed, on arrival in Cairo in September 1940, that he was assigned to Pubsec his friends lamented that "I might have enjoyed more interesting and rewarding employment if Sir Miles Lampson had named me to be Assistant Sanitary Man in the local asylum, or Deputy Corpse-Washer at the local lazaret."[68] Grafftey-Smith was brought in to lead the embassy's oral propaganda efforts as part of the summer 1940 reorganization of its publicity efforts after the fall of France and the Italian declaration of war in June 1940 (see Chapter 3). The embassy sent out bulletins to supporters throughout Egypt that provided arguments that they could use to respond to Axis propaganda lines. Individuals were tasked with sharing these talking points with specific targeted audiences, such as the religious scholars of al-Azhar or the patrons of Cairo's coffee houses.[69]

The famous travel writer Freya Stark was seconded from the Information Office in Aden in autumn 1940 and attached to Pubsec to strengthen these oral propaganda campaigns.[70] She initiated the *Ikhwan al-Hurriya* (Brotherhood of Freedom), a cell-based organization designed to combat fifth columnists in Egypt. By January 1941 she reported 400 members divided up into cells of no more than 20 people, who met to discuss a printed bulletin that equipped them to respond to the issues of the day. Rather than trying to win over those who were convinced of the Axis cause, Stark wanted to focus on bolstering Britain's friends: "Our first aim is–like that of a good bridge player–to make the fullest use of the cards in our own hand before attending to those of the enemy." This propaganda should be, as much as possible, written by Egyptians for Egyptians, in order to address the frequent criticism that British propaganda sounded like lines written by Englishmen translated into Arabic.[71]

The formation of the Special Operations Executive (SOE) in 1940 bolstered the arsenal of black propaganda.[72] GHQ ME recruited Dr. James Heyworth-Dunne, an Arabic language instructor at the School of Oriental and African Studies in London, to undertake propaganda and intelligence work under Brigadier Clayton and also to develop black propaganda for SOE. Heyworth-Dunne claimed to solve one of the most pressing publicity challenges: limited contact with the local population outside of official circles. Ministry of Information propaganda was ineffective because, as he argued, "We can only deal with Egyptian and Moslem propaganda with Egyptian and Moslem technique." A frequent visitor to Cairo where he maintained a home, Heyworth-Dunne had converted to Islam and as Lampson observed, "His contact with Egyptians is therefore on a different footing from that of an official Englishman and for that reason of special interest."[73]

The expansion of Britain's propaganda apparatus in Egypt was accompanied by an infusion of funds, and Rushbrook Williams estimated in November 1940 that Britain was spending over £120,000 on propaganda in Egypt, funded from various offices.[74] Pubsec at the Cairo embassy, now the headquarters for both covert and overt propaganda distribution throughout the Middle East and the eastern Mediterranean, became the largest Ministry of Information overseas post after the one in the United States.[75] This expansion created new problems: "The local propaganda world," Grafftey-Smith observed, "had far too many mansions."[76] The entry of Italy into the war and the inclusion of the Balkans in the purview of GHQ ME exacerbated military-civilian tensions, as Wavell and Lampson often sparred over control of propaganda.[77] The disruptive presence of SOE's "cloak and dagger wallahs," as the embassy called them, and the sheer complexity of these overlapping agencies, with their frequent renaming and reorganization, led one London official to note in exasperation that he "reached the conclusion that it was impossible to try to disentangle and readjust it from this end."[78] Conflicting loyalties and turf wars would leave SOE in the Middle East severely discredited by 1941 and contribute to local conspiracies and paranoia about British influence.[79]

Some propaganda lines, while well intentioned, had unintended consequences and officials had to keep constant sight of the policy implications. Films sent out from

London did not necessarily resonate with local audiences. Only selected portions of the film "London can take it" were screened in Cairo as Pubsec feared that if this film documenting the Battle of Britain was shown in its entirety it would "have a terrifying effect on a public which is itself liable to bombing attacks while it has neither the natural stamina nor the passionate will to victory which enable the British public to support these ordeals." As for "Convoy," they decided not to show it in Cairo at all as "for the unsophisticated majority in Egypt, heroic defence by British naval units against superior German forces is not a theme which inspires confidence in British victory."[80] In reviewing Britain's propaganda initiatives, Colonel MacKereth warned that "Britain as the protector of small nations" would ring hollow in the Arab world, and the idealism of the Allies presented dangers, both for the present and the future. Not only would it seem hypocritical but, as he noted in a prescient comment that would prove to be prophetic by the end of the war: "it may generate false hopes in the breasts of Arab politicians. Incautious phrases may later be dug up as promises by His Majesty's Government."[81]

The reality of this danger and the growing movement in Egypt for a quid pro quo for cooperation in wartime became apparent in a petition that the Wafd Party presented to Lampson on April 1, 1940.[82] Addressed to the Egyptian people, the petition repeated the Wafd's commitment to the treaty but also made demands for five concessions from Britain: the withdrawal of British troops after the war, Egyptian participation in postwar peace conferences, postwar negotiations to recognize Egyptian rights in the Sudan, withdrawal of Britain's request for an *état de siège* in Egypt, and for Britain to address the serious economic problems the war was causing Egypt with respect to the cotton crop.[83]

The Foreign Office, angered by the petition, instructed Lampson to inform Nahhas that this was "a deliberate attempt to play at internal politics at a moment when Great Britain is involved in a struggle in which the fate and independence of Egypt is as much at stake as our own."[84] It lay the groundwork for the Wafd to potentially instigate an anti-British movement, and was also a way to reassert its status as a nationalist party. Lampson warned of the petition's potential long-term implications as it "may possibly prove to have marked a turning-point in the history of Anglo-Egyptian relations since the Treaty. The Wafd's demand for the withdrawal of our troops from Egypt on the conclusion of peace looks like becoming the theoretical basis of Egyptian policy."[85] It gave the British a sense of what the Egyptians might demand after the war, setting the bar much higher than had previously been expected.

The Wafd petition did not go unnoticed in Iraq. In fact, a member of the Iraqi Chamber of Deputies asked Rashid 'Ali if his new government would follow the Wafd's example in asking the British to clarify Iraq's position in postwar negotiations. The prime minister responded by reaffirming his predecessor's dual approach to foreign policy. He acknowledged Iraq's commitment to the Anglo-Iraqi alliance but also declared that his first duty was:

> To strengthen the foundations of Arab Alliance and to continue to work for the realization of the aspirations of other neighbouring Arab countries, whose ties with Iraq and Arab States and whose need for independence and freedom should

> be the mutual aim of them all. This aim is a complement to Iraq's foreign policy as applied to the obligations and promises contracted by the Allies and the aims announced by them.[86]

He could not offer more open support to the Allies unless "he could at the same time declare the establishment of an agreed policy between the Allies and the Arabs for the realisation of Arab ideals," by which he meant a settlement of the Palestine issue and independence for Syria and Lebanon.[87] The Allies had already made commitments regarding this independence and they were now asking them to follow through, a theme that would continue throughout the war.

3

Calling Britain's Bluff in the Middle East, May 1940–January 1941

Events in Europe in the spring and summer of 1940 transformed the wartime situation and forced Britain to reconsider the status quo policy for the Middle East. Lacy Baggallay, observing the situation from the Foreign Office, reflected in June 1940 that:

> Up till a month ago our policy in Iraq was, I am convinced, paying in spite of all appearances to the contrary. That is to say, we were, by and large, getting what we needed without creating a situation in which we might have to have a row. At that time that was just what we wanted. Everyone agreed that a quiet time in the Middle East suited our book. But in the last month something has happened which up till then had never entered into our calculations, or at any rate into my calculations, that is to say, the total collapse of France.[1]

The fall of France and the Italian declaration of war had seismic implications for British strategy in the Mediterranean and the defense of Egypt. Britain would be unable to rely on French reinforcements for British forces, negating months of Anglo-French military planning. French troops in Tunisia were no longer a threat to the Italian forces in Libya, increasing the likelihood of an Italian invasion of Egypt and placing the Fleet Base at Alexandria in even greater danger. Lampson, reflecting on the implications of the fall of France for Britain's position in Egypt, concluded: "In short, our garrison, which was judged adequate so long as the French were acting with us, seems to me in all probability to be inadequate in the event of the French having run out."[2] All naval calculations were placed in disarray with the loss of French naval support, and Britain lost access to French air bases for refueling. Vichy French and Italian control of most of North Africa effectively closed off the Mediterranean to British shipping, forcing both military and civilian transport to use the much longer route around the Cape.[3] As for Iraq, the Italian presence in East Africa undermined the security of the Red Sea route, making the overland route via Iraq even more important for imperial security at the same time as the Vichy French presence on Iraq's western border in Syria threatened the lines of communication to India.[4]

Winston Churchill's new coalition government, formed in May after the collapse of Neville Chamberlain's government, asserted the importance of holding the eastern Mediterranean as a vital part of Britain's wartime strategy for the defense of the British Empire. The ongoing dilemma in 1940 was how to balance calls for shoring up the defenses of the Middle East with the desperate need for supplies for home to protect Britain. As Churchill recalled,

> Until the battle of Britain had been decisively won, every reinforcement of aircraft to the Mediterranean and Egypt had been an act of acute responsibility. Even in the winter months, when we felt we were masters of our own daylight air at home, it was very hard under the full fury of the Blitz to send away fighter aircraft either to Malta or to Egypt.[5]

Italy's declaration of war on June 10, 1940, was not unexpected. When an Italian declaration had appeared likely in early spring, Lampson asked the Foreign Office for authorization to again use pressure on the Egyptian prime minister "on the ground that in the case of Italy nothing short of a declaration of war would enable Egypt to fulfil her obligations under the Treaty of Alliance."[6] In the end, both Egypt and Iraq refused to comply with this request. 'Ali Mahir announced that Egypt would break off diplomatic relations but it would not take military action against Italy unless Egyptian territory was attacked.[7] Britain expected that Iraq would quickly follow suit to at least break off diplomatic relations with Italy, but Rashid 'Ali's government hesitated. Newton goaded the regent on Iraq's failure to do so, commenting in an audience that "I thought it was all the more pitiful that the Iraqi Government should apparently merely wait on the Egyptian Government and fail to get credit for taking the inevitable decision sooner rather than later."[8] Rashid 'Ali, supported by his Cabinet, tried to use the severing of relations as leverage for concessions on Palestine and Syria, and Iraqis were hesitant to declare war at a time when an Axis victory seemed likely. On June 17 the Cabinet ended its deliberations and passed a resolution that reinforced Iraq's commitment to the treaty but also stated that they would maintain "a waiting attitude" on the question of breaking off relations with Italy.[9]

Britain was willing, for the moment, to accept these limited responses. As Edmonds noted, as troubling as this hesitation was, it was not completely unexpected: "The collapse of France, the second Empire of the world, is a big thing; we must expect Iraq as a whole to have difficulty in assimilating it without some strong digestive tonic. The best tonic would of course be some striking success in Europe or North Africa, but that is unobtainable at the local chemists."[10] However, behind the refusals to declare war or, in Iraq's case, even break off relations with Italy, British officials saw more troubling developments and blamed this obstructionism on the individuals they considered to be most responsible: the prime ministers. As a member of the Egyptian Department observed, "There has always been a tendency in the Residency or Embassy at Cairo to have some 'Public Enemy No. 1.'"[11] During the early years of the Second World War Britain's "Public Enemy No.1" in Egypt was Prime Minister 'Ali Mahir while in Iraq it was his counterpart, Rashid 'Ali. Officials believed that if only these leaders could be removed from power, relations would improve, and yet by doing so the British raised the stakes and turned their resignations into an issue of prestige. Britain's response to the crises facing Egypt and Iraq in 1940 reflects the full implications of this attitude for official British policy.

Britain's Public Enemy Number One in Egypt: 'Ali Mahir

Although 'Ali Mahir technically adhered to the letter of the Anglo-Egyptian Treaty in meeting Britain's wartime demands, in the embassy's opinion his actions in spring 1940 clearly did not reflect the treaty's spirit. The prime minister was being "systematically obstructive" over the issue of counter-propaganda, was unwilling to cut off all ties with Italy, and had not yet interned all Germans in Egypt, leading Lampson to the conclusion that he needed to be replaced.[12] But how to foster this change without visibly violating the treaty and actively intervening in Egyptian internal affairs? As far back as January 1940 Lampson suggested that 'Ali Mahir should leave office due to internal pressure, rather than from embassy influence, so that British intervention would not be apparent.[13]

Three new internal developments in Egyptian politics in spring 1940 signaled that the time was ripe to press for a new government: increased cooperation between the opposition parties, growing discontent within the Egyptian administration itself, and the Wafd petition of April 1940, discussed in the previous chapter. The British viewed the declaration as a sign of the Wafd's desire to return to office and the embassy increasingly came to see it as a viable partner. The Wafd in power could mobilize popular support for the war effort; a Wafd in opposition was a focal point of nationalist agitation.[14] Both the embassy and the Egyptian opposition were now actively working to replace the 'Ali Mahir government and Lampson gave hints of encouragement to the backroom intrigues of the Egyptian political parties.[15]

As the deteriorating war situation in June made the issue more urgent, Lampson broke the façade of non-interference and demanded that Farouk dismiss 'Ali Mahir's government. Both the king and prime minister responded by sending protests to London in an attempt to circumvent the embassy.[16] Lampson informed the Foreign Office: "For all practical purposes we are now without a government with which we can co-operate." He proposed a three-stage plan for dealing with the situation that would have led to British administration of Egypt under martial law. The Foreign Office vacillated but ultimately agreed to support active measures, including the forced abdication of the king if necessary. Wavell assured Lampson on June 23 that they could impose martial law as early as that evening as he was bringing in British troops from Palestine. The ambassador visited King Farouk and insisted that he consult Nahhas in forming the new government, giving him until sunset to agree to this condition. Four days of intense political wrangling followed as Egypt's political leaders tried to form a new government, held up by Nahhas's insistence on new elections for the Chamber of Deputies.[17]

In the midst of these machinations the king seized the upper hand and asked Hassan Sabri to form a government. Lampson later observed that this was a "master-stroke" on Farouk's part, putting in power a pro-British politician whom the embassy could not possibly object to who was also politically weak and unable to threaten the position of the palace.[18] This crucial about-face came as a result of two developments, the first being the Wafd's unwillingness to compromise with the embassy on their demand for new elections. From the Wafd perspective, they could afford to bide their time and return to office when conditions were more favorable. The second development was the changing war situation. Wavell had informed Lampson just five days earlier that they could impose British martial law in Egypt, but in a meeting with the service chiefs on June 28 they decided that this would put too much of a strain on the British military at a crucial moment in Europe.[19] Brigadier Shearer later told the Foreign Office that "we had come within an ace of being stampeded into an entirely unnecessary complication" and Wavell was determined to avoid a repeat of this situation.[20]

By the end of June the political crisis in Egypt was resolved. King Farouk was still on the throne, 'Ali Mahir was out of power, and Hassan Sabri, a friend of the embassy, was prime minister and head of a government with neither Wafd participation nor Wafd support. The ambassador reflected, "I am aware that this Government is not ideal ... But then things seldom work out exactly as one would wish and I felt I had to shape my action yesterday to quickly changing situation." The Wafd had refused to cooperate and at least "King Farouk has had a wholesome jolt and is well aware of the narrowness of his escape." The Foreign Office was not as convinced and saw troubling trends in this show-down. While they got rid of 'Ali Mahir, their "Public Enemy No. 1," both the king and Nahhas were left with the impression that they had "out-smarted" Britain.[21] As this episode demonstrated, Britain's intervention in internal politics throughout the war years would be shaped by the overarching question: was the moment militarily opportune, as well as politically opportune for British intervention, and was the threat so severe that it was worth the sacrifice on other fronts? In 1940 in Egypt the answer was no, while in 1942, in similar political circumstances, the answer would be a qualified yes.

Facing the Italian Threat

In the months since the outbreak of war Britain's military presence had been steadily expanding. By June 1940 Britain had 36,000 troops in Egypt and 85,775 in the area under Middle East Command, "none of which were organised in complete formations," against 505,000 Italian troops.[22] With the Italian declaration of war British troops crossed the frontier into Cyrenaica (eastern Libya), taking the Italian troops at the frontier posts by surprise. These initial forays were successful, gave the British forces valuable experience, and bolstered Egyptian morale but they were not sustainable. General Wilson noted that "The collapse of the French altered the whole strategical aspect of the Western Desert campaign" as Italy could now turn its attention to the east, and "By the end of July our troops were back on the line of the frontier wire."[23] The war came closer for Egypt when Italian troops crossed into Egyptian territory on September 13, 1940, and captured Sidi Barrani. Air raids on Alexandria and the Canal Zone led to 155 deaths and 425 injuries in autumn 1940, once again raising fears of Egypt's vulnerability to air attack.[24]

The Italian offensive raised all of the old debates about an Egyptian declaration of war and the role that the Egyptian military would play. Egyptians debated whether this was an imperial war between Western powers or a direct attack on Egyptian sovereignty. Young Egypt, in a statement to the embassy, suggested that the Egyptian army should withdraw from the Western Desert until they knew Italian aims and only fight if Italy demonstrated that it planned "to transgress Egypt's independence and suzerainty." The palace took a similar line.[25] Ahmad Mahir, the leader of the Sa'dist Party who had advocated for an active Egyptian role since the Munich debates in 1938, renewed his push for an Egyptian declaration, asserting that "this invasion necessitated Egyptian participation in the defence of the country, and that her failure to do so would amount to a recognition of a status of protectorate."[26] The Sa'dist ministers in Hassan Sabri's Cabinet resigned in September in protest against the government's refusal to declare war.[27]

The British Cabinet had decided that as long as Egypt provided all necessary assistance they would not be pressured to declare war unless they were directly attacked. Now that this line had been crossed, the issue was raised again. The Foreign Office argued that an Egyptian declaration of war would have a positive impact in the Arab world, most notably in Iraq and, by having Egyptian troops engaged in their own defense, they could free up British troops. The embassy and the service chiefs, however, were all agreed that for the moment it was better if Egypt refrained from taking this step. A perplexed Churchill asked for the rationale. From a political perspective Egyptian sentiment was still strongly against entering the war, and doing so would require another change in leadership that would cause instability at a time when the military authorities wanted to keep Cairo calm. As Egyptians had already made clear their postwar desiderata, a declaration of war would also give Egypt more of a justification to make postwar claims for representation at a peace conference or treaty revision. There were also general fears, not unfounded, that if Egypt declared war it would lead to the bombing of Cairo, which Egyptians could then blame on the British for provoking them into the declaration.[28] The service chiefs were agreed that the Egyptian military was not in a position to play a greater role in Egypt's defense and a declaration would make key British naval bases, ports, and the Canal Zone targets for bombing campaigns, disrupting naval operations.[29]

In the midst of the ongoing debates about Egypt's response to the Italian offensive in November 1940, Prime Minister Hassan Sabri had a heart attack while addressing the Chamber of Deputies and later died. His successor, Husayn Sirri, was valued as a reliable embassy contact. Lampson and Sirri enjoyed a longstanding friendship and his wife, the aunt of Queen Farida, supplied the embassy with palace gossip.[30] The new prime minister was as pro-British as his predecessor, but he was also equally weak in his political influence, raising concerns as to whether or not he would be able to deliver on Britain's wartime demands in the difficult months of autumn/winter 1940.

While British officials agreed that there were benefits to Egypt not declaring war, it did complicate matters for Anglo-Egyptian military cooperation. As part of defense planning Wilson and the Egyptian minister of national defense discussed the role the Egyptian military would play in time of war, primarily with respect to internal defense. The Frontier Force was responsible for monitoring the Libyan border, which not only relieved British troops of this task but was a way to avoid provoking Italy.[31] Egyptian troops formed part of the garrison at Mersa Matruh, were stationed at various points along the Libyan border and in the Delta, and Egyptian anti-aircraft units were assigned a critical role in defending Alexandria. Despite all of the prewar demands for additional military supplies, Wavell reported that the Egyptian army "was in many respects much better equipped than most of the British forces" but while Egypt was "the main base of operations for the Middle East, yet the country is not at war, and has still large numbers of enemy subjects at large."[32] Wilson noted that, given the Egyptian responsibility for anti-aircraft defenses, "one was confronted with the problem of having a non-belligerent ally manning the main A/A and searchlight defences of the ports and capital."[33]

The British Military Mission's relations with the Egyptian army had already been damaged by the dismissal of ʿAziz al-Masri (see Chapter 2). After it became clear that the Egyptian state of non-belligerency was not going to change, Wavell withdrew the Egyptian troops that were part of the force at Mersa Matruh and Wilson proposed that Britain might buy back some of the military equipment it had sold to the Egyptian army. The latter proposal was dropped after it caused an uproar in Egyptian military circles.[34] At a dinner with the Egyptian prime minister in October, Secretary of State for War Sir Anthony Eden expressed concerns about whether or not the Egyptian troops stationed at Siwa would fight if the Italians attacked.[35] Anwar al-Sadat later pointed to this episode as evidence of Churchill's plan of "neutralizing the Egyptian Army," leading to talk of a revolt in the army.[36] To Egyptian army officers these were clear attempts by the British to once again deliberately undermine the effectiveness of Egypt's military, building on the suspicions planted by the debates over the supply of arms in the interwar period.[37]

Britain's Public Enemy Number One in Iraq: Rashid ʿAli

As the war moved closer to the Middle East the concentration of power in Cairo created new tensions among diplomatic representatives. Ambassador Lampson blamed his counterpart in Iraq, Sir Basil Newton, for not doing enough to fight Axis influence, in particular controlling press attacks on the Allies. Newton was frustrated by Lampson's critique, noting that "when he talks of force he seems to overlook that Iraq is probably more jealous of its independence than Egypt and that it is much less civilized and that we neither maintain large land forces here nor presumably wish to have to do so."[38] A Foreign Office official observed in Newton's defense that it was hard enough to get the Egyptian government to comply with British requests, even with large numbers of British troops in the country: "In Iraq, we can really only urge and persuade."[39] The most powerful forces in the Iraqi army and many of Iraq's politicians were strongly pro-German, making it unlikely that the relatively weak but pro-British regent and a British embassy that lacked military backing could unseat the prime minister. The area liaison officer in Mosul pessimistically estimated in May 1940 that "less than 5% of the population of ʿIraq (excluding Christians and Jews) is possessed of a pro-British sentiment."[40] Rashid ʿAli's government was supported by the four army colonels known as the "Golden Square": Salah al-Din al-Sabbagh, Kamil Shabib, Fahmi Saʿid, and

Mahmud Salman. These pro-German pan-Arab nationalists were in close touch with the mufti of Jerusalem, still resident in Baghdad. The Iraqi government provided the mufti with funds and public recognition, and he became an important actor in Iraqi politics in 1940.[41]

As in Egypt, Britain's relations with the Iraqi army were hampered by the question of military supplies. The prewar period saw repeated Iraqi requests for the supplies that Britain was committed to providing under the terms of the Anglo-Iraqi Treaty and, when Britain failed to deliver, the Iraqi army approached both Germany and Italy. In April 1940 the Eastern Department of the Foreign Office drafted a memo that asked the question: "Has the apparent inability of His Majesty's Government to meet the orders which foreign governments have endeavoured to place in this country meant that the Allied cause has suffered in those countries?"[42] With respect to Iraq, the memo noted that Britain had a prewar commitment to supply material to Iraq under the terms of the treaty. British assurances that they did not have any arms to spare for Iraq rang hollow in light of British propaganda that was projecting British military power and publicizing Britain's increased military production: "no Iraqi believes (especially in view of the propaganda which is always being put about in this country regarding our enormous output in arms and aircraft etc.) that we do not give them arms because we cannot spare them. At the back of their minds is the conviction that this country wishes to keep Iraq weak and dependent."[43] Italy exploited Britain's repeated failure to meet Iraq's requests for military equipment, including anti-aircraft weapons, with propaganda that warned that these deficiencies were leaving Iraq vulnerable to air attack.[44] The projection of British military power solved one publicity dilemma in Iraq but created another that had a long-term, detrimental effect on Anglo-Iraqi relations, especially in light of the growing political power of the Iraqi army in the early years of the war.

Concerned about growing Axis influence and anti-British sentiment in Iraq, Ambassador Newton made the first of many requests for British troops in May 1940.[45] Discussions about opening the lines of communication through Iraq, a right accorded to Britain under the treaty, were revived numerous times over the subsequent months. On June 14, 1940, the same day that German troops entered Paris, the Chiefs of Staff Committee in London recommended that the War Cabinet take definitive action to fight anti-British feeling in Iraq, which was particularly strong in the army. They proposed demanding that the government implement "not merely the letter, but the spirit of the Treaty," but they stopped short of agreeing to send troops. Their recommendations included heavy investment in propaganda, encouraging France to make concessions to Syria, and "Since we are dealing with Eastern Countries and people, the power of gold applied personally, should not be forgotten."[46] The following week the treasury approved £30,000 for Newton to use toward these ends, with an additional £20,000 reserved for later use. The money was earmarked for buying influence over the newspapers and wireless stations and gifts to individuals as well as the Euphrates tribes to prepare them for the eventual arrival of Indian troops. Yet bribery was a problematic policy, as was well recognized. Officials looked to the cautionary tale of the First World War, when large sums of money were spent in the Middle East with little accountability. For his part Newton was conservative in his use of these funds, and hesitant to spend money on bribes.[47]

Later that month the issue was revisited once again, and on July 5 Newton was informed that Britain intended to send troops from India to Iraq as soon as the Government of Iraq agreed to receive them. Operation Trout would serve three purposes: pressure the Iraqi government to act against Axis interests in the country, amass troops at Basra ready to protect the Abadan oil refinery in Iran if necessary, and keep the lines of communication open with Palestine. The Italian declaration of war put the Red Sea routes in danger, making the land route through Iraq even more important, and the infusion of troops from India would strengthen the resources available for the Middle East Command.[48] Troops would also have a salutary effect on local public opinion, as even a small force would send the message that the disastrous turn of events in Europe was not preventing Britain from defending its positions in the eastern Mediterranean.[49]

The War Office initially supported the proposal to send troops to Iraq, but as the plan solidified it raised a whole host of issues that reflect the real weakness of Britain's position in July 1940 and the rapidly changing war situation. Wavell and the Government of India expressed concern that the proposed Trout force was too small to accomplish the aims set out for it, and the War Office wanted assurances from the Foreign Office that troops would not be asked to perform political functions.[50] The British were embroiled in a conflict over oil concessions in Iran, and military officials feared that sending troops to Iraq might provoke the Soviets to send troops to northern Iran in response.[51] Any force sent to Iraq would be poorly equipped and under-manned as India did not have any anti-aircraft or anti-tank guns for its own defense, let alone any to send with the Trout mission.[52] The Battle of Britain began in the midst of these debates, making the issue of anti-aircraft guns even more important. Guns for the Trout forces would have to be sent from Britain as India had none to give, and "the War Cabinet would have to decide between reducing to some extent the air defences of this country, or running the risk of losing the oil output from Abadan."[53]

Newton and the Foreign Office appreciated these difficulties, and suggested that even if the troops did not stay in Iraq it would be helpful to have them at least pass through "in order to accustom the Iraqis to the sight of British troops and to make it easier to station troops in Iraq later on."[54] London ultimately decided in August that any available reinforcements from the east should be sent to Egypt in light of the Italian threat from Libya.[55] The troops would not be sent via Iraq, as Newton had requested, because Wavell did not want to open the overland route unless absolutely necessary, and utilizing the land route would cause delay in their arrival in Egypt.[56] If the question was Egypt or Iraq, the answer in 1940 was clearly Egypt. Wavell would make similar arguments in 1941.

Given the lack of troops the British had to explore alternative means of forcing Iraq to break off relations with Italy. Financial tactics were one option; Britain was the main purchaser of agricultural products such as barley and dates, and oil was a major source of revenue for the Iraqi government. But financial pressure brought its own challenges, as barley and dates were needed to meet Britain's own food requirements, so cutting these off would hurt the war effort at home. Oil was already a source of tension in Anglo-Iraqi relations. Italy's entrance into the war and the closing of the Mediterranean had led to the closing of the Tripoli pipeline and the flow of oil on the Haifa line was reduced by more than half, leading to a dramatic decrease in oil revenue.[57] The stick of financial pressure is only effective if the carrot is available to reward compliance, and as Baggallay admitted in July 1940 there might not be funds available for an oil subsidy if Iraq did cooperate, and they certainly would not be able to give them the aircraft and machinery they had requested. As a result, he concluded that since troops were not available to send to Iraq "we shall have to swallow our pride and accept the Italian Legation at Bagdad indefinitely."[58]

The summer saw the intensification of Iraq's commitment to Palestine and Syria and Rashid 'Ali's government was now supporting a policy of "complete neutrality" in the war, by which he meant that "without satisfaction over Palestine he would not go one inch beyond the bare letter of the Treaty."[59] The British received troubling intelligence of Rashid 'Ali's advances to the Axis and his intention to foment trouble over Syria and Palestine, including news of a planned attack on the embassy to be followed by targeted assassinations.[60] In August two Palestinian Arabs were caught on the Iraq-Transjordan border with a military permit for access to the Rashid Camp in Baghdad. The information revealed through the investigation of this event provided the evidence to confirm rumors that the Iraqi military had been training and arming Palestinian Arabs and planning uprisings against the British in Palestine.[61]

Britain's failure to address these regional issues in summer 1940 led to a significant shift in Anglo-Iraqi relations. The colonial secretary, Lord Lloyd, sent Colonel Newcombe on a last-ditch mission to discuss Arab grievances but it was, by all accounts, a disaster. British officials were horrified by his meddling in Palestinian affairs in the name of brokering a settlement, there were rumors that he was sent to foment a revolt in Syria against the French, and Arab nationalists were frustrated by still more empty British promises.[62] Naji Shawkat left for Turkey, ostensibly for health reasons, but in reality to build contact with the Axis powers, taking a letter from the mufti to Hitler. Edmonds pointed to August 29, soon after Nuri's return from a failed trip to Cairo to meet with Wavell, as the turning point in Iraqi policy. In a meeting on September 17 Rashid 'Ali informed him that Iraqis "had come to the conclusion that the Arabs had nothing more to hope for from the British; Nuri Pasha had come back from Egypt thoroughly disillusioned; and the disillusionment had been finally confirmed by a communication from you to the effect that nothing would be done for Palestine."[63] After this disappointing trip Nuri made his own overtures to the Axis.[64]

At the end of September 1940 one Foreign Office official had noted that "I have an uneasy feeling that we are allowing Iraq to drift too freely towards the Axis … We are watching, but we are not taking a sufficiently positive and firm line to deter them."[65] These fears were realized when, in October 1940, Germany made a public declaration of a new Arab policy that included German and Italian support for Arab independence:

> Germany has always sympathised with the Arab question and hoped that the Arabs will one day regain their position in the world which will honour their race and their great history. The German Government has followed with interest the struggle for independence in the Arab countries. In that struggle the Arabs can rely unhesitatingly on the entire Germany sympathy. In this declaration Germany is in full accord with her ally Italy.[66]

There were also signs of Japanese overtures to the Iraqi government with offers of supplies and trade deals.[67]

The Axis declaration emboldened the Iraqi government, which still refused to break off diplomatic relations with Italy and even announced that it was reinstating telegraphic communications with both Germany and Italy on October 31, 1940. The government's neutral stance provided a cover for Rashid 'Ali's refusal to announce an active policy of cooperation with Britain, and there was growing evidence of Iraqi secret contacts with all three of the Axis powers. The Axis declaration was also a big propaganda blow to Britain. Anti-declaration articles were deleted by the Iraqi censor as were British cartoon images, and Iraqi newspapers began publishing pro-Axis news, disguised as coming from nonexistent news agencies, directly from Axis radio broadcasts.[68]

In light of these threats, Britain was in a weak position in Iraq with no troops available to demonstrate British power. In October Wavell warned that the window of opportunity for sending a small force under the guise of the treaty without Iraqi opposition was closed, and in any event he could not spare the troops. The only response was "a much stronger diplomacy and propaganda. Iraq should be made to understand that we are going to win this war and that we mean business," starting with the removal of Rashid 'Ali and economic and diplomatic pressure.[69] The mufti of Jerusalem was a particularly troubling pro-Axis influence in Baghdad, and the War Cabinet discussed the possibility of having him assassinated, an extreme step which the Foreign Office opposed.[70] Projecting ahead they already had plans in place to destroy Iraqi oil wells and pipelines in the case of a German invasion, and hoped to have forces available by spring 1941 to assist Turkey and occupy Syria and Iraq. Given the lack of troops the autumn campaign in Iraq would rely instead on what the War Cabinet described as "threats and money."[71]

The Foreign Office made Rashid 'Ali's removal from power a priority and instructed Newton to let the Iraqis know that continued economic and trade benefits were dependent on cooperation: "In fact he that is not for us is against us and will be treated accordingly." Echoing Lampson's earlier declaration in Egypt, Newton informed Rashid 'Ali on November 26 that "he had now lost the confidence of His Majesty's Government in his ability to collaborate with them," a serious accusation to be made by any diplomatic representative against a host government.[72] As the ambassador noted: "It is this refusal properly to carry out the policy based on the Anglo-Iraqi Alliance, which is the basis of most of our charges against Rashid 'Ali."[73] And yet, even this extraordinary statement was not enough to bring about the fall of the Rashid 'Ali government. Britain had no carrots to offer Iraq as they could provide neither policy concessions on Palestine nor the anti-aircraft guns that the Iraqi military had been repeatedly requesting, and the stick of a military response was of limited impact given the status of the war and other commitments and, ultimately, the need to maintain quiet.[74]

Changing Tides: Operation Compass

In November 1940 a Foreign Office official pessimistically observed: "During the past ten years or more our position in the Middle East has been founded on bluff and I am afraid that this is now realized," a conclusion echoed in the assessment of military intelligence as well.[75] The launch of Operation Compass on December 7, Wavell's counter-offensive against Italian troops in the Western Desert, raised hopes that Britain's fortunes might be changing. The next two months saw a series of British victories in the Western Desert, including the Battle of Sidi Barrani, the capture of Bardia and Tobruk, and the surrender of Benghazi on February 7, 1941, ultimately leading to the removal of Italian troops from Cyrenaica. Wavell reported that in its two-month advance over 500 miles of territory in the Western Desert, the Army of the Nile achieved "the destruction of the Italian Tenth Army" and "the capture of 130,000 prisoners, 400 tanks, and 1,290 guns."[76]

One of the key assumptions of British propaganda in the Middle East since the beginning of the war was that military successes would be the best publicity. Lampson reported that the British victories in the Western Desert, "coming on top of the Greek victories, shattered any Egyptian illusions regarding Italian power and changed the whole atmosphere of fear which had so long prevailed in Egypt. There was great jubilation at the removal of the imminent menace of invasion and British stock soared to a high level."[77] In Iraq, however, these victories were not enough to overturn years of anti-British sentiment. The British embassy tried to leverage these battlefield successes to push for a change of policy by the Iraqi government, taking the opportunity to once again press the government to remove the Italian legation, but without success.[78] As Newton explained to Eden, while they had tried to make use of military successes in Egypt:

> we have found that cold water is skilfully poured on the iron by Berlin and Bari. What they broacast [*sic*] this evening is whispered tomorrow (or even earlier) in a hundred coffee shops by the army of Palestinian and Syrian political refugees, with Iraqi birds of the same feather, who frequent every place where two or three are gathered together .... If London says that Britain has won a great victory, the cue is taken from Berlin to pass the word round that the battle was only an affair of outposts with no effect on the real course of the war and that anyhow it profits the British little to have emptied Sidi Barrani if London and Coventry are laid in ruins by German bombers.[79]

As 1941 dawned Britain's Public Enemy No. 1, Prime Minister Rashid 'Ali, was still in office two months after Newton formally declared his inability to work with him. The Chiefs of Staff once again examined the possibility of sending troops to Iraq but in a recap of earlier debates they concluded that air strikes would be ineffective, and a small contingent of British troops could spark an aggressive response from Iraq but would not be enough to effectively deal with the outcome, thereby requiring the supply of additional troops that could not be spared from other theaters. Landing troops at Basra "would be little more than a bluff" and there were no plans in January 1941 to open the overland route through Iraq in the near future.[80] The alternative was to continue financial pressure and urge the regent "to bribe his way out of the present situation by using the tribes to threaten the Army." While Newton had been hesitant to resort to bribery the previous year, he now agreed that they should provide funds to the regent to buy support and help offset the influence of Axis money.[81]

The Iraqi Constitution limited the parameters within which the regent could take action against the government. He did not have the power to dismiss the prime minister, which made it difficult to remove the government by constitutional means, but at the same time the Parliament could only be dissolved with his approval. Rashid ʻAli pressured the regent to take this step but he refused, left Baghdad to avoid having to sign the order by force, and went to Diwaniyya to build support among the tribes in southern Iraq. The shifting dynamics of Iraqi political faction-building ultimately led to Rashid ʻAli's fall from power. Britain's economic pressure undermined confidence in his leadership, and the prime minister finally relented when two members of his Cabinet threatened to resign themselves and after he received news that the army at Diwaniyya and the southern Shiʻi tribes would support the regent. His Cabinet resigned on January 31, and Taha al-Hashimi formed a new government the next day.[82]

4

Iraq and the Rashid 'Ali Coup, January 1941–May 1941

The British embassy in Baghdad viewed Taha al-Hashimi's appointment as prime minister in January 1941 with misgiving. Ambassador Newton's list of desiderata for the new prime minister included severing relations with Italy and improved Anglo-Iraqi cooperation on propaganda and economic issues. To address anti-British sentiment they also prioritized the "elimination from politics of hostile military elements," the expulsion of Palestinian political refugees and their removal from positions of influence, particularly in the field of education, and control of the mufti.[1] The new prime minister's past record on all of these issues was troubling. A former president of the German-supported Palestine Defence Society Taha al-Hashimi, while serving as minister of defense in 1939, had been behind the decision to use a declaration of war as leverage for concessions on Palestine. As chief of the general staff he had played a key role in fostering the Iraqi military's intervention in politics in the 1930s. As Edmonds later observed, "If there has been no abrupt reversal of policy it is because Taha was himself largely responsible for the policy pursued by Rashid 'Ali's Cabinet."[2]

The prime minister assured Newton upon taking office that Iraq would cooperate with Britain, yet in public he declared that his government's foreign policy would be the same as that of his predecessor. While prepared to honor Iraq's treaty obligations, he would do everything possible to keep Iraq out of the war.[3] The new government created as many problems as it solved, but once again, Britain found its options were limited. One official noted that while it was easy to suggest that they should occupy Iraq this would have serious repercussions for the war effort and "For better or worse (rather the latter!) Iraq, like Egypt, is independent and we can't put back the clock."[4] The British returned to the tactic of financial pressure accompanied by secret disbursement of funds behind the scenes through SOE in order to build support for the regent.[5] The British did have some economic leverage in the supply of dollars and the provision of military equipment. For months the Iraqi government had requested that Britain supply requested military equipment in accordance with the annex to Article 5 of the Anglo-Iraqi Treaty. From the Iraqi perspective, the weapons were a British obligation under the terms of the treaty; from the British perspective, they would be a reward for good behavior. When the Iraqi representative in London asked Foreign Secretary Sir Anthony Eden for the release of dollars for Iraq to purchase war supplies in January, he responded that given the real limitations to Britain's dollar supply they must first go to the needs of "our loyal Allies, such as the Greeks, Turks and Egyptians." Until Iraq reconsidered its position "and showed the marked friendship and loyal co-operation we were entitled to expect" there was no hope that Britain would fulfill Iraq's request. The expulsion of the Italians would be the litmus test of Iraq's commitment to the treaty.[6]

By the end of March the British had grown increasingly frustrated with Iraqi dithering on breaking off relations with Italy and little progress had been made in weakening the political power of the officers. The regent proposed a more drastic step. He would press the prime minister to clamp down on the military, which he would be unable to do, forcing him to resign. The regent would then take the royal family to Basra for safety in case of retaliation. In the end, the plan was never put into action due to the intervening military coup.[7] Like Rashid 'Ali, Taha al-Hashimi fell afoul of the complicated factional politics of Iraq and internal tensions within his circle when he attempted to transfer two members of the Golden Square to posts outside of Baghdad in order to weaken the army's political influence. They refused to leave, and on the evening of April 1 Iraqi soldiers occupied various government buildings. The military clique tried to get Taha to replace the regent, but he refused and resigned his post as prime minister. The Golden Square planned to force the regent to appoint Rashid 'Ali as prime minister, but the regent, warned that he might be seized, had taken refuge at the American legation and from there proceeded to Habbaniya in the American minister's car.[8]

The departure of the regent complicated the plans of the military officers, as he had to give his approval of any new government under the terms of the Iraqi Constitution. The chief of staff of the Iraqi army rationalized the coup by arguing that the regent had neglected his duties, tried to claim the throne for himself, harmed the army, and undermined the Constitution.[9] The new Government of National Defence called a joint meeting of the two houses of the Iraqi Parliament who then unanimously approved a resolution deposing the regent and replacing him with Sharif Sharaf, another member of the royal family, who duly asked Rashid 'Ali to form a government. To counteract rumors of his contact with the Axis powers, Rashid 'Ali assured Parliament that he represented "a purely domestic movement having nothing to do with any foreign state. It was inspired by patriotic zeal and national enthusiasm, and the guiding spirit in it was loyalty to the nation." They would continue to respect and carry out the provisions of the Anglo-Iraqi Treaty "both in letter and in spirit" but at the same time "We are only most anxious that the honour of Iraq shall be fully maintained."[10]

The timing of the April crisis was particularly unfortunate for the British, as they were between ambassadors. The Foreign Office had begun investigating the possibility of replacing Newton as far back as autumn 1940 in the hopes that "a more forceful character" with knowledge of the local situation might be more effective given the delicate situation in Iraq, and they found the experience they were looking for in Sir Kinahan Cornwallis.[11] After serving in the Arab Bureau during the First World War, he held the position of adviser to the Iraqi Ministry of the Interior from 1921 to 1935 and personal adviser to King Faysal. With the outbreak of the Second World War he reentered government service as a member of the Middle East division of the Ministry of Information in London and he spent the early war years in the Political Intelligence Department of the Foreign Office, analyzing the internal situation in Iraq.[12] He was a well-respected Arabist and, in a post where personalities were considered to be the most crucial factor in politics and diplomacy, Cornwallis's extensive personal contacts were seen as a real benefit.[13] At the same time, his long tenure in Iraq had also given him a chance to make enemies, most notably Rashid 'Ali, who was partly responsible for his departure from Iraq in 1935.[14] The regent had warned that Rashid 'Ali would not support this appointment, giving the British another reason to push for the prime minister's removal from power.[15]

The new ambassador was in a difficult position because, as a Foreign Office official pointed out, it would be problematic to have a new ambassador expressly chosen for his longstanding relations with Arab leaders call for armed intervention on his first day in office.[16] Cornwallis was not scheduled to officially present his credentials to the regent until April 5 and he refused to recognize or meet with the new prime minister.[17] Instead he relied on Edmonds, who as British adviser to the Ministry of the Interior was a Government of Iraq employee, as the unofficial point of contact between the Iraqis and the embassy.[18]

A War of Nerves, April 1941

The British had limited options in responding to this turn of events. Recognizing Rashid 'Ali's government would harm British prestige and military force would take time to arrange, so Crosthwaite suggested a *Nervenkrieg* (war of nerves) to buy time. The embassy cut off the Iraqi government from its funds through the currency reserve stock in Baghdad and money held in London. Cornwallis met with the regent at Habbaniya, and, alarmed by his failure to respond to his deteriorating position, urged him to proceed to Basra and form a new Cabinet. The regent's efforts to rally military support proved ineffective, and when the Iraqi army tried to capture him in Basra he boarded a Royal Navy ship with his supporters. Lamenting that the regent "is severely handicapped in the matter of publicity," the new ambassador sent money for him to use to gather support but this proved easier said than done.[19]

Newton had been criticized for his staid response to unconventional propaganda initiatives. Cornwallis had no such qualms, and the embassy coordinated with other British agencies, including SOE, to increase its publicity through a wide variety of channels. Cecil Hope-Gill, a member of the embassy staff recruited to undertake SOE work in Iraq, mobilized the 220-strong British community in Baghdad to interact socially with English-speaking Iraqis and to spread oral propaganda, providing funds as needed. Volunteers were arranged into cells of six who met with a member of the embassy staff and, as Hope-Gill colorfully described it, "passed on the dope" which they then transmitted to their secondary cells at work. This verbal propaganda was reinforced by broadcast propaganda from an SOE station in Palestine, illustrated weeklies, and pamphlets.[20] Britain's professional propagandists also sought to exploit religious and ethnic differences in the country. The pro-Axis political and military leaders were overwhelmingly Sunni, and so the British sought to win over Shiʿi Iraqis in an anti-Axis campaign.

Cornwallis urged British officials to institute a more forward policy in Iraq: "Nothing short of armed intervention on our part can hurt Rashid ʿAli at present."[21] The Chiefs of Staff reexamined the possibility of sending reinforcements to Iraq, an action they first considered in spring 1940 (see Chapter 3) but the pendulum of Britain's wartime situation would ultimately limit the response. In the three-month period from December 1940 to February 1941 the British had an impressive victory in the Western Desert with the success of Operation Compass, pushing the Italians out of Cyrenaica. Yet that same month Rommel landed in Libya and the Axis offensive was launched in late March, pushing back the earlier British gains and culminating in the siege of Tobruk. The German invasion of Greece and Yugoslavia in April led to the disastrous Greek campaign that resulted in the British evacuation.

The Government of India, alarmed by developments in the region, warned that events in Iraq had implications for India, Iran and its oil supplies, and the larger Gulf region. General Sir Claude Auchinleck, commander-in-chief, India, had been pressing the British government to dispatch reinforcements to Iraq, not only to send a message to the government but, more importantly, to lay the groundwork for a base at Basra that would serve the larger war effort.[22] Wavell vehemently refused, as the conflict in Iraq could not have come at a worse time for the Middle East Command, still reeling from the fall of Greece and the siege of Tobruk while also mounting the defense of Crete. To give a sense of the scale of the challenge Wavell faced, his biographer Harold Raugh observed that:

> During the crucial period from February to July 1941 … Wavell was directly responsible for the conduct of some eight campaigns, with three on hand at any one time and five running simultaneously in May 1941. This fact is all the more spectacular when one considers the immensity and geographical diversity of his 2,000 by 1,700-mile command, and the resources he had available with which to conduct those campaigns.[23]

The Anglo-Iraqi Treaty limited Britain's military options in Iraq while at the same time providing a possible means of breaking the impasse. It would be difficult for Britain to take any military action unless it could be shown that Iraq had violated the treaty in some respect, and Rashid ʿAli could portray any British use of force as an attack on Iraqi independence. Cornwallis suggested that they put the prime minister's verbal assurances of support for the treaty to the test, informing him that they planned to move troops through Iraq to Palestine and open the lines of communication, a right they were guaranteed under the treaty:

> This will be an acid test for him. If he refused we have a perfect right to take any action we think fit and be in good position to counter his invasion propaganda. If he agrees we will gain military foothold in the country and be in much better position to recover the vast amount of ground which we have lost.[24]

India committed troops and the Foreign Office informed the ambassador that they would be sent to Basra on April 13. When the troop ships were in sight of Iraq Rashid 'Ali "should then be told that His Majesty's Government have noted his declarations that treaty will be observed, that His Majesty's Government are exercising their treaty rights to use line of communication through Iraq to Palestine, and that troops will arrive immediately." The Foreign Office prepared pamphlets to be printed in Arabic and distributed during the troop landing that stated that the troops were "entering your country not as enemies but as friends," that the Anglo-Iraqi Treaty allowed for the passage of troops, and that Britain respected Iraqi independence.[25]

Cornwallis decided that he would have to go back on his decision not to have any contact with Rashid 'Ali in order to make the troop landing in Basra successful, and they held a series of secret, unofficial meetings at Edmonds' home, which the official PAIFORCE history later described as "a diplomatic duel."[26] Cornwallis informed the prime minister that if he cooperated with the troop landings Britain was prepared to open "informal relations" and recognize the new government. The Government of Iraq consented to the landings but then soon qualified this response with three conditions that would have limited the number of British troops allowed in Iraq at one time to only those actually moving through the lines of communication.[27]

The first set of troops arrived without incident in Basra on April 19, but two days later the Ministry of Foreign Affairs sent a note to Cornwallis restating the previous three conditions and adding a new one that the "total strength of forces within the frontier of Iraq at any one time [was] not to exceed 1 mixed brigade."[28] Britain refused to accept these conditions. The Foreign Office informed the embassy that, not only were the British troops in Basra to stay but a second brigade was set to leave India in mid-May, with a third to follow in June:

> Our chief interest in sending troops to Iraq is the covering and establishment of a great assembly base at Basra … Our rights under the Treaty were invoked to cover disembarkation of troops and to avoid bloodshed, but force would have been used to the utmost limit to secure the disembarkation if necessary. Our position at Basra is of course covered by Article 4 of the treaty, but it also may be regarded as a new event arising out of the war. No undertakings can be given that troops will be sent northwards or moved through to Palestine, and the right to require such undertakings should not be recognised in respect of a Government which has in itself usurped power by a coup d'état, or in a country where our Treaty rights have so long been frustrated in the spirit.[29]

As the diplomatic crisis transformed into a military one, both sides turned to the treaty to provide a public rationale for their actions. Britain framed the dispatch of troops to Basra in terms of their treaty rights, and officials in London scoured the old correspondence relating to the details of the treaty to make their case while Iraqi officials did the same. Iraq protested that the establishment of a base at Basra was outside the scope of the treaty, to which the British responded that the Iraqis were trying to apply the narrower peace time provisions, which were no longer applicable: "Iraq is bound in time of war to furnish in Iraqi territory *all* facilities in her power" under Article 4.[30]

The two views were fundamentally irreconcilable because, as a Foreign Office official admitted, "we consider it necessary, on military grounds, to establish a base at Basra whatever the treaty position may be, whereas Rashid 'Ali is determined to oppose the establishment of British forces in Iraq, whatever the treaty position may be."[31]

By the end of April as these troop movements were underway Cornwallis suggested delaying tactics as Rashid 'Ali's government might be replaced by an even less cooperative one, and German progress in Cyrenaica and Greece was bolstering German prestige in Iraq.[32] He informed the Iraqi government that, in light of their cooperation on landing troops in Basra, he "had been authorised to enter into informal relations with the new administration forthwith." Yet this concession was not enough and the Iraqi government would not agree to allow any more troops from India to land in Basra. Cornwallis responded that "ships will proceed and His Majesty's Government will hold … Government responsible for any incident that may occur as consequence of this refusal."[33]

The Military Crisis

As the Anglo-Iraqi situation grew increasingly tense, Cornwallis ordered the evacuation of all British women and children to Habbaniya to then be transported to safety in India via Basra. Habbaniya, one of two British air bases in Iraq under the terms of the treaty, was, in the words of Air Vice-Marshal H. G. Smart, the air officer commanding in Iraq, "our biggest advertising feature," a visible sign of Britain's military presence in the country.[34] Yet as the political situation deteriorated, air officials were increasingly concerned by the weakness of their position there. Primarily used as a training base, Habbaniya lay in a geographically vulnerable position at the base of a plateau, many of its planes were inoperable or obsolete, and most of the pilots were inexperienced.[35] Smart wrote to Air Marshal A. W. Tedder, deputy air officer commanding-in-chief, Middle East in March 1941 that his position in Habbaniya reminded him of the Baghdadi tale of the farmer fighting locusts who stole his corn grain by grain: "my locusts arrived from the Middle East, they wore uniforms and were perfectly charming, but, after they had had a good look round, each took his grain of corn away, or sent for it by letter after his departure." As men and equipment were drawn away from Habbaniya to reinforce positions elsewhere in the region, local officials took note and he warned that they would only be able to "play a bluff hand" for so long.[36] Tedder's response to Smart's request for additional resources reveals the difficult situation of the British in early spring 1941: "You should know that situation Libya has deteriorated and German armoured forces progressing faster than anticipated. You will know of German attack on Yugo-slavia and Greece. With these two major commitments both Army and Air Force have nothing to spare for Iraq and you must do your best with what you have got."[37]

Smart's concerns proved well founded when, on April 30, an Iraqi army unit occupied the hills around Habbaniya under the guise of training exercises. Iraqi authorities asked the RAF to stop all flights and threatened to fire on any British airplanes leaving the base. British military officials protested that any armed response by the Iraqi army would violate the treaty and "will be considered an act of war and will be met by immediate counter action."[38] This demand threatened the British civilians now trapped at Habbaniya and contradicted the assurances Rashid 'Ali had given for their safety. Cornwallis saw this threat as an opportunity to challenge the Iraqi government and Churchill agreed, sending a telegram to Smart that if they had to act, "hit them quick and hit them hard."[39] On May 2, British planes bombed the Iraqi army unit, transforming the diplomatic crisis into a military one.

The Iraq crisis revived the First World War struggle between military headquarters in Cairo and the Indian army for control of policy in the Middle East. On May 5 Wavell was given operational control of British troops in northern Iraq, and on May 8 this was extended to southern Iraq as well, under the rationale that reinforcements would need to come from Middle East Command.[40] As vociferously as Wavell opposed military action in Iraq, officials in London and in India were just as determined that military action was necessary. Wavell was instructed to defend Habbaniya "by all possible means," while Cornwallis was instructed to put pressure on the Iraqi government by threatening not only the bombing of Baghdad, but also the destruction of key infrastructure such as dams and oil stations and the blockade of Basra port.[41] Wavell responded with strongly worded warnings of the perils of expanding the military conflict in Iraq. As he explained to Lampson: "*It was a question of Egypt or Iraq.* Which was the more important?" Lampson was alarmed when Wavell made this suggestion, but for both the general and the ambassador the obvious choice was Egypt at all costs.[42]

Wavell called for a political settlement rather than a military one, including resumption of normal relations with Iraq and limiting British troops to Basra for the moment. The commander-in-chief, Middle East viewed the situation in Iraq from the perspective of the war in North Africa. Two-thirds of Britain's bombers had been diverted from the Western Desert to Iraq, which greatly limited Britain's ability to effectively bomb Tripoli and Benghazi. Organizing reinforcements to send from Palestine to Iraq would mean that there would be no means of transporting the Free French force to Syria, where the situation was also growing tense, and the departure of troops from Palestine would leave it vulnerable at a time when there were signs of an impending rebellion.[43] Any expansion of Britain's military presence would appear to be a reoccupation of Iraq and risked all-out revolt in the region at a particularly sensitive time in the war. From India's perspective, Britain could not afford anything less than a strong response, because negotiations would be taken as a sign of British weakness and hurt Britain's prestige in the entire Muslim world.[44]

After a flurry of heated exchanges between Cairo and London Wavell ultimately conceded, but the military campaign did not go as expected for Britain during the early days of May. Detailed analysis of the military operations is outside the scope of this work and has been ably undertaken by others, but a brief summary is helpful to contextualize the political considerations.[45] There were three main forces involved on the British side: the RAF in Habbaniya, the troops from India at the base in Basra under the command of Lieutenant-General Edward Quinan, and the Habforce contingent from Palestine named for its first objective, the relief of Habbaniya. In the short term the sizeable troop presence in Basra proved to be of limited use, as their movement was hindered by spring floods and transportation issues. By the time the main body of the Basra force was able to mobilize the armistice had been announced.[46]

British military advisers had predicted that the Iraqi army stationed outside Habbaniya would fall apart when the British began bombing. Initially they held together against all expectations but Iraqi luck quickly changed. The Iraqi army did not storm Habbaniya even though they had superior numbers and the British base had no artillery. The base mobilized its aircraft, flying hundreds of sorties and bombing the Iraqi positions outside. The Iraqi troops were forced to withdraw at heavy cost on May 6, and the next day the British civilians were safely evacuated to Basra and then to India, allowing the British troops at Habbaniya to move out.[47] By May 7, the Royal Iraqi Air Force was out of commission due to British bombing raids, and the few intact planes were of little use as the British withheld replacement parts from India.

Habforce, the rapidly assembled body of troops from Palestine commanded by Major-General J. G. W. Clark and supported by the Arab Legion, proved instrumental in the offensive.[48] Habforce's 2,000-person Kingcol flying column, named after its commander, Brigadier J. J. Kingston, crossed the desert in record time, arrived at Habbaniya on May 18, and joined in the attack on Fallujah the next day. The official operational history noted that the capture of Fallujah "was the first airborne operation carried out by Imperial troops in this war," and also praised the Assyrians in the RAF Levies for their part in the attack.[49] The combination of spring flooding and Iraqi sabotage of the embankments on the Euphrates slowed Britain's response.[50] Oil installations were another target, and Wavell reported that after Iraqi troops occupied Rutba "by 3rd May all the refineries and oil installations were in their hands."[51] Iraqi troops also destroyed bridges on the approach to Baghdad and cut the supply of oil in the pipeline to Haifa.[52]

When the Iraqi troops had moved to surround Habbaniya the British embassy sent the signal to implement pre-arranged plans for 350 British subjects to take refuge in the embassy compound and 170 more at the American legation. Iraqi police immediately surrounded the embassy to prevent anyone from leaving or entering and cut off its wireless and telegraphic communication. Those who found themselves outside of the capital when hostilities began were not so lucky; a number of British officials and civilians in the provinces were arrested and kept in custody for the duration of the conflict.[53]

Freya Stark was one of those trapped at the British embassy, and she published a three-part series of articles in the London *Times* in June 1941 recounting her experience.[54] F. J. Harris, senior manager of the Ottoman Bank in Iraq, provided a colorful account of the life of the internees at the American legation. Harris praised the Americans for their hospitality and willingness to share living space and food stores, even including the liquor ration, "a true example of democracy!" They kept themselves busy by organizing language classes, lectures on topics "ranging from seventeenth century literature to wild game in Iraq," concerts, and producing their own newspaper.[55] Stark's account, written for public consumption, emphasized the sense of adventure, the British fighting spirit to raise morale, and the esprit de corps among those confined to the embassy grounds. Her diary entries tell a different story of anxiety over limited information and records of aircraft flying overhead. Vyvyan Holt, the oriental counsellor, was tasked with all of the negotiations for food and necessities for those at the embassy. While public programs and entertainments helped to relieve the sense of boredom, the British were, in effect, hostages, with the Iraqi government informing Cornwallis that if the British bombed any Iraqi government buildings in the capital they would retaliate by bombing the sites where the British civilians were staying. Stark lamented the "Lucknow atmosphere" in the embassy during the siege, as they lived in fear of bombing, sniping, and mob attacks.[56]

Those in the embassy had little news of what was taking place outside the compound walls and, as Stark reported, they endured the audio assault of the Baghdad radio, "blaring a holy war by wireless to all its hearers" as "The ex-Mufti preached religious war, the radio in every coffee shop was heaping insults."[57] The Iraqis demanded that the British flag be removed from the roof of the embassy, that British bank managers turn over their keys, and that all Iraqis in the compound be sent out. Cornwallis cooperated on all but the last point, although, in an act of defiance, the Union Jack was flown from the embassy grounds and later laid out on the roof.[58] He also ordered the destruction of the secret archives and ciphers to prevent them from falling into Iraqi hands. Stark described seeing, on her arrival at the embassy, "a mountain of archives smouldering to cinders … as if the sins of diplomacy were being dealt with in one of Dante's milder circles."[59] After the crisis the ambassador justified his compliance by pointing out that the people in the embassy were completely reliant on Iraqi authorities for food, water, medical supplies, and electricity, while the women and children who had been evacuated to Habbaniya were particularly vulnerable.[60] Stark observed that Adrian Bishop, assistant public relations officer (and SOE representative) was "not too optimistic" and they "must admit that in the map of the whole Middle East we are not so very important, but console ourselves by reflecting that our neighbourhood to Oil will prevent us from being forgotten."[61]

"A Family Affair" or "Imperialist War"

Both sides of the conflict drew on the terms of the treaty to provide a rationale for their actions. Rashid 'Ali's government circulated an official memo to diplomatic representatives in Baghdad at the outbreak of hostilities that reviewed the Anglo-Iraqi negotiations in April and concluded: "the acts violating the treaty continued, as well as the violations of sovereignty of the state, on its independence and dignity, which provoked worry among the general population" so the stationing of troops around Habbaniya was, in the eyes of the Iraqi government, "a simple measure of precaution." Britain's May 2 airstrikes on these troops were an attack on Iraqi sovereignty, and Iraq "proclaims to the world that it was not responsible for the consequences of this aggression, responsibility for which rests on the British government."[62] British aggression proved that, as Iraq had long claimed, the British used the treaty as a pretext to cover their war of imperial expansion.

Eden stated in the House of Commons debate on May 6 that it was not Rashid 'Ali's unconstitutional coup that led to British military action, it was his failure to observe the treaty obligations, made all the worse by the fact that "It is we who assured the independence of modern Iraq, and it is we who have assisted her and in every respect have kept our word."[63] Britain did not intend to control Iraq, but to see in place a government that would "honour the Anglo Iraq Treaty in letter and in spirit." The Foreign Office asserted that full implementation of Britain's right to move troops into Iraq would not threaten Iraq's sovereignty, as the experience of Egypt had proven.[64]

The developing conflict was watched with great interest by other actors in the region. Axis broadcasts reinforced the message of imperialist aggression, projecting the image of Iraq defending itself against Britain and fighting for Arab independence, and hoped to use the conflict to spark unrest in other Arab countries.[65] Pro-Iraqi demonstrations were held in both Damascus and Beirut, and in Damascus the Arab Guard distributed anti-British pamphlets and there were calls to establish an Iraq Defence Committee. In Turkey the British ambassador received information on 2,500 Syrians who left for Iraq to support the uprising.[66] Rashid 'Ali tried to capitalize on regional interest and recruit support from neighboring states, framing the conflict as a holy war with himself as the head of a movement that would unite not only Arabs but all Muslims. The Iraqi government publicized the names of religious leaders who had issued fatwas declaring the struggle a jihad, and instructed its representatives in India and Afghanistan to get this information published in the local press to win the support of local Muslims. He called for consultation with the members of the Saadabad Pact and sent representatives to both Turkey and Saudi Arabia to try and rally support for the Iraqi position.[67]

The British Ministry of Information tried to limit the appeal of these regional campaigns, urging representatives to downplay the importance of the operations in Iraq and avoid any suggestion that it was a real war: "We suggest the use of phrases such as 'dissident elements' instead of 'enemy' and that normal war communiqué jargon should be studiously avoided." Instead they should "treat the Iraq revolt as family affair wherein mighty parent Britain is about to administer sound slapping to a naughty child."[68] As Wavell observed, treating it as a war only gave credence to Rashid 'Ali's claims as an Arab leader. The BBC was instructed to avoid any implication that Britain was conquering Iraq or denying its independence. SOE printed leaflets attacking the attitude of Syrian and Iraqi students for distribution at al-Azhar.[69]

The Rashid 'Ali government was banking on assistance from Germany, but despite the propaganda it was too little too late. Not only were they caught by surprise, but they were unhappy at the timing, as the conflict was unfolding in Iraq at the same time as Germany was planning its attack on the Soviet Union and engaged in operations in Crete.[70] Germany sent weapons and air support via Syria but these reinforcements arrived late and were far more limited than what the Iraqi government had expected. Fritz Grobba returned to Baghdad to serve as liaison with the Rashid 'Ali government, which was requesting German officers to train the Iraqi forces.[71] Grobba brought a treaty with him that would have obliged Iraq to transfer all oil concessions, the Baghdad Railway concession, and all aerodromes to Germany. While Rashid 'Ali was willing to accept the terms, some of his colleagues were not, resulting in a Cabinet split.[72] Sir Hughe Knatchbull-Hugessen, British ambassador to Turkey, reported that the Germans suggested that Rashid 'Ali move his capital to Mosul but: "Germans are very ill supplied and state that they can produce no more help for two months."[73]

As the military operations proceeded, Wavell suggested they have the regent set up an alternative government, which Britain would then recognize and finance, as a way to assuage concerns that Britain might be using military operations as cover to occupy Iraq.[74] The regent arrived back in Iraq on May 22 and convened a Council of State charged with forming a government.[75] To help prepare the way for a change of government, Britain began an intense propaganda campaign. By May 26 the RAF was dropping 40,000 pamphlets a day to targeted populations.[76] Kingcol moved on to Baghdad on May 27 and British officials received vague reports that Rashid ʿAli's government was falling apart and losing support. Confirmation came on May 30 when the mayor of Baghdad informed Cornwallis that Rashid ʿAli and his government, as well as the officers of the Golden Square, the mufti, and their followers, had left Iraq to seek refuge in Iran. The mayor and a committee of four local leaders took over administration and asked for an armistice and the return of the regent to the capital.[77] Gerald De Gaury reported that the formal surrender took place on May 31 "at an eerie rendezvous in waterlogged country west of Bagdad" at 4:00 in the morning.[78]

The Foreign Office suggested terms for an armistice that dealt with both political and military issues and a government that would fulfill the treaty "in both letter and spirit."[79] Britain would aid the regent in restoring a "legal government" and "abstain from any infringement of Iraq Independence as formally laid down by Treaty." The British recognized that events in May had not resulted from any division between Iraq and Britain but "that these incidents were engineered solely by a small political party for their own private ends." The new government agreed to allow British forces to remain in Iraq for the duration of the war, and that British military authorities could remain in Basra under the condition that they not interfere with domestic affairs.[80] On June 8, 1941, Iraq broke off relations with Italy, finally meeting one of Britain's most important tests of loyalty.[81]

While the armistice settled official relations between Iraq and Britain, it did not bring calm to Baghdad. Cornwallis described the temper of Baghdad as "hostile," with the Italian legation actively spreading propaganda and pamphlets in support of Rashid ʿAli's return.[82] British military intelligence had reported anti-Jewish propaganda in late April, and in the aftermath of Rashid ʿAli's departure the city was wracked by violence targeting the Jewish community.[83] Known as the *Farhud*, the two days of violence on June 1–2, 1941, resulted in the death of 180 Baghdadi Jews and the injury of many more, as well as widespread destruction of property. The Foreign Office sent instructions preventing British troops from entering Baghdad to put down the riots as this would have reflected poorly on the regent.[84] Cornwallis reported that Iraqi army and police officers instigated the violence to "take advantage of the temporary absence of responsible authority." They also participated in the looting and refused to crack down on the riots without the direct order of the regent. Cornwallis was frustrated that the new Cabinet, while generally cooperative, was still very weak and hesitant to aggressively counter the damage created by the propaganda of the Rashid ʿAli regime. The army was "sullen and in no mood to obey unpleasant orders." He concluded: "In those few hours however hundreds of families were ruined and brutal outrages were committed which all right minded persons will for long remember with shame and horror."[85]

The Rashid 'Ali coup highlights the way in which the ebb and flow of progress on the military front of the war affected diplomatic calculations. In March, when the war was going well for the British, military officials supported a forward policy, but by April they were discouraging military action. Facing criticism at home for his government's response to the Iraqi crisis, Churchill argued that the coup was not the result of an intelligence failure, but rather lack of troops. He noted in a House of Commons debate on May 7, 1941:

> We have been told that the Foreign Office never knows anything that is going on in the world, and that our organisation is quite unadapted to meet the present juncture. But we have known only too well what was going on in Iraq, and as long ago as last May, a year ago, the Foreign Office began to ask for troops to be sent there to guard the line of communications. We had not the troops.[86]

However, by sending in troops through Basra the British were able to disrupt Rashid 'Ali's plans to play for time until the Germans were ready or able to provide assistance.[87]

Was Britain's gamble in Iraq worth the risk? When Wavell called for negotiations rather than sending additional troops, the War Office argued that Rashid 'Ali had planned to delay action until the Axis could provide substantial support: "Our arrival at Basra forced him to go off at half cock before the Axis were ready."[88] Germany's feeble response to Iraqi requests for help was largely determined by its own larger war commitments. The Iraqi decision to push the envelope in spring 1941 proved to be a grave miscalculation; Britain took the risk of responding with a more aggressive policy, and, despite serious military shortages, was successful. Egypt and Iraq had called Britain's bluff in 1940, and as Wavell observed after the conclusion of operations in Iraq: "I must say I very much doubted whether the bluff, for it was almost entirely bluff, would succeed."[89] In the end, the military response set in motion a series of events, culminating in operations in both Syria and Iran, that presented Britain with a far more stable Middle East for the remainder of the war.

While often referred to as the "Rashid 'Ali coup," the Iraqi prime minister's actual role in this dramatic confrontation with Britain was overshadowed by that of the army officers who put him in power. As Cornwallis admitted after the fact:

> In the light of later events it may reasonably be concluded that the rebel Government was the Government of the Golden Square, and not a Government of Rashid 'Ali relying on the unqualified support of the army. As a politician of practised cunning with a considerable following he was certainly more than a figure-head; as such a politician, indeed, he was indispensable, but at the same time far from all-powerful.[90]

This episode reveals the dangers inherent in Britain's focus on Rashid 'Ali as the "Public Enemy No. 1" in Iraq. As with the crisis leading up to 'Ali Mahir's removal from power in Egypt in 1940, it caused the British to overlook the deeper structural issues underlying local discontent.

Many Iraqi historians use the term "revolution" to describe the coup, but its result was far from revolutionary. Mahmud al-Durra, who offered one of the most-cited Iraqi accounts of these events, noted that the outcome was a reassertion of the conservative social order of Iraq with British support.[91] As will be demonstrated in the chapters below, as the war progressed Britain's response was ultimately to fall back on Nuri. Yet the use of revolutionary language in accounts of the coup reflects its important place in the historical memory of Iraq. One Arab historian later described the Rashid 'Ali coup as "the first Suez in modern Arab history," comparing it to the 1956 Suez crisis in the passionate zeal it inspired in the Arab people.[92] Mahmoud al-Durra observed that the 1958 revolution was "one of the fruits of this war and a link in the chain which strengthened the Iraqi people to face the journey which lay before them."[93] A new Iraqi historical narrative of the war was developing, with the main participants in the revolt taking on the status of martyrs in the eyes of many Arabs.

5

Getting the "Muddle out of 'Muddle East,'" June 1941–December 1941

Air Marshal Tedder, the recently appointed air officer commanding-in-chief for the Middle East, surveyed the situation in July 1941. Using a nickname for the Middle East Command (MEC) that had been circulating since the early months of the war he lamented, with good reason, that "there is a devil of a lot to be done to get the 'muddle' out of Muddle East."[1] The transformative events of 1941 in the Middle East and Mediterranean: the Rashid 'Ali coup, operations in Syria, the ongoing siege of Tobruk, the loss of Greece and Crete, and events further afield, most importantly Operation Barbarossa, the German invasion of the Soviet Union, would dramatically change the Allied presence in the region.[2] Britain found itself, in the case of Iraq, occupying a country with which it had treaty relations and, in the case of Egypt, using its ally as a staging ground for the North African campaign. Reflecting on the new year Lampson envisioned that Britain "shall gradually establish in Egypt a sort of bastion to which we shall pour men and material to enable us to take on an eastern front."[3] Despite all of Britain's announcements that they were only in Iraq to oppose an unconstitutional government, the reality was that, once the dust settled in summer 1941, Britain had a far more extensive system of military and political advisers, intelligence organizations, and propaganda machinery. Officials were keenly aware of the need to balance very real wartime needs with sensitivity to local fears that the terms of the treaties were being ignored and overstepped.

In spring 1941 British planning for the region was predicated on the assumption that Hitler was moving east through Greece, Crete, and then into the Middle East in a pincer movement. The fact that this German offensive never materialized makes it easy to downplay the threat, which was very real at the time, particularly from 1941 to 1943. The German invasion of the Soviet Union on June 22, 1941, shifted the projected path of a German offensive, raising fears that Germany would sweep south into Iraq and Iran, seizing oil installations and cutting off Britain's lines of communication. A July 1941 War Cabinet Joint Planning Staff report emphasized the importance of Iranian oil and the need to hold defensive positions in Egypt, Syria, and Iraq as they would strain Germany's lines of communication and supply networks. Withdrawing to only the most vital areas in the region would hurt morale, lead Spain and Turkey to join the Axis, cause economic damage, and give Germany free rein in the Mediterranean: "She must be made to fight for every inch."[4]

Britain had an uneasy acceptance of the Vichy presence in Syria, and had discouraged upsetting the status quo there but the experience in Iraq brought home the potential danger. Britain had issued a declaration in July 1940 on Syria after the fall of France "to the effect that they could not allow Syria or the Lebanon to be occupied by any hostile Power, or to be used as a base for attacks upon those countries in the Middle East which they are obliged to defend, or to become the scene of such disorder as to constitute a danger to those countries."[5] Germany's aid to the Rashid 'Ali government during the events of May 1941 was limited in scope but their use of Vichy-controlled Syria as a landing base for planes and source of supplies to aid Iraq violated this declaration.[6] There was a sense that Britain had lucked out in Iraq, but may not be as lucky with Syria. Air Vice-Marshal Smart noted that "We won the 'Rebel' war with training aircraft and were extremely fortunate in defeating the few Huns with what we had in the way of operational aircraft. But if he really pushes much stuff over here, we shall be in a bit of a mess."[7] The result was the June 1941 campaign to install the Free French in Syria and remove the Vichy threat from the Levant.[8]

The events of spring 1941 brought home a number of lessons that shaped Britain's presence in the region for the remainder of the war. The first was a reinforcement of the conviction that propaganda was closely tied to policy and, as a result, the unpopularity of Britain's actions in the region would hamper the effectiveness of their publicity efforts. It was against this backdrop that Churchill asked Eden for a reconsideration of Britain's Arab policy. While acknowledging that support for Arab unity might open the Pandora's box of Arab demands for the independence of Palestine, Syria, and Lebanon, Eden concluded that it would be impolitic to oppose the principle. Arabs should make such a declaration themselves but he did not think it was likely due to dynastic rivalries and the fact that Iraq wanted Baghdad to be the center of such a federation. He concluded: "Arab federation is not at the moment practical politics … Nevertheless, Arabs generally agree that some form of 'Arab federation' is desirable, and I think that we should not only refrain from opposing such vague aspirations, but even take every opportunity of expressing publicly our support for them."[9]

Eden's Mansion House speech of May 29, 1941, echoed these sentiments. After addressing developments in Iraq and Syria he declared:

> The Arab world has made great strides since the settlement reached at the end of the last War, and many Arab thinkers desire for the Arab peoples a greater degree of unity than they now enjoy. In reaching out towards this unity they hope for our support. No such appeal from our friends should go unanswered. It seems to me both natural and right that the cultural and economic ties between the Arab countries, and the political ties too, should be strengthened. His Majesty's Government for their part will give their full support to any scheme that commands general approval.[10]

The speech was well received in the Arab world and would frequently be referred to in subsequent years as a formative moment in the wartime Arab unity movement.[11]

The second lesson that Britain took from the tumultuous events of 1941 was that Britain's command structure for the Middle East was flawed. General Wavell was forced to wear too many hats, with political and propaganda responsibilities in addition to the military ones and multiple operations in progress simultaneously over a vast territory. In autumn 1940 Wavell had first called for the establishment of an "outpost" of the Ministry of Information in the Middle East to coordinate propaganda work, and he continued to repeat this call through spring 1941.[12] Recognizing the growing complexity of Britain's war effort in the Middle East and the need to coordinate information and decision-making throughout the region, the British created the new position of minister of state, Middle East to address these challenges. Based in Cairo the new minister was charged with carrying out the policy of the War Cabinet on the spot, relieving the Commanders-in-Chief of some of their duties and providing political guidance. He was also well placed to address issues that fell under the purview of multiple departments, such as Anglo-Free French relations, enemy-occupied territory, economic warfare, and issues tied to American supplies.[13]

When Oliver Lyttelton arrived in Cairo in July 1941 to take up this newly created position, one of his first priorities was reorganizing the propaganda field. Each of the three military branches had their own propaganda organizations, SOE was engaged in black propaganda, and the embassy had charge of open civilian propaganda.[14] As part of the reorganization much of Pubsec's staff was removed from the embassy and placed in the new Directorate of Propaganda, which took control of both production and distribution of propaganda for the Middle East as a whole and fell under the Ministry of Information. The remaining embassy section was left to focus on Egyptian propaganda, which had been somewhat neglected given its enlarged scope in the early months of the war.[15]

The military losses of 1941, including the failure of Operation Battleaxe to relieve besieged Tobruk in June, led to a change in leadership in MEC. In July 1941 Wavell was transferred to India to serve as commander-in-chief, India and was replaced by General Auchinleck. This was followed by a reorganization of Britain's command structure in the Middle East in order to more effectively respond to the multiple challenges Britain faced. Forces in the Western Desert composed the new Eighth Army under General Cunningham, while "the Headquarters, British Troops in Egypt, became in effect a large Base and Lines of Communication Area Command operationally responsible only for the internal security and anti-aircraft defence of the Egyptian base."[16] General Wilson was given command of the new Ninth Army in Palestine and Transjordan.

The question of whether Iraq fit best within MEC or India remained a point of debate through the rapidly evolving wartime situation in 1941: "On June 18th, Lieutenant-General Quinan re-assumed command of all troops in Iraq, now to be known as FORCE IRAQ, and was made responsible to GHQ, India. Thus the problem of dual control between India and Middle East was solved for the time being." RAF Iraq remained under MEC, however. The growing threat of a German invasion through the Caucasus in autumn meant that "It was essential to have a unified command in Syria, Palestine and Iraq" and in January 1942 Force Iraq became the nucleus of the Tenth Army and returned to MEC.[17]

In order to keep the Middle East quiet for the duration, especially in light of this quickly expanding military presence, Britain also needed to meet the region's material needs and limit wartime disruption of supplies and economic activity. This became increasingly difficult with the closure of the Mediterranean to British shipping in 1940, which not only added at least ten weeks to the travel time for supplies to Egypt but also disrupted internal shipping, as ships were rerouted from the well-established port facilities in Alexandria to the less developed ports on the Red Sea. The opening of the Red Sea to shipping from the United States in April 1941 promised some relief, but civilian supply needs had to be balanced against the heavy demand military supplies placed on Allied shipping, especially by summer 1941 when the ration strength of Britain's army in the Middle East approached a million men. While military needs were paramount, disruptions in food supplies could spark local unrest, leading to the diversion of troops from the front to restore order.[18] The Middle East Supply Centre (MESC) was established in April 1941 to address the supply challenges caused by the shortage of shipping. MESC was tasked with building reserves from within the Middle East to limit the draw on shipping from Britain and the United States and to ensure that local resources were used effectively.[19]

Britain had to balance this rapid reorganization and expansion of Britain's military, propaganda, and intelligence structures in the Middle East against the sensibilities of the local populations and governments. Rushbrook Williams reminded his colleagues in the midst of the discussions surrounding an expanded Ministry of Information presence:

> Has anyone considered the constitutional position? Egypt is an independent country and there are only two "British" official bodies who have the necessary locus standi in Cairo: namely, the Embassy and G.H.Q. A "branch office" of the Ministry will have, I think, to be attached (in name at least) to one or the other. And this, plainly, may lead to difficulties.[20]

As Britain's footprint in both Egypt and Iraq continued to expand throughout the war, the question of how to square this with the terms of the treaties would remain a perpetual concern.

This preoccupation shaped the parameters of the new MESC as well. London officials debated whether or not the center should be given executive or merely consultative authority, and ultimately concluded that it would be limited to a supervisory role, as "it would be politically impossible for a British authority to assume direct control of the imports and exports of independent sovereign states." MESC's power to ensure compliance was more indirect, as it could reward cooperative governments by granting access to shipping space and import supplies. MESC staff in Egypt and Iraq were based in the local British embassies, in keeping with the guidelines of the treaty.[21]

"Sweetening the Egyptians" in 1941[22]

Ambassador Lampson reported that the Egyptian public's response to the events in Iraq was muted by their preoccupation with events much closer to home.[23] Rommel's offensive in March 1941 brought him to the Egyptian border by April, signaling a new and more dangerous stage of the war in the Western Desert. By the end of April the ambassador lamented that "the average Egyptian now believes that Turkey will rat and let German troops through to Syria and Palestine. The more sophisticated Egyptian realises how easily the Germans can now get into Syria without even passing through Turkey."[24] The timing of events in Iraq with the attack on Tobruk and the fall of Greece all added to this sense of gloom. The influx of refugees from the Balkans, including the royal families of Greece and Yugoslavia, provided sobering visual reminders to the residents of Cairo of the disastrous operations of spring.[25]

At the same time, Lampson warned that the situation in Iraq had serious implications for Egypt that could not be ignored. The Egyptian government was generally helpful during the Iraqi crisis but there were troubling signs emanating from Cairo including reports that 'Ali Mahir and his supporters were trying to contact the Iraqi prime minister and that there were plans in the works for a coup in Egypt as well.[26] The 'Aziz al-Masri affair turned all of these forebodings and rumblings into reality. On May 16, 1941, the former Egyptian chief of staff who had been forced to resign due to British protests in 1940 (see Chapter 2) attempted to fly to Iraq in a stolen airplane and was caught. After his capture 'Aziz al-Masri defended his actions, explaining that he was going to Baghdad to try and stop the revolt by offering Iraq Dominion status "on instructions from the British Military Authorities."[27] Colonel Thornhill, a member of SOE operating in Egypt, had had lunch with al-Masri four days before his flight. While Thornhill was adamant that he did not encourage the mission to Iraq, he did agree to pass his contact's suggestions on to Brigadier Clayton who concluded that "the proposal was too fantastic to be acted upon and no further action was taken by him." Lampson first heard of the British connection in this case from the Egyptian prime minister, and the involvement of SOE only exacerbated his frustration with military authorities operating in Cairo. While Egypt wished to prosecute 'Aziz al-Masri for treason, a trial would bring up the uncomfortable question of British involvement in Egypt and threatened to expose the whole British intelligence apparatus.[28]

'Aziz al-Masri's true intention may have been to join Rommel's forces and bring Egyptian troops with him, and the episode is indicative of Britain's growing concern of a potential security threat from inside the Egyptian army. Major A. W. Sansom, British chief field security officer in Cairo, later recalled that, when he heard of the hostilities at Habbaniya: "Nothing could stave off an Egyptian Army revolt, I thought … Our position in Egypt and in Iraq was so similar that a revolt in one country seemed almost bound to spark on an insurrection in the other."[29] Future Egyptian President Anwar al-Sadat's description of the response of the young Egyptian army officers to news of events in Iraq reveals that Sansom's fears were well founded: "It was the first sign of the liberation of the Arab world, and we followed the course of the revolt with admiration … We, the young officers, wanted to attack the British and make Egypt a second Iraq."[30]

Lampson described Egypt's attitude to the war in spring and summer 1941 as "one of despondency," caused by setbacks in Cyrenaica in April, the campaign in Iraq in May, and air raids on Alexandria in June, leading to a revival of the "open city" calls and vociferous demands for British evacuation of Cairo. Over 650 residents of Alexandria died during the air raids of June 7–8, and the ensuing mass exodus of

250,000 people from the city threatened the ability of the port to keep functioning.[31] At the same time, as C. H. Bateman noted in June 1941: "Our policy in Egypt is based purely on military necessity. General Wavell has insisted that everything must be done (and certainly while the enemy is on Egyptian soil) to keep the great body of Egyptians sweet and tranquil … he cannot afford to run the risk of 'another Iraq' in his rear."[32] The Foreign Office revived the issue of an Egyptian declaration of war, but the service chiefs were satisfied with Egyptian cooperation and did not demand a greater commitment.[33] Maintaining internal stability in Egypt to avoid any disruption to the war effort or the diversion of British troops from the front became the priority.

While Britain dropped the issue of a declaration of war for the moment, it was no longer willing to turn a blind eye to fifth columnists operating in Egypt. Amidst reports of growing defeatism and xenophobia it renewed its demands for the internment of the Palace Italians and other suspected fifth columnists. The Foreign Office tried to embolden Egyptian Prime Minister Husayn Sirri to act and offered assurances that Britain would support him "should he find it necessary to take most drastic action now that the enemy is on Egyptian soil."[34] The former Prime Minister 'Ali Mahir was one of the key targets, as he was out of power but not out of Egypt. In April 1941 Sirri had assured Lampson that 'Ali Mahir would be sent abroad or confined to his home in the country, yet he refused to leave Cairo and protested that forced internment violated the parliamentary immunity he enjoyed as a senator.[35] Ahmad Husayn of the Young Egypt group was arrested in May, and in autumn 1941 Hassan al-Banna, leader of the Muslim Brotherhood, was interned as well, although Sirri had him released in November out of concern that his internment would lead to a "religious revolution."[36]

Economic dislocation caused by the war effort further heightened tensions and exacerbated the income disparity in Egypt due to rampant inflation, with the overall cost of living index up 38 percent by autumn 1941. Food prices had been particularly hard hit, and those on fixed wages, including most government officials, were feeling the pinch. Bread supplies had long been the bellwether of Egyptian economic conditions, and shortages threatened unrest. In June 1941 as grain prices increased bakers threatened to strike in protest against limits in supplies. Grain purchases from British military authorities alleviated the immediate crisis, and loaves of mixed grains were introduced to stretch the supply of wheat.[37] Matches, small change, and cotton cloth were some of the other items in short supply, and meatless days were introduced twice a week.[38] Tramway and bus workers went on strike in September, and there were rumors of a planned railway strike, which would potentially disrupt troop movements.[39]

The British brokered an agreement with the Egyptian government to limit Egyptian cotton production in order to increase food production and address food shortages. Cotton made up 70–80 percent of Egypt's exports, and Britain purchased the Egyptian cotton crop at a price of £25,000,000, with a 50/50 cost-sharing arrangement with the Egyptian government in 1941.[40] Yet British officials believed that Sirri failed to properly sell the deal, missing out on its propaganda value and reinforcing the British dilemma of finding themselves, as Lampson noted in September, "backing a minority though entirely friendly Government, against a hostile majority." It appeared that the Wafd and the palace were joining up against the embassy, which, in Bateman's estimation, was "the worst of all possible Egyptian combinations." This meant that the embassy, as the sole remaining backer of the Sirri government, could be held responsible for all of its failings.[41]

The difficult lesson British officials took away from the 1940–1 Sabri/Sirri administrations was that having a pro-British government in power was not enough to secure their interests in wartime. The Foreign Office was now convinced of the need to bring the Wafd back to power as the only party that had real popular support in Egypt. Lampson agreed but it would be difficult to convince King Farouk to accept a Wafd administration and it would require removing Sirri from power and, as Lampson admitted, "We must be loyal to our friends: and Hussein Sirry with all his faults is supremely loyal to us." Given their past record the Wafd would likely demand treaty revision, it would be hard to remove them from power, and it would alienate other Egyptian politicians. The question was, on what issue should Britain take a stand, and when would the moment be opportune? The best time to move would be when the situation in the Western Desert was clearer.[42] Autumn 1941, with the assemblage of troops and supplies in Egypt in preparation for Operation Crusader, Auchinleck's offensive against Rommel at Tobruk in November 1941, was not the right time to risk political upheaval in Egypt.

Post-coup Iraq: The "Second British Occupation"

The new British ambassador to Iraq, Sir Kinahan Cornwallis, was finally able to formally present his credentials to the regent on June 14.[43] He then faced the daunting task of dealing with the short-term fallout of the coup, facilitating the return of a legitimate and cooperative government, and rooting out pro-Axis influences, all while keeping within the parameters of the treaty. At the same time, Iraq would be called on to play an even greater role in the war effort. Air Vice-Marshal D'Albiac, the new RAF commander in Iraq, pointed out in June that Palestine and Iraq had been on the periphery of the air campaigns but: "The recent German advances into Greece and Crete and her infiltration into Syria have, however, altered the situation materially and from now on we must regard both Palestine and 'Iraq as operational theatres of war."[44] The German invasion of the Soviet Union only increased Iraq's importance and over the next two years securing Iraq became increasingly vital as neighboring Iran developed into a critical transit point for Lend-Lease supplies. Britain's military presence was no longer limited to the RAF contingent allowed under the Anglo-Iraqi Treaty, but swelled to include a significant army presence with the creation of the Tenth Army in January 1942.

Iraqi historians refer to this period from 1941 to 1945 as the "second British occupation," a time during which Britain intervened in internal Iraqi affairs at a level unmatched since the end of the mandate.[45] To the British, this was not an occupation but the exercise of their rights under the treaty to face the extenuating circumstances of world war. When the BBC Arabic broadcast used the word *ihtilal* (occupation) to describe Britain's post-coup role, Cornwallis urged the Foreign Office to ensure that this word was removed from any future statements relating to the

British troops in Iraq, as it would only reinforce local concerns about their ultimate purpose.[46] However justified this presence may have been to the British in light of the status of the war, to many Iraqis it represented a substantial violation of the terms of the treaty.

The coup was a vindication of those who had warned that Britain was not taking the German threat in Iraq seriously and one of the embassy's most pressing concerns was removing pro-Axis influences from the country. The political clubs that had been focal points of Axis propaganda were a key target; the Palestine Defence Society was shut down, the Muthanna Club got a new president, and the premises of other political clubs were seized by the government.[47] Beyond immediate damage control Britain instituted a long-term campaign to restore faith in British motives, promote effective government, and address the economic issues created by the war. This involved creating an extensive publicity and intelligence apparatus in the country, bolstered by the growing presence of Allied troops. The embassy Public Relations Section (PR Section) was reorganized and Cornwallis brought in new publicity staff from across the region, including Stewart Perowne from Aden and Freya Stark from the British embassy in Cairo.[48] Many of these new publicity officers used their positions as cover for intelligence work, and the PR Section and Oriental Secretariat served as the home for SOE operatives in the early months after the coup.[49] The restructuring was not limited to Baghdad, as there were plans to establish PR Sections at the consulates in Basra and Mosul for publicity work and to set up a British Institute in Mosul.[50] A member of the Indian Political Service was seconded to head the new PR Section in Basra, a reflection of its importance as a regional crossroads with the potential to influence public opinion in Iran and India.[51]

British officials were divided in their estimation of the extent of the support that Rashid ʿAli had enjoyed. Cornwallis believed that most Iraqis had not supported the revolt and it "came as a profound shock to them. They were ashamed, and wanted to make amends."[52] Other observers pointed to larger existential questions. Freya Stark, reflecting on the origins of the crisis in her series of articles in the London *Times*, cited the unpopularity of Britain's policies on Palestine and Syria and its inability to provide Iraq's military with the equipment it requested under the terms of the treaty. But there was also another deeper social challenge, the generation gap and what she viewed as Britain's failure to mobilize youth in support of its cause: "It is regrettable that in most nations of the world youth is not with us. In Iraq the fact that for 20 years power has been in the hands of a small set of elderly men friendly to Great Britain has driven into an opposing camp the restless young for whom no room was made." She contrasted the situation in 1941 with that of the earlier global conflict: "One must remember that in 1914 our position was the exact opposite of what it is now. We were then the apostles of change; we are now upholders of the *status quo*. We then made common cause with young and ardent ferments of revolt; we are now holding them in check as best we can," creating a situation that Germany was poised to exploit.[53]

Stark's solution to this generational divide was to import the Brotherhood of Freedom model from Egypt. She and Stewart Perowne had dreamed up the original model for the Brotherhood while they were both stationed in Aden, and now she hoped to use it to harness Arab nationalism as a pro-British and progressive force.

However, this required winning over youth and the army. They focused on the need to build personal relationships and recruited the British community to support their cause, reaching out to those with local networks such as the members of the military mission, Iraq Petroleum Company employees, the British colony, British officials in the Iraqi government, and teachers.[54]

In the post-mortem of British policy following the events of May 1941, officials pointed to two main factors leading to the coup. The decline of British influence in the 1930s made Iraq fertile ground for Axis infiltration, and the decrepit state of Iraqi politics spiraled into a cycle of coups and intrigues far removed from the representative government promised in the Iraqi Constitution. The British framed their response within the terms of the treaty as a way to restore constitutional rule. Cornwallis was, in the British view, the perfect person for this job, given his previous experience in Iraq. Stark noted that at the time of the armistice on May 30, 1941, Cornwallis "made a wonderful speech in Arabic telling them that as he and King Feisal *made* the constitution, it is safe in his hands."[55] Political rebuilding required a cooperative prime minister. The regent chose Jamil al-Midfa'i, who had served as prime minister after the 1936 coup and had a reputation for remaining politically neutral. Cornwallis pledged "that I would give him my full support providing he carried out the Treaty in the letter and spirit." The ambassador had his doubts about his ability to deliver, but admitted that "he was the only available candidate with any public support."[56]

Britain's second political priority was to restore the legitimacy of the regent by increasing his popularity and visibility.[57] The monarchy in Iraq did not play as active a role in politics as it did in Egypt and had not figured strongly in the Iraqi political equation after the death of King Faysal. In the constitutional chess match that played out in spring 1941 the real limitations of the monarchy's power had proven to be a key vulnerability. A number of amendments to the Iraqi Constitution passed in 1942 addressed some of these weaknesses. In addition to provisions that made it more difficult for the Cabinet to dismiss the Chamber of Deputies and allowed Parliament to meet outside of Baghdad in an emergency, the amendments also gave the regent, acting on behalf of the young king, the ability to dismiss the prime minister.[58] And yet, these enhanced constitutional powers did not change the fact that the regent had returned to Baghdad after the coup only because he had British support, and he paid the price in the loss of local popularity. Having lost its nationalist credentials, the monarchy came to rely more heavily on both British support and conservative interests in the country, in particular the tribal shaykhs.[59]

Neither Iraq's Shi'i majority nor its Kurdish minority had supported the coup; in fact, Rashid 'Ali's inability to convince them to fight against British forces was often cited as a contributing factor to the coup's failure.[60] Leaders of both communities called for increased participation in the political process as a reward for their loyalty, a demand which also complemented British objectives of revitalizing Iraqi politics and administration and infusing new blood into the system. As Cornwallis warned: "We must not give the Shiahs the impression that we seek their support in time of trouble and ignore then when things go well." The post-coup Midfa'i government did make some progress in addressing Shi'i and Kurdish demands, including representatives of both communities in the Cabinet.[61] Yet these concessions were limited, and the

British were disappointed in the prime minister's unwillingness to move on this issue. The Shi'i leader Sayyid Muhammad al-Sadr, the president of the Senate, expressed his "deep feeling of dissatisfaction" with the Sunni's "virtual monopoly" of political offices.[62]

C. J. Edmonds, the British adviser to the Ministry of the Interior and himself an expert on Kurdish affairs, advocated a gradualist approach, urging both the Shi'a and Kurds to avoid making drastic, concrete demands but rather allow the British to put pressure on the Iraqi government to meet legitimate grievances.[63] At the same time, he grew frustrated by the government's unwillingness to give more than lip service to these reforms. Cornwallis reported that Edmonds sensed when talking to Iraqi politicians, "a vindictive feeling that they would prefer to lose Kurdistan rather than secure them as loyal Iraqis by acknowledging their existence qua Kurds; they are ready to contemplate evacuation of the Kurdistan areas but never a really liberal policy."[64]

As with Sirri's government in Egypt, Britain quickly became frustrated with the limitations of the Midfa'i government and its unwillingness to actively counteract the impact of Rashid 'Ali's propaganda and bases of support, particularly in the army. Cornwallis deprecated the prime minister's "business as usual" approach to politics:

> The Madfai Cabinet acted as though the events of May had been comparable to any of the other *coups d'État* by which one Government had succeeded another since the death of King Faisal I—one more lamentable episode over which it was charitable to draw a decent veil .... Iraqi offenders, ... were so tenderly handled as almost to give the impression that the Cabinet themselves lent belief to Rashid Ali's promise to be back shortly with a German army.[65]

Britain's Iraqi supporters found the continued presence of known Axis sympathizers in the bureaucracy and army demoralizing, but, as the oriental counsellor observed, sympathy for Rashid 'Ali was so pervasive among Iraqi officials and military officers that they could not simply remove anyone with these sympathies from power or they would have a huge group of disgruntled, unemployed officials.[66] The Iraqi army was a particular cause of concern and while it was not dismantled it was purged. It had grown in size from 20,300 men in 1936 to 47,000 men in 1941. In the aftermath of the Rashid 'Ali coup its size fell to 25,000 men and "over 605 officers were either arrested or retired, including all division and brigade commanders."[67] The army would now be removed from the political equation for the remainder of the war and maintained in a perpetual state of weakness, with its duties limited to internal security and defense along the borders and lines of communication.[68]

The weaknesses of the government became increasingly evident by autumn 1941 and revived the perennial question of British intervention. British officials viewed the inefficiency of Iraqi politicians with alarm, as the stagnant nature of Iraqi politics had repercussions for Britain as well as for Iraq, but there was widespread disagreement on the best solution. How much administrative control did they want to exert? Should they support the installation of a more representative government, and could they do so within the confines of the treaty and while protecting wartime aims? J. Chaplin, a second secretary at the embassy in Baghdad, posed the question in a different way, namely whether it was in British interests to have a "well-run Iraq," which would require greater British intervention, or a "friendly Iraq." The first option, an Iraq "where all men are equal before the law, where officials serve the public and not their own interests, where economic resources are developed and trains run to time," would require greater British intervention in day-to-day administration. Such a country would not necessarily be pro-British and it would resent this intrusion into its internal affairs: "the right of a country to go to the devil in its own way (more commonly known as 'independence') is a powerful fetish."[69] The question remained how to ensure enough stability in Iraq to avoid disrupting the war effort while keeping within the confines of the treaty in a way that did not provide proof to those who argued that Britain's main objective was to use the war as cover for a reoccupation of the country.

When Midfa'i's government resigned in October 1941 it proved to be difficult to find a replacement. The regent's first choice for prime minister was unsuccessful in forming a cabinet, and the regent refused to offer the position to Cornwallis's choice. The only options left were a reorganized Midfaʿi government or one led by Nuri al-Saʿid.[70] While Nuri was an experienced prime minister, his return to power brought new complications. After the Rashid ʿAli coup British officials both in Baghdad and London had hoped to keep him out of Iraq and out of power. His pro-British credentials had the potential to discredit him; Iraqi communists called him "the agent of imperialism," a reflection of his history of cooperating with Britain, and yet his loyalties were also suspect to the British as he had remained in Rashid ʿAli's government a little too long for their comfort.[71]

Nuri quickly laid out a policy that addressed all of Britain's demands for cooperation under the Anglo-Iraqi Treaty, including reorganization of the army, diversifying the sectarian and ethnic make-up of the Cabinet, appointing a Shiʿi minister of the interior for the first time in Iraqi history, and a promise not to pursue Arab confederation or a resolution of the Palestine and Syria issues until the end of the war. Nuri agreed to the internment of Rashid ʿAli's inner circle and a trial in absentia. Cornwallis was pleased but skeptical of his ability to deliver on these promises: "If he fulfils half of his assurances the millennium will have arrived but they show at all events that his heart is at present in the right place."[72]

The challenges presented by post-coup Iraq also required a restructuring of Britain's presence in the provinces. Military authorities and the embassy in Baghdad took advantage of their renewed influence to bolster their intelligence gathering capabilities through a network of organizations such as the Combined Intelligence Center Iraq (CICI), established in summer 1941 and RAF area liaison officers (ALOs) in the provinces, in addition to the SOE operatives already working under diplomatic cover.[73] While ostensibly put in place to smooth British relations with provincial and tribal leaders and maintain calm on Iraq's borders with Iran, these organizations also served as an elaborate surveillance apparatus which strengthened the perception amongst many Iraqis of Britain's extensive control of the country.

The new ambassador was a great advocate of personal relationships as the bedrock of diplomacy in the Arab world, investing lots of time in face-to-face conversations with Iraqis and renewing his old contacts. Cornwallis recognized the great gaps in

British intelligence in Iraq and proposed creating an organization to allow him to follow developments in the provinces and maintain contact with local leaders. He established the Political Advisory Staff (PA Staff) to serve as a two-way channel, communicating British policy and publicity lines to the provinces, and at the same time gathering valuable political intelligence for the embassy.[74] Political advisers (PAs) would serve as liaisons between military authorities and regional civil and tribal leaders, and mixed propaganda and intelligence functions, allowing Britain to respond more quickly to any future crisis in Iraq.[75]

The PA Staff was, in many ways, a throwback to the days of the mandate. Edmonds observed that "Without going so far as to say, 'Scratch the Embassy and you will find the High Commission,'" most Iraqis remembered the days of mandate rule and "even before the war the Embassy in Iraq could not be exactly like an ordinary diplomatic mission." This was particularly true for the period after 1941, as with the appointment of PAs the embassy "pushed its tentacles into the internal administrative machine even more deeply than the High Commission in its later days."[76] Cornwallis had served as adviser to the Ministry of the Interior from 1921 until 1935, and it is perhaps unsurprising that he tried to recreate the mandate-era advisory network as ambassador. Some of the new PAs had even served as administrative inspectors in the 1920s and 1930s, providing a continuity in personnel as well as structure.[77] Cornwallis envisioned the PAs to be an extension of his own personal influence outside of the capital and he insisted that they remain under his direct supervision, reporting directly to him through the Oriental Secretariat, even though they officially fell under CICI, the new military intelligence organization.[78]

Cornwallis's first appointees were Captain C. C. Aston and Wallace Lyon, land settlement officers with extensive experience in Iraq.[79] E. Kinch was recruited from the employees of the oil companies, while Dowson had managed an estate for Hills Brothers dates before serving as an ALO.[80] The PA Staff provided an effective cover for intelligence work, and among the ranks of the assistant PAs were men with ties to other organizations, for example, Hugh McNearnie who was recruited from MI6.[81] Iraq was divided into three regions: northern, central, and southern with headquarters for the PAs at Kirkuk, Baghdad, and Basra, respectively. While their duties would evolve over the course of the war, their initial primary objectives were "to fight Nazi influence in all its forms in this country, to prevent the possibility of the recurrence of another rising against us and to make such preparations as are possible to meet a German advance."[82] PAs were instructed to support the regent and Iraqi government, cooperate with the propaganda efforts of the embassy staff, and submit weekly political reports. As one official noted, they would be "most useful in 'showing the flag.'"[83] Cornwallis did not share any of his predecessor's squeamishness about using bribery, and the PA Staff utilized extensive personal contacts backed up by money to win the support of tribal and local leaders and pro-British businesses.[84]

The PAs faced a challenging task as they began work in 1941, first needing to regain the confidence of the Iraqis after the Rashid 'Ali coup. Their task was made even more difficult by the fact that Britain was suffering serious losses in the war, and the British believed that wartime victories were the most effective form of propaganda. As a reflection of the tense situation in Iraq, Lyon noted that in his PA office in the north he had three specialists seconded to train under him:

> These were officers specially trained in the use of explosives who, in the event of the enemy driving over the Caucasus and occupying Iraq, would stay behind in command of guerrilla bands to disrupt their organization and lines of communication. While under my care they were to learn Kurdish and make friends with the various tribal chiefs whose co-operation would be needed in the event of a British withdrawal.[85]

The PA system was not just about addressing the short-term needs of Iraq but also preparing for the long-term postwar requirements. Military authorities in Cairo approved of a plan to train a number of young officers as deputy assistant PAs to gain experience not only in Iraq but in Syria, Transjordan, and Palestine as well, with the plan that they would be equipped for political work after the war.[86]

By the end of 1941, many aspects of the Middle East muddle had been sorted out. New command structures were implemented in response to the continuously evolving strategic considerations that shaped British policy in Iraq, most importantly the German invasion of the Soviet Union. In August 1941 British and Soviet troops moved into Iran, ostensibly to replace an obstructionist shah revealing pro-Axis sympathies with his more compliant son. The more urgent motive behind the Anglo-Soviet occupation was to facilitate the movement of Lend-Lease supplies to the Soviet Union.[87] The new Iraqi government of Nuri al-Sa'id proved its worth during these operations, giving full facilities to the British forces and favorable press coverage.[88] These events in neighboring Iran would shape Iraq's experience through the rest of the war, and the agreements that the Allies signed with Iran would provide models for the Arab states in their own demands of Britain. In November 1941 Iran received assurances that it would have a seat at any postwar peace conference, and with the January 1942 Anglo-Soviet-Persian Treaty of Alliance Iran agreed to provide all necessary wartime facilities. In return British and Soviet forces committed to withdrawing from the country within six months of the end of hostilities. Arab leaders saw in these agreements an important precedent: wartime cooperation would lead to a postwar voice in the peace settlement.

Laurence Grafftey-Smith, from his vantage point at the British embassy in Cairo, recalled that in 1941 "The ebb and flow of desert war was an alternation of climax and anti-climax, emotionally exhausting. Triumphal progress, stimulant of a hundred talking-points, would suddenly become retreat, with an ominous crescendo of German gunfire."[89] December brought the welcome news of the relief of the siege of Tobruk with the success of Operation Crusader and raised hopes for the turning of the tide in North Africa. The US declaration of war that same month changed the calculus of the war, as it would lead to the landing of American troops in North Africa in autumn of the following year as well as a vital American role in the Persian Corridor to supply the Soviet Union. By the summer of 1942, however, both Egypt and Iraq would find themselves under the most serious threat of Axis invasion of the war.

6

Abdin Palace and "British Bayonets," January 1942–October 1942

In the aftermath of the 1942 Abdin Palace crisis, Prince Muhammad 'Ali shared a joke circulating in royal circles, that "the British Army are running so fast away from Rommel that they bumped into Abdine."[1] While the British were surely less than amused, the joke reflects the intersection of the internal political crisis in Egypt with the larger events of the war. In January 1942 King Farouk provoked a cabinet crisis that Lampson felt was a serious enough threat to British interests to warrant issuing an ultimatum to the palace, culminating in the events of 4 February 1942. The confluence of the events of the war with internal developments in Egypt pushed Britain beyond its status quo policy, and the Abdin Palace incident was the closest Britain came to unseating the Egyptian monarch in order to gain compliance on war aims. It was also the rapidly evolving wartime situation which ultimately convinced British officials to pull back at the last minute and leave the king on the throne when he complied with their political demands.[2] Yet the damage had been done, and the fact that Britain imposed its political will on Egypt "by British bayonets" became a trope revived periodically throughout the war by opposition forces, a phrase that reminded Egyptians of British perfidy and the fact that the Wafd was in power due to Britain's violation of Egyptian sovereignty.

British bayonets were also more widely visible throughout the region for another reason, as summer 1942 was the point when the fear that the Middle East might fall to the Axis, a preoccupation of British planners since the earliest days of the conflict, seemed most likely to become a reality. It saw "the Flap," the lowest point in the North African campaign when Rommel came closest to taking Egypt, and it was also a time of danger in Iraq as British planners anticipated a German offensive through Turkey. The British in the Middle East were pushed from both the west in North Africa and from the north and, as one military appreciation later reflected,

> By September 1942 the position of the Allies was as precarious as England's fate had been after Dunkirk. Rommel was within fifty miles of Alexandria and the rich delta of Egypt was almost within his grasp. Stalingrad was invested and German troops were pushing down towards the Caucasus. For Persia and Iraq–always a sensitive barometer–there seemed to be stormy weather ahead.[3]

The increasing shadow of British military power shaped Anglo-Egyptian and Anglo-Iraqi relations during the crucial year 1942.

"Send for the Wafd"[4]

It was a source of concern to Britain that, with the Axis powers on their doorstep in North Africa, Egypt was still harboring the Palace Italians and maintained ties to Vichy. On January 6, 1942, Sirri's government finally decided to sever relations with Vichy France in response to British requests, although it would not intern French citizens or sequester their property.[5] King Farouk was on vacation at the time of the announcement, and on his return to Cairo he called for the minister for foreign affairs, Salib Pasha Samy, to resign, charging that the decision to sever relations with Vichy had been taken without consulting him.

This request appeared at first glance to be a relatively normal development in Egyptian politics, and Lampson's advisers suggested that Britain should consider this an internal affair and stay out of it. Lampson disagreed and viewed the conflict in terms of British prestige. The constitutional issue of whether or not Sirri could take this action without consulting the king was irrelevant to the British position and Lampson told the prime minister that this "would amount to the sacking of an Egyptian Minister for Foreign Affairs by his Sovereign for loyally complying with a request by His Majesty's Ally formulated for perfectly legitimate and sufficient war reasons."[6] Lampson attributed Farouk's actions to the anti-British sentiment of his advisers, whom he viewed as destructive influences on an impressionable monarch.[7] Secret reports indicated 'Ali Mahir was behind the palace's attitude and that Farouk was being pressured to return him to power to lead a new government that would enforce a narrow interpretation of the Anglo-Egyptian Treaty. The crisis provided the perfect pretext to demand the dismissal not only of Abdel Wahab Talaat, whom the embassy considered to be "Ali Maher's tool," but also all of the Palace Italians. The Foreign Office, however, was not convinced that this development was a real danger to British interests. As Scrivener noted, "The criterion is the safety of our base in Egypt: it has not yet been endangered by the King's action."[8]

The situation grew more urgent on January 26 when Sirri announced that if the minister for foreign affairs was not reinstated in office then he would resign himself. Embassy and military officials met and reviewed correspondence from crises in 1940 to find a precedent. They concluded that Farouk's actions violated Article 5 of the treaty, in which both parties agreed "not to adopt in relation to foreign countries an attitude which is inconsistent with the alliance," and would justify the implementation of martial law.[9] Lampson remained convinced that the king would ultimately back down and he did not think they would need to resort to these drastic measures, but he wanted them prepared.[10]

Farouk allowed the minister to remain in office for the moment, but the calm proved to be short lived. Student strikes on February 1–2 fomented by forces opposed to the government compelled Sirri to resign, as he stated that he would not stay in office when he had clearly lost the "King's confidence."[11] The protests were well-timed as they took place at a very difficult moment in the war effort, not only in North Africa but also in the Far East. On January 18 Lampson reported that recent successes in Libya and Russia had strengthened support for Britain but only days later the situation changed drastically with the launching of Rommel's renewed offensive in Cyrenaica. German radio broadcasts exploited the bad news from the Western Desert and the embassy received reports that the palace was not only organizing protests at al-Azhar but was also in regular contact with Germany. Cairo erupted into public demonstrations with thousands of protestors shouting "Long live Rommel" and other pro-Axis slogans in support of Rommel's advance.[12]

The military was committed to backing up Lampson and enforcing British martial law if necessary but it would have been a real strain on their resources. The news that Britain was sending reinforcements from Egypt to the Far East at the same time as Benghazi was under attack caused local alarm. Despite the reinforcements Malaya fell, and just days after the crisis in Egypt was resolved, Singapore fell on February 15.[13] It had been university protests that ultimately sparked Sirri's resignation and provided the catalyst that turned the Vichy issue into a cabinet crisis in the first place. While troubles with the war had frequently been reason to pull back, in this case Lampson wrote: "It was made clear that present crisis had been timed and worked up by anti-British elements to take advantage of our present difficulties in the Far East and in Libya; and that if we failed to show firmness now the country would remain under the influence of these elements."[14]

When Lampson asked Sirri who he thought should replace him, he replied "Send for the Wafd"; Lampson responded that he had been thinking the same thing.[15] Before doing so the Foreign Office wanted assurances that Nahhas would cooperate in the war effort. Eden asserted a maximalist interpretation of the treaty, as Britain had done in Iraq in the months leading up to the Rashid 'Ali coup, and instructed Lampson to inform Nahhas that:

> they have no intention of departing from that settlement but they would welcome some sign of understanding on Nahas Pasha's part that in time of war and in the interests of the Ally who is doing the fighting every point which may arise cannot be measured by yard stick of a Treaty and that in such circumstances the Egyptian Government may reasonably be expected to adopt an attitude favourable to the prosecution of the war effort and to military exigencies.[16]

He also requested confirmation that Nahhas would support the purge of pro-Axis officials at the palace, and that Farouk would offer some form of recognition for the outgoing prime minister in order to avoid the impression that Sirri was being punished for his cooperation with the embassy.[17]

The Foreign Office repeatedly asked Lampson to meet directly with Nahhas to secure his support on these three key issues before agreeing to the new government. Despite this clear directive he failed to do so until after the latter had been asked by Farouk to assume office. As he explained to London, he believed getting in touch with Nahhas might not only embarrass him, but dissuade him from following through with the meeting with the king.[18] Lampson preferred to wait and work through Amin

'Uthman, who had served as a valuable intermediary between the embassy and the Wafd on past occasions.[19]

On February 2 Lampson met with Minister of State Lyttelton and the military chiefs. Lyttelton agreed with Lampson on the need to take action, but the military chiefs were not convinced and expressed concerns about possible unrest. That same day the ambassador telegraphed London with his plan for dealing with Farouk, which was similar to his proposals during the crisis of 1940: if the king failed to call on Nahhas to form a government, he would ask him to abdicate and put Prince Muhammad 'Ali on the throne. If he refused, he would have him deposed and impose British martial law if necessary. The rationale for forced abdication would be Farouk's failure to adhere to Article 5 of the treaty by refusing to expel the Palace Italians.[20]

The events of 1941 in the Middle East set two precedents that shaped Lampson's response. His insistence on having the option of using force to back up his requests to King Farouk was a cause of tension with the British military authorities but Iraq had demonstrated that, despite their protestations, at the end of the day the troops could be found. While he agreed that they should not weaken their defenses in the west, he had observed in his diary at the time of the Rashid 'Ali coup that "I am learning by experience that when the military say categorically (as they have done on many occasions) that troops, transport, etc. are not available, experience proves that in fact if the issue is pressed something is usually forthcoming. The technique of the military, and especially of Wavell, is to announce dogmatically that such and such can't be done."[21] Recent events in Iran, where the British had removed the shah from power and replaced him with his son, set a second powerful precedent for Lampson's ultimatum, one which, given the ties between the two royal families, would not have been lost on Farouk. Frustrated at the need to "frighten the boy at periodical intervals," Lampson observed that "Persia should surely serve as a reminder to the King of what happened if it was overstrained."[22]

Lampson met with Farouk that same day and lay out the rationale for a Wafd government under Nahhas: "We must have a government that is loyal to the treaty and able to implement both its spirit and letter, calling particular attention to Article 5" and they needed a strong government to meet wartime requirements. Only Nahhas as the leader of the majority party could provide this. To reinforce his point, Lampson read the terms of Article 5 of the treaty to Farouk and set a deadline of noon the next day for an answer. Farouk agreed to meet with Nahhas.[23]

On February 4 Lampson met with the Middle East War Council and they decided that the ambassador should inform Muhammad Hasanayn, the king's chamberlain, that the king had until 6:00 p.m. to ask Nahhas to form a government or Farouk "must accept the consequences." As of 5:45 Lampson had not received a reply, so he sent a telegram to the Foreign Office explaining his decision. He also noted in his diary that while Eden had given him "full discretion" in dealing with Farouk, "there is no specific sanction to abdication or deposition," but they had decided to proceed with the plan if necessary. Lampson called on Walter Monckton, the recently appointed deputy minister of state, to draft the letter of abdication, as he had experience with this, having also drafted Edward VIII's letter for the same purpose. At 6:15 p.m. Hasanayn returned with a message from the king that he had summoned the leaders of all the political parties to meet with him, and they had all agreed that the British ultimatum infringed the Anglo-Egyptian Treaty. Those present at the meeting had signed a resolution to this effect, including Nahhas. Lampson informed Hasanayn that he would visit the palace at 9:00 p.m.[24]

The War Council had decided that the damage was past repairing and Farouk must be forced to abdicate. Lampson was determined to follow through with this threat but during a dinner with Lyttelton and his wife before proceeding to the palace, the minister of state changed Lampson's mind. Lyttelton pointed out that it would look bad if they ended up "throwing the boy out for giving us at 9 p.m. the answer which we should have welcomed at 6 p.m." Perhaps most importantly, he was concerned about drawing the military into the situation unless absolutely necessary. Lampson recounted: "it was up to us, the civilian side, to prevent if we reasonably could the possibility of embarrassment of a grave kind in the country which might conceivably occur if the King were removed."[25]

Lampson recorded his visit to the king in great detail. He arrived at the palace accompanied by General Stone, the general officer commanding, British Troops in Egypt, and emphasized the show of force made by the British military. They were joined by

> an impressive array of specially picked stalwart military officers armed to the teeth. On the way, we passed through lines of military transport looming up, through the darkened streets … Whilst we waited upstairs I could hear the rumble of tanks and armoured cars, taking up their positions round the Palace … this caused no little stir and added to the growing anticipation of coming events.[26]

Once Lampson was admitted to see the king he read his prepared statement, which concluded that Farouk was "no longer fit to occupy the throne" due to his breach of Article 5 of the treaty, for provoking a cabinet crisis, and for refusing "to entrust Government to the leading political party which by commanding general support of the country is thus alone in a position to ensure the continued execution of the treaty in the spirit of friendship in which it was conceived." Lampson then presented him with the letter of abdication. Farouk hesitated but after consulting Hasanayn agreed to summon Nahhas and ask him to form a government.[27]

Lampson considered the events of February 4 to be "a complete victory," but Maurice Peterson at the Foreign Office had serious doubts. Reflecting his ongoing concern with Lampson's reliance on intermediaries, he warned of the implications of Lampson's failure to meet with Nahhas in person to get his assurance on the three British demands until after he had accepted the premiership: "As a result not only is it open to Nahas publicly to deny (and he will certainly deny it) that he either owes anything to our support or is under any obligation towards us, but we really have nothing to flourish, even privately, in his face when the next crisis arises." Messages sent through intermediaries were liable to distortion, and Peterson predicted that within three months Eden would be wondering, "Why on earth didn't we do anything except put the Wafd into Office?"[28]

While the crowds of Cairo could not have helped seeing the British troops and tanks outside Abdin Palace on February 4, Farouk asked British officials to keep the truth of what happened during Lampson's visit a secret. The ambassador complied, and it was only much later in the war that the details became public in Egypt, causing a great uproar.[29] It was generally known that the British had used force to return the Wafd to power, but not that Lampson had threatened abdication or the deeper issues underlying the demand. Lampson tried to limit the damage by speaking to Hasanayn, who had been present at Lampson's audience with the king on February 4, and taking the palace to task for allowing the idea of "the Wafd having been imposed by British bayonets" to circulate and not putting a stop to it: "As Pasha was present at the interview, he knew full well that was a distortion of the facts: British bayonets had been present for quite another purpose which we on our side had loyally not disclosed."[30] British officials assumed that if the underlying issue of the Palace Italians and the threat of abdication were widely known then the Egyptian public would be more understanding of Britain's methods.

The perception that the British had used force solely to return the Wafd to power seemed to provide proof for all of the warnings that Britain was using the war as a pretext for greater intervention in Egyptian affairs. Egyptians made their disapproval known through a social boycott of the British community. The king, on his first meeting with Lampson after February 4, publicly snubbed the ambassador in front of a large crowd gathered to welcome the empress of Tehran at the airport. Lampson, with his keen sense of protocol and the need to maintain British prestige, was extremely angry and demanded a formal apology.[31] Pamphlets and petitions arrived at the embassy, protesting Lampson's actions as a violation of Britain's pledge that it was fighting the war to protect democracy. One petition, signed by 1,000 Egyptian women including Huda Sha'rawi, a prominent Egyptian feminist, as well as the wives of Egyptian politicians, asked: "Where, Your Excellency, is the treaty between you and Egypt? Did you honour your pledges in such a heedless act? Can it be, after this aggression, that you can convince us that you are defending Democracy, and that you have embarked upon this war in defence of the freedom of nations?"[32] The Sa'dist Party protested that Egypt had met all of its treaty obligations and the London newspapers and Lampson himself had praised the Egyptian government for its cooperation, and yet: "Egypt found herself back in the time of the Occupation and the Protectorate, when ministries were made and unmade at the will of the British representative, but never in this visible and palpable fashion as that of Your Excellence."[33]

The fact that the British brought back the Wafd, which had caused trouble with its periodic manifestos and anti-government campaigns, smarted for the Sa'dists and Constitutional Liberals who had consistently supported the war effort in the early years. Even worse, Nahhas was insisting on elections which would result in these parties losing seats. Amin Bey Yussef, a long-time British supporter, told an embassy official of an Arabic saying: "'The English take a friend as a lemon, take the juice out of it, then throw away the skin and forget that it was a lemon.' We had this reputation of throwing away our friends; it was very important that we should do our utmost to prevent its growing, especially in the present case." The embassy proposed to give attention to the contribution of these parties in newspaper articles and BBC broadcasts as a sign that their loyalty had not been overlooked.[34]

The lesson of the early war years in Egypt was that to meet wartime requirements Britain needed a government that was both cooperative and enjoyed popular support.

With ʿAli Mahir Britain had an effective but non-cooperative prime minister; with Hassan Sabri and Husayn Sirri Britain had cooperative but weak and ineffective prime ministers. Lampson drew the following lesson from Sirri's fall: "no unrepresentative Government could hope, at that time, to govern in the spirit of the Anglo-Egyptian Treaty in view of the fact that any effort to do so must lead to conflict with the Palace; equally, without popular support in the country, no Government could fight the Palace."[35] The return of the Wafd to power promised both a cooperative and effective government with a popular base of support. This became a bedrock of Lampson's policy for the rest of the war, and yet this very act undermined their nationalist credentials.

General Wilson, who had command of the Ninth Army in Palestine and Syria, recalled that when he heard of the events of February 4 "I was astounded and horrified at this news as one felt that all one's efforts at getting the goodwill and co-operation of the Egyptians in the early days of the war had been thrown away." He was particularly concerned about the potential impact on the Egyptian army at a critical time of the war.[36] His fears proved well founded, as the events of February 1942 further alienated the military leadership in Egypt. Officers cancelled a scheduled reception for General

Figure 1 British Ambassador Sir Miles Lampson, Oriental Counsellor Sir Walter Smart, and Crown Prince Muhammad ʿAli at an embassy party in Cairo, April 1942. Smart was Lampson's most important adviser and directed the Oriental Secretariat, which took on expanded propaganda and political intelligence roles during the war. Imperial War Museum (E11060).

Stone in protest at the slight on Farouk, as the king was the official head of the Egyptian army. Two British agents reported on the anger of the officers at a meeting on February 7: "There was considerable feeling against Nahas Pasha for having accepted to form the new Ministry and above all because he was aware of British demands which were made to the King and which could only be regarded as threats. The Officers declared that in the future there would be no co-operation between themselves and the British."[37] The Egyptian army would continue to be a center for anti-British activity and a point of tension in Wafd-palace relations.[38] Lampson reported in August 1942 that Nahhas "spoke of recent arrest of the two German officers and consequent arrest of certain Egyptian Officers and of Aziz el Masri. Also the flight to the enemy of the two Egyptian Army aviators. He also referred to the reports of a secret society amongst Army officers which he believed to be true."[39] The first episode he mentioned was the August 1942 Eppler and Sandy case, a plot to assist German agents in establishing a wireless transmitter station in Cairo to send information on British troop movements to Rommel.[40]

Egyptian Politics after Abdin Palace, Spring 1942

Had the ultimatum to the king achieved what Britain had hoped? Lampson had his doubts, and one of his friends warned him that "whereas in the past I had only to spend 12 hours a day watching the Palace, it would in future be question [*sic*] of 24 hours a day watching not only the Palace but the Wafd!"[41] As the opposition parties feared, the new prime minister lost no time in targeting them. Nahhas had always made the holding of elections a condition for his return to power, and one of his first acts on taking office was to dissolve Parliament and call for elections. The Foreign Office suggested that

> while we cannot, of course, suggest that the elections should be "rigged," we shall be on the fairly safe ground of an established practice if we suggest that, in war-time, every care should be taken to make the elections pass off as quietly as possible and that with that end in view the Wafd might even be prepared to consider some "allocation of seats."[42]

Nahhas originally agreed to this proposal, but he ultimately decided not to give any seats to the opposition parties beyond those to which they were elected in retaliation for their protests against his return to office. The Liberal and Sa'dist Parties then threatened to boycott elections.[43]

As the February crisis unfolded, the Foreign Office had expressed concern that the embassy was losing sight of the key issue: continued Axis influence in Egypt.[44] With the new government in place, Britain drew up a list of security requirements: the internment of fifth columnists; the dismantling of organizations such as the Muslim Brotherhood, Young Egypt, and Abbas Halim's labor organizations; and the expansion of censorship to include the postal system, telegraphs, and telephones. Britain continued to see 'Ali Mahir as a threat and sensed his hand behind the palace decision to subsidize political candidates from Young Egypt and the Muslim Brotherhood.[45] Nahhas agreed to have the former prime minister confined to his country estate but in April 1942 he escaped from his home, gave a speech at the Senate to invoke parliamentary immunity, refused to leave and was eventually captured. He then began a hunger strike to protest the decision to send him into exile in the Sudan. Lampson was concerned that if he died as a result of this strike, he would be viewed as a martyr and Britain would be held responsible for his death. Instead, he was sent to Gharbaniyat, near the Western Desert, where he could be guarded by the Frontier Force.[46]

Organizations that had fallen outside of the three-legged stool model attracted new members who were disillusioned by the Wafd Party. A December 1942 GHQ Middle East assessment of the Muslim Brotherhood estimated that it had between 100,000 and 200,000 members and "admitted that the nationwide organisation of the Ikhwan far surpasses that of the official opposition parties and is comparable only with that of the Wafd itself."[47] In spring 1942 British intelligence officials, Walter Smart, and Amin 'Uthman held a meeting on the Brotherhood at which they discussed a variety of initiatives to win them over rather than allowing them to fall into the palace's orbit. Hassan al-Banna would be allowed to start a newspaper and encouraged to publish pro-democracy articles and the Wafd would provide subsidies to the Brotherhood via the government, with the embassy providing some of the funds. Nahhas met with Hassan al-Banna in October 1942 but the British became increasingly concerned by the implications of the Wafd's outreach to the Muslim Brotherhood and withdrew their support.[48] The Wafd's relationship with the Muslim Brotherhood oscillated over the course of the war between attempts to win them over and periods of and arrest.[49]

The Palace Italians proved to be more problematic as Nahhas wanted to let them remain as long as they stayed on good behavior, much to the frustration of the Foreign Office.[50] A final settlement was not reached until autumn when all but four of the Palace Italians were removed, after which Muhammad Hasanayn, the king's chamberlain, emerged as the most powerful voice in the palace.[51] The embassy generally found Hasanayn to be cooperative and a positive influence on Farouk, although they recognized that his pro-British attitude was due to political pragmatism rather than conviction. Nevertheless, he provided a channel for both the Wafd government and the embassy to communicate with the king.[52]

In the eyes of the Egyptian public, the Wafd had only been able to return to power by the strength of British bayonets, a conviction that had profound implications for Anglo-Egyptian relations after Abdin Palace and also shaped the decisions of the Wafd in power. As Egyptian historian al-Rafi'i explained, by cooperating with the British in 1942 Nahhas made his Cabinet "a client of the English, reliant on them to solve any crisis between the government and the palace."[53] Sensitive to this perception, the embassy's relations with the Government of Egypt after February 1942 were defined by the desire of both parties to avoid any overt signs of British influence over internal politics. As a result, contacts between the embassy and the Nahhas government were frequently carried out through local intermediaries. Amin 'Uthman was offered a ministerial position but having learned from 'Ali Mahir's earlier criticism of neglecting his work, he declined it on Lampson's advice, preferring to serve as secretary-general to Nahhas's Cabinet. He was also appointed auditor general in March 1942 but Lampson informed London that this title was "nothing but an official cloak for his real function, which is that of liaison officer between the Prime Minister and this Embassy."[54] Not everyone was pleased with this arrangement, which held a number of pitfalls. The Foreign Office renewed its concerns that it would make it difficult to hold Nahhas accountable, and Wafdists were angered that a relatively junior official was given such weighty responsibilities.[55]

The efficiency of the Wafd government was undermined by struggles within the party, most importantly a growing rift between Nahhas and Makram 'Ubayd. In part the rift was personal, as Nahhas's wife used her husband's position to garner preferential treatment for her relatives, which angered Makram.[56] There was also a religious dimension, as Makram represented the Coptic contingent within the Wafd. In the aftermath of Abdin Palace religious rhetoric reemerged as a key to solidifying anti-British sentiment around the monarchy, and critics labeled the Wafd as a "Coptic Party," leading to Coptic fears of a backlash. The rift between Nahhas and Makram had potentially serious consequences for British policy in Egypt, as Makram was the organizational genius of the party. If the party structure crumbled, its utility to the British would be undermined. At the same time, the embassy had to be careful in intervening in this internal dispute. In the end, the rift proved irreparable, and in May 1942 Nahhas formed a new Cabinet without Makram.[57]

Walter Smart reassessed British policy toward the Wafd government in light of this party conflict. It was in Britain's interests to keep the Wafd in power at least until the war turned in favor of the Allies. Echoing the language of the days of Cromer and the veiled protectorate, Smart suggested that they should offer the Wafd "all possible veils to cover up our intervention" but in return they would have to accept British guidance in crucial areas of concern for the war effort, such as supply issues. Smart justified this increased intervention on the principle of "he who pays the piper, calls the tune." Having put the Wafd in power, Britain had both the right and the responsibility to ensure sound administration and compliance with British aims and "I feel that we must take Nahas in hand, just as Cornwallis has taken Nuri, and prolong the Wafd's uncertain tenure." No alternative government would be able to provide the domestic support needed for the war effort. Wafdist leaders were "playing the English card heavily" by blaming their repressive measures on British pressure. Smart reasoned that if the Wafdists were going to pass the blame to the British like that, then they had even more right to intervene and guide the government.[58]

As British officials had anticipated, Nahhas in power was haunted by his 1940 petition which had attacked British intervention in Egypt in wartime (see Chapter 2). The new prime minister raised the issue of treaty revision and representation at the peace conference to be held at the end of the war, admitting privately that he was doing so in response to pressure from Parliament to act on his earlier demands. The Wafd government also undertook measures to decrease foreign influence in Egypt, including an Arabic language bill that made it obligatory for foreign firms to use Arabic in their transactions, another to prevent foreigners from owning agricultural property, and new limits on foreign missionary schools. Lampson viewed these measures as Wafdist attempts to deflect criticism by showing "its nationalist impeccability by excessive assertion of Egyptism."[59]

Upon taking office Nahhas inherited the economic difficulties and supply shortages created by the vast British wartime presence in the country. The government had not restricted cotton acreage in 1941 so there was a danger of bread shortages in cities due to insufficient wheat supply. Axis attacks on Allied shipping limited food imports just at the time when they were most needed to make up for a poor 1941 harvest and tide the country over until the 1942 harvest was ripe. The region as a whole was facing shortages, and the minister of state warned that the grain supply situation "was such as to foreshadow an outbreak of famine which might imperil security in the Middle East."[60]

For Britain, the supply issue was shaped by the need to avoid heavy burdens on the civilian population which might lead to unrest and divert troops from the front lines in the Western Desert. For the Wafd the supply issue had potential political implications, as their opponents charged that they were sacrificing the well-being of their citizens to supply the British who had, after all, put them in power. The spring 1942 grain shortages convinced the Egyptian government to implement cereal collection and distribution plans and manage supplies on a national scale. An Anglo-Egyptian Supplies Committee was established and the MESC worked with the government to provide imported grain, set up a collection system for wheat, limit cotton acreage, and regulate the use of other cereals as adulterants to spread out the diminishing wheat supply. A cold snap in late spring further delayed the harvest, but it was finally collected with only days to spare before supplies were completely depleted.[61]

The Flap

The new Wafd government was put to the test in the summer of 1942 during "the Flap," the most dangerous period of the war for the British in Egypt. On May 26 Rommel launched a new offensive in Libya and Tobruk fell on June 21. By the end of the month the Axis army was on Egyptian territory and made its closest approach to Cairo until it was finally stopped at El Alamein. At times Rommel seemed sure to reach the city. Jean Lugol, a newspaper editor in Egypt during the war, recalled that during the summer of 1942 "Night and day the convoys rumbled through the streets of Cairo on their way from Suez to the front line and back. In the whole of one part of the town, civilian traffic was forbidden in order to clear the way for the endless procession of military vehicles passing through."[62] Lampson publicly demonstrated British resolve to stay put in Cairo at the height of the crisis and continued with his normal activities: shopping in the Mousky with his wife, dining at the Mohamed Aly Club, attending church services, and having the railing around the embassy painted. Grafftey-Smith recalled: "At that moment in time, the fresh green paint on the railings of what had been written off as a doomed property was more effective for good than any whisper of propaganda that his publicity section could have thought up in a month of Sundays."[63]

This veneer of "business as usual" did little to relieve the seriousness of the situation. The embassy and GHQ burned their archives, a sure sign that an invasion seemed imminent.[64] They developed contingency plans for the evacuation of King Farouk and the Egyptian government and for the destruction of Egyptian goods such as wool, cotton, and oils that the Germans were short on in case a scorched earth policy became necessary. The Italians struck medals in anticipation of a victory in the Western Desert, Egyptian officers sympathetic to the Axis powers made overtures to Rommel, and there was a general air of fear and anticipation in both Cairo and Alexandria, with a run on banks and departures of European and Jewish community members from Egypt. The fall of Mersa Matruh led to "signs of panic amongst all classes" and the Italian occupation of Siwa, first air raids on Heliopolis, and the setbacks in Russia further damaged public faith in the Allies.[65]

Although Lampson's ultimatum to Farouk and the imposition of a Wafd government in February 1942 proved destructive to Anglo-Egyptian relations in the long term, it did serve Britain's short-term wartime requirements by providing a local partner who was both willing to cooperate with Britain and strong enough to impose the necessary wartime measures. Nahhas proved his worth as a British ally during "the Flap," and at the end of June 1942 Lampson noted that, despite British reverses in Libya, Egypt

Figure 2 Egyptian air raid wardens in Cairo during the Flap, July 1942. Imperial War Museum (E15054).

was generally friendly, which he attributed to the "admirable and most courageous" attitude of the Wafd government, including public statements by the prime minister. This situation provided "a remarkable example of what can be done by a friendly Government even in adverse circumstances. The Government of Sirry Pasha, in spite of evident friendliness of Sirry, was unable to produce this atmosphere during Rommel's much less serious advance last January/February."[66] Yet he also conceded that if the Wafd had been out of power, the result might have been the opposite. It was much better to have the Wafd in power, where they held responsibility, rather than out of power where they could cause trouble, and potentially turn the Egyptian masses against the Allies.[67] Overall, through the tense summer of 1942 British officials were pleased that there was not more fifth columnist activity and that many of those who had previously been anti-British were being more cooperative.[68]

Iraq and the Northern Front, 1942

Britain's fortunes in Iraq in 1942 were also shaped by the rapidly changing events of the war both in North Africa and closer to home. In early spring the looming threat to the north on the Levant-Caspian Front emboldened fifth columnists and, as in Egypt, the Iraqi army remained a focal point of lingering anti-British sentiment.[69] Crosthwaite gloomily noted that the army would probably "stab us in the back" if Germany invaded Iraq but disbanding it would "involve us in tearing up the Anglo-Iraqi Treaty and reversing the whole policy that goes with it" so they had to continue with the policy of reform.[70]

By May 1942 British officials noted an improvement in the morale of the Iraqi army and pro-Allied sentiment, largely due to British action against Axis influences in neighboring Syria and Iran and the presence of the Tenth Army. The American entry into the war played a key role as well, given visible effect with American aircraft landing in Basra, American ships in the Shatt-el-Arab, American technicians, and the inclusion of Iraq in Lend-Lease aid.[71] Yet the summer 1942 setbacks in North Africa caused renewed alarm and were accompanied by an increase in pro-Axis activity. In order to bolster support for Britain, the Iraqi government arrested thirty-eight high-profile pro-Axis Iraqis and interned them in 'Amara.[72] But by August 1942, Cornwallis called for cautious optimism about the political situation in Iraq despite bad news on the war front: "thanks in some measure to the work of our Public Relations Department, there is evidence that at last a belief in the rightness of the principles of democracy is beginning to grow … provided the enemy can be kept from her frontiers, Iraq will now stand true to her alliance to the end of the war."[73] The supporters of the Rashid 'Ali coup had been forced into exile or interned, and pan-Arab nationalist sentiment quelled through censorship.

Iraq's place in the Allied war effort shifted with the creation of the new Persia and Iraq Command (PAIC) in August 1942, with General Wilson as the commander in chief. The new command would relieve Middle East Command of some of its responsibilities at a critical time in the war in North Africa. Wilson was charged with defending oil installations in case of an eventual Axis invasion and facilitating the transport of supplies and aid to the Soviet Union.[74] To prepare for this first objective PAIC developed oil denial schemes to render oil installations inoperable if they fell into enemy hands.[75]

GHQ PAIC opened in Baghdad in September 1942 with a staff of 460 and with it came a host of personnel and ancillary organizations.[76] An embassy official noted: "Bagdad is fast emerging from being a relatively peaceful backwater and we are confronted with an imminent invasion of literally hundreds of staff officers and General Headquarters followers."[77] Iraq was now experiencing some of the challenges Egypt had faced with the ballooning of the British military presence in the country. In Basra, the heart of Britain's expanded operations, tensions between the local Iraqi and British military authorities developed over economic issues, such as British delay in paying rents and the impact of military spending on the local economy. Administrative disagreements and cultural strains when, for example, the British protested the closure of local restaurants during daylight hours in Ramadan, all added to the tension.[78]

Iraqis read the creation of PAIC in 1942 as a sign that the war in the Caucasus was going poorly, and Nuri made a public statement in August to the effect that if the Germans threatened Iraq's borders by breaking through the Caucasus then Iraq would declare war. His critics argued that even Egypt, which had Axis troops within its borders, still had not taken this step, and therefore Nuri was only trying to curry favor with the British.[79] By November though, the British Military Mission reported that the presence of so many British troops in Iraq had a salutary effect in convincing the general public that the Allies would win the war as they could "see in Iraq itself GHQ at Baghdad, a whole division just outside the town, very large forces between Khaniqin and Mosul and also at Basra and finally the Poles," a reference to the thousands of Polish troops that formed the Polish Army in the East.[80]

Interest in the war was overshadowed by the economic problems at home. While the Iraqi crop should have been sufficient to meet domestic needs, the country was beset by widespread hoarding, motivated by memories of severe grain shortages during the First World War, and smuggling of grain across the border to Syria and Palestine for higher prices. The northern part of Iraq was experiencing a drought, leading to famine conditions in Kurdish areas, a situation made worse by a harsh winter and pests. Britain was responsible for some of these economic challenges, as military requirements in Iraq led to an increase in the amount of currency in circulation, fueling inflation. All of these developments exacerbated the shortage in staples due to wartime reductions in imports. This would be a persistent problem for both the Government of Iraq, criticized for its inability to resolve the grain situation, and the British, who faced rumors that they were either deliberately limiting grain as revenge for the events of 1941 or encouraging the shipment of grain to neighboring states to ruin the Iraqi economy.[81] By November the situation had become so serious that, as CICI reported, "bribes are paid by almost everyone carrying a sack of almost anything almost anywhere to almost anybody."[82] Fifth column activity was increasing in the north, and a British adviser in Mosul responded that the best way to counteract Axis influence would be to address the severe food shortage.[83] Britain had to tread lightly in its response, however, as local officials resented interference in these economic matters.

The events of 1942 brought the war closer to the Arab states than it had ever been before with Rommel's advance across North Africa and the threat of a German invasion via the Caucasus seemingly imminent. While the tides of the war shifted dramatically by November, the British drew a number of conclusions from the dramatic days of 1942. Cooperative prime ministers in both Egypt and Iraq proved their worth in the difficult summer months. While Britain's response to these threats was ultimately successful, the actions required strained the terms of the Anglo-Egyptian and Anglo-Iraqi Treaties. At the same time, the civilian populations of the region increasingly felt the economic impact of the war and the presence of Allied troops in their midst. Addressing these concerns was a political and strategic as well as economic concern, and one that would result in far greater British intervention in the internal affairs of both countries through the remainder of the war.

As for Lampson, his 1942 showdown with the King of Egypt earned him "a reputation as a hard man," which endeared him to Winston Churchill, who even toyed with the idea of appointing him as viceroy of India so that he could use his heavy-handed techniques there. In 1943 he was elevated to the peerage, taking the title 1st Baron Killearn. Egyptians took this honor as a sign of the British government's approval of Lampson's methods during the Abdin Palace crisis. Lampson noted that this recognition "strengthened the Embassy position and discredited the suggestion by anti-British elements of disagreement on policy between London and Cairo."[84] For an ambassador who highly valued the role of prestige as a tool of diplomacy, this recognition emboldened him for future conflicts with the palace.

7

"The Cause of the United Nations Is the Cause of the Arab Nation," November 1942–June 1943

The dramatic change in the war situation in autumn 1942, with the Allied victory at the Battle of El Alamein, turned the attention of Arab leaders toward the postwar world. In the Speech from the Throne opening Parliament in November 1942 the Government of Iraq drew attention to the public statements that both Churchill and Eden had made regarding Arab independence and declared: "the Cause of the United Nations is the Cause of the Arab Nation."[1] Iraq was now looking ahead to the end of the war for the fulfillment of all of these promises and the Iraqi Parliament passed, by a two-thirds majority, the government's proposal that Iraq join the 26 Power Pact and ultimately enter the war on the Allied side, stating: "The best and surest way to realize these noble aspirations is for 'Iraq to adhere to the principles of the Atlantic Charter in order that she shall take her proper place at the Peace Conference."[2] Nuri believed that the dramatically changing wartime situation would ensure general public support for a measure that, in spring, would have been viewed far less favorably.

The British were lukewarm in their response to the proposal, seeing it as another attempt by Nuri to use wider Arab politics to deflect attention from Iraq's domestic difficulties. Eden's response best sums up the view of British officials: "I am not impressed; nor distressed."[3] On the other hand, the minister of state saw the potential to use Iraq's declaration and their request for assurances to push for greater cooperation on supply issues and the imposition of economic controls, vital actions which had been "obstructed by inertia due to a considerable extent to peace time mentality and tendency to argue, 'this is not our war.'"[4]

That same month the Egyptian Senate was also engaged in a heated debate surrounding Egypt's postwar goals. In the context of the Allied offensives in North Africa Ambassador Lampson had stated that Britain would ensure that Egypt would have representation at peace negotiations on any issue "which concerns Egyptian direct interests," and that "H.M. Government will not go into negociations [*sic*] about matters touching the direct interests of Egypt without consulting the Egyptian Government." While the British intended this to serve as an assurance of an Egyptian voice, many senators found the letter insulting because it amounted to, as Senator Barakat Pasha stated, "an exterior protectorate," since Egypt would not have a say in other matters at the peace conference, and Britain was, in essence, speaking for her on those issues. He dismissed the argument that it was inopportune to demand these rights from Britain in wartime, noting that other countries were seizing the opportunity "except here in Egypt where we are volunteers for imaginary sacrifice for good, and other chatter that we are supporters of humanity, this thing if said by the strong is good but if said by the weak it is only unacceptable, weakness." Allied propaganda about fighting for democracy was, in his view, merely a pretext for greater British intervention. Other senators turned this Allied rhetoric against Britain, with Haykal Pasha noting that Britain's declaration to speak for Egypt contradicted "the present international tendencies and the Churchill-Roosevelt Atlantic pact which gives the small and conquered countries the full right to choose their own Government." The speech provided an opportunity to expose the ways in which the Nahhas government was using wartime controls for domestic political gain through censorship and other limitations on the very freedoms that these wartime declarations claimed for the Allied countries. Most troubling to British observers, senators expressed concern about the 1936 treaty serving as the basis of any postwar representation, an early indication that Egypt might try to "internationalise the Egyptian problem" at war's end.[5]

Both Egypt and Iraq saw the potential to use the wartime declarations and the postwar vision as leverage to demand not only greater autonomy for themselves but also for the other areas of the Arab world still under imperial control, namely Syria, Lebanon, and Palestine.[6] In this changing international environment, Egypt and Iraq followed two different models. The Wafd government worked to secure British assurances on a postwar voice without a declaration of war, using Egyptian cooperation in the war effort and Allied promises as the rationale. These sacrifices, Egypt reasoned, were a sufficient demonstration of Egyptian support. The Iraqi government took the formal step of declaring war in January 1943 and Nuri then used this declaration to launch a renewed campaign for Arab unity with the first bilateral talks between himself and Nahhas.

The United States and the Soviet Union, now allied with Britain after the events of 1941, would become increasingly visible players in the region and challenge British influence and status. The landing of American troops on November 8, 1942, to fight in North Africa, the growing American presence to bolster the Persian Corridor to provide relief to the Soviet Union, and the growth of an Allied, and not merely British, internationalist vision changed the publicity message. This provided the opportunity to assuage concerns that this was another imperialist war by focusing on the promises of democracy for a transformed postwar world far removed from the Axis nightmare. However, as the Egyptian debate revealed, it also held British officials and the governments they supported to a higher standard.

Iraq's declaration of war

Nuri had been exploring the possibility of declaring war since the release of the United Nations Declaration in January 1942, but the events of the war and domestic challenges put this on hold. Building on the momentum of the Allied advances in autumn 1942 and the November parliamentary vote, Nuri determined to move ahead with a formal Iraqi declaration of war in January 1943. Ambassador Cornwallis counseled that this would require extensive preparation to avoid the appearance that the declaration was foisted on them by the British. He instructed the public relations attaché to work with the prime minister to initiate an oral propaganda campaign supported by articles in the Arab press on the benefits this would bring which the British publicity organizations could then quote and circulate, emphasizing that Iraq was taking this step on its own initiative and driving the timeline. He agreed to inform the British PAs and asked Nuri to warn provincial leaders.[7]

When Iraq declared war on the Axis powers on January 16, 1943, the newspaper *al-Akhbar* declared that by this act Iraq earned its "place in the sun" and rightful status in the international community.[8] Cornwallis did not expect the declaration to have much effect on the actual prosecution of the war but he acknowledged its deep symbolic importance: "For the first time in history an independent Moslem state entirely of its own free initiative has declared war as Ally of Great Britain thereby setting example to the whole Moslem and Arab world by coming down unequivocally on our side."[9] The embassy PR Section made much of the Iraqi declaration, widely distributing posters and postcards displaying the flags of the United Nations, with the United States, Britain, and the Soviet Union prominently displayed up front, and Iraq among the many nations arrayed in a long line behind them. The Axis tried to counteract the impact of the declaration with their own propaganda campaign. Former Prime Minister Rashid ʿAli, now in Berlin and broadcasting on Germany's Arab radio programs, announced just days after Iraq declared war that: "I hereby declare … in the name of the Iraqi people … Iraq remains in a state of war with the British."[10]

Maurice Peterson, viewing this development from the broader perspective of the Foreign Office, did not share Cornwallis's optimism as to the positive example being set by Iraq. He warned that "Iraq's action is causing ripples on the Middle East duck-pond." The other Arab states were not so much inspired by Iraq's example as fearful that they were missing the opportunity to make their own demands of the Allied powers at the end of the war.[11] Britain grew increasingly alarmed at rising Iraqi expectations as to the benefits to be reaped from this declaration. Rather than a solemn obligation demanding great sacrifice, Iraqis were treating it as a quid pro quo, an attitude exemplified by a speech former Prime Minister Jamil al-Midfaʿi gave to the Iraqi Senate:

> By adhering to the Atlantic Charter and by the declaration of war we have done more than we are required to do under the Treaty of Alliance … It is therefore within our rights to demand from our Allies an appreciation of our stand … I pray God will help the Government and the whole of ʿIraq to enable us to benefit from our new position.[12]

Embassy officials acknowledged that Nuri and his supporters needed to emphasize the potential benefits of a declaration of war to win Cabinet approval, but they were dismayed when the prime minister took a similar line in his correspondence with

Churchill, expressing his hope that he and Roosevelt, as the "authors of the Atlantic Charter," would find a way to secure the independence of the Arab states.[13] Albert Hourani, who had embarked on a fact-finding tour of the region for the Foreign Office Research Department, warned that among those who supported the declaration, "there were those … who regarded the declaration as a masterpiece of political cleverness, by which Iraq secured automatically and without effort a share in the fruits of victory."[14] The British embassy found itself engaged in a delicate balancing act, on the one hand publicly praising Iraq's declaration while also trying to convince Iraqis of the responsibilities such a declaration would entail and reining in the extravagant expectations it created. The embassy used the news columns it submitted to the *Iraq Times* and *Basra Times* to remind Iraqis of their new responsibilities.[15]

Nuri followed up the declaration of war with the release of his Blue Book on Arab unity. This document was intended as a means of publicizing the Arab cause to a Western official audience, shaped by both the changing tides of the war and growing concern about Zionist publicity efforts in the United States.[16] As Nuri explained in the document's cover letter,

> The recent successes of the United Nations are leading many of us to hope that the collapse of the Axis Powers is much closer than we dared to expect. Therefore, I feel that our case should be properly prepared and that British and American public opinion should be informed of it, well in advance of the conferences which will decide the peace Settlement.[17]

The Blue Book reflected the lessons the Arabs learned from both world wars, with a historical narrative that emphasized the destructive effect of the First World War in breaking up the Arab peoples and their sense of betrayal and frustration at the postwar settlement. The mandate system, in Nuri's assessment, not only undermined Arab unity but was the root cause of Arab ill will toward Britain and France and the unrest in the region during the interwar period. If Britain adopted policies that addressed Arab concerns, they would undermine the appeal of Axis propaganda and ensure the peace and stability that the Allies so desperately needed in the region at a crucial time in the war. Nuri explicitly tied the movement for Arab unity to the campaign for independence in the remaining mandated territories, calling for the union of Syria, Lebanon, Palestine, and Transjordan into one Arab state and the formation of an Arab League for the other Arab states to join. As for the Jews in Palestine, Nuri turned to the model of the semi-autonomous Maronite community under the Ottomans for inspiration, suggesting that a similar system would provide the rights and security that they desired within the framework of a broader Syrian state.[18]

Nuri's arguments about Fertile Crescent unity had been in circulation for years, but the Blue Book is significant in using the lessons of the Second World War as part of the rationale for implementation at this point in time. Nuri echoed an assumption common in British official circles during the war: that one of the most important lessons of the war was the vulnerability of small states, and that the postwar settlement must necessarily involve placing these smaller states into larger regional organizations for their protection. Former Iraqi Prime Minister Taha al-Hashimi warned Nuri in

1942 that "The events of this War showed that the mere independence of the Arab countries would not be useful if they did not unite with one another. Only union would safeguard their existence and independence in the best form … we must work for the formation of this unity and to achieve it before this War has ended."[19] The debates and declarations surrounding Arab unity in the later war years reflect a growing awareness of a rapidly closing window of opportunity for Arabs to shape their own political future. Thus, Nuri appealed to the vision that the movement would not be toward smaller states, as after the First World War, but larger states, as a means of justifying Arab unity to the British.

Nuri assumed that Britain would expect the Arab states to provide for their own defense after the war and argued that a separate and independent Palestine, Syria, and Lebanon would be unable to do so. A unified Arab state, however, would have the resources and manpower to defend itself.[20] After declaring war Nuri offered to send Iraqi troops for service in Syria and explored the possibility of sending troops to North Africa as a way to demonstrate Iraq's commitment to the war and also its ability to contribute to the defense requirements of a future Arab state. Britain declined the offer due to the potential political complications and Nuri's recruitment drives for volunteers had little success.[21] The British did not want Iraqi troops but rather greater cooperation on the economic challenges the country faced.

Nuri's ideas were widely circulated, both in the Arab world and in British officialdom.[22] On February 24, 1943, Eden once again publicly addressed the question of Arab unity and reaffirmed his 1941 Mansion House statement, an act which, coming so soon after the release of Nuri's Blue Book, led to renewed focus on Arab unity. The rapidly improving wartime situation in early 1943 further galvanized the movement. Watching from Cairo Abd al-Rahman 'Azzam welcomed Eden's statement and pressed for the Arabs to take up the call, declaring in a letter to *al-Ahram*: "Something … must be done."[23] Nahhas took the initiative in responding.

Egypt's Foreign Policy Turn 1942–3

The Iraqi declaration of war took Egypt by surprise and revived the latent Egyptian-Iraqi rivalry. Ambassador Sir Miles Lampson, now Lord Killearn, noted that Egypt was upset that it was not consulted first, and "Egypt's amour propre is offended because Iraq is now assured of a place at the peace conference on a par with other belligerents and Egypt's position is therefore inferior. It is also feared that Iraq may wrest from Egypt the leadership of the Arab world."[24] Egypt responded with its own series of foreign policy initiatives, trying to get the benefits through every means short of actually declaring war and competing for the advantage of opening Arab unity talks under Egyptian auspices.

Egypt's role in the Arab unity movement was unclear and it was generally viewed as a nation apart from the rest of the Arab world. British officials and Arab leaders doubted whether Egypt could be brought into an Arab union due to the negative feelings between Egypt and the other Arab states and because they viewed Egyptian nationalism as distinct from its Arab counterpart. Yet for Nahhas, facing opposition at home due to the way in which he returned to power in 1942, seizing leadership of the Arab unity movement held the potential to bolster his reputation.[25] Egypt's foreign policy turn started with the issue of Syria and Lebanon. In the aftermath of the Abdin Palace incident the new Wafd government finally broke off relations with Vichy France, but it was an embarrassment to Britain by summer that Egypt had still not opened diplomatic relations with the Free French and had not recognized the new Syrian and Lebanese governments. At the same time, the British balked when Nahhas took the initiative to meet with General Georges Catroux, the Free French delegate plenipotentiary in the Levant, and presented him with a set of proposals developed by Syrian and Lebanese nationalists. As Walter Smart noted: "It is quite possible that Nahas, in his endeavour to make political capital out of foreign policy in order to strengthen his political position internally, may be indulging in dreams of an Egypt playing through him a grandiose role in the Arab world."[26]

British officials had a complex relationship to this movement, and debated whether it was inherently anti-British or if it might be channeled into a pro-British direction. An MI6 officer posted in Baghdad noted that while sentiment in the Iraqi army had improved, underneath "lurks a strong feeling of pan-Arabism, which is naturally closer to Nazism than to democracy," primarily due to Arab interest in the status of Palestine. Cornwallis disagreed, and criticized the alarmist nature of these intelligence reports:

> It is a mistake to regard Pan-Arabism as being necessarily an evil or a crime. In itself it is a perfectly legitimate ideal for which many good Arabs have worked for many years, and it only becomes dangerous to us when we are accused of thwarting their ambitions in this respect. Responsible Arabs have decided to allow the question of Arab independence to lie until after the war when they will turn to negotiation as an option.[27]

As the war progressed British officials were caught between the movement's potential to complicate their position in Palestine and relations with the French over Syria and Lebanon, while also fearing that openly opposing it would increase anti-British sentiment in the region. British views are perhaps best summed up by Maurice Peterson's assessment: "My own views on Arab Federation are a) that we must let the Arabs arrange it, and, b) that they never will."[28] Britain ultimately took the position of publicly supporting the movement while working behind the scenes to temper Arab nationalist sentiment. Minister of State Richard Casey suggested that they offer Arab leaders "friendly advice to slow down the momentum of the movement" and encourage them to undertake consultative meetings before holding a conference.[29] The official British line was that "much spade-work should first be done" and Arab leaders should hold bilateral talks in the form of confidential discussions that might lead to a coherent plan of action before a conference was called.[30]

Galvanized by their collective intervention in Lebanon in 1943, the turning tide of the war, and concerns about an Arab place at the peace conference, Nahhas announced to the Egyptian Senate on May 30, 1943, that his government would invite representatives of the Arab states to a "friendly meeting" in Egypt to discuss the possibility of an Arab union.[31] The announcement was followed by a series of meetings at Alexandria over the summer of 1943 between Nuri and Nahhas to start laying the plans for an eventual conference. The leaders reached an agreement that a single, united Arab state was not viable for both internal and external reasons. Instead, they explored the possibility of a Greater Syria, encompassing Palestine, Syria, Lebanon, and Transjordan, as well as a larger organizational body to which all Arab states could belong. As it would be difficult to convince the Arab states to cede some of their sovereignty, Nahhas suggested an organization modeled on the Pan-American Union, not a political union but one focused on commercial, economic, and cultural cooperation.[32] The leaders were keenly aware of the rapidly changing wartime situation in summer 1943 and Nuri observed that the evolving Anglo-American relationship and the growing influence of the United States in the international arena would shape the way in which an Arab unity plan would have to be sold to the world. From the very first meeting the leaders revealed their preoccupation with the postwar environment by discussing how the union would be represented at the eventual peace conference.[33]

The diplomatic talks were accompanied by a wide range of cultural and educational initiatives, yet the façade of Arab cooperation belayed deep tensions and divergent visions for what Arab unity might look like.[34] During the early 1943 bilateral talks Nahhas, who was ill at the time, met with Nuri's envoys while in bed, and the Iraqis were not only offended by this informality but also alarmed by the Egyptian leader's ignorance of the complex issues in the wider Arab world. Nahhas wanted to limit conference participation to official representatives as this would serve his domestic political ends by excluding the Egyptian opposition, which, as is examined in Chapter 8, was engaged in a heated attack on his policies while the talks were taking place. For the Iraqis, this would exclude some of the best-informed Egyptian politicians as well as any Palestinian or Syrian representation.[35] The mutual suspicion that developed between Nuri and Nahhas as to their respective motives and their rivalry for leadership of the movement would shape its development through the war years. Despite these tensions, the Egyptian-Iraqi talks resulted in the joint communiqué of August 6, 1943, that signaled their intention to solicit the views of various Arab leaders.[36] In the ensuing months the leaders met with representatives from Saudi Arabia, Transjordan, Syria, Lebanon, and Yemen.[37]

Propaganda: From Projection of Power to Projection of Ideals

By the summer of 1943 the resurgent Allies, now the United Nations, equipped with the inspiring vision of the Atlantic Charter and the United Nations Declaration, had a new opportunity to reframe the propaganda war. Stewart Perowne, public relations attaché at the Baghdad embassy, explained that British publicity agencies in Iraq had been "devoted to convincing the public that we have bombs and aeroplanes. They can just as easily be used for convincing them that we have civilized ideas."[38]

The January 1943 declaration of war made the Allies' fight Iraq's fight. While Allied victories helped the propaganda campaign, they also bred assumptions that the end of the war was approaching just as quickly as the actual fighting was moving away from their borders. The likelihood of an Axis invasion of Iraq had faded and so "It is therefore no longer necessary to guard against the possibility that a country which included a considerable pro-Axis element might become the springboard of a German advance, but rather to prevent undue complacency when the war goes well for the allies, with a corresponding swing in the other direction in the case of any temporary set-back." Declaring war brought obligations as well, and Britain would look to Iraq to not only support the war through economic policies that would provide for local needs and fight inflation, but also, in a nod to pan-Arab sentiment, to serve as a leader "to obtain respect from the rest of the Arab world for the principles on which she took this initiative."[39]

As for Egypt, it was vital to convince Egyptians "that their interests and aspirations are closely bound up with the victory of the United Nations." They should emphasize democracy as a shared Anglo-Egyptian value which would also help to bolster the new Wafd government in its struggles with the palace. The 1942 Ministry of Information propaganda directive noted though that "Egyptian ideas of democracy are largely old-fashioned and out of date, and it is becoming increasingly necessary to educate the Egyptians in the problems of working a democratic system under modern conditions."[40]

Egypt remained at the heart of Britain's propaganda machinery for the Arab world, which by 1943 included not only the various Ministry of Information-sponsored enterprises but also the public relations offices of each of the three service branches, the British Council, and SOE publicity services.[41] The proliferation of such agencies exacerbated tensions with the embassy, which continued to try and maintain control.[42] Britain also poured resources into the PR Section of the embassy in Baghdad, which was, by 1944, its largest department, employing over 100 people and with branches in the major cities of Basra and Mosul. Perowne, as public relations attaché, answered directly to the ambassador, a sign of the importance Cornwallis placed on this work.[43]

British publicity used a wide range of methods to reach as broad an audience as possible. Glossy magazines and pamphlets were aimed at the more influential segments of the population, while cinema vans, display cases, cigarette cards, and radio broadcasts ensured that the message reached those outside of circles of power, even in remote locations.[44] Radio was a valued medium but receivers were in short supply. In December 1942 money was approved to buy 300 radio sets from enemy property to be refurbished to only receive BBC and Egyptian State Broadcasting because "the listening channel is an essential one in doing propaganda among illiterate people, and also that communal listening is equally essential when the illiterate audience is very poor."[45] Touring officers carried battery-powered radio sets so that they could share the Allied news in Arabic and give talks, which were well received.[46] The Vanguard Players, a repertory company that toured Egypt, performed English plays in Arabic translation. By 1944 Pubsec in Egypt had twenty-seven cinema vans, which offered 300 shows per month and played recordings of popular Arab musicians and BBC broadcasts, in addition to showing films. It was difficult to keep the vans in repair and secure spare parts, but they were a crucial part of the publicity machine and Pubsec estimated that these shows were reaching 500,000 people per month.[47] In Iraq the publicity staff's

Figure 3 Publicity for the elite: A film viewing in Baghdad, December 1941. Original caption: "The intelligentsia of Baghdad are taking a great interest in the film shows which are held every Thursday afternoon. 20 to 30 guests come to tea and stay to see British news reels and shorts." Imperial War Museum (K1364).

Figure 4 Publicity for the masses: The river steamer *Showboat* hosts viewings of British publicity films along the Euphrates River, July 1944. Imperial War Museum (K7174).

seven cinema vans were supplemented by a cinema steam boat which showed films to the marsh Arabs of the south. The PR Section in Basra took the boat on a month-long cruise and showed war films from the deck, reaching 50,000 people "most of whom had never seen moving pictures before."[48]

By 1944 Britain had a sophisticated system for the distribution of both print and oral propaganda throughout the region. Newsprint shortages limited the size of Egyptian newspapers to four pages, but Pubsec found it fairly easy to buy influence in the Egyptian press to get its material published.[49] Public Relations in Iraq pioneered the publication of *Fatat al Rafidain,* "the first magazine exclusively for women to be produced in Arabic," with a circulation of 8,000. The magazine included a colored insert highlighting the latest fashions. The Baghdad embassy reported a positive relationship with the local press in Iraq and found that 90 percent of the contents of its twice daily news bulletin made their way into the newspapers.[50]

Iraqi scholar Majid Khadduri later noted that wartime Iraq was buried in an "avalanche of declarations, broadcasts, and propaganda literature extolling merits of the democratic way of life and promising improvement in the internal conditions of the country if the democratic countries won the war."[51] Thousands of Ministry of Information propaganda pamphlets were distributed each month, including a booklet of KEM cartoons, printed in Iraq but circulated throughout the region. The embassy supported 120 showcases that provided a venue for displaying publicity photos and exhibits around the country. Small enlightenment bureaux managed by local residents were established in Iraqi provincial towns and provided a place for residents to listen to radio broadcasts and view publicity materials. There were thirty-six reading rooms which not only provided access to Arabic-language reading materials but also had lending libraries and highly coveted wireless sets.[52] The reception manager at the Baghdad reading room distributed propaganda materials to the 90–120 visitors who came each day and helped them to find work, another way to build a cadre of loyal pro-British Iraqi citizens. He also served as a valuable point of contact and source of intelligence for public opinion on the ground, receiving concerns that could then be passed along to British authorities for remedy.[53]

The British Council held a special place in these propaganda efforts. It started work in Egypt in 1938, and by 1943 had institutes in both Cairo and Alexandria as well as seven other institutes in provincial towns and sponsored the Anglo-Egyptian Union, a jointly funded project with the Egyptian government.[54] The British Council was also active in Iraq, opening a British Institute in Mosul in 1942 and in Basra in 1944.[55]

All of these efforts had to overcome the suspicions of the local population as to their intent, a challenge that would hamper British publicity throughout the war. Public relations attachés were assigned to the consulates at Basra and Mosul but a report from Mosul noted that their parties were not popular because "Many people believe that the Public Relations Section is the centre of the Intelligence Service at Mosul and so they are avoiding it."[56] As a result, the British Council went to great lengths to position itself as a non-political body and an independent organization, which allowed its staff to stay in contact with those who might otherwise avoid official British circles.[57]

Iraq presented some unique challenges in the realm of propaganda. Sahib Tahir Hussain Quraishi, the Indian vice-consul at Baghdad and a Shi'i Muslim, served as a valuable liaison with Shi'a notables in the cities of Karbala and Najaf, the heart of the Shi'i pilgrimage traffic.[58] The shadow of 1941 hung heavy over these propaganda efforts. In 1942 Eden called for the formation of British Community Councils as a way to foster Anglo-Iraqi social interaction. The embassy sent letters to the consuls in Basra and Mosul to encourage British women to meet with their Iraqi counterparts. In Mosul this initiative was hindered by both the hesitance of local leaders to allow their daughters and wives to attend functions in British homes, and the fact that many of the British women still resented the poor treatment of their property during the events of May 1941. Since tea parties proved problematic, another suggestion was sewing parties to benefit the local poor or the Red Crescent. In Basra these efforts were hampered by the limited number of British women available and the closed mentality of the British community there.[59] The wife of one oil executive was, however, recruited to serve as the assistant public relations officer, a position to which she was able to bring her extensive local contacts.[60]

The Ministry of Information's campaigns targeted youth as a particularly important demographic. Allied military and civilian officials in London and Washington and stationed across the Middle East were all agreed on the potential threat posed by Arab youth as a source of unrest and latent anti-British sentiment.[61] This issue was also tied to the economic challenges of the war due to growing Soviet influence and the danger of "black coated unemployment" among the new *effendiyya*, a term whose exact definition is subject to debate but which, when used by British officials in this context, referred to the generation of educated Arab youth who came of age during the interwar period.[62] The wartime publicity message provided a new opportunity to win over the next generation, not only for the duration of the conflict but as a way to secure their allegiance in the postwar world as well. Rushbrook Williams urged: "What we need to 'get across' to Iraq—to the youth particularly—is that Britain is alive and progressive and vital, and not old, tired, and backward looking," what he identified as "the 'Perowne' outlook."[63] Smart, writing from Cairo, concurred with this assessment: "we must get hold of the youth of Egypt by showing sympathy for their ideas of social progress and by guiding these ideas into reasonable channels advantageous to ourselves. The old fogies of today, including the Wafd leaders, are not going to be the leading spirits of the post-war period."[64]

The events of the Rashid Ali coup and the growth of organizations such as Young Egypt and the Muslim Brotherhood, which built support among the *effendiyya* in the interwar period, made this issue particularly acute.[65] The Iraqi government, in its official investigation into the causes of the 1941 Farhud, identified the role that German propaganda, Arab nationalist teachers from Syria and Palestine, and the youth organizations such as al-Futuwwa played in driving Iraq's youth to violence, a legacy of pro-Axis influence in the Iraqi Ministry of Education.[66] As a result, the education system was a key target for reform. Nuri's government took numerous steps to repair this damage, including the appointment of a British adviser to the Ministry of Education and the replacement of Syrian and Palestinian teachers with Egyptian teachers who were not considered to possess the same radical Arab nationalist ideals of their Levantine counterparts. C. R. Grice, assistant adviser to the Ministry of the Interior, organized what he described as a "Sixth column" of British volunteers who helped to screen textbooks and started English-speaking groups in local schools.[67] In Egypt, the Association of British Schoolteachers adopted texts in their English reading and writing exercises that reinforced propaganda messages aimed at fifth-year students and the Ministry of Information in Cairo published an illustrated magazine for students, *al-Taleb,* which was also circulated in Iraq.[68] Publicity staff also worked to create social opportunities. The American mission in Basra had a room with a ping-pong table and other games, as well as a canteen widely used by the city's youth. British troops stopped by as well, with over 100 people meeting nightly. These gatherings fostered the kind of social interaction that the British wanted to encourage.[69]

The Brotherhood of Freedom had a critical role to play in these efforts to win over Arab youth. The cell-based organization had been developed as a behind-the-lines initiative to fight fifth columnists but as the threat receded from the region Brotherhood leaders reconceptualized their purpose with the postwar period in mind. In autumn 1942 the Brotherhood took on a second long-term objective, "to prepare a body of democratic public opinion for postwar Iraq."[70] The following year Freya Stark left Iraq and embarked on a speaking tour of North America and leadership of the Brotherhood fell to Christopher Scaife, a former English professor at an Egyptian university who, after being wounded during the siege of Tobruk, joined the Ministry of Information. Scaife was the perfect individual to lead the Brotherhood as it increased its focus on youth as he brought to this position not only years of contacts in Egypt but also experience in the 1930s working with innovative educational movements in England, including work camps for the unemployed, a summer school for the arts, and traveling drama groups.[71]

The language of democracy was a double-edged sword that could be used against the British as well. The Brotherhood tried to limit this danger by keeping its definition of democracy purposefully vague. The organization was defined primarily by its opposition to fascism, and Freya Stark was adamant that her organization "apart from being democratic, is a non-political society."[72] Stewart Perowne reassured critics by noting: "Discussion of internal politics is taboo." Vyvyan Holt, the oriental counsellor in Iraq, saw the inherent flaw in this argument and pointed out that an organization designed to promote democracy as a form of government could not, by definition, entirely avoid internal politics.[73] The PR Section encouraged abstract discussions of democracy as a means of bolstering the war effort, but distanced itself from grassroots efforts to apply these ideals to local administration. Britain experienced similar problems in Egypt as well. As they would see through the rest of the war, the vision of democracy laid out in Allied wartime propaganda was dimmed by the political and economic realities on the ground in Egypt and Iraq, with governments that enjoyed British support but also were widely viewed as corrupt and ineffective.

The Anglo-American troop landings in North Africa in November 1942 and the opening of the Persian Corridor to channel Lend-Lease supplies to a besieged Soviet Union via Iran changed the calculus of the publicity campaigns. The United States was now both a partner and a rival in the publicity work in the region and a cause of endless frustration to British officials who, on the one hand, acknowledged the value of the US contribution, while also feeling threatened by American attempts to extend their influence into a decidedly British sphere.[74] In April 1943 Killearn commented on "the extent to which the whole Middle East area is now compelled to draw upon United States sources for consumption goods of all kinds." It was important to avoid "another American lapse into isolation and self-sufficiency" and keep the US "international-minded," but "On the other hand American cultural and political influence with its ignorant prejudice against 'imperialism' and its constant vague talk of democracy and liberty is just the thing to cause us the maximum of embarrassment in oriental countries like Egypt."[75] These tensions were exposed during the visit of Wendell Willkie, Roosevelt's personal representative, in autumn 1942 as part of his worldwide tour.[76] Before his arrival the Ministry of Information asked its staff to draw Willkie's attention to "the seriousness and the extent of British effort and sacrifice" and to ensure that he would "gain as good an impression as possible of British Middle East propaganda methods and machinery."[77]

Willkie's visit to Baghdad in September was, from the embassy's perspective, a success as it demonstrated to the Iraqis the American determination to win the war and facilitated Anglo-American cooperation on publicity.[78] His visit to Egypt was less productive. While highly complementary of General Montgomery, with whom

Figure 5 Wendell Willkie at a British embassy luncheon in Baghdad, 1942. Notable figures include Oriental Counsellor Vyvyan Holt (first row far left), Wendell Willkie (first row third from left), Ambassador Sir Kinahan Cornwallis and Iraqi Prime Minister Nuri al-Saʿid (first row second and third from right), Embassy Counsellor G. Thompson (back row second from left), and Public Relations Attaché Stewart Perowne (second row, second from right). Imperial War Museum (K3578).

he toured the front at El Alamein, he criticized the "lacksidaisical" attitude he saw in Cairo, reflecting a frequent American criticism that the British had not done enough to get the population of the region behind the war effort.[79] Willkie described his surprise when, in dinner conversation with British military and civilian officials in Alexandria about the future of the empire, "What I got was Rudyard Kipling, untainted even with the liberalism of Cecil Rhodes." At a time when Arab nationalists were appropriating the Allied rhetoric of the Atlantic Charter to support independence, he found that: "The Atlantic Charter most of them had read about. That it might affect their careers or their thinking had never occurred to any of them." As for his conversations with the public in his travels through the region, he recalled that "Again and again I was asked: does America intend to support a system by which our politics are controlled by foreigners, however politely, our lives dominated by foreigners, however indirectly, because we happen to be strategic points on the military roads and trade routes of the world?"[80] These were not merely personal ruminations buried in a report to the president, but rather his public conclusions outlined in his 1943 book *One World,* which sold over a million copies in seven weeks.[81] The book was suppressed in Egypt because Willkie described Killearn as "for all practical purposes, its actual ruler," an uncomfortable observation at a time when the embassy was facing harsh criticism for its support of Nahhas's government.[82]

The Turning Tides of the War

By spring 1943 Cornwallis reported that the situation in Iraq was "tranquil" and the country was fulfilling all of its wartime obligations as outlined in Article 4 of the treaty. He attributed this to three factors: "the turn of the tide of the war in our favour, the presence of strong British forces, and the comparative calm of the contemporary political situation in Palestine and Syria."[83] With news of the Axis defeat in Tunisia: "Public opinion has now finally awarded victory to the United Nations and feels itself free to discuss the future of the world on this basis, encouraged by the comfortable assumption that so far as Iraq is concerned, the war is over."[84] The embassy received mountains of congratulatory messages from across the country. In Mosul the *mutasarrif* declared a public holiday and the British consul, whose predecessor had been murdered during the anti-British protest in 1939, found himself "receiving homage of school-children in processions." As Geoffrey Thompson commented in his report to London, "Nothing succeeds like success."[85]

With the end of the North African campaign the Middle East was removed from the front lines of the war, but it continued to have strategic importance to the Allies. This radically transformed wartime situation had deep implications for both Egypt and Iraq. General Wilson left PAIC and became the new commander-in-chief, Middle East, returning to Egypt where he had started the war. Lieutenant-General Sir Henry Pownall, who replaced Wilson as commander of PAIC in March 1943, found that his responsibilities had shifted. As the threat of an Axis invasion of Iraq and Iran receded, British troops were moved to other theaters and "The number of operational troops remaining was no greater than FORCE IRAQ had been, two years before." Priorities included protecting oil supplies in transit via the Kirkuk/Haifa pipeline and internal security and Basra had a new role as the landing base for supplies being transported to Russia via Iran. There was still the danger of fifth columnists and Axis sabotage plans exploiting unrest in tribal areas but by spring of 1943 PAIC "was now more of an administrative than an operational command."[86]

Yet Iraq still had an important role to play as a major transit point, with the official PAIFORCE history reporting that:

> In the six months which ended on 30th September, 1943, the Iraq railway system carried 29,000 soldiers and 4,000 vehicles, in addition to the normal movement of military stores. In the same period Transport Companies of the R.A.S.C. and I.A.S.C. were ferrying troops across the desert by the all-weather through road from Baghdad to Haifa, and every vehicle in these companies was covering 1,500 miles a month. Seven hundred thousand soldiers passed through the transit camps at Baghdad.[87]

While this impressive show of British military strength was passing through Iraq on the way to other theaters, the local presence was greatly reduced, with real implications for British policy. As Thompson noted in July 1943 from the perspective of the embassy: "it is now evident to all that our local forces are reduced virtually to clerks, care-maintenance and labour formations, our military strength here and heavy commitments elsewhere would scarcely justify the sudden adoption of an aggressive policy over questions that are difficult and important, but scarcely vital."[88]

On the anniversary of the signing of the Anglo-Egyptian Treaty on August 26, 1943, Ambassador Killearn gave a broadcast speech against the backdrop of these victories in which he reflected on the ways in which the events of the war had proven the treaty's worth. After reviewing the tumultuous events since the signing of the treaty in 1936 and the treachery of the Axis powers in breaking their own treaties, Killearn declared: "Standing out against this background of treachery, slaughter, destruction and spoliation, as a small but morally by no means insignificant symbol of hope for the future, there is one Treaty which has been loyally kept by both parties—that Anglo-Egyptian Treaty whose anniversary we commemorate to-day." He reminded his audience that even though an Allied victory was within reach they still had a heavy fight ahead, and while Egypt had made a great contribution, more sacrifices were necessary.[89] For Killearn victory in North Africa proved that the treaty had fulfilled its purpose, but as will be explored below, opposition forces in Egypt took quite a different lesson: the threat to Egypt had passed, Egypt had made a contribution to this outcome, and the treaty had now lived beyond its usefulness.

8

"Let Us Stand by Our Friends," March 1943–December 1943

With the surrender of Axis forces in Tunisia on May 13, 1943, the conflict in North Africa, which had begun in September 1940 with the Italian offensive and brought the war to the doorstep of Cairo multiple times in the ensuing three-year period, was over. The last Axis troops departed from North Africa and the Allied troops massed in Egypt were now focusing their attention across the Mediterranean to Italy. The Soviet victory at Stalingrad in February 1943 meant that the long-feared invasion through the Northern Front was increasingly unlikely, and the Tenth Army was reabsorbed into Middle East Command.[1] With Allied troops landing in Italy, the Middle East and North Africa were now peripheral to the fighting in Europe. While the threat of Axis sabotage remained, Egyptian and Iraqi leaders declared that their governments had fulfilled their treaty commitments through the dark days of the war and they were now looking ahead to the postwar world.

For the Allies, the Middle East still had a vital role to play in the conflict. The base at Basra became the massive staging ground for the Lend-Lease operations to supply the Soviets through the Persian Corridor, and both Egypt and Iraq could provide much-needed food supplies locally, thereby relieving pressures on Allied shipping. Egyptian cereal exports could meet demand in other parts of the Middle East, sugar exports were needed in the Sudan, and Iraqi cereals could be shipped to India in the midst of the Bengal famine. A Foreign Office official noted in April 1943 that: "200,000 tons of white rice and 25,000 tons of grain and 75,000 tons of sugar, all of which according to M.E.S.C. the Egyptians could easily spare would be more important to us in the present juncture, from the point of view of getting on with the war, than keeping 'Ali Mahir and Nabil Abbas Halim locked up."[2]

British publicity now pivoted to fighting Arab apathy and convincing the public that the war was not over and as Allies they still had an important contribution to make. The receding immediacy of the conflict in 1943 coincided with the maturing of what the American legation in Iraq called "the British control apparatus," the network of intelligence, publicity, and administrative advisers spread throughout the country in the interest of the war effort. Britain had cooperative governments to work with in both Egypt and Iraq, and yet they were also corrupt and inefficient, a reality which, in the eyes of critics, stood in stark contrast to the Allied rhetoric of the United Nations and the Atlantic Charter. Britain found it increasingly difficult to balance its wartime requirements with the growing calls for political and economic reform.

Nahhas and the Black Book Affair

Two days before Nahhas announced the preliminary conversations with Iraq on Arab unity, Egypt was rocked by an internal political scandal. On March 28, 1943, members of Egypt's opposition parties gave the king a lengthy petition called the Black Book, which purported to document all of the Wafd government's abuses of power. While many of these accusations of corruption and nepotism had been spreading as rumor for months, the Black Book included documents to back up these assertions. Many of the charges exposed the Wafd's vast patronage network, from the granting of lucrative government contracts to supporters to securing promotions or admission to the military college for the children of Wafd officials. Nahhas's wife and her extravagant lifestyle at government expense served as another target and reflected her acrimonious relationship with Makram, who blamed her in part for the political split within the Wafd party that led to his departure.[3] The document was widely circulated, with Smart estimating that between 20,000 and 35,000 copies were printed, some even making their way outside Egypt to Palestine.[4]

Before deciding on their response, the embassy investigated the accusations. The crown advocate concluded that many of the more sensationalistic charges appeared to be exaggerated and unsubstantiated.[5] Most British officials took a pragmatic approach to Egyptian corruption and favoritism, accepting it as part of the cost of doing business in the country. In fact, they sometimes worked within this system to secure appointments for their own local clients. The Wafd faced distinct challenges as it was a popular party and had to reward its supporters on its return to power. Killearn observed: "The trouble with the Wafd is that having a larger *clientèle* to satisfy than the minority parties, its misdeeds on these lines must be wider spread and thus better known."[6] One Egyptian official pointed out that while the Wafd's reputation had been hurt by the corruption charges, it had been strengthened in the provinces through the extension of patronage, as it widened the net of Egyptians dependent on the Wafd for economic gain.[7] It was this widespread support that made the Wafd such a valuable collaborator in time of war and enabled the party to deliver on Britain's wartime requirements.

Killearn sensed a joint opposition-palace initiative behind the Black Book. In response to the petition King Farouk began a public boycott of the government, placing Britain in the middle of the struggle between the palace and the Wafd. Farouk had been improving his relationship with the embassy in recent months, and the British valued good relations with the palace because it was a permanent presence in the country, unlike the ephemeral Egyptian governments. As for Nahhas, the prime minister had delivered the goods in the darkest days of "the Flap," keeping Egypt steady when the threat of Axis occupation seemed greatest, although he had not proven as cooperative on supply issues.[8]

The British often faced the charge of letting down their friends when the situation became difficult. Nahhas tried to use this guilt tactic to win the embassy's support, chiding Killearn that the British got rid of Egyptian governments as soon as they had served their purpose.[9] Eden himself weighed in on this debate, concluding: "Surely Nahas is our friend and the king is not. Let us stand by our friends."[10] Charges of abandoning the prime minister after the loyalty he had shown in the most difficult days of the war in Egypt would damage British prestige more than the charges of overlooking the corruption of the regime they put in power. The Foreign Office acknowledged that Nahhas may not be able to completely refute the charges, but he should be able "to confuse the issues successfully."[11]

Killearn welcomed these instructions, but his oriental counsellor, Sir Walter Smart, was deeply troubled by their implications: "The substance of this telegram is that it is better to condone corruption than to let down our friends. This theory, surely novel in our imperial history, is developed with a cynicism astonishing in an official telegram."[12] The palace and opposition leaders highlighted the hypocrisy of British support for Nahhas as a betrayal of their principles. Hasanayn pointed out that "From the days of Cromer the British had never tolerated corruption of any king on the part of Egyptian Governments and it would certainly be a very grave mistake to do so now. Surely we were not prepared to sacrifice our prestige in order to keep a man like Nahhas in power."[13] Since the British brought the Wafd to power through the threat of force, they bore responsibility for this government. For Smart, this was not just an ethical issue, but one with practical ramifications for the work of the embassy as it would reflect poorly on British prestige: "I have always found that the legend of British honesty was of the greatest help to me in many different positions where often I had not force on my side," and he warned that ceding the moral high ground would be disastrous for Britain's ability to secure its wartime requirements.[14]

Churchill took Smart's side on this issue: "It is a very serious thing for the occupying Power to shield a corrupt Government. Our position in Oriental lands, including India, has always been the opposite." Given the large British military presence and recent Allied successes Churchill suggested that they could afford to let Nahhas's government fall and wait to intervene later if necessary.[15] The Foreign Office, however, supported Killearn: the charges against Nahhas were no worse than those that could be made "against any oriental potentate in any oriental country at any time in history," and it was important for the long term to keep the Wafd's friendship.[16]

Both the Wafd and opposition parties took the issue to the streets. Pubsec received reports that the Sa'dist Party was planning demonstrations and a whispering campaign against the British with the goal of inciting a rebellion and urging the people to "join in a 'Jihad' for independence." In response, the British mobilized their own oral propaganda networks to counteract rumors that Killearn had presented Farouk with another ultimatum. British contacts in the provinces and the Egyptian army were asked to gauge public opinion toward the Wafd to determine whether or not they still had widespread support.[17]

The embassy tried to place the responsibility for resolving this dispute back on the Egyptians by arguing that, rather than dismissing the Wafd government outright, the palace should give it the opportunity to defend itself. The king reluctantly agreed and debate opened in the Chamber of Deputies. As the deliberations dragged on through the spring Killearn decided to try a new tactic, "shifting the issue from corruption charge to democracy principle." The majority of the people should decide the fate of Nahhas's government through elections, rather than the king or the embassy. As with the corruption charges, Killearn took a pragmatic view of Egyptian elections. They would be rigged whether they were held by a Wafd government or an opposition one, but he was convinced that the Wafd still had a majority in the country and as a result "it will matter less if they fake the elections than if the other parties were to have."[18]

The palace objected to the election proposal as it would inevitably lead to a manipulated Wafd victory and the opposition would boycott it.[19] On May 17 Farouk informed Killearn that he had taken the ambassador's advice and given Nahhas's government a chance to clear its name before Parliament but after five weeks of debates he concluded that a new government was necessary as "the present Cabinet has lost all moral authority in the country." However, he would keep the Wafd government in power if the British insisted that doing so was necessary for the war effort, in effect trying to pass the responsibility back to the embassy. Killearn was alarmed by the implications of this proposal, as it would allow the palace to blame Britain any time the Wafd government did something unpopular.[20]

While the embassy was negotiating the terms of the political settlement with the palace, British officials were also debating the viability of using force to support the Wafd and unseat Farouk, once again pitting the diplomats against the military authorities. One of the lessons Killearn took away from the 1942 Abdin Palace incident was that when King Farouk realized the British were serious about using force he backed down and compromised, making the threat of force a useful tool to ensure palace compliance.[21] From the perspective of the service chiefs, they had lost the element of surprise. Britain had "played the force card" in 1942, and the Egyptian army would be prepared for such action in the future.[22] General Stone warned that, given the Wafd's unpopularity with the army, police, and most of the upper classes, British military action would foment anti-British sentiment and interfere with the war effort.[23] The service chiefs opposed the politicization of the British troops present in Egypt and their use for internal matters and, much to Killearn's frustration, Minister of State Casey supported their view, suggesting that they should instead take any action "short of threat or use of force" as he did not believe that the alternative of a non-Wafd government was as bad as Killearn portrayed it.[24]

After hearing their reservations Killearn wrote to the Foreign Office to make his case for having force on hand as an option. The ambassador was deliberate in the language used in this telegram, noting in his diary that he chose the phrase "weakness never pays" because it was "just the sort of phrase that would catch our Prime Minister's attention."[25] The ploy worked; Churchill agreed and instructed General Wilson, now commander-in-chief, Middle East, to support Killearn as necessary by providing troops because a simple demonstration of force would most likely be sufficient.[26]

In the end the Black Book crisis was resolved without the use of force. The debate in the Wafd-dominated Chamber of Deputies resulted in a vote of confidence for Nahhas when, as expected, the opposition boycotted the vote.[27] Killearn finally dropped the idea of holding elections as summer 1943, on the eve of the Allied invasion of Sicily, was an inopportune time to risk unrest in Egypt and the possible diversion of troops. Nahhas himself seemed unenthusiastic about the idea of elections, which a Foreign Office official attributed to his realization of the Wafd's declining popularity.[28] Nahhas remained in power and Farouk took a more conciliatory attitude to the embassy, which the ambassador credited to "the foreknowledge of rods in pickle." While disappointed that the planned elections had fallen through Killearn concluded that "we have at least achieved our main object—namely no change likely to upset local stability of our base in the immediate future."[29]

Having twice intervened on behalf of Nahhas, the embassy felt some responsibility to ensure good government and grew increasingly concerned about the Wafd's abuse of wartime power, particularly because the Wafd regime was so closely associated with the British in the Egyptian public's mind. In the aftermath of the crisis Killearn reported: "I have impressed on Nahas Pasha the necessity of a conciliatory attitude towards the Palace, of cleaner, abler administration, of a constructive policy for the welfare of the people." The warning had limited effect as in July 1943 the Wafd led a motion to strip Makram of his seat in Parliament, part of a larger backlash against the Coptic contingent in the aftermath of the 1942 party rift.[30] This set off a spiral of recrimination and retribution that would continue to the end of the war and haunt Nahhas after he eventually fell from power.

The political turmoil of the Black Book crisis took place against the backdrop of the dramatically altered wartime landscape in spring 1943, creating new challenges for British policy. The continuing presence of large numbers of British troops in Egypt despite the removal of the immediate Axis threat led to increasing xenophobia and the Wafd capitalized on this sentiment to deflect attention from its cooperation with Britain and to regain its reputation as a nationalist party.[31] In assessing the potential fallout of the Black Book affair Killearn warned that Britain would now become the focal point of attack by the opposition. The rhetoric of these protests was no longer against the government in power, but against British influence in the country. Now that the fighting had left Egypt it would be increasingly difficult to justify British intervention in terms of Allied war interests.[32]

The embassy dated this new offensive to a series of speeches by opposition leaders at Menoufia on June 1, 1943.[33] Ahmad Mahir, who was one of the most vocal supporters of Egypt declaring war, announced: "we have returned to the past days of occupation and protectorate ... The English are colonizers and are now depending on a dishonest Government. Our struggle is against foreign administration." In an analogy that carried heavy implications of collaboration and betrayal, he then described Nahhas as "an Egyptian Quisling," put in power by the British on February 4 just as the Germans supported a puppet government in Norway, concluding: "I see no difference between the two conducts."[34]

Economic Challenges in Egypt and Iraq

The opposition speeches at Menoufia included a critique of the government's financial policies, a reflection of the growing preoccupation with economic matters throughout the region. It was here in the financial realm that the war most impacted the average citizen, with rampant inflation combined with shortages of key commodities and fluctuating demand for crops affecting the local economy. British officials were keenly aware that British military spending in Egypt and Iraq had exacerbated these economic challenges and local shortages in either country would undermine support for the war effort. Economic problems might lead to unrest and could open the door for greater Soviet and American penetration of local markets. For all of these reasons it was vital to tackle the persistent economic problems and yet the process of doing so also exposed the weaknesses of the governments in power.

Britain's support of Nahhas during the Black Book affair came at the price of greater British control over supply issues and the appointment of British financial experts. Amin 'Uthman, longtime intermediary between the Wafd and the embassy, was rewarded for his work during the crisis with an appointment as minister of finance in Nahhas's Cabinet reorganization in May 1943. Britain and Egypt were engaged in tense negotiations over supply issues and Killearn noted that with this appointment "seventy-five percent of our day to day difficulties should disappear." Yet even while this served the war effort it created new problems, including rumors that Nahhas was exporting food that was needed in Egypt as payment to the British for helping him.[35]

The question of supplies remained highly politicized and the Wafd government had to navigate the difficult waters between Britain's demands and the charges of their political opponents. During the summer of 1943 Nahhas and 'Uthman proved their worth to Britain by resisting demands from their supporters to raise the price of wheat in Egypt, a decision that would have limited supplies in Egyptian cities but also had a ripple effect throughout the region, undermining wheat collection in the Levant and inflating the price Britain would have to pay for Iraqi barley.[36] Later in November 1943, when Egypt changed course and raised the price of rice and wheat, British officials charged that the government was using "blackmail" on the question of cereal supplies by forcing the price higher, with one official noting that this was "an unheroic attitude on the part of an ally living in plenty while other territories in our fold were in danger of starvation."[37] The Egyptian opposition was also critical of this decision, but for different reasons, as higher prices on cereals benefited wealthy landowners and placed an additional burden on the poor, increasing the economic gap in Egypt. This action only provided further proof of the corruption and ineptitude of the Wafd government and its commitment to its supporters at the expense of the general public.[38]

Egyptian agriculture was heavily reliant on imported nitrates from South America, which took up valuable shipping space. Without the nitrates agricultural production would suffer, with implications for both Egypt's own food supply and its ability to support the broader Allied war effort. Britain and Egypt held negotiations in late 1943 for an agreement by which Egypt would receive 300,000 tons of nitrates in 1944 in return for letting Britain buy any excess crops that resulted. As part of the settlement Egypt agreed not to increase cotton production in 1944, and areas usually given to cotton cultivation were turned over to cereals and rice.[39]

Amin 'Uthman was a success from the British perspective in his position as minister of finance. He implemented conversion loans which absorbed some of the excess money in Egypt due to the Allies' military spending in the country as a way to try and curb inflation and he facilitated the appointment of Mr. Baxter as a financial expert within the Ministry of Finance.[40] For Britain this appointment was critical to managing Egypt's supply challenges, while the Wafd's political opponents viewed it as yet another concession made by Nahhas as the price for British support. The opposition attacked Baxter's appointment as a return to the days of the protectorate, when Britain had advisers in various Egyptian ministries, and also exposed the fact that Baxter's salary was more than that of a government minister, echoing a frequent critique of Cromer's "veiled protectorate."[41] The minister of finance did not get along well with the new adviser, who complained that Amin 'Uthman's methods were "highly unorthodox" and involved maintaining his own patronage network but also spending "an immense amount of time on quite extraneous duties." As a result, Baxter had to create paths to work around 'Uthman to achieve objectives for the ministry and meet wartime goals.[42]

Iraq's declaration of war opened up similar opportunities to move forward on economic issues. As a belligerent Iraq would be expected to make a real contribution to the war effort, and one of the most important avenues for doing so would be in the economic realm, providing grain for export to the region. Iraq faced a myriad of economic challenges in 1943, many of them similar to those faced by Egypt, but exacerbated by the limited reach of the central government in the provinces. The amount of currency in circulation had more than quadrupled since 1941, and the resulting rise in the cost of living and inflation led to speculation and hoarding. Britain had to balance the pressure it put on the Iraqi government to control prices and the distribution of imports with the need to maintain enough good will to allow them to negotiate favorable prices to purchase Iraqi barley and Basra dates.[43]

Managing this economic contribution required a more extensive system of bureaucratic control, leading to greater British intervention but also exposing the real weaknesses and inefficiencies in the Iraqi system, sparking calls for internal reform. Nuri was cooperative but also part of the problem and Cornwallis repeated the perennial refrain of his predecessors, that the prime minister was more concerned with grand schemes of Arab unity than with the mundane day-to-day administration of Iraq. His frequent absences from the country, either for health reasons or to promote his pan-Arab agenda, left the government without its leader and encouraged intrigues.[44]

Like his Egyptian counterpart Nuri's politics were driven by personal connections and patronage, and corruption and nepotism remained a serious problem both in Baghdad and in the provinces. While the British believed that Nuri himself was an honest politician, those who surrounded him were not. British reports portrayed him as being too blinded by his friends to notice their failings and too loyal to put them out of office even when it was in the country's best interest, and they lamented the unwillingness of Iraqi politicians to set aside personal interests and allegiances for the greater good in time of war.[45] The Iraqi army had been purged but not reformed, and it still functioned on a patronage model driven by loyalty to Nuri. One Foreign Office observer noted that the corruption in Iraq was no worse than in other Arab countries, but a "higher standard" was required in Iraq because "the elements which comprise the country are more difficult to handle than those of, say, Egypt or the Levant States."[46]

Not only had this hindered the purging of pro-Axis government officials, but as in Egypt these patronage networks also complicated Britain's agenda for economic reform. Nuri's supporters and members of the government were drawn from the class of landowners who benefited from inflation and had the most to lose if wartime controls were implemented.[47] As Cornwallis noted, Nuri's administration was criticized for its slow response on economic challenges and also "for their continued subserviency to powerful agricultural and mercantile vested interests. The fact is that the Prime Minister with his head full of Pan-Arab dreams, is reluctant to offend any potential political 'friends.'"[48] Once again, economic reforms threatened to undermine the delicate and complex patronage networks keeping Britain's allies in power.

While Britain wanted Iraq to provide supplies to neighboring states, they did so with one eye on local prices, cognizant of the need to keep prices reasonable in order to avoid unrest. In spring 1943 the Iraqi Parliament passed a "Law for the Regulation of the Economic Life of the Country" which assisted with these measures. The law gave the Ministry of the Interior more power over supply issues through a new department with British advisers and led to the creation of a Cabinet Committee of Supplies. The United Kingdom Commercial Corporation (UKCC) would purchase barley and wheat for export to other countries in the region and the law required growers to sell a portion of their crops to the government for a set price, with the option to sell more at the same price if desired. Other measures were designed to improve the distribution of imports, to keep import prices down, and to monitor available stock levels.[49]

Passing the law was one thing; enforcing it was another. After some initial success the law was not enforced so costs rose, with the embassy reporting in summer 1943 that cotton goods were in high demand and "Meat, fruit and vegetables are now dearer than ever and a large proportion of the working classes cannot afford to buy them. Many townspeople are therefore obliged to do without these very important foods."[50] Transportation of goods was another challenge and so British and Iraqi officials developed plans to ensure that Iraqi trucks were available for local transport and had access to spare tires and parts. A new British officer was appointed to organize road transportation and to smooth over tensions regarding military and civilian use of roads and supplies. No motor vehicle could be purchased or sold without the approval of the director general of transport.[51]

As in Egypt, the supply situation laid bare the inefficiencies of the Iraqi government. In October 1942 Saleh Jabr had been moved to the Ministry of Finance and it was hoped that he would initiate real changes to prepare Iraq for the economic impact of the war and also be open to bringing in British personnel. Saleh Jabr represented the new younger generation of progressive leaders the British hoped would take over the reins from Nuri's old gang and was considered to be a potential future Shiʿi prime minister.[52] In the end he proved to be a disappointment to the British when he dragged his heels on the appointment of British economic advisers. He was sent back to the Ministry of the Interior in June 1943 and Cornwallis lamented the missed window of opportunity to get ahead of supply issues.[53]

By the autumn of 1943 the impact of these efforts was uneven. Farmers were benefitting from high prices but there were shortages in the north and in urban areas. Britain was concerned the urban poor would be hard hit in winter due to limited clothing supplies. One solution was to import cotton goods from India in return for shipping excess barley to help relieve the Bengal famine, and yet the Foreign Office had difficulty securing support for this plan. Thompson warned Eden in September 1943: "As I have urged ad nauseum, loss of Iraqi goodwill over this question may well react against our efforts to relieve India's grain crisis."[54]

To meet these economic challenges Britain once again proposed bringing in British financial experts to develop rationing programs and controls on import distribution who would be granted executive, as opposed to purely advisory, powers. After Saleh Jabr's departure the Iraqi government opened discussions for a British "Director-General of Imports and Economic Adviser to the High Supply Council." Colonel Bayliss from the Middle East Supply Centre (MESC) was appointed to this position in November 1943, along with a staff of five controllers who held executive powers in their respective sections of the Directorate-General of Imports. Bayliss also served as chairman of a number of new committees to address economic issues. There was a lot riding on the success of Bayliss's appointment. Britain had imposed this new system of British advisers with executive functions on the Iraqis and any failures they might experience would reflect poorly on British prestige.[55]

Iraq's economic issues were not just affecting life in the capital, but also reflected the limited reach of the capital in the provinces. CICI reported that provincial officials warned that the presence of Allied troops was the only thing keeping the country from experiencing protests and unrest due to the economic situation, and that they were frustrated that Britain was not taking action to address the problem.[56] The Kurdish north was particularly hard hit by these economic problems, a region viewed as strategically significant yet vulnerable. While the changing tides of the war made an Axis invasion increasingly unlikely, British military intelligence was on the guard against potential acts of sabotage. The British had made contingency plans to destroy Iraq's oil infrastructure, concentrated troops in northern Iraq, and recruited the Kurds to construct defenses such as earthworks and trenches.[57] Britain's preoccupation with security in the northern provinces appeared to be well founded when three German parachutists and a Kurdish-speaking Iraqi were captured in June 1943 near Mosul. During their interrogation they stated that their objective was to stir up the Kurds against the Allies and gather information, with a later party to undertake sabotage. While the unit had outdated political intelligence, the episode was troubling because the parachutists received local assistance in hiding after they landed and it exposed the continued vulnerability of the Iraq-Iran border.[58]

In addressing these economic and security concerns the British preached action to the Iraqi government and patience to the Kurds. Baghdad made some token concessions, but a combination of discriminatory government policies, wartime pressures, and natural disasters exacerbated the economic difficulties of the Kurdish areas, creating widespread shortages and famine conditions in 1943.[59] The impasse was broken in July when Mulla Mustafa, a leader of the Barzani Kurds, escaped from detention in Sulaymaniya. In September he and his followers raided police posts, gathering arms when the posts surrendered.[60]

The Iraqi army intervened but it suffered humiliating defeats, revealing its weakness and lack of organization, a legacy of the 1941 conflict. Cornwallis observed: "It was found that the men were quite untrained for mountain operations and, furthermore, that they had no heart in the business."[61] The size of the army had dropped dramatically after 1941 as a result of purges, the failure to enforce conscription, and high rates of desertion. The British, considering the Iraqi military to be a potential threat to stability during the war given its role in the 1941 coup, had supported Nuri's policy of keeping it weak by limiting supplies and rations.[62] At the same time, they expressed frustration with his neglect of Iraqi military affairs and the need for a drastic reorganization of the army. His patronage networks extended to the army and his continued support of older officers, the last remnant of the Ottoman-trained soldiers, built resentment among younger officers, who saw their chances at promotion blocked.[63]

The Political Advisory Staff, originally appointed to root out Axis influence in the provinces, came to play an important role in addressing the intertwined issues of supply shortages in rural areas and tribal revolts, of which the Kurdish uprising was only the most serious. Cornwallis observed that the inability of the central government to address the famine conditions in the north had led tribal leaders such as Mulla Mustafa "to take the law into their own hands, to pursue private feuds and to flout orders of local officials."[64] The revolt had the potential to disrupt Iraq's contribution to the Allied war effort, particularly its grain shipments, its role in imperial communications, and its oil supply. The situation in Kurdish areas over the border in Iran was particularly tumultuous in the wake of the 1941 Anglo-Soviet occupation, and British officials in Baghdad were perpetually worried that this instability, and with it Soviet influence, would spread into Iraq. Kurdish leaders in Iran and Iraq frequently took refuge on the opposite side of the border, resulting in complicated negotiations between tribal leaders, embassy officials, and local governments for their return, either to amnesty or internment.[65]

The British were divided as to the best response to this Kurdish revolt. The Foreign Office insisted that Britain not get involved in local issues unless absolutely necessary to protect Allied war interests. By contrast, many of the British PAs believed that the Kurds had been cheated out of an independent state after the First World War when the state of Iraq was formed, and that Britain had a duty to right this long-standing wrong.[66] Since this would potentially lead to military intervention, which Britain wanted to avoid at all costs, Cornwallis felt it was necessary for him to use his political influence in order to "localise the present conflict."[67] The Foreign Office agreed; the Iraqi government was responsible for maintaining internal order, and British troops would only be used to protect British interests, such as the lines of communication and the Assyrian Levies who were under threat of attack by "the insurgents."[68]

Executive Control and the British Control Apparatus in Iraq

The Kurdish issue encapsulated all that the British believed was wrong with Iraq's administration and the embassy was growing increasingly frustrated by the lack of what it called "courageous leadership." Yet there seemed to be no suitable alternative from the British perspective: "There is a great dearth of material, for those who are able … are not reliable, while those who are reliable are either incompetent or insignificant."[69] The impending parliamentary elections in 1943 raised again the issue of the closed nature of Iraqi politics and seemed to provide a perfect opportunity to remedy this situation.

Nuri was in poor health and so the embassy anticipated the need to find a new prime minister in the near future, but he resisted British pressure to infuse the government with "new blood," arguing that it was difficult to find suitable new candidates with experience, and "he could scarcely be expected to sacrifice old friends in favour of new, untried and possibly hostile critics."[70] In the end, the elections resulted in only twenty new deputies, and while all the supporters of Rashid 'Ali had now been eliminated from the government, the embassy concluded that the new Chamber was much like those that preceded it and would most likely vote in a similar manner.[71]

Cornwallis held a marathon talk with Nuri in October 1943 in which he expressed his concerns with the Iraqi administration: the government's failure to deal with economic issues and Kurdish unrest, as well as the "weakness and corruption" of the police, "unreliability" of the army, and "dishonesty and inefficiency" in public administration. The people of Iraq were no longer as patient as they had been in the past and if the government did not adjust to the changes, particularly in urban areas, "the old order might be very rudely disturbed at no very distant date."[72] The administrative problems in the north were growing so serious that Edmonds and Cornwallis were considering radical options, including a proposal to have the PAs employed directly by the Iraqi government under the Ministry of the Interior for six months with the goal of directly reforming local administration. Nuri agreed to this idea and was even willing to give the PAs the power to suspend Iraqi officials if they deemed it necessary. They would remain under the ambassador's authority for their regular duties, and Edmonds would supervise their new administrative work. The Foreign Office was alarmed at this "retrograde step" of giving the advisers real executive power as this proposal, "even allowing for our heightened war prestige in Iraq, runs dead against our general policy in the Middle East, which is to achieve our ends by use of influence rather than the direct exercise of authority."[73]

While never implemented this scheme reflects the persistence of the mandate mentality among British officials in Iraq, in particular a growing conviction that smooth administration required British supervision. The ambassador argued: "There is at present a widespread realization that Iraq cannot hope to solve any of her politico-economic ills without expert foreign guidance."[74] Cornwallis noted that even though they were not given the title "a number of the Mutasarrifs treat their Political Advisers as though they were Administrative Inspectors and have frequently invited them to settle difficult tribal disputes." It was also in line with a growing trend as before 1941 Britain only enjoyed this executive control in the Port of Basra and in the administration of the railways, but under Nuri they now had "British executive control in the Irrigation, veterinary, Transport, Imports, Foreign Exchange and Internal Produce departments" as well as greater British influence in the Ministry of Education.[75] Yet this control also contained the potential danger that they would get blamed for shortcomings, as the embassy warned with Bayliss's appointment.

The implications of this plan were not lost to the Iraqis. Ibrahim Kemal, an Iraqi politician widely viewed as a likely future prime minister, complained to Edmonds that this proposal would "reimpose the Mandate."[76] The establishment of so many British organizations under the guise of public relations added further fuel to the belief that the British were pulling the strings of the government. Newspapers and speeches mentioned by name the various British organizations trying to influence public opinion in order to expose the reach of the embassy.[77]

Iraqis were not alone in drawing attention to creeping British controls. On November 20, 1943, Loy Henderson presented his credentials as the new minister plenipotentiary of the United States to Iraq, the first to hold this title as his predecessors had been ministers resident. The appointment was a sign of growing American interest and influence in Iraq. Henderson threw himself into his new post with a series of reports that recounted his first impressions and travels around the country, as well as a lengthy document that outlined what he called "Britain's control apparatus," an elaborate network of British civilian and military officials "which endeavors to safeguard British interests in practically every field of Iraqi national life and to direct trends of Iraqi internal and external policies into channels which will serve the well-being of the British Empire." He noted with frustration that, due to the wide array of British advisers who had been added to various government ministries in the post-coup period, "It is practically impossible for this Legation to have any dealings with the Iraqi Government which do not eventually come under the scrutiny of some British subject connected with that Government."[78] The embassy was at the heart of this apparatus and while Ambassador Cornwallis preferred to use indirect methods of influence rather than direct control when possible, his power in Iraq was not left in doubt, with Richard Gnade, a member of the American legation staff, noting that the British ambassador even had precedence over the Iraqi prime minister at events attended by the regent.[79]

This civilian authority was bolstered by the military structure of PAIC (the troops of which were also referred to as PAIFORCE), whose "activities and expenditures affect every class of Iraqi." The prewar British Military Mission, with its limited function, was now supplemented by the work of British Army Public Relations of PAIFORCE as well as the Combined Intelligence Centre Iraq (CICI) of the RAF, whose area liaison officers (ALOs) were stationed throughout the Iraqi provinces. The British military organizations complemented and at times competed with the Political Advisory Staff and the embassy PR Section's own network of satellite offices and publicity bureaux. Britain was expending vast sums in maintaining the embassy and its networks, but British officials believed that this was far less than it would cost to maintain order through a military occupation.[80]

As in Cairo, the United States viewed the British embassy in Baghdad as complicit in shoring up a corrupt regime: "Although the British control apparatus begins to function immediately when it observes that an Iraqi official is following an anti-British line, it remains quiescent when his activities are not of an anti-British nature," leaving officials who support Britain and the Allied war effort free to benefit financially from corrupt practices, while those who criticize this arrangement face punishment, including in some cases internment.[81] Given these shortcomings, Henderson doubted whether Britain's "somewhat too obvious" attempts to win support in Iraq through its publicity machinery and intelligence networks would meet with success.[82] All of the embassy's efforts could backfire with the approaching end of the war if the British failed to address underlying economic issues and good governance.

The Call for Reform

After the removal of Rashid 'Ali and 'Ali Mahir from power, Britain turned from the principle of "Public Enemy No. 1" to what Maurice Peterson called "the doctrine of irreplaceability." He defined this as "that type of diplomacy and that type of diplomatic mind which seizes on a single figure in the country concerned-generally a dictator or a semi-dictator-and holds it indispensable," and then cited Nuri in Iraq and Nahhas in Egypt as prime examples of this doctrine.[83] Britain supported both leaders out of a sense of obligation. Having brought them to power, they could not be seen to be abandoning their friends after they had supported the Allies at a crucial time in the war and their replacements might prove to be even less cooperative. This concern resulted in a greater degree of administrative intervention in the internal affairs of both countries, which Britain justified on the basis of the demands of the war. The presence of British troops allowed them to intervene despite local opposition, yet this policy brought its own dangers. In Egypt, Britain found itself supporting an admittedly corrupt government that was losing popularity, and in Iraq their support for Nuri bolstered the old gang of politicians at a time when these politicians were losing favor.

In both cases, administrative reform provided a useful cover for British intervention and this call was picked up by the local governments. The December 1943 Speech from the Throne at the opening of the newly elected Parliament in Iraq set out a domestic program that included a new draft election law and a wide range of infrastructure and development projects.[84] The Wafd took up a similar call at its November 1943 Congress, held to celebrate the twenty-fifth anniversary of the party's founding. Party leaders presented programs for the kinds of internal reforms that Britain had advocated to address endemic poverty and the minister of health unveiled initiatives to improve living conditions: "Egypt, he declared, must adopt the principles of the Beveridge Report in drawing up plans for sanitary and medical services." Killearn did not hold much hope that the government would follow through on these proposals, but "the tendency is healthy, not only because it is high time that the Government of Egypt did something for the masses of Egypt, but also because attention to the realities of social reform may give Egyptians less time to waste on sterile discussions of impracticable foreign policies."[85]

The autumn of 1943 also brought signs of increased unrest and violence in Egypt. The opposition leaders took to the offensive again in November 1943, presenting a petition to the king which highlighted the corruption of the British-backed Nahhas regime. It protested against British interference in internal affairs; demanded an end to martial law and censorship; and, foreshadowing Egypt's postwar demands, also called for the withdrawal of foreign troops, Egyptian control of the Suez Canal, Egyptian unity with the Sudan, and a place for Egypt at the peace conference. They also had a broader audience in mind, as they planned to present their petition to the Allied leaders gathered for the Cairo Conference that same month.[86]

The opposition's confrontational rhetoric was accompanied by violent protests that originated in Egypt's response to an important regional issue, French policy in Lebanon.[87] King Farouk was injured in an automobile accident in November 1943 and, in an eerie echo of the protests after King Ghazi's car accident in Iraq in 1939, the embassy received reports of anti-British violence in the provinces aimed at British residents and Egyptian collaborators. Rumors spread that Britain was behind the car accident and was holding Farouk hostage at a British military hospital. Students and workers held demonstrations in support of the king, British propaganda displays in the provinces were vandalized, and Killearn's niece, a NAAFI driver, and a number of British officers were pelted with stones. According to British reports Egyptian authorities in the provinces did nothing to stop these events. While the protests were widespread, the violence was isolated, but even so it worried embassy officials, who observed that the situation required "careful watching."[88] The embassy interpreted these protests as a sign of growing discontent with the Wafd administration and the fact that in the eyes of the Egyptian public, the British were responsible for its maintenance in power and therefore its shortcomings. Opposition leaders had warned that keeping a corrupt government in office would lead to unrest, a trend that would grow with the approaching end of the war.[89]

9

Democracy and Development, January 1944–September 1944

In January 1944 Ambassador Cornwallis embarked on a tour of southern Iraq. While the main purpose was to attend the opening of a new British Institute in Basra, the tour also took him to Nasiriya and ʿAmara. Basra had been transformed by a massive Allied troop presence as a launching ground for the Lend-Lease operations to support the Soviet Union via neighboring Iran, which had also created tremendous strains on the local population. Cornwallis was pleased by the warm reception he received, noting that, when he arrived in Nasiriya, "The town was gay with flags of the United Nations and the streets were lined with schoolboys."[1] In addition to the formal opening of the new British Institute in Basra, he attended receptions and tea parties that drew local Iraqi notables and members of the British community.

The message he gave in his many speeches was one of progress and development, as well as the continuing responsibility to support the war effort through grain production. In Nasiriya he highlighted the improved infrastructure such as roads, electricity, an updated hospital, and the Kut Barrage, a massive irrigation project that opened in 1939. He contrasted the good fortune of Iraq, which "has ample supplies of home grown food while imported goods come in a steady stream from across the seas thanks to Allied might," with the deprivation in Axis-controlled areas, where people were not only starving for food, but "They also starve for freedom and are shot by the hundred when they express their desire to be free."[2] In ʿAmara, Cornwallis reminded the crowd that the recent Allied victories that local leaders celebrated in their speeches were "victories of war" but they should also look to "the future realization of our shared desire to achieve the perhaps more difficult but certainly not less glorious victories of peace, which will bring to Iraq, if Iraq has the will for democratic freedom, progressive agriculture and industry, roads and services and a happier more united people."[3]

Cornwallis's message was the same as that which was being relentlessly projected by Britain's publicity apparatus, from well-placed newspaper articles to pamphlets and posters to the bulletins of the Brotherhood of Freedom: Iraq still had a role in this war in producing grain for the war effort, and development and good governance would ensure Iraq's well-being in the postwar period. British, Kurdish, and Arab commentators alike adopted the call for a "New Deal for the Kurds," or "a Beveridge Report for the Arabs," indicating that economic development and freedom were part of the expectations of the modern world. For Britain, taking hold of this vision was also a way of ensuring that the United States and the Soviet Union, who were selling alternative versions of this message, did not get the upper hand.

Back in Baghdad, the reality of Iraqi politics was a far cry from the promise of these speeches. Nuri reorganized his Cabinet once again in December 1943 but this "Christmas Cabinet" was poorly received by Iraqi officials and the public, to Britain's great disappointment. As Edmonds so colorfully described it:

> The birth was greeted, not with the usual signs of rejoicing, but with a chorus of cat-calls and abuse just as if yet another girl had been born to a family already overburdened with them instead of the boy everybody had been hoping for. Actually there was, as I shall show, nothing much wrong organically with the child, but parental neglect caused it to ail.[4]

Cornwallis observed that the new Cabinet was not any worse than previous ones but public expectations for good governance had changed. This was a positive development and in fact the very thing that Allied publicity efforts had been encouraging and hoping for, but it was difficult to find candidates who met not only the Iraqi public's rising standards, but also those of the British.[5]

The new Cabinet inherited a range of stubborn economic challenges and tensions in Kurdish areas which would contribute to the ultimate downfall of Nuri's government. In autumn 1943 the Ministry of Finance and the Price Control Committee set prices on a wide array of goods, from cotton cloth and lightbulbs to carbon paper and typewriter ribbons, in order to control the spiraling price of imports. These policies had, by January 1944, achieved some success, resulting in a drop in the cost of living index. Cornwallis noted that the citizens of Baghdad adapted quickly to the textile rationing scheme, which utilized a point system, aided by a large-scale press and radio campaign.[6] Britain's publicity network was mobilized to support this effort as well. The Brotherhood of Freedom bulletins in February 1944 provided the details of the new textile rationing scheme, instructing members to share this information with their friends and also report any difficulties faced with implementation, mobilizing the two-way exchange of information the Brotherhood was designed to facilitate.[7] One of the more controversial measures was the decision in January 1944 to ration tea and coffee. The ration size was very small and the embassy admitted that these were items readily available at a reasonable price before the scheme was implemented, leading to local backlash. The result was that merchants hid stocks and they were soon only available on the black market at inflated prices, undermining the rationing plan.[8]

While some economic problems were the result of local inefficiencies, others were clearly tied to the war and British military spending, which led to vast currency reserves in the country. The most vexing challenges remained supply and distribution. As Cornwallis emphasized during his tour of southern Iraq, the most important contribution that Iraq could make to the war effort was selling excess grain to bolster regional food supplies, including relief of the Bengal famine in India. Iraqi barley was an important adulterant for bread in light of wheat shortages. The supply issue required forecasting crop output and advance commitments on purchases, but the rapidly evolving war situation made it increasingly difficult to anticipate demand. By 1944 Britain no longer had need of surplus barley but the embassy was deeply concerned that failure to purchase Iraqi supplies after months of pressure to increase output would have serious political implications. The MESC had to balance the economic need to buy stocks of grain at the best possible price, not only in the interest of the British treasury but also to limit inflation, against the political imperative of avoiding any provocation of unrest.[9]

Col. Bayliss's appointment as director general of imports was supposed to ease Iraq's economic challenges. Cornwallis advised him to avoid "'blitz' tactics" and to instead work closely with the British advisers in Baghdad and the political advisers in the provinces. Despite these warnings, Bayliss's tenure got off to a rocky start, as he moved quickly to implement controls and ignored advice, alienating potential supporters. While he had promised to be more cooperative after the ambassador shared his initial concerns, by March 1944 Cornwallis was reporting Bayliss's ambition to become the "economic dictator of Iraq," bringing all supply issues under his control, which put him on a collision course with not only Iraqi ministers but British officials as well. He had succeeded in bringing prices down through his policies, but "his pace has tended to be too fast for a country such as Iraq with a comparatively primitive economy and a weak Administration in which, moreover, corruption has, unfortunately, become rife in the past few Years." Bayliss clashed with Arshad al-Umari, acting minister of supply, ultimately leading to the British adviser's dismissal and damaging Britain's economic initiatives in Iraq.[10]

The embassy reported that Iraq enjoyed a good harvest in 1943 and that, along with heightened British spending, brought "the country as a whole to a remarkable level of domestic prosperity" with low unemployment. But the impact was uneven and a number of economic challenges remained. The rationing schemes proved far more difficult to implement in the provinces and exposed the administrative inefficiencies and corruption in outlying areas.[11] The supply situation remained particularly acute in northern Kurdish areas, and the Government of Iraq attempted to address the issue within the framework of economic development.

Nuri appointed a minister without portfolio to deal with Kurdish issues as part of his December 1943 Christmas Cabinet. Majid Mustafa had served in the Ottoman army and supported Kurdish leader Shaykh Mahmud during the 1920s, later joining the Iraqi government. He had been suspended from government service for five years as a result of actions during the 1941 Rashid 'Ali coup but he was brought in before that period had expired to deal with Kurdish issues because, as a British military official observed, "there seemed no other Kurdish nationalist of the calibre needed to meet the situation created by the Barzani revolt." Majid Mustafa's first task was to negotiate a cease-fire agreement with Mulla Mustafa.[12] He then turned his attention to the underlying causes of the uprising.

After a January 1944 fact-finding mission Majid Mustafa suggested that the government should rectify the administrative problems in the region and alleviate the economic difficulties of the Kurds. Local authorities deserved blame for not suppressing the movement at the beginning and for neglecting Kurdish areas, making them fertile grounds for revolt. He described the difficult conditions in the Barzani territories: famine, destitution, deserted villages, little cultivation, and a restless population. Baghdad should provide immediate relief in the form of grain and supplies "in order that the inhabitants should feel the benefits of the presence of government organisations in their midst." He also called for long-term infrastructure development through repairs to phone lines and roads. The use of local labor would provide much-needed employment and income and better roads would tie outlying villages more closely to the towns and facilitate the travel of government officials and, if necessary, troops, to places of unrest.[13] The Cabinet accepted these proposals and began taking tentative steps toward their realization.

The embassy supported this approach, putting pressure on the central government to provide what it described as a "New Deal" for the Kurds.[14] Majid Mustafa's proposals complemented the embassy's own view that the Kurdish revolt was yet another installment in the ongoing struggle between a modern centralizing state and traditional tribal authority. Development projects in the Kurdish areas would "tranquillise turbulent people and make them useful citizens of the country," bring credit to Iraq on the international stage for treating its people well, lessen the chance of frontier disturbances, and save money on military operations.[15] The Kurdish New Deal would also buy time until the Iraqi army was strong enough to impose a military solution if needed, and limit Soviet influence in the north.[16] The army's poor performance in responding to the revolt convinced the British Military Mission under General Renton of the need to undertake a program of reorganization to maintain internal order, but Britain continued to face criticism for failing to meet Iraqi requests for weapons.[17]

The political advisers were an invaluable source of local intelligence and, as the lynchpins in the embassy's efforts to encourage the Kurds to submit to the Iraqi state, were called upon to act as intermediaries. As the Kurdish situation grew increasingly tense, however, their sympathies with the Kurds conflicted with their official mandate. They became increasingly disillusioned by the embassy's unwillingness to take full advantage of this window of opportunity to right old wrongs and its double standard with respect to the competing demands of Kurdish and Arab nationalism. Political Adviser Wallace Lyon recalled: "We frequently hear of Arab aspirations but if a Kurd lifts up his voice he is sent to Coventry."[18] Edmonds received reports from his Iraqi contacts that Lyon was being "most indiscreet and thereby doing great harm" by attacking Iraqi and British policies.[19] Col. Wood, the head of CICI, British military intelligence in Iraq, warned his officers in the provinces in a June 1944 letter: "If you agree openly and sympathise with adverse comments on the Embassy policy, i.e. the policy of His Majesty's Government … you are in fact committing what is tantamount to treason."[20]

Ultimately, lack of will on the part of the Iraqi government derailed these efforts. Majid Mustafa's reform agenda was not popular in Baghdad and provided a rallying point for politicians who opposed Nuri for other reasons.[21] The regent was lukewarm as well and he reported in March 1944 that politicians were pressing him to abandon the new Kurdish policy, charging that Majid Mustafa was using his position to lobby for Kurdish independence. The minister submitted his resignation in March 1944 out of frustration at his inability to carry out the necessary reforms and only changed his mind once he received assurances of support from Nuri and the regent.[22]

The British acknowledged that Nuri's current Cabinet was as cooperative and efficient in implementing wartime policies as possible under such difficult conditions, and yet it had become deeply unpopular with wide sections of the Iraqi population. The dedication of both the embassy and the government to greater Shiʿi representation waned as the war proceeded. The Shiʿa had been given only three minor seats in the December 1943 Cabinet while the overall size of the Cabinet had been expanded, further diluting their representation and increasing sectarian tensions in the developing political crisis.[23] Nuri also faced a resurgent palace and the weakening of the patronage network that held him in power. By 1944 this network had become a liability, as he had reorganized his Cabinet nine times since October 1941 but had not introduced new faces. As Cornwallis lamented, "Having used and discarded twenty-four different colleagues, he seemed to be coming to the end of possible combinations."[24] These frequent changes hampered the work of the government as ministers were rarely in office long enough to implement programs and reforms and see them through.[25] The inclusion of three members of Taha al-Hashimi's Cabinet from early 1941 provided further proof of Nuri's attachment to the old guard. As Thompson observed, if politicians who had been deeply implicated in the 1941 crisis could be appointed to Cabinet positions at a time when Britain had a strong military and administrative presence, what would happen after the war when the British presence was drawn down?[26]

In March 1944 Edmonds predicted that the current administration should last at least a year but in fact it lasted only three more months.[27] The climax came May 21 during a heated budget debate in the Chamber of Deputies. Nuri confided in Cornwallis: "this incident had made his position impossible. Many of his supporters had come to him afterwards and said that if he could not protect them from personal insults he should resign" which he would do if the regent did not agree to provide him with open support and call elections in the autumn. Cornwallis did not encourage the regent to keep Nuri's government in power "against his will" and it fell in June 1944.[28]

Given the short-lived nature of Iraqi governments, Nuri's almost three-year term as prime minister from 1941 to 1944 was remarkable. Having a cooperative leader in power during a crucial turning point in the Allied war effort during 1942–3 was vital to Britain's interests in Iraq. Overall, the British admitted that Nuri's government met all their wartime requests "with a reasonably good grace" but had "proved themselves monumentally incompetent to set their own house in order."[29] Patron-client relationships are dependent on the protection offered to clients and their loyalty to the patron, and by 1944 Nuri proved unable to provide this protection and his reliance on clients had led him to turn a blind eye to their corruption, a position that became increasingly untenable in the later wartime environment with the calls for reform and good governance.

The regent appointed Hamdi Pachachi, a wealthy landowner in poor health, as the new prime minister. As he was ill when he was appointed the palace formed the new

Cabinet, a reflection of the regent's attempt to reassert the power of the monarchy.[30] Cornwallis was concerned that the new administration might overturn the Kurdish policy of its predecessor and sought assurances from the regent that he would appoint a government that would follow through on implementation.[31] In the end, the New Deal for the Kurds stalled in Baghdad.

The "Abdine Incident without Tanks" and the Fall of Nahhas[32]

Nahhas's government was also facing a crisis in early 1944 that highlighted its inefficiencies, but unlike with Nuri, the embassy intervened to keep him in power. After the Black Book affair, Egyptian politics reached an impasse as relations between the palace and the Wafd remained tense. Scrivener, observing events from the Foreign Office, noted that "both sides have so manoeuvred as always to leave outstanding at least one issue which could be worked up instantaneously into a first-class quarrel."[33] The stalemate was broken with a serious outbreak of malaria and food shortages in Upper Egypt which both the palace and the opposition exploited to move against the Wafd and the British. In January 1944 Makram issued a sequel to the Black Book with new accusations, including the government's mishandling of the malaria problem in Upper Egypt.[34] The malaria crisis put the embassy in a difficult position. On the one hand, Britain blamed the Wafd for neglecting the developing situation and for the inefficient distribution of food. They needed to act against rumors on the street that the British were responsible for the problems. On the other hand, if they were too critical of the government they would further weaken their authority.[35] The British took a defensive position in the press both in Egypt and in London, with articles pointing out that Britain had warned of a possible malaria outbreak two years earlier and had offered medical assistance to deal with malaria that the Egyptian government had refused.[36] The *Egyptian Gazette* published an official British statement in February 1944 directly responding to the rumors that Britain's wartime policies and purchases had created the crisis, noting:

> There is no scarcity of food in Egypt. If there is undernourishment it is only because the available food is not properly distributed. the peasants are at the mercy of a system which forces them to live below subsistence level, and naturally the first attack of disease finds their undernourished bodies an easy prey. Even after four years of war the Egyptian government has failed to work out a system of food distribution which ensures adequate supplies to the whole population.[37]

Nahhas protested against these articles that placed the blame on the Egyptian administration, but in this case the embassy concluded it was more important to defend Britain's reputation than to support the Wafd government.[38] In private officials admitted that Britain's long-term policies over decades had in fact contributed to this situation. The development of perennial irrigation through improvements to the Aswan Dam brought increased prosperity but also overpopulation, malnutrition, and ultimately an increase in diseases such as tuberculosis, malaria, and bilharzia. The solutions were difficult, as only a response on the scale of a "nationwide health scheme" would be able to address the sanitation issues, but growing Egyptian xenophobia and sensitivity to outside intervention had made it difficult for the United States or Britain to suggest changes. The war exacerbated these challenges, as the poor suffered most at a time of high cost of living and hoarding.[39]

After a March 1944 visit to Cairo Scrivener wryly observed: "It is an extraordinary paradox that the country which saved Egypt from extinction and ruin in this war should now be threatened-if distantly-with an outbreak of popular fury engendered by the ineptitude and venality of an Egyptian administration. But there it is."[40] Nonetheless Killearn, repeating his persistent refrain from the days of the Black Book affair, still felt that they should support the Wafd for three reasons: he did not see any alternative except a palace-supported government, the Wafd had and would continue to support the war effort, and the Wafd "stood by us in the black days of 1942 and … we should stand as long as reasonably possible by those who have proved themselves our friends in the foulest of foul weather."[41] Smart resumed his earlier warnings of the long-term consequences of such a policy, and once again argued that they should relinquish their role of propping up the Wafd as it was turning all the other bases of power in the country against the British. The Wafd was a destabilizing force and was building ties with organizations that opposed British interests, courting both the Muslim Brotherhood and Young Egypt and trying to organize the workers of Egypt. Farouk, on the other hand, was opposed to the politicization of the army and al-Azhar and the government's wasteful financial policies, and at the moment British and palace interests aligned.[42]

The question was, what type of issue would be the best pretext for allowing the government to fall? Smart considered it of paramount importance that the Wafd should leave office over a dispute with the king on a purely internal issue rather than one directly involving Britain that they could capitalize on while out of office; the Foreign Office agreed. Nahhas's government would face the risk of being turned out of office twice in 1944, and both times Britain's response would be shaped by this set of criteria: (1) the Wafd should fall on an internal issue that did not involve Britain, and (2) it would need to happen at an opportune moment from the perspective of the war effort. As Terrance Shone pointed out, if the military situation developed in Britain's favor in the coming months, "we can better afford to experiment with something different in the way of a Govt; and if they go well, I should doubt whether the Palace could afford to make trouble for us."[43]

Both the palace and the Wafd, as part of their struggle for control, continued to politicize the malaria crisis. In April 1944 the king visited areas that were suffering from the malaria outbreak and Nahhas, in response, made his own provincial visits which the palace felt were "characterised by semi-Royal procedure and amounted to an encroachment on Royal prerogatives."[44] In response, Farouk handed Killearn a memorandum calling for a new government, suggesting that Hasanayn, his own chamberlain, should be appointed prime minister. Killearn noted that while the king was friendly, "it is clear that His Majesty does not in the slightest degree appreciate that the war is still in the balance or that we need worry ourselves any further with the political stability of our base here in Egypt." In response, Killearn suggested to London that they be prepared to replace Farouk and use force in Egypt until the war ended, although hopefully the threat would be sufficient.[45]

The minister of state and British military authorities opposed this proposal because the outcome would be more threatening to wartime interests than any protests that might arise if the Wafd fell.[46] Killearn was convinced that it was highly unlikely that Britain would actually have to resort to force and Farouk would most likely give in just as he did in 1943: "But what I did not like was going down and giving such advice if I knew that I had only an empty gun in my pocket." General Sir Bernard Paget, the commander-in-chief, Middle East, argued that they just did not have the troops available and told the ambassador that "the gun was definitely empty."[47] The Foreign Office heard these concerns and suggested that elections be held instead, but Churchill overrode them and supported his ambassador: "I think we should stand by our friends. The King is no friend of ours, but an intriguing despot embodying many of the worst Oriental vices."[48]

Churchill's decision was based partly on the larger war situation, in the midst of planning for the D-Day landing: "Now, on the morrow of great military operations, we cannot have disorders in Egypt." The War Cabinet supported Churchill's decision, noting that the "gloomy prophesies" of the military at the time of the Black Book crisis had proved to be unfounded and endorsed Killearn's conviction that Farouk would back down at the mere threat of force. They recommended that the Commanders-in-Chief should prepare to provide Killearn with whatever support was required.[49] In the end, Farouk backed down and decided to leave the Wafd government in power. Once the crisis ended, Killearn resolved to speak with both Nahhas and Farouk, impressing on the prime minister that they were only supporting him because they wanted a quiet time in Egypt during a crucial stage of the war and urging the two leaders to cooperate. In future, though, Nahhas should be prepared to fight his own battles with the palace.[50]

In the midst of these crises the newly unified opposition parties issued a series of five joint manifestos between February and June 1944 that reinforced many of Britain's fears as to the cost of supporting Nahhas. The February petition, addressed to the Egyptian people, stated that they were not fighting the Wafd, but "against the British Imperialists who have renewed their ambitions and who cannot be satisfied or convinced by any means whatsoever." The government was merely a figurehead for the embassy and was beholden to the ambassador for its power.[51] In light of this situation the opposition parties were joining together in their demands for internal reform, including an end to martial law and British interference in internal affairs, the release of political internees, and corrective measures to address the rampant corruption and nepotism of the Wafd administration, including free elections.[52]

The second declaration issued the next month exposed the patron-client relationship between the embassy and the government, the "British representative and her Egyptian Agent. The Agent gets his pay in power and wealth, and England gets all Egypt as if it were a spoil of the war."[53] British interference in internal politics in the context of the malaria crisis was a violation of the treaty and reduced Egypt to a position of subservience to imperial interests even worse than in the days of the protectorate. The opposition also referred back to the exchange of letters on Nahhas's assumption of power in February 1942 and Britain's assurances that she would not interfere with internal politics. As a result of all of these abuses, the National Front declared supporting the Nahhas Cabinet to be "high treason against this country."[54] The manifestos clearly linked Britain's wartime policy in Egypt to the hardships the country was facing, including British requisitioning policies leading to food shortages and disease.[55] They raised the question of Egypt's sterling balances and warned that Britain was using the war as a pretext for imposing a form of economic imperialism.[56]

These manifestos resonated with Egyptians in light of the economic impact of the war and they reinforced British fears that the hardships of war could lead to postwar unrest as it had after the First World War. In many ways Egypt was better off economically than other parts of the Middle East, but its importance as a base and its influence over the Arab world justified preferential treatment. The embassy saw troubling parallels to the conditions that led to the 1919 postwar Egyptian revolution and Killearn warned that if either the opposition or the Wafd successfully exploited the Egyptian peasantry, the fellaheen, against the British the situation would be even more serious than in 1919 due to the proliferation of weapons from the war in the Western Desert: "In 1919 the fellaheen were armed with little more than clubs. Now they would be able to muster quite a considerable number of men armed with modern rifles."[57]

Before departing Egypt to spend his leave in South Africa during late summer, Killearn told the government and the palace in no uncertain terms that the chargé d'affaires, Terrence Shone, would act with full authority in his absence and that it was not the time for political maneuvering or raising questions about Egypt's postwar status. Despite this warning, a serious crisis erupted soon after his departure. While traveling to a mosque in Cairo on the last Friday in Ramadan, Farouk noticed that streamers stating "Long life to Nahhas Pasha" hung next to the streamers proclaiming "Long life to King Farouk." The king ordered Ghazali, the director of public security, to remove the offending banners. In response, the minister of the interior, acting at the direction of the government, suspended him for complying with the king's demand.[58] As Amin 'Uthman explained, the king could not constitutionally give a direct order to an official and Ghazali should have consulted the minister of the interior before complying. Britain had an interest in this matter because Ghazali had been "an extremely staunch friend" and "very valuable" to the British military.[59] For British officials who believed in standing up for their friends, they were now faced with a situation in which one client was being undermined by another and they would be forced to choose between them. Despite this difficulty, the Foreign Office instructed Shone to let Nahhas's government fall and make it clear to both parties that Britain was not going to intervene. On October 8 Nahhas received his dismissal and Ahmad Mahir was appointed prime minister.[60]

The Wafd held office for two and a half years during the Second World War. The British actively intervened to the point of threatening to depose the king three times in that period to maintain the Wafd in office despite charges of corruption. The Ghazali crisis in September 1944 met the criteria that Smart had laid out earlier that year for the ideal change of government. The war situation did not require absolute calm in Egypt and they could risk whatever resulted. It was also an issue that was purely between the king and the government that could not be presented as a nationalist question or an anti-British one. Killearn philosophically reflected: "Taking the broad view I think that probably was no bad thing and it certainly was all to the good that it happened whilst we were away in South Africa."[61]

The Democracy Principle

The challenges of 1944 brought home to British officials that a cooperative government was no longer enough; charges of inefficiency and corruption, and British support for those who engaged in these activities, would undermine their long-term position and development initiatives would stall without a more effective government. The flawed democracy of both Egypt and Iraq underlay these issues. Killearn had long seen the struggles in Egypt as the tension between "democracy (rule by the Government and elected Parliament) versus autocracy (rule by the Palace)." As he expressed on the eve of the war (Chapter 1), Britain had a role as the protector of democratic interests which, in the period after Abdin Palace, meant the Wafd Party as it had the support of a majority of the country. As long as that fact remained it was in the interest of the war effort to keep the Wafd in power. The corollary to this assumption was that in the end Farouk would have to be removed from power. Killearn remained convinced that Farouk would never be content to rule as a constitutional monarch and he admitted to Eden before he left for leave that "I rather hope—selfishly perhaps—that this may happen in my time here. For I should like, as a matter of pure personal sentiment and romance, to see this drama played out to its final act."[62]

The Foreign Office expressed deep concern at Killearn's suggestions that they impose democracy by force. Scrivener, acknowledging Egypt's continued importance in the war, suggested that instead they could "'support the growth of democratic institutions in Egypt' without recourse to measures of coercion."[63] As for the palace, it still had an important role to play in Egypt: "While it is no doubt desirable that Government in Egypt should evolve on lines more akin to modern constitutional and democratic systems, we must surely bear in mind that we are dealing with a backward oriental country which is not yet ripe for democracy with a big 'D' and in which the Throne is (or ought to be), a valuable brake on the activities of self-willed political leaders and unfledged political parties."[64] At the same time, the opposition parties, the Muslim Brotherhood, and the growing labor movement were all articulating different visions of a democratic Egypt. The opposition saw British support for the Wafd as anti-democratic and a violation of all of the principles and ideals Britain purported to protect in their propaganda. Comparing the Wafd government to "an absolute dictatorship similar to a Nazi regime" they expressed surprise at Britain's willingness to condone the Wafd's actions.[65] They asked: "This is, Egyptians, the Democratic rule imposed on you by your Democratic British Ally, and which she finds suitable for you ... If this is what they call democracy, what will then anarchy be."[66]

The British faced a similar dilemma in Iraq. Both British and Iraqi observers cited two inherent weaknesses in the Iraqi political system: the personal nature of Iraqi politics and the public's limited knowledge of the inner workings of a healthy democracy. In a 1944 pamphlet Iraqi constitutional scholar Majid Khadduri argued that the inherent tension between the "form" of the Iraqi government, which was shaped by the British on Western democratic models, and local "forces," in particular the socio-economic status of Iraq at the time of the mandate, ultimately undermined the effectiveness of the constitutional structure. The scaffolding of Iraqi democracy was built on a weak foundation, and the absence of viable political parties meant that Iraqi politics centered on personal loyalties and patronage rather than party platforms.[67] The result, as one Iraqi commentator later observed, was that "though the Constitution was formally retained, it went into cold storage."[68] The intervention of Britain's control apparatus, while vital from a British perspective for the war effort, added further stress to this system. Albert Hourani observed after his 1943 fact-finding mission to the region that "the Government's inability to last a day without the approval of Great Britain" has meant that all problems were blamed on Britain. If Britain stepped back and allowed a "social revolution" to take place, a better government might come to power but not without serious short-term risk of political instability which was unacceptable in wartime.[69]

If democracy was difficult to impose by force, then they needed to train the next generation of leaders. The Brotherhood of Freedom would have a key role to play in this effort, and in 1943 its purpose shifted from the immediate wartime goal of counteracting Axis propaganda to what Major Scaife, Stark's successor as leader of the Brotherhood, described as "education for citizenship." The Brotherhood's democracy message fused the internationalist rhetoric of the war with local concerns as it aimed to help both Egyptians and Iraqis to better understand the democratic principles on which their own constitutions were based while, at the same time, ensuring the preservation of British influence into the postwar period.[70] The rhetoric of development that was circulating in 1944 was enfolded into this message, and Killearn reported that the Brotherhood "is becoming a means of interesting its members in such matters as public health and education, and generally fostering their nascent sense of civic responsibility."[71]

In April 1944 the Brotherhood opened a new club in Baghdad. The location was significant, as it was located in the same premises as the former Muthanna Club, which had been a center of pan-Arab and pro-Axis sentiment in the early years of the war. Major Scaife, in his opening speech, urged his audience to have faith in the Allied declarations, as "it is a very serious error to think that the millions of British and American soldiers do not take seriously the professions made by public men on their behalf that they are fighting for a better world." This better world was not just about political freedom but economic freedom as well, and there was a growing conviction, "a feeling that under modern conditions an absolute increase of well-being is possible, and that by social and economic adjustment a good life can be opened for the many as well as for the few."[72]

The focus on development and economic issues also turned attention to the question of labor organization. The British were determined to channel this in a pro-British direction and Hankey endorsed the idea of getting British trade unions in touch with their counterparts in the Arab world: "In all these countries we are identified with a ruling class everywhere corrupt and often oppressive and selfish as well. It is useful for us to use them to run these countries in a way that (more or less) suits us, but we are getting tarred with their failings. A link with our Trade Unions would show another class a quite different side of the British character."[73] The publicity section at the embassy in Cairo initiated contacts with local unions, providing funds directly to the Chauffeurs' Union, for example, as well as informational materials.[74] The Brotherhood of Freedom had influence among the dock-workers in Alexandria and so there was an opportunity to use the Brotherhood to steer labor in a pro-British direction.[75] The Government of Iraq authorized the formation of trade associations in summer 1944 and the embassy reported that the publicity drawing attention to labor conditions in Britain was having a "noticeable influence … on working class opinion" in Iraq.[76]

Winning over youth had been a goal early in the war to limit the appeal of fascism; winning over youth was vital later in the war as a way to ensure British influence after the conflict ended. The messaging of democracy might prepare a new generation of leaders, but it did not address the pesky issue of how to get the old gang to turn over power. Britain faced a dilemma in this regard: continued support for the old gang would alienate the same youth the embassy hoped to win over through the Brotherhood of Freedom, yet by placing the tools of democracy in their hands the Brotherhood might undermine the authority of the governments ensuring cooperation in the war effort. Major Scaife reassured British officials that the Brotherhood of Freedom would serve as a "moderating influence" on the agents of change and also equip future leaders knowledgeable in the working of democracy.[77] As one Ministry of Information official noted, "We do see its dangers—namely that unless carefully handled it might develop into a kind of opposition movement to political regimes which hold their position by corruption. We think, however, that the risk is worth taking."[78]

The democracy principle became increasingly urgent in the later years of the war as the growing American and Soviet presence in the region added additional critiques to British policies, as well as alternative models and new potential allies for the postwar period.[79] Egypt established diplomatic relations with the Soviet Union in August 1943 and Iraq followed suit in September of the following year, but not without some trepidation. Cornwallis reported that "In a country where the Government is almost entirely in the hands of the rich, the 'Communist' bogey seems a very dangerous beast," but the Iraqi government acknowledged they would have no choice but to deal with the Soviets after the war.[80] Soviet influence offered a new locus of political activity for those discontented with the stagnant political situation. Wadie Jwaideh, an Iraqi historian who toured the Kurdish provinces during the war through his work as an inspector of supply, observed that the Soviets and the British were selling the same message: "Both Soviet and Western propaganda denounced the Axis for enslaving and exploiting other nations, extolled political freedom and the self-determination of peoples, and promised the inevitable overthrow of the tyranny of the strong over the weak."[81] The communist threat galvanized the British push for real political reform. CICI kept close watch over the communist movement, interning suspected members and seizing caches of pamphlets. A significant portion of the monthly Security Intelligence Summary compiled by the Defence Security Office was devoted to communist activity and summaries or complete translations of communist pamphlets, particularly the monthly *al Qa'ida* publication and the writings of Fahd, the pseudonym for Yusuf Salman Yusuf, the general secretary of the Iraqi Communist Party.[82]

Other movements on the left raised similar critiques. The moderate leftist Ahali group reopened its newspaper in 1942, publishing under the new title *Sawt al-Ahali*, or "Voice of the People." Taking advantage of the loosening of government controls on the press in 1944, it soon became an influential advocate for government reform.[83]

Democracy was an important cornerstone of the Ahali group's platform well back into the 1930s, and it fused the idea of political participation and economic well-being in its vision of this term. The Ahali group's ideology was shaped by a variety of forces, including the British Fabian Society, Marxism, early socialist organizations in the Arab world, Egyptian political thought, and the Indian independence movement. Its newspaper was of interest to the embassy because its target readership, which the American legation described as "the working class and young intellectuals," included the same Iraqis, the *effendiyya*, who were the focus of the Brotherhood of Freedom and the democracy campaign, and they remained suspicious of its complex relationship with the Iraqi Communist Party.[84]

As with the Egyptian opposition parties, the Ahali group, through its newspaper *Sawt al-Ahali,* worked to hold Britain accountable for the failings of the government it supported while also calling for both political and economic reform. In an August 1944 editorial the paper argued that by adhering to the Atlantic Charter and joining the United Nations through its declaration of war, Iraq became beholden to the standards embedded in these documents. The government had an obligation to improve the general public's standard of living as well as opening up the political system to democratic reform. Failure to do so would mean violating both international responsibilities and the government's duties to the people.[85]

The tension between Britain's desire to maintain its position in the Middle East, the growing American and Soviet rivalry for influence in the region, and nationalist demands for greater autonomy, resulted in the debates over diplomatic representation that erupted during the second half of the war. Britain's allies, the United States and the Soviet Union, pressed for the raising of their legations to embassies and an end to diplomatic precedence for Britain. For British officials, this was more than a mere symbolic gesture; it went to the very heart of British prestige in both countries. Cornwallis was willing to recognize the raising of the US legation in Baghdad to an embassy but warned against abandoning Britain's traditional privileges as protected in the treaty. Just as Iraq needed to feel the burden of responsibility that came along with its declaration of war, the United States and the Soviets needed to appreciate that the greater economic role they hoped to play in the region would also bring greater responsibility.[86]

Killearn strongly objected to the idea of ceding his diplomatic precedence and, as he observed in March 1944: "As regards political sphere my whole instinct is to say politely 'Hands off Egypt.'"[87] The ambassador had a good working relationship with the US legation but the Americans were far more sympathetic to the complaints of the palace and Alexander Kirk, the American minister in Cairo, lost no opportunity to point out Egypt's political failings.[88] American encroachment in the economic sphere was an even greater cause of concern. James Landis, whom Killearn described as a "Super Trade Commissioner *cum* Economic Dictator," arrived in Cairo in December 1943 to take up the newly created position of director of American operations in the Middle East. Landis held the personal rank of minister, a reflection of the importance the US government placed on his mission to coordinate American economic interests in the region and chair the Executive Committee of the Middle East Supply Centre. The United States had criticized the British control apparatus in Iraq, but Killearn reported that the Americans were building their own economic control apparatus in Egypt, taking over the MESC and undertaking a coordinated "policy of economic penetration followed by the U.S. Legation, Lend/Lease, Office of War Information and Army authorities in Egypt." Development projects provided another avenue for growing American influence in Egypt looking ahead to the postwar period.[89]

The United States was also increasing its cultural diplomacy and publicity efforts, importing massive quantities of newsprint for English and Arabic versions of *Reader's Digest* at a time when local newspapers still faced strict rationing of newsprint.[90] This greater American role in the region was not without its own dangers, and the United States became a target for criticism on the basis of the hypocrisy of its propaganda. Egyptian journalist Mustafa Amin published an editorial in *Ithnein* in summer 1944 titled "Will our hopes in America be lost?" in which "He reminded the Americans of their own struggle for independence, referring to the exquisitely printed and illustrated pamphlets which the O.W.I. circulated and which deal with 'the honeyed terms of freedom, independence, etc.', remarking that there must be deeds to support such excellent words."[91]

Against the backdrop of the dramatic wartime events of 1944, British publicity repeated the message that the war was far from over and the Middle East still had a role to play. From the perspective of Arab nationalists, the war had receded from the region, the Axis threat had been neutralized in the Middle East, they had fulfilled their obligations under the terms of the treaties, and the expanding British presence and intervention in internal affairs could only be interpreted as European imperialism in the guise of the war effort, the very danger they had warned about from the beginning of the conflict. Britain's extensive control apparatus was of limited value if they were unable to address the pressing needs of the region, as both Egypt and Iraq faced challenges in 1944 that laid bare the long-term cost of administrative inefficiencies and corruption. Britain had succeeded in projecting power with its wartime successes, but it was struggling with the equally important projection of ideals.

10

Fighting the New Protectorate and the New Mandate, September 1944–May 1945

The cover of a September 1944 issue of the Egyptian satirical weekly *Ruz al-Yusuf* showed a shop called the "Patisserie l'Atlantique." The waiter John Bull tells his customer Misri Effendi, the personification of Egypt, that the big cake in the window labeled "Treaty Revision" is expensive, to which Misri Effendi replies: "Yes, I know ... but I have already paid the price."[1] This cartoon, which appeared the opening week of the Alexandria Conference on Arab unity, reflected the belief that the internationalist rhetoric of the war, encapsulated in the Atlantic Charter, held the promise of treaty revision as a reward for wartime sacrifices.

Dr. Fadhil al-Jamali, an Iraqi official in the Ministry of Foreign Affairs, expressed a similar sentiment in a letter to the American legation in October 1944. He hoped that the Arab states would benefit from the provisions of the Atlantic Charter and that the Allies would thereby avoid the errors of the post-First World War settlement, as the Arab states were using the Allied wartime declarations as the yardstick by which they judged the actions of the Western powers.[2] In a frequently repeated history lesson, Jamali warned: "The Arabs were deeply disappointed by the breach of promise by the Allies after the last World War. The nationalist hope did not materialize; no Arab unity; Palestine promised to the Jews; Syria cut to pieces; Iraq under mandate. President Wilson's promise of self-determination was thrown in the waste-basket."[3] The Second World War provided the Arabs with an opportunity to hold the Western powers accountable for the promises made and broken during the earlier conflict.

As the earliest debates about declaring war in autumn 1939 demonstrated, this rhetoric had been present throughout the conflict. The changing wartime situation in 1944, the dramatic events that heralded an approaching end to the war, and the Allied wartime conferences all seemed to indicate that the time was now to push for the long-awaited postwar concessions. Albert Hourani observed after his 1943 fact-finding mission throughout the region, "many people still believe that after the war the Arabs will be called to account for their actions. They imagine the Peace Conference as a school-prize giving, with rewards for good conduct."[4] The Arab states could be excused for reaching this conclusion, as British and American officials frequently conveyed this message as a way to ensure compliance with wartime demands and push for domestic reforms. In 1943 Scrivener informed the embassy in Cairo that "Our strongest weapon in fact seems to be the influence we are capable of exerting in the peace settlement, and our ability to make it clear, if necessary, that we should not exert it very much on behalf of a country whose policy is a generation, and a war, out of date."[5]

The uproar over the Wafd's extended tenure in office in the context of the Black Book affair and malaria crisis indicated that Egyptians were still not masters of their own political house on internal issues, despite British declarations to the contrary. Yet neither were they in control of their own external affairs as the war had made clear, and the preliminary talks on Arab unity at Alexandria in autumn 1944 and the growing demands for treaty revision were all attempts to break this British hold on Arab foreign policy. The failures of the British and the local governments they supported would lead to a postwar reckoning and with other actors such as the United States and the Soviets sensing opportunity to penetrate Arab markets, the cost of failure was even higher than before.

Debating Treaty Revision

In February 1944 Maurice Peterson raised the question of postwar strategic requirements in Iraq in an exchange of letters with Ambassador Cornwallis. Britain's main postwar concerns for Iraq were the maintenance of British land and air lines of communications and protecting not only Iraq's own oil reserves, but also those in neighboring Iran. British troops would have to be withdrawn from Iran after the war in accordance with the Tripartite Agreement, and Iraq was the next best location from which to ensure the security of Iranian oil assets. From the Foreign Office perspective, Britain would likely want to have a greater postwar presence in Iraq than the treaty allowed.[6]

Cornwallis expressed confidence that British facilities in Iraq under the treaty were sufficient to protect British interests in all but the most extraordinary of circumstances. Unlike in Egypt there were no cries for treaty revision as of yet but he was doubtful that its leaders would agree to an expanded British presence: "We must expect after the war a tendency in all Arab countries to get rid of wartime controls and to whittle down foreign privileges ... the spirit of nationalism is very strong and we are most unlikely to be accorded any facilities or privileges which can be held to restrict the independence of the country." Cornwallis concluded that it would be difficult to achieve their goals "on the old unilateral imperial basis," and instead they should look to the new international organizations envisioned in the postwar settlement and cooperate with the United States. He endorsed Churchill's suggestion of "a United Nations Commission for the Middle East," within which Britain's special position in the region would be recognized. Yet he warned that this plan would only work if they addressed Arab demands over Palestine, as otherwise even these proposals would be unworkable.[7]

In January 1944 the issue of postwar requirements and the potential for treaty revision was also being discussed in Cairo in the Egyptian press and Chamber of Deputies. Killearn's response was that this question was "eye wash": under the terms of the treaty itself the possibility of revision could not even be raised until 1946, and either party had the right to decline until 1956. Walter Smart warned that regardless of the terms, the reality was that a movement in support of revision was developing in Egypt and they would do well to take it seriously.[8]

Killearn was alarmed at the service chiefs' expectations that they would be able to get a continuation of some of the wartime concessions on troop numbers and access to facilities into the postwar period, expanding Britain's role in the region. From the embassy's viewpoint, it was far better to try and make the existing treaty work to cover their strategic requirements, as they had a firm basis for refusing revision, rather than open the Pandora's box of negotiations. As for the argument that a United Nations presence could provide cover for a greater British role, Killearn believed that the established position in Egypt under the terms of the treaty should be fitted into a postwar UN framework, rather than using the framework to replace the treaty. Egyptians would be more likely to want to keep British control of facilities rather than including the United Nations: "Egyptians are not favourably impressed by a united front of foreign nations—it reminds them too much of the capitulatory regime—and they are sceptical of the ultimate coherence of the Powers at present fighting together." Shone noted that the Egyptian government had "Russo-phobia" and the Egyptian Parliament was critical of the "grant to the American and other forces of privileges similar to, but not so extensive as, those granted to the British forces under the Treaty."[9]

From a strategic perspective much of the discussion centered around the future of the Suez Canal Zone base, port access in Alexandria, and air facilities. If, by 1956, Egypt was able to demonstrate its ability to defend the canal then under the terms of the 1936 treaty Britain would have to withdraw its troops. Killearn assured the service chiefs that, based on the Egyptian military's wartime performance, this was unlikely, and in fact the treaty had been drafted in such a way as to make it very difficult for Egypt to meet these criteria. Terrence Shone admitted that the current British position in the port of Alexandria extended beyond the terms of the treaty as they could be interpreted in peacetime, but they should be able to work within the parameters of the treaty to secure their strategic priorities by other means. The embassy's recommendation was: "Let us leave well alone."[10]

The question of treaty revision remained a focal point of debate in Egypt. In April 1944 the General Assembly of the Wafdist Bloc, the group under Makram's leadership that had broken away from Nahhas's party in 1942, passed a resolution protesting against Britain's intervention in internal affairs, a situation that "can be considered as declaration of a British protectorate over the country and even places Egypt in the position of the Crown Colonies because even a protectorate has a free hand in its internal affairs. This declaration takes the country back fifty years to the time when Lord Granville said that 'British advice in Egyptian affairs is obligatory.'" Britain's actions exceeded the parameters of the treaty "which recognizes Egypt's independence and sovereignty," violated the assurances given after the Abdin Palace incident that

Britain would not intervene in Egypt's internal affairs, and on a larger scale, was a direct violation of the Atlantic Charter.[11]

In a reflection of the move to internationalize Egypt's grievances, the Bloc shared their protest with "Governments of the U.S.A., Russia and other countries which have signed the Atlantic Charter, to intimate how Britain by her action has given an example of what small nations may expect under the Atlantic Charter, of violence, tyranny, loss of rights, and breach of promises, in a manner which is unimaginable even from Nazi and Fascist Dictatorship." The Bloc also warned other Arab nations not to follow Nahhas's lead on Arab unity, as Nahhas "has been commissioned by the English to favour and execute Arab unity under British patronage in the same way he has accepted it in the form of a protectorate over his own country." As to Britain's claims that it was acting to defend Egypt, the Wafdist Bloc responded that its actions were self-interested and had only brought hardship. They used these arguments to call for Egyptian neutrality on the model of Switzerland, and also argued that Britain's actions would justify not only an end to the treaty but the Anglo-Egyptian alliance itself.[12] Other opposition petitions joined in the demand that Egypt be represented at any postwar peace conference on the same footing as other nations and called for the revision of the Anglo-Egyptian Treaty in line with the principles of the Atlantic Charter, citing Egypt's support of the war effort.[13]

While many opposition figures in Egypt and their party organs had been calling for treaty revision, the embassy in Cairo was shaken when *al-Ahram*, the most influential Arab newspaper with the widest circulation in the region, published articles calling for this as well in June 1944. Its reputation gave its article, "National Demands at Which All Meet" far greater authority than previous calls in the press.[14] Now was the time to publicize Egypt's contribution to the war effort "in order to obtain our rights" and support Egypt's claims for treaty revision. This was an issue that united Egyptians regardless of political affiliation: the evacuation of British troops, the unity of the Nile Valley, and treaty revision in recognition of Egypt's loyalty during the war. Egypt had participated in a wide range of regional and international conferences "including the Food Conference, the Labour Conference and the Monetary Conference … and in all these conferences we have taken our place as an independent sovereign country to a great extent." But they must not overlook the most important conference:

> the supreme conference which will be held after the war in order to organise the world and define the various political position [sic]. In the nature of things, Egypt's complete independence should *ipso facto* be acknowledged, so that Egypt may play her role in the Mediterranean, having become one of its principal countries, and having been acknowledged as the leader of Arab nations who also aspire to independence.[15]

Egyptians should not take for granted that these goals will be recognized: "The time has come to work for this."[16] Later that month Smart observed that many opposition figures were moving beyond a call for treaty revision to a call for treaty abolition and "the incorporation of Egypt in a new international system of security and co-operation under the terms of the Atlantic Charter."[17]

The Alexandria Conference and Arab Unity

As the *al-Ahram* statement noted, Egypt was claiming not only her own independence but also her leadership role in the Arab world. The 1943 Nahhas-Nuri meeting on Arab unity was followed by a number of meetings with other Arab leaders, and British officials would later point to these talks as the turning point when Egypt adopted internationalism as the best tactic to achieve its goals.[18] Once the bilateral talks were complete, Nahhas turned his attention to the next step: a regional conference. In June 1944 he sent a letter to the Arab governments calling for delegates to be sent to a preparatory meeting with a sense of urgency driven by the war: "Public interest necessitates acceleration of Arab unity scheme so that events which today quickly succeed one another should not outstrip us."[19] The rapidly changing events to which he referred were the developments of the war during summer 1944: the Normandy invasion, the upcoming American presidential elections, and the possibility of an armistice in the near future all made it urgent for the Arabs to organize themselves to prepare a united front for the postwar conferences.[20]

The Foreign Office saw that it would be difficult to oppose the proposed conference and that they must not appear to be obstructing it, but they also mobilized Britain's diplomats in Cairo and Baghdad to slow the movement down.[21] Britain lay out some parameters: a conference would need to be well planned in advance and they were particularly concerned that it might become a forum to attack British policy in Palestine and French policy in the Levant. They would require assurances from Nahhas that he would ensure that the conference discussions would not worsen Arab-Jewish relations in the region and damage the war effort. Cornwallis gave similar instructions to the new Iraqi prime minister, Hamdi Pachachi, informing him in July 1944 that "H.M. Government did not wish the Palestine issue to be raised at a time when all their efforts were directed against the common enemy."[22] This argument fell flat, and Pachachi turned Cornwallis's argument back against him, explaining in a public statement in July that if the Arab states were united they would actually be able to provide much greater assistance to the Allies.[23]

As these negotiations indicate, Palestine remained a dominant issue in the Arab world in the summer of 1944, sparked by the election cycle in the United States and the declarations by both the Democratic and Republican Parties in summer 1944 in support of Zionist immigration. Arab leaders closely followed these developments, a reflection of the growing role that the United States played in Arab calculations for the postwar period. On July 27 *al-Ahram* called on the Arab representatives at the upcoming conference to formulate a response in protest, and Killearn lamented the timing of the Democratic Party's resolution so close to the opening of the conference as it would make it increasingly difficult to keep Palestine out of the discussion.[24]

Nahhas's original plan was to hold the preparatory conference in summer 1944 but he ran into multiple roadblocks, largely a result of the conflicting goals of the Arab states. As it became evident that the Iraqi delegation, led by Nuri, wanted to speed up the timeline to push their own agenda, Nahhas pivoted to slow things down. Despite their public professions of unity, it was well known that the rivalry between Nuri and Nahhas for leadership of the Arab unity movement was both national and personal, and the tensions between the two leaders played a role in the timeline.[25] Nahhas, already in a precarious political position due to the fallout of the Black Book affair and malaria crisis, hoped to use the Arab unity agenda to bolster his reputation at a time when his internal power base in Egypt was rapidly eroding. Nuri was no longer prime minister in Iraq but he was still a prime driver in the Arab unity movement. Nahhas received secret information that Iraq, Syria, and Lebanon planned to use the conference to go ahead with their own plan for federation as a way to mobilize a united front to address their grievances with the French, thereby removing Egypt from the Arab unity equation.[26]

The British tried to use the rivalries between the Arab leaders to their advantage. Killearn pointed out that Nuri had left office and therefore Nahhas no longer faced competition for leadership of the movement and could justify stalling the conference. They also hoped that Ibn Saud would use his influence to get the conference delayed until after the war.[27] Nahhas ultimately decided to postpone until after Ramadan ended in late September since not all states had replied to his invitation.[28]

The opening of the Alexandria Conference on September 25, 1944, was greeted with great fanfare and *al-Ahram,* despite wartime rationing of newsprint, issued a lavish multi-page special issue that included a map of the region as well as maps and profiles of each individual state represented, highlighting the idea of sovereign states joining together to form a regional body.[29] The Preparatory Committee met for ten days with representatives from Egypt, Iraq, Syria, Lebanon, Transjordan, Saudi Arabia, and Yemen, as well as a Palestinian Arab representative.[30]

The delegates had multiple goals: to achieve their own independence but also that of the remaining mandates of Syria, Lebanon, and Palestine. Early on the delegates recognized that a political union was not practical at the time but a regional organization would be helpful in postwar negotiations and on October 7, 1944, they signed the Alexandria Protocol, which included a resolution to form a "Council of the League of Arab States."[31] It also called for cooperation on a range of economic, social, and cultural matters, including commerce, communications, and public health. The Alexandria Protocol was preliminary in nature and it included plans for subcommittees that would meet to draft the statutes of the new league. All independent Arab states would be invited to join and participate in council meetings with the aim to strengthen Arab ties and "protect their independence and sovereignty against every aggression."[32]

As the conference unfolded British and American officials had to balance their desire for information to monitor the proceedings against the need to avoid the appearance of outside intervention. The embassy reported that one US intelligence officer was so desperate for information that he "ran round the delegates armed with boxes of Chesterfields as bribes: apparently he had a low opinion, not only of their integrity, but even of their price."[33] The embassy in Baghdad mobilized its networks in Iraq to monitor and control the message reported back to the public. The Public Relations Section ensured that local papers would take all news about the Preparatory Conference from the dispatches of the Arab News Agency, and the minister for foreign affairs arranged with the Iraqi newspapers the lines that they would follow in covering the conference before he departed for Egypt. As British officials had feared, much of the Iraqi commentary focused on Palestine, but the Government of Iraq restricted this coverage by limiting the number of articles the Iraqi press could publish on this topic.[34]

British officials viewed the provisions of the Alexandria Protocol and the development of the Arab unity movement as both a real opportunity and a potential liability. Lord Moyne, the minister of state, observed that the protocol represented an Arab world with "one orientation, and one only, towards the outside world," and at this moment after the Alexandria Conference this orientation was pro-British.[35] Cornwallis affirmed this view, noting that Nuri and the Iraqi minister for foreign affairs assured him that the goal of the conference was "to unite the Arab World in co-operation with Britain." If Britain would follow through on the White Paper on Palestine and endorse Syrian and Lebanese independence, they could maintain the good will of the Arabs in the postwar world. However, this orientation could change quickly if they failed to do so, and the all or nothing implications of this unity meant that it could either work to Britain's benefit, by bringing the whole Arab bloc behind them, or it could work against them, with the Soviet Union as a likely beneficiary.[36]

Despite the best efforts of its advocates to portray Arab unity as the deepest desire of all Arabs, there was opposition from various fronts. The Egyptian opposition parties worked to undermine the movement, portraying it as tainted by association with Nahhas and against Egypt's interests. They exposed Nahhas's attempts to use the conference to deflect attention from the corruption charges he faced and the way in which he had tried to limit the participation of opposition leaders.[37]

Cornwallis observed in early 1944 that while there was a general sentiment in Iraq in support of the idea, "to take a metaphor from the technique of electricity, it is doubtful whether the current of enthusiasm which this ideal generates has a high enough voltage to overcome the resistance of the circuit along which it will have to flow." The Shi'a opposed the move because it would subsume them in a larger Sunni Arab entity, and yet they had to be careful in articulating this opposition. The Shi'a of Iraq "as good Arab patriots" had to at least give outward support to the Alexandria Protocol, and could not appeal to the Shi'a of Iran for assistance or this would make them suspect as Iraqis, forcing them "into uneasy acquiescence." But after noting the reservations of the Shi'a, Cornwallis reported that the general Iraqi public was "flattered and pleased" by the result: "It has made them feel that it is something after all to be an Arab; and Arab Unity undoubtedly appeals to the Iraqis very much as the reunion of Christendom appeals to Christians, namely as an ideal which, if incapable of immediate realisation, is nevertheless devoutedly to be wished."[38]

The idea that the Arab League was a result of British machinations persisted for two reasons. First, many Arab nationalists strongly criticized Nuri and Nahhas, the Arab leaders who spearheaded the preliminary talks, for their collaboration with Britain. The extent to which these leaders were implicated in Britain's colonial policies is reflected in the Egyptian opposition's assumption that, because Nahhas was involved in promoting Arab unity, the British must ultimately be behind it. Killearn noted that the Egyptian opposition "are inclined to suggest that the British, through their agent Nahhas Pasha, are trying to put something undesirable across the Arabs."[39] Secondly, while the British certainly tried to temper and show down the movement for Arab unity, Arab leaders, Nuri in particular, seized on British declarations of support for the project, in particular Eden's 1941 and 1943 statements, as a means of furthering their pan-Arab projects. While this tactic was intended to legitimize the movement to the international community, to Nuri's political opponents it could be viewed as further evidence that Britain was the guiding hand behind the Arab unity talks. In the end, Britain aimed to channel something that they viewed as inevitable in as pro-British a direction as possible.

While the British were disappointed that Palestine came up at all as they had encouraged Arab delegations to avoid discussion of this issue, the Arab press expressed frustration that the Arab states did not do more. As a result the period after Alexandria saw increased Arab mobilization on Palestine. Building on their collective response to pro-Zionist declarations during the 1944 presidential election, in November the Iraqi papers published messages of protest from Iraqi politicians to their American counterparts.[40] The seriousness of the Palestine issue as a stumbling block for British policy was brought home when, on November 6, British Minister of State Lord Moyne was assassinated in Cairo by members of the Zionist extremist Stern Group. The high-profile trial of the two assailants in the Egyptian courts dragged on through the winter and they were sentenced to death and executed in March 1945. As much as the British wanted to keep Palestine out of the equation, it was clear that, for all parties involved, a Palestine settlement was vital to moving ahead with other British objectives for the region.[41]

Egypt after the Wafd

Soon after the signing of the Alexandria Protocol Egypt, Transjordan, and Syria all experienced changes of government. While they fell due to domestic issues, Axis propaganda capitalized on this situation by charging Britain with orchestrating the demise of the governments as punishment for their role in the Arab unity movement.[42] The fall of Nahhas's government put a damper on the celebrations and threatened to weaken public confidence in the conference's work. As one observer noted:

> It was something of an affront to their pride that the very day after they published their Protocol the leading member of the Conference was dismissed from office. And though the delegates are aware of the details of the case, public opinion in their own countries is not, and thus the delegates fear that public confidence in their plan must have been weakened.[43]

Nahhas's Wafd government was succeeded by a new coalition government drawn from the opposition parties and led by Ahmad Mahir, the Sa'dist Party leader. The British considered Ahmad Mahir to be an able politician but they had opposed him taking office earlier in the war because he had been implicated in the Stack murder in the 1920s.[44] The new prime minister assured Britain of his intentions to honor the Anglo-Egyptian Treaty and cooperate on the war effort but the embassy was unsettled by this change from an openly cooperative government to one that was untested.[45] The fall of the Wafd led to a reorganization of political power in Egypt. On the one hand, King Farouk reasserted his influence behind the scenes; the palace leg of the three-legged stool was in the ascendant. The new prime minister, however, tried to avoid being drawn too far under the influence of the palace, maintaining his independence of action.[46] On the other hand, the new government was riven by divisions among the various political parties involved, each vying for influence.

The fall of the Wafd also had serious implications for Killearn's policy of maintaining relations with the Egyptian government through intermediaries as it signaled Amin 'Uthman's fall as well. Killearn's system was further undermined by the serious illness of Hasanayn, the palace chamberlain who had effectively served as intermediary between the embassy and the palace throughout the war.[47] The embassy extended its policy of standing by Britain's friends to the Wafd as Killearn was concerned that the new government was coordinating a campaign of revenge against the former one. With Foreign Office support, he pressed Ahmad Mahir to refrain from bringing charges against Wafd officials.

The British had supported the Wafd in power for so long partly out of fear as to what the majority party might do in opposition. Having been put in office through British intervention they had a certain obligation to cooperate with British authorities; while out of power they would be free to challenge British demands. These fears were soon realized when the Wafd organized large-scale student demonstrations in December 1944 against British policy in the Sudan, with an estimated 15,000–16,000 students involved.[48]

The embassy believed that Ahmad Mahir was committed to supporting the treaty and the Allied war effort but was unsure as to whether or not he had the power to impose these plans. If he proved unable to control a politically divided Parliament Britain could be faced with a number of embarrassing issues, such as treaty revision and the Sudan, potentially leading to even greater palace intervention in politics. This was not as dangerous a threat in late 1944 given the recession of the war from Egypt. With characteristic paternalism, Killearn argued that "we can afford to let the children play their games to their satisfaction or dissatisfaction during the present lull." Yet once the war switched focus to the Far East Egypt would again become a crucial base for supplies and troop movements, which might necessitate further British intervention.[49]

Ahmad Mahir's government was composed of members of the various Egyptian opposition parties. These were the same politicians who had drafted the many opposition pamphlets earlier in the year that sought to expose British complicity in supporting the corrupt Wafd regime. While they assured the embassy of their cooperation and intention to honor the treaty, British officials were nonetheless concerned the demands in those manifestos might now receive wider circulation, especially in light of Ahmad Mahir's policy of relaxing censorship and press restrictions.[50] One of the new prime minister's first acts was to release a number of Egyptian prisoners detained on political grounds by the Wafd government, including his brother, former Prime Minister 'Ali Mahir, and the former Wafdist official Makram 'Ubayd, whom Nahhas had arrested earlier in 1944 for his inflammatory speeches.[51]

Egypt's Declaration of War

At Yalta in February 1945 Churchill, Roosevelt, and Stalin finally answered the question of who would be invited to the upcoming conference to establish a new world organization. In addition to states that had declared war and joined the United Nations as of February 8 they would also invite any of the "Associated Nations" who had severed relations with the Axis powers if they declared war by March 1.[52] Egypt was included in this formula, and on their way home from Yalta Churchill and Eden stopped in Cairo for conversations with both Farouk and Ahmad Mahir. They had two main messages: one was the invitation to declare war and participate in the upcoming conference, and the other was the importance of social reform in Egypt, addressing the great wealth disparities in the country.[53]

Ahmad Mahir had supported a declaration of war from the very beginning. He saw the restrictions of the 1936 treaty as a reflection of British "lack of confidence in Egypt." Egypt's wartime cooperation had demonstrated that these fears were unfounded, and as a result he believed that it was an opportune time to reexamine the terms of the treaty. As he stated in an interview with foreign correspondents outlining Egypt's foreign policy:

> I believe that war has definitely proved Egypt's goodwill towards her Ally in particular, and towards the Democracies in General. Egypt has fulfilled her Treaty obligations with the spirit of a sincere desire to co-operate, this is testified by the services which Egypt rendered and the sacrifices she offered in support of the Allies. It is for this reason that I find no place for this … lack of confidence and that these restrictions should be ultimately raised so that Egypt could have her complete independence.[54]

Even at this late date there were misgivings about declaring war in multiple quarters. The Wafd warned that a declaration of war would not only expose Egypt to harm, but it was unnecessary. In November 1942 Nahhas had received assurances that Egypt would be consulted on issues of concern without a declaration and the new requirements coming out of Yalta were, in their view, a betrayal of that earlier agreement: "This makes a declaration of war the price of entering the Peace Conference. Egypt is now required to pay this price contrary to the unanimously agreed policy of [the] previous Egyptian Government as approved by Parliament and the nation when there were stronger reasons for entering the war than there are now."[55] The Wafd also argued that Britain was pushing for a declaration of war only so that they could gain additional votes at the San Francisco Conference, "in the same way as she had formerly strengthened her position in the League of Nations by recruiting the Dominions as members."[56] This Wafdist declaration, which Killearn later described as the "stupidest of stupid blunders," frustrated the ambassador as the party was undermining Britain's position in Egypt at the same time as the embassy was actively working to protect Wafdist officials from persecution and trial.[57] Despite these efforts, Makram 'Ubayd provided the momentum behind the movement to proceed with charges against Nahhas, leading to heated debate in the Egyptian press and Chamber of Deputies.[58]

The declaration of war faced strong opposition within Egypt, and on February 24, 1945, Ahmad Mahir was assassinated while leaving a secret session of the Chamber of Deputies to discuss the issue. The assassin was Mahmoud Issawi, a lawyer and member of the Watanist Party who had been interned by the Wafd and released by the prime minister himself as part of his amnesty program on coming to office. The assassination of Ahmad Mahir, so soon after the assassination of Lord Moyne in November, raised fears that Egypt was facing a resurgence of the political violence that followed the First World War. In a portent of things to come, on March 2 Amin 'Uthman survived an attack by an assailant with a knife. Ahmad Mahir's assassination led to a reimposition of the wartime censorship measures that he had eased and a new round of arrests. Young Egypt and Muslim Brotherhood meetings were banned as part of the crackdown.[59] Mahmud al-Nuqrashi, Ahmad Mahir's successor as prime minister, succeeded in passing the declaration of war on February 26, 1945, meeting the deadline for participation in the San Francisco Conference.

"World Organisation Intoxication": Treaty Revision and the San Francisco Conference

In March 1945 the Preparatory Committee reconvened and approved the proposals for the new Arab League in a single session. On March 22 the Covenant of the Arab League was signed by delegates of Egypt, Syria, Transjordan, Iraq, Saudi Arabia, and Lebanon.[60] The Covenant declared that "The object of the League is to strengthen relations between member States, to co-ordinate their political action with a view to ensuring collaboration between them and protection of their independence and sovereignty, and generally to consider all questions concerning the Arab countries and their interests." The council of the Arab League would hold regular meetings twice a year, with each member state having one vote and the presidency of the council rotating among the member states. The permanent seat of the League would be in Cairo and 'Abd al-Rahman 'Azzam of Egypt was chosen to serve as the first secretary-general. The Covenant also included annexes addressing the Palestine issue, calling for Palestinian independence and participation in the Arab League, and providing a mechanism for cooperation with non-member Arab countries.[61]

One of the Iraqi representatives admitted that "preoccupation of all concerned with preparations for [the] San Francisco Conference" was largely responsible for expediting the proceedings of the Preparatory Committee.[62] After the signing of the Arab League charter in March 1945 Arab leaders turned their attention to the upcoming conference. Their strategy was to internationalize Arab demands regarding Palestine, Syria, and Lebanon, as well as treaty revision for Egypt and Iraq, using the new international organization as a means of bypassing the bilateral relationships with Britain and France. In addition to their participation in the conference halls they prepared an extensive public relations campaign with an array of social opportunities to demonstrate to the other delegates that the Arab states were prepared to take their place in the postwar world.

British officials viewed these preparations with alarm. In Killearn's estimation, the Arabs were getting above themselves in the postwar euphoria. He portrayed the Egyptian delegation to the San Francisco Conference as "in a thoroughly tiresome mood, swollen headed, self conceited and elated by what I might call 'world organisation intoxication.' … they seem to have got it into their heads that we, the British, were finished so far as the Middle East was concerned." The Egyptian delegation included a number of high-profile politicians, an indication of their expectations for the conference. The Foreign Office, sensing that the Arabs would have little of substance to do at the conference and use it to raise uncomfortable issues, aimed to keep close tabs on them.[63] They also instituted "corrective publicity" in the Arab press to try and limit the expectations of the general public, going to great lengths to impress on them that the upcoming conference would be based on the Dumbarton Oaks proposals and the supplemental decisions made at Yalta, and would not address issues outside the wording of the invitation. As the Foreign Office stated in a circular to its representatives, "The Conference will thus have nothing to do with particular current political or economic questions, or with particular aspects of the post-war settlement."[64] Despite these warnings, the conference remained a focal point of attention throughout the spring of 1945, with the director of the Brotherhood of Freedom in Egypt observing that "Even the spectacular events in Germany appear to be causing less interest than the account of proceedings at San Francisco."[65]

Egyptian Minister for Foreign Affairs 'Abd al-Hamid Badawi drafted a paper in May 1945 titled "the Anglo-Egyptian Treaty of 1936 and the Dumbarton Oaks Agreement," in which he argued that the termination of the League of Nations rendered the 1936 Anglo-Egyptian Treaty null and void and that the treaty, which recognized nominal Egyptian independence but included real limitations on its sovereignty, was incompatible with the Dumbarton Oaks proposal. As a result, Britain and Egypt would have to negotiate a new treaty under the terms of the San Francisco Conference and the new United Nations.[66] In fact, he argued that Egypt would not be able to sign the resulting charter in good faith unless Britain at the very least agreed to the need for treaty negotiations before the conference. While embassy staff acknowledged that portions of the Egyptian argument had some validity, the official Foreign Office response was that the 1936 treaty was a "regional arrangement" as defined by Dumbarton Oaks and therefore the timeline for renegotiation did not need to be changed.[67] The Egyptian delegation at San Francisco introduced proposed amendments to inscribe a different definition of regional arrangement in the United Nations Charter, a tactic that ultimately failed.

The British dilemma was whether to fight the calls for treaty revision or to revise the treaties before the United Nations had established itself, thereby presenting the Security Council with "a fait accompli" before the Egyptian leadership could "internationalize their problems."[68] Ambassador Killearn was highly skeptical of what would emerge from the San Francisco Conference and its implications for the British position in Egypt: "with due respect it seems indefensible to jeopardise (if such be the case) our treaty arrangements with Egypt for the safety of our imperial life-line by idealistic commitments in regard to world security which may or may not prove effective in practice."[69]

As the summer progressed, Arab hopes for the San Francisco Conference turned to disappointment. The Arab delegations were unsuccessful in securing passage of their proposed amendments in the conference halls or in achieving their objectives regarding the remaining mandates. The political cartoons that appeared in the Egyptian humor weekly *Akhir Sa'a* surrounding the San Francisco Conference provide useful glimpses of how the events of the conference were projected back to the Arab public and reflect the transition from hopeful optimism to disillusionment. A March 1945 cartoon shows Misri Effendi heading to the San Francisco Conference pushing a wheelbarrow loaded with papers and petitions, labeled hopes and plans. As news from the conference reached Egypt, these hopes were replaced with warnings that these dreams were in danger: a cartoon from April shows a doctor giving a delegate a transfusion of blood from four women, each labeled with one of Roosevelt's Four Freedoms, while a May cartoon shows a doctor desperately trying to resuscitate a dying woman labeled "the Atlantic Charter." The message here is that the conference was failing to live up to the promises of Allied wartime declarations.[70] As the Iraqi newspaper *al-Iraq* lamented in July, "The four freedoms of the Atlantic Charter have been melted in the pots of trusteeship."[71]

Iraqi observers were disappointed not just with the outcome but also with the performance of their delegation, a sentiment perhaps best reflected in the fact that, when it came time to sign the new document, this task fell not to the Cabinet members who were at the conference but to Fadhil Jamali, the director general of foreign affairs.[72] Mahmud Abu al-Fath, an Egyptian politician and editor of *al-Misri* who accompanied the Egyptian delegation to San Francisco, reported home his sense of disappointment at the representatives of the small states who, despite their many speeches and proposed amendments, in the end voted in accordance with the great powers. The new Charter was, in the consideration of *Wafd al-Masri*, a "catastrophe" for the small nations.[73] The attempt to internationalize the question of Arab independence had, for the moment, failed and the long-anticipated postwar peace conference on the model of the 1919 Paris Peace Conference never materialized.

11

War's End, May 1945–September 1945

Victory in Europe in May 1945 was celebrated throughout the Arab world with declarations of support for the Allies, but also with hints that now was the time for the Allies to deliver on their wartime assurances. While Killearn's V-E Day radio address from Cairo praised Egyptians for their loyalty, it also reminded them of Britain's sacrifices on their behalf and Egypt's continued role in the war in the Far East. In response, Egyptian leaders highlighted the way in which the country not only met the requirements outlined in the treaty but exceeded them. *Al-Ahram* urged "It was now time to get to work" and achieve Egyptian independence by assembling documentation of the country's contribution to the war to support its claims.[1] In Egypt, the British rightly feared that the political model of the three-legged stool of the palace, Wafd Party, and Britain, which had served them so well thus far, might acquire some unwieldy and inconvenient appendages in the postwar world. In Iraq the concern was that Britain's support for the old gang of Iraqi politicians would push opposition elements into the arms of a nebulous communist threat.

Britain responded to these challenges on two fronts, on the one hand addressing the calls for treaty revision with a reexamination of British postwar military and strategic requirements, and on the other hand by developing a new cover for British intervention: economic relations and British expertise. The approaching end of the war provided the opportunity to capitalize on the rhetoric of development that Allied propaganda had fostered. Strengthening the Anglo-Arab bond could be accomplished by building up commercial relations and providing British officials to implement development projects and social reform.[2]

The debates surrounding treaty revision and Britain's postwar strategic priorities for the Middle East were multi-faceted, a reflection of local, regional, imperial, and global considerations as well as domestic politics at home in Britain.[3] The focus in these two chapters is how, in keeping with the themes of this work, the wartime experience and the lessons drawn from the conflict shaped both the case that Egypt and Iraq made in pursuing treaty revision, as well as some of the strategies that Britain developed in response. It is this question that illuminates the place of the war in the evolving Anglo-

Iraqi and Anglo-Egyptian relationship in this critical period that bridged the Second World War and the era of decolonization.

Treaty Revision

The war was nearing its end but Britain still had a towering physical presence in Egypt, including over 200,000 troops. The Suez Canal Zone base was the largest military installation in the world in 1945, a vast "network of roads, railways, harbours, ports, military garrisons, airfields, and a flying-boat station," training grounds, and supply dumps.[4] Cairo remained, in the words of Sir Edward Grigg (Lord Altrincham), "an occupied city." In an April 1945 report he painted a powerful visual image of the statue of Sa'd Zaghlul, the Egyptian leader of the Wafd delegation after the First World War and hero of the 1919 revolution, gazing out over a city scattered with barracks, military camps erected in parks, and wartime headquarters in hotels, all built to accommodate the British military presence: "Egypt has been the centre of an essential war-base, even since the war passed out of Africa. But Egyptians may be forgiven for feeling that the magnitude of our military occupation three years after Alamein has not been entirely justified by the needs of the latter phases of the war against Germany or the war with Japan." Speaking from his vantage point as minister resident in the Middle East, Lord Altrincham noted that "Our military organisation in the Middle East is all-pervasive; and though it is well within our Treaty rights, it is of great political importance that all signs of military occupation should now be rapidly withdrawn."[5]

This report provides a powerful reminder of what was at stake for both Britain and its Arab allies with the end of the conflict and why the future of the Suez Canal Zone base was at the forefront of the earliest discussions regarding treaty revision. If, for the Egyptians, the war had proven their loyalty to Britain and that the treaty was outdated, for many British officials the war had only reinforced their conviction of the Middle East's vital place in the British Empire. Eden stated in April 1945 that the Middle East was "one of the most important strategic areas in the world, and it is an area the defence of which is a matter of life and death to the British Empire since, as the present war and the war of 1914–18 have both proved, it is here that the Empire can be cut in half."[6] Lord Altrincham advocated a regional approach to British defense issues and described Egypt, Palestine, Transjordan, and Iraq as "a strategic spine in which all four are essential vertebrae. We cannot afford to lose our position in any one of them or even to see it seriously weakened. They support and depend on each other." Continuing with the anatomical analogy, he advocated for a reduction in the permanent troops stationed in the region and instead "What we should aim at is a well-planned skeleton with bases and communications adapted each to each, which can be rapidly clothed with muscular flesh should the emergency arise."[7]

With the end of the war in Europe the issue of treaty revision was propelled forward by the Wafd Party, now out of power, and the opposition parties when, in July 1945, Nahhas sent a statement to Killearn reflecting his party's demands. After describing Egypt's loyalty to Britain during the war and contribution to the war effort, it stated that the cessation of hostilities provided an appropriate opportunity for Egypt to exert its independence and called for treaty revision before the anticipated peace conference. Nahhas offered a thinly veiled threat, implying that Britain's position was based more on the goodwill of Egyptians than the strength of its military presence: "The experiences of the present war have indeed clearly proved that Great Britain relies in such circumstances on the friendly sentiments and loyalty of the Egyptian people. This is indispensable and cannot be replaced by the presence of a limited number of British Forces either in Egyptian towns or on the banks of the Canal."[8] Implicit in this statement was the threat of unrest in Egypt if the request for treaty revision was not granted.

Nuqrashi's government and the British were both feeling the pressure for treaty revision from the Wafd and other political elements in Egypt.[9] The original treaty had been negotiated by a United Front of Egyptian parties in 1936. Killearn argued that the Wafd would reject any treaty negotiated by Nuqrashi's government and that they needed the Wafd, as the majority party in Egypt, to endorse any proposed revision.[10] Yet the chances of achieving a new United Front seemed slim. The prime minister was stalling due to fears that Britain would demand the return of the Wafd to power as the price of negotiation; British officials were delaying because they were still debating what exactly their military requirements were for the region. Smart saw this as an opportunity for Britain to buy time. They should "wait and see as long as possible," and when the Egyptian government did raise the issue, they should suggest that they would only negotiate with a United Front and say "we were ready to talk when Egyptians were agreed among themselves."[11]

The surrender of Japan on September 2, 1945, provided additional motivation for the Egyptian demands for treaty revision. At a meeting that same day, the consultative committee of senior Egyptian politicians proposed that the government should formally raise the issue.[12] Although the official request would not come until December 1945, the British continued to plan their potential response and assess Britain's postwar requirements.

The growing demands for treaty revision opened an opportunity for a realignment of allegiances in Egypt. Patrick Scrivener of the Foreign Office Egyptian Department suggested that they should focus their attention on the king and take advantage of his fear of growing Soviet intervention by pointing out that treaty revision could weaken Britain's ability to protect Egypt and open the door for greater Russian encroachment.[13] King Farouk also recognized that teaming up with Britain might be the best way to break the impasse and he proposed "a gentleman's agreement with the British Government that they would lend him their moral support and withdraw it from Nahas Pasha … In return for our moral support of the King … His Majesty would guarantee to take the necessary steps to safeguard our vital defence interests in Egypt" and implement the requested social reforms. Rapprochement between Britain and the palace would allow Britain to meet its strategic requirements while the king could avoid having to call a United Front government.[14]

At the British embassy in Cairo there was a divergence of opinion between Killearn and Smart as to an appropriate British response to these demands, reviving many of the debates that had taken place in 1944. Smart believed that the postwar planning of the British military authorities was out of touch with the reality of British limitations and the strength of local nationalist opposition. They proposed an even greater postwar military presence beyond the treaty limits, and Smart observed that "I cannot help feeling that all this is rather in the realm of fantasy," and Egyptian acquiescence on larger troop movements would require the use of force: "Is it probable in the new world circumstances that Great Britain will be prepared to use such force?"[15] Given that this did not seem like a viable option, Smart took the side of conciliating Egypt. They should first of all decide what their minimum requirements were, and then ensure that "our requirements must be as little irksome as possible, internationally and locally."[16] The ambassador, for his part, did not share Smart's hesitation in using force if necessary. As he dramatically stated in his diary: "if retaining our predominance entails being a little rough with Egypt, I would be fully prepared to be as rough as required."[17]

In January 1944 Cornwallis had observed that the issue of treaty revision had not been raised in Iraq, but the situation had changed by the spring of 1945. Britain had to balance the need to recognize the contributions of the Arab states to the war effort with the need to avoid provoking demands for concessions as a result. The presentation of a message to the regent from King George VI acknowledging Iraq's wartime contribution in March 1945 sparked demands in the Iraqi press for treaty revision. The newspaper *al-Nida* pointed out that Transjordan had requested the renegotiation of its treaty and Syria had refused to sign a treaty with France, instead viewing the United Nations as the best protector of freedom in the postwar world. Egypt, whose own treaty was based on the Anglo-Iraqi model, was also demanding revision. All of these examples demonstrated that bilateral treaties were "not consistent with the present age." This was, as a pro-Soviet newspaper declared in a June 7 headline, "The Auspicious Opportunity" for Iraq to demand her rights.[18] When Iraq raised the treaty question with Britain in July 1945, the British saw the influence of Egypt behind this act. Foreign Office officials concluded that "this unwelcome development is mainly due to the ideas picked up at San Francisco by the Iraqi delegation to the Conference … The Iraqis and Egyptians doubtless feel that if they both shout together for treaty revision, they are more likely to secure a hearing … Their next step will probably be to mobilise the Arab League."[19]

The treaty revision discussion in Egypt centered on British evacuation and the unity of the Nile Valley. In Iraq the conversation focused on the removal of British troops and the status of British diplomatic representatives and advisers. Iraq requested an end to the permanent precedence of the British ambassador in Baghdad along with raising the status of its own diplomatic representation in London to an embassy, and removal of the stipulation that Iraq should hire British advisers for any posts unless a suitable candidate could not be found. While Britain allowed the establishment of a Soviet legation in both Egypt and Iraq, the Foreign Office informed the State Department that "in view of the responsibility which we have undertaken for the defence of Egypt and Iraq" Britain preferred to retain its precedence in both countries and the United States agreed to maintain its representation at the level of legations for the moment.[20]

Britain would later concede the issue of diplomatic precedence and diplomatic representation in London but held firm on the question of advisers: "it is the Advisers and other British servants of the Iraqi Government who are the real vehicles of our influence here. We should do all we can to maintain them."[21] The call for treaty revision within Iraq grew through the summer, and to the requests regarding advisers and diplomatic representation was added a new demand that struck at the very core of British interests: to end Britain's rights to maintain air bases "on the ground that these bases are inconsistent with the sovereign independence of Iraq."[22] At the same time, British military officials were hoping to station ground troops in Iraq in addition to the RAF bases.

As the issue of diplomatic precedence demonstrated, growing American and Soviet influence in the Middle East was a complicating factor in these considerations regarding treaty revision. An April 1945 article in the *Times* that suggested that the great powers should share Britain's burden in the Middle East led to a heated debate in the Egyptian press about postwar demands. Egypt did not intend to replace British imperialism with new ties to the Western powers or, as Dr. Taha Husayn described it, replace Britain with "four mandatories instead of one, but complete and unconditional independence."[23]

British officials in Egypt and Iraq viewed this encroachment on their turf with a combination of alarm and resignation. Smart observed, "I think we must take it for granted that we shall not be allowed to be so politically exclusive as we have been in the Egypto-Arab world during the period between the two wars." Given this threat, it was even more imperative that Britain "should gain the maximum amount of local acquiescence as is compatible with our strategical interests" to balance these new interests.[24] Some officials put this in terms of a sort of British "Monroe Doctrine" for the eastern Mediterranean.[25] Cornwallis advocated a combination of British retrenchment and concessions to Iraq: "In these circumstances, it obviously behooves us to take nothing for granted. We must be zealous in preserving the predominant political position which we have gained, and in so acting we must realize that the Iraqis have grown up and must be treated as adults."[26] Local cooperation therefore was necessary not only to fight radical elements in Iraqi and Egyptian society, but also to curtail the influence of Britain's allies in the region. The key for Britain was to build support so that, once the shine wore off of America in Arab eyes, Britain would be ready to step forward once again.

The Changing of the British Guard in Iraq

On May 9, 1945, C. J. Edmonds, the British adviser to the Ministry of the Interior, retired and left Baghdad. It was thirty years, almost to the day, from his first arrival in Iraq in 1915 and observing the significance of the date in his diary he noted: "I arrived in Iraq this tour on Sept. 1, 1939 the day the Germans marched into Poland. I therefore saw through the war exactly, without a superfluous day at either end, in Iraq." Edmonds had earned the nickname "the Cerberus of the Orient" for the way in which he controlled access to the circles of power in Iraq, a perception that provides insight into the reasons why the Iraqis made the removal of British advisers a priority in treaty revision.[27] His departure was part of a much larger sea-change in British personnel in the closing year of the war. At the end of 1944 Wallace Lyon, political adviser in the north, left Iraq for a new position as consul in Ethiopia, disillusioned by the lack of progress on the Kurdish issue. Vyvyan Holt, who had held the position of oriental counsellor since the death of Gertrude Bell in 1926, was transferred to the Foreign Office and replaced by Stewart Perowne. Holt did not stay in London long, as he was soon assigned to accompany the Arab delegations to the San Francisco Conference.[28]

The departure of Edmonds and Lyon, Britain's most experienced and influential Kurdish experts, in such a short period of time was noticed by the Iraqis and was keenly felt by the remaining staff. Rumors circulated that the change signaled that Britain was altering its traditional policy and pursuing an anti-Kurdish agenda. Major R. Wilson, who succeeded Lyon as political adviser in the north, noted that the PA and ALO staff in the Kurdish areas were "in a very awkward position" because the senior Kurdish experts had all either left Iraq or were on leave, and of those who replaced them: "our total experience is only a few years as compared to half a century."[29]

Many of these officials, like Edmonds, had begun their careers in Iraq during the First World War or in the early years of the mandate and their departure was, in the eyes of many observers, long overdue. The regent, during his autumn 1943 visit to Britain, had called for younger British officials to be sent to Iraq, complaining that "the Advisers were all too old" and the British Military Mission was "not up-to-date nor composed of modern soldiers."[30] All had held challenging positions in the difficult war years with very little leave and with the approaching end of the war there was a sense that new personnel would infuse energy into the embassy and the advisory staff.

These departures left deep gaps in the embassy's local networks. Iraqis who had enjoyed Edmonds' support now found themselves removed from their positions, a reflection of the changing power dynamic and a weakening patronage system with broader ramifications. The American legation drafted a report in November 1944 titled "Evidences of a somewhat more independent attitude on the part of the Iraqi Government towards the British Government," a reflection of the significance of this development. Pachachi's government was distancing itself from some of Nuri's pro-British policies and officials were thinking twice before implementing British recommendations because they feared that "if in following British lines of policy they should become unpopular with their colleagues, with the members of the Iraqi Parliament, with any influential groups of Iraqis, or with the Regent, they may not be able to depend upon the continued support of the British Government."[31]

The most significant change was the departure in March 1945 of Ambassador Cornwallis. He had struggled with poor health for two years and the winding down of the war provided a window of opportunity for new leadership. His four-year tenure in Iraq was, by all British accounts, a success.[32] Cornwallis noted in his Valedictory Dispatch that he had had three main tasks after the 1941 coup: to secure Britain's wartime requirements, purge Iraq of pro-Nazi sympathizers, and shape public opinion in favor of the Allies. He also had an unofficial fourth task, "to influence the administration as far as possible, but not to the extent of causing a crisis" which might threaten the other, more important aims. He concluded that he had achieved the first three tasks but the fourth goal, governmental reform, proved far more elusive and, in the long term, destructive to British interests in Iraq. The British were blamed for all of the shortcomings of the Iraqi administration but Cornwallis rejected these charges: "The real trouble lies not with us, but with the rulers themselves, who obstinately refuse to give up any of their privileges or prerogatives to others."[33]

Despite these reservations Cornwallis was optimistic about the state of Iraq at the end of the war: "On the whole, therefore, in spite of much corruption and inefficiency, it is only fair to record that the Iraqis have risen well to the occasion. Everywhere public security is good and taxes are collected." At the same time he was concerned that once British troops withdrew, the situation would deteriorate as he was convinced that Britain alone would be able to ensure the stability needed to reform Iraq's administration and address local discontent. Given the atmosphere in the Middle East, it would be impractical to exert British influence by force or by exceeding the bounds of the treaty, but Cornwallis believed Britain could increase its influence by taking a more sympathetic approach to Iraq's grievances, ensuring a continued supply of good British officials to work within the government, and maintaining the personal contacts that were reestablished during the war. He called for the extension of the Political Advisory Staff and the PR Section of the embassy into the postwar period to ensure this, to eventually be replaced by administrative inspectors or, at the very least, more consulates. The Oriental Secretariat should have an even greater role in Anglo-Iraqi relations in the postwar period after these wartime organizations were gradually dismantled.[34] He was therefore advocating for the extension of British influence through advisers, much as had happened under the mandate. Cornwallis's assessment was very much at odds with the pulse in Iraq.

Intervention through Experts

The victory of the British Labour Party in the July 1945 election led to speculation as to what this would mean for treaty revision as well as for the reformist agenda. Egyptian Minister of Finance Makram 'Ubayd expressed confidence that "the labor party is the most inclined to respect the independence and liberties of small nations." However, as the American legation reported, the general sense among Egyptians was that, while the Labour victory might lead to real changes at home, British policies abroad were likely to stay the same.[35] CICI officials observed that this development was a topic of much interest in Iraq, and "while it is only natural that leftist elements should be delighted, there seems to be a general assumption that the terms 'Labour' and 'Communism' are synonymous, and that British will now, in the field of foreign policy, more easily give way to Russian demands." In August 1945 the communist publication *al-Qa'ida* expressed optimism in the aftermath of the Labour victory as "Any social change in England must naturally re-echo here." Yet the following month, CICI's summary of *al-Qa'ida*'s September 1945 issue observed that: "One can detect a note of disappointment in the report rendered by 'Fahad' wherein he says 'The coming to power of the Labour Government has brought no change in the British Government policy with regard to the colonies and countries which desire to shake off the yoke imposed on them.'"[36]

The clearest indication of the new Labour government's policies toward the Arab world came at a meeting Foreign Secretary Ernest Bevin convened in London with the heads of mission in the Middle East during September 1945. The meeting aimed to address two critical concerns: how to maintain influence in the region at a time when local nationalist movements were calling for less foreign intervention, and how to ensure that the sterling balances built up by these states during the war were not used to cause further economic problems for Britain. Economic and social initiatives were the answer, as they would improve the lives of Arab populations and also benefit Britain by absorbing the sterling balances. Many of the decisions made at this meeting reflected this new approach. Communist propaganda, for example, could best be countered by addressing the social and economic concerns that made it an attractive ideology. The lifting of wartime economic controls could lead to greater economic rivalry with the United States, and therefore the conference asserted that Britain "should not make any concession that would assist American commercial penetration into a region which for generations has been an established British market" except in the area of oil.[37]

As part of Bevin's plans for the postwar Middle East, Britain would provide technical experts to local governments to encourage these states to use their sterling balances wisely and in a way that took into consideration Britain's postwar economic limitations. These experts were a crucial component of the plan: "It cannot be too strongly emphasised that the proposed policy of economic and social development in the Middle East can only succeed if it is based on an adequate supply of first-rate scientific and technical advice."[38] This initiative faced a number of logistical problems: how to locate the necessary experts, convince their employers to release them for short-term missions, make them available to Middle Eastern governments, and ensure that they were well qualified and suitable for work in the region. The meeting proposed the creation of a bank of available experts in a wide variety of scientific and economic fields, from agriculture to public health. The mechanism for exerting this influence in the economic and commercial sphere would be a new British Middle East Office, which would act as a successor to the Minister of State's Office and serve as the headquarters for these technical experts who would then be available to consult with Middle Eastern governments.[39] The Arab Centre, established in Jerusalem in 1944 to train the next generation of British experts for the Arab world, was designed to fill this need.[40]

The policies of the Labour government coincided with the determination of British officials in both Egypt and Iraq to promote social reform, a trend that began in 1943. Geoffrey Thompson, chargé d'affaires at the embassy in Baghdad, expressed his support for the recommendations that arose from this conference with the heads of mission because

> it referred to the 'financial, economic and social' needs of the area in question. Too long, it seems to be, have we refrained in our official pronouncements from registering any interest whatever in the well-being of the ordinary inhabitants, the countless little people, in countries such as this. Now that we have started on this path of emphasising our concern with public welfare, let us continue bravely

> ahead, for here is one way of promoting a growing and necessary appreciation of the progressive element in British policies.[41]

By becoming agents of change rather than conservatism in Iraq, the British could seize this popular sentiment in support of reform from the Soviets. Bevin's new policy for the Middle East complemented embassy officials' own sense of responsibility for reform in Iraq, as exemplified in the conclusions Cornwallis reached in his valedictory. Cornwallis's successor, Sir Hugh Stonehewer-Bird, warning of the "disruptive forces" at work in Iraq, suggested that

> It is of great importance that Great Britain should recover her reputation as a leader of material progress. Practical assistance in recruiting technical experts, training Iraqi technicians and craftsmen (the latter are still almost entirely lacking in Iraq), together with judicious advice upon internal problems and wide distribution of carefully chosen propaganda, appear to be the right methods, and these are being assiduously applied.[42]

Social Reform and British Clients

The implications of this policy were not lost on the Arabs and postwar Labour plans for influence through experts collided with the legacy of distrust built through British wartime control. Egyptian politicians compared Bevin's new policy of social reform to Cromer's policies toward the Egyptian fellahin, with *Ruz al-Yusuf* stating that: "Both policies, it is suggested, should be regarded as cover for British political aims."[43] Fahd, secretary-general of the Iraqi Communist Party, issued a scathing critique of British influence in a 1944 speech, targeting the many avenues of British influence in the country, from the political advisers in the provinces, to the print and broadcast propaganda, to the Brotherhood of Freedom, which claimed to be fighting Axis propaganda with democratic propaganda, but was in fact spreading British imperial propaganda instead. The staff of the various British Institutes spread throughout the country were "missionaries" propagating new political ideas rather than religious ones.[44] The usually pro-British newspaper *al-Zaman* published an article in November 1944 written by Professor Taha al-Rawi, dean of the Higher Teachers' Training College, in which he exposed the damage caused by Western imperialism. He singled out Western education programs and institutions in the Arab world as "centres for sowing the seeds of discord among the people of the nation," and added that "among these weapons are the social services which look attractive and fascinating while they are really poisons undermining the body of society."[45]

The personal relationships that Cornwallis so highly valued were also suspect. Muhammad Hadid, an Iraqi politician and industrialist whose views were representative of Iraqi leftist reformers, noted that many of the new staff added to the embassy PR Section after 1941 were "intellectuals" with expertise in Arab affairs. Their democratic and leftist sympathies and social contacts helped them win the favor of young men who were attracted to Roosevelt's declarations and the postwar promises of the Allies. The British Council and the embassy held parties and cultural events to which Iraqis were invited, but those who joined Stark's organization and attended these events were, in Hadid's estimation, merely British clients.[46] Iraq's demands for the removal of the treaty requirement to hire British advisers reflected these sentiments.

In February 1945 the Iraq bulletin of the Brotherhood of Freedom announced the opening of a new public exhibit at the club's headquarters in Baghdad titled "Iraq, Know Thyself." Consisting of a colorful cartoon narrative drawn by Iraqi artist al-Hajj Su'ad Selim and calligrapher Lt. Sabri al-Khattat, the exhibit would

> present some of the most vital and fundamental social problems which stand in the way of progress in Iraq in such a way that anyone who has learnt to read may be impressed with a sense of their seriousness and urgency against the background of the struggle against social evils which is being carried on all over the world even in the midst of war, by men of good will.[47]

The three focal points were "ignorance, infant mortality, and disease." These three "enemies of Iraq" and their accomplices "figure as personalities in an allegorical world in which Iraq appears as victim and protagonist."[48]

Over the next few months the Iraqi bulletin would include statistics on the number of visitors to the exhibition as it traveled the country, as well as articles using the exhibit as a starting point. Special days were set aside for women to view the display and other days for army officers. This major publicity initiative is reflective of the "education for citizenship" campaign and the particular vision of democracy espoused by the Brotherhood's British leaders in the later war years, with its focus on social issues.

The March 26 issue of the Iraq bulletin opened with an imagined dialogue between an Iraqi man and his two sons, who visit the "Iraq, Know Thyself" exhibit and, deeply troubled by the social problems presented, blame the government for its inability to solve them. The father, well traveled in both the Middle East and Europe from his years in the Turkish army and as a merchant, expresses his frustration with this attitude. He encourages his sons, who might one day enter government service, to work for the good of all Iraqis.[49] As the comments of Fahd, Muhammad Hadid, and others indicated, the motives behind the Brotherhood of Freedom were suspect due to its close association with the embassy. The Iraq bulletin addressed these critiques directly in an April 4, 1945, article that included another imagined dialogue between the same father and his sons. Impressed by the "Iraq, Know Thyself" exhibit, but acknowledging that the British had created both the exhibit and the Brotherhood, they muse that there must be "something behind it," but are unsure what that would be. The British would not invest in something that did not support their interests. One son observes:

> You notice how they steer clear of anything which could possibly be interpreted as having a political bias. You see, my dear Jawad, the one thing our Western Allies do not want our people to think too long or too deeply about is politics, and particularly our political relationship with themselves. So they hit on the brilliantly cunning idea of founding a thing like the Ikhwan al Hurriyah Society

> which exhorts us to get together and fix our minds on our social problems—on anything in fact but on the problem of our political and economic rights in relation to the dominant power.[50]

The wise father dismisses these conspiratorial ideas, and instead states that the war taught the great powers the importance of economic development for "more backward countries ... In my opinion, political activity which does not arise from a passionate and practical concern for social problems is nothing but a sordid scramble for personal privilege and empty dignity."[51]

The sons in these dialogues exemplify the new *effendiyya* that the Brotherhood of Freedom viewed as its target audience.[52] The Iraqi and Egyptian bulletins of the Brotherhood of Freedom were carefully crafted documents designed to facilitate a "two-way traffic," as Stark described it, between the British and local readers. Articles provided talking points for members to refute circulating rumors and also encouraged reporting back of issues and concerns heard on the street.[53] The inclusion of these lengthy articles over multiple issues directly addressing the question of British motives in supporting social reform provides an indication of the challenge Britain would face in implementing the new Labour Party program for the Middle East.

Dismantling the Wartime Control Apparatus

Just as it was reaching maturity and the peak of its influence, Britain began exploring the inevitable postwar task of dismantling the complex assemblage of intelligence organizations, economic missions, and publicity offices that evolved to support the war effort in the Middle East. Some were abolished with a celebratory sense of "mission accomplished"; others were expected to evolve into new postwar organizations to extend British influence. In 1945 the Minister of State's Office was closed and many of its functions were inherited by the new British Middle East Office, which fell under the Foreign Office and was housed in the British embassy in Cairo, making it the "second largest British diplomatic mission, surpassed only by Washington."[54] The Middle East Supply Centre, while it shut down operations in November 1945, had transformed the economies of the states with which it had worked.[55]

Others had much shorter afterlives than anticipated due to a combination of financial considerations and growing local opposition to British influence, even when it came in the guise of development and technical expertise. The Iraqi Ministry of the Interior inquired in September 1945 when the political advisers and area liaison officers would be withdrawn. Perowne reported that "His Excellency said that their work had been very good during the war, but now the war was ended there was no longer any reason for them to continue."[56] Britain saw a host of postwar security concerns that would make a continuation of these positions helpful but also recognized that doing so would lead to Iraqi protests. The dismantlement of the sixteen-member Political Advisory Staff was scheduled for March 1946, but Stonehewer-Bird proposed the creation of five new vice-consul positions to take on some of their functions at a reduced cost and within the traditional diplomatic structure more in keeping with the treaty.[57] The Iraqi government dismissed many of the remaining British advisers in various government ministries in 1946–7. The British Military Mission in Iraq would grow increasingly unpopular after the war, and General Renton was criticized for exceeding his powers under the treaty, leading the British government to withdraw the mission in 1948.[58]

The Brotherhood of Freedom was one of the organizations for which the British saw great postwar potential as a way to extend British influence. When Col. Scaife became adviser to the Iraqi Ministry of Education in December 1944 there were hopes that this would facilitate the transformation of the Brotherhood of Freedom into the adult education department of that ministry.[59] The organization flagged, however, without his leadership and by September 1945 membership had dropped. The Ministry of Information decided to close the Iraqi men's branch in November 1945 and disbanded the women's branch in June 1946.[60]

The Egyptian branch of the Brotherhood of Freedom was still active after the war, claiming over 50,000 members in 1948. British officials hoped that the organization would prove useful in providing pro-British oral propaganda in the midst of contentious postwar negotiations on revision of the Anglo-Egyptian Treaty.[61] Instead, members increasingly faced periodic opposition, press campaigns attacking the organization, bomb threats, and harassment, and it was ultimately dismantled in 1952. The Brotherhood was designed to project British interests, which brought it under increasing suspicion, with its members viewed as British agents.[62]

This was in fact one of the deepest legacies of the war for Britain's presence in the Middle East: in building its vast publicity and intelligence network to monitor Axis activity and win Arab support, Britain was never able to fully assuage Arab suspicions of its motives. This dilemma predated the war and serves as a critical point of continuity with the interwar period. David Kelly, serving as acting high commissioner in September 1936, had observed that "hitherto the Egyptians have attributed a very exaggerated significance to the Residency. The belief in the all-pervading activity of His Majesty's High Commission and in the network of intrigue spread by the crafty oriental secretariat has survived a hundred shocks and has remained a fundamental datum of Egyptian political theory."[63]

Ten years later the wartime experience had only reinforced these assumptions. As a result of the work of the "cloak and dagger wallahs," political advisers, oral propagandists, and publicity officials, so vital in wartime, these assumptions about the power of the British embassies and their work abounded and continued long after their decline as a locus of influence, complicating the implementation of Britain's postwar developmentalist agenda for the region and shaping many of the debates about Britain's postwar role in the Middle East.[64]

12

The Postwar "Bill of Reckoning" and the Decline of Imperial Power, 1945–6

The end of the Second World War raised new questions about its legacy for the Middle East.* The conflict had stretched the terms of the Anglo-Egyptian and Anglo-Iraqi Treaties: what now did it mean to return to a peacetime footing? What did the Arabs owe Britain for protecting them from Axis control, and what did Britain owe the Arabs for cooperating in wartime, at the expense of their sovereignty? At the heart of the issue was the debate over the contributions the Arab states made to the war effort. Throughout the war British officials weighed expressions of appreciation for Arab support to boost morale with private exasperation at the demands for concessions to be made after the war that these statements often elicited. For example, Wavell's January 1941 letter to the Egyptian prime minister thanking him for "the help and cooperation received by us from the Egyptian military authorities in the course of our campaign in Libya" which "greatly facilitated the task assigned the Imperial Army under my command of defending Egypt against the attacks of the enemy" was recirculated at the end of the war as evidence of Egypt's contribution.[1]

This was not merely a question of gratitude for services rendered, but a key part of the Egyptian and Iraqi arguments in favor of treaty revision. The issue was of such vital importance that in 1944 Egypt began compiling a dossier of its many wartime contributions in the hopes that it might provide ammunition for postwar treaty negotiations. Pamphlets outlining Egypt's contribution were circulated in the United States after the war to support these demands.[2] The postwar debates over the future of Egypt and Iraq's hefty sterling balances, £400 million and £70 million respectively, reflect the political implications of these questions.[3] When Churchill suggested in December 1945 that Egypt might cancel some of its sterling balances as a mark of gratitude for British protection during the war, Isma'il Sidqi replied that "Mr. Churchill overlooked the fact that if Egypt was saved it was due to the Anglo-Egyptian Treaty of 1936 which changed Egypt into a big land, air and naval base for the Allied Forces and thereby paved the way to victory."[4]

* Elizabeth Monroe, *Britain's Moment in the Middle East 1914–1971*, 90–1.

To the end, Cornwallis denied any intervention in Iraqi internal affairs, noting that "in a war in which so many frontiers have been obliterated we have held these inviolate without ever, even after 1941, encroaching on Iraq's internal independence."[5] Ambassador Stonehewer-Bird, his successor, believed that, other than in the economic field, the war had little direct impact on the lives of most Iraqis.[6] In fact, measures instituted by British military and civilian authorities in the Middle East as short-term solutions to the immediate needs of wartime proved to have deep and long-lasting effects. As Elizabeth Monroe commented, "All these arbitrary British acts may have been necessities of war, but they were by local standards never-to-be forgotten indignities, and all were entered on a bill of reckoning for presentation after the war."[7] The bill was partially financial, in the form of the large sterling balances, but it also included the potential loss of bases that still held great strategic value after the war and the growing sense of disillusionment with the local governments that Britain had supported. For groups challenging the postwar status quo the pivot point of the conflict in the Middle East was not the 1943 victory in the Western Desert but rather British intervention in response to the 1941 Rashid 'Ali coup and the 1942 Abdin Palace incident.

Egypt's Postscript: Postwar Violence and Treaty Revision

On November 13, 1945, designated "National Struggle Day" in Egypt, Nahhas gave a speech in which he defended his actions during the Abdin Palace incident over three years earlier (see Chapter 6). He denied having any role in the planning leading up to the confrontation at the palace and emphasized the steps he took after accepting office to minimize British interference in internal affairs, namely issuing protests to both the ambassador and the minister of state. He portrayed his acceptance of the premiership as "evidence of his manly conduct, patriotism, and extreme loyalty to the Throne and country," rather than a betrayal of the Egyptian nationalist cause. Refusing the premiership would have given Britain a pretext for even greater interference in Egypt and so, from his perspective, cooperation with Britain was an act of real patriotism that allowed Egypt to avoid the greater evil of a renewed British military occupation.[8]

The speech set off a barrage of articles in the Egyptian press either defending or attacking Nahhas's role in these proceedings. With the lifting of press censorship, an action that the Wafd party had been demanding through the summer months after V-E Day, Egyptian newspapers were now free to publicly debate the legacy of the war and reveal the true details of what had happened on February 4, 1942. The pro-palace newspaper *Akhbar al-Yawm* published for the first time the complete text of the British ultimatum to Farouk. The editor of the paper Mustafa Amin argued that Britain had insisted on a Wafd government as part of a divide and rule policy that made Nahhas beholden to Britain as he would be "aware that he owes his existence to their tanks and that they are the source of his power. The intelligent British wanted to escape the consequences of Egypt's unity, so they did this master stroke."[9] Nahhas's political opponents emphasized the role that British military force played in the unfolding of events. His acceptance of this plan was not an act of patriotism, as Nahhas insisted, but rather signified "approval of foreign intervention … To accept the premiership under such circumstances means attaining it with the help of British bayonets."[10]

The strength of public sentiment in Egypt in favor of treaty revision became evident in the debates in the Egyptian Chamber of Deputies and Senate in October 1945. One representative noted that the issue went beyond the demands for British troop evacuation and the Sudan: "that it was necessary to add to these two issues freedom for the Egyptian government to legislate without any foreign intervention in order to attain national prosperity … in order to attain the freedom to legislate, we do not need to adopt an attitude of weakness but to speak to the English in a language that they will understand."[11] Prime Minister Nuqrashi faced similar criticism from senators who compared the situation to that after the First World War, when Sa'd Zaghlul taught them that "the remaining questions between us and England are not the domain of the government but belong to the entire nation."[12] Nuqrashi's hesitation to call for treaty negotiation and his unwillingness to publicly articulate his stance on the issue threatened to undermine his government.

British military officials concluded that their postwar strategic requirements would require even greater concessions from Egypt and Iraq with respect to the stationing of troops in these countries. The challenge was how to sell this to local governments.[13] The military authorities accordingly tried to convince both Egypt and Iraq that it was in their own interests to continue the "partnership" with Britain as neither country was prepared to defend itself. Only a great power could afford the "great technical complexity and expense of modern war" and while they would require bases, they would not need a large number of permanent troops to man them. Britain also pointed out that troops could not be moved into Egypt at short notice so it was in Egyptian interests to keep British troops there even in peacetime. At the end of the day, they argued that the true interests of both countries lay with Britain: "it is only to Great Britain that these countries can look for help in their national defence, since she is the only great power whose interests coincide with theirs and who, as an ally, would be willing to come to their aid."[14]

Britain proposed a number of possible options, including base leasing and a regional arrangement to square the circle of Egyptian demands for evacuation with British military priorities. Killearn, who had strongly opposed Egyptian attempts to internationalize treaty revision earlier in the year, now suggested that Britain could sweeten its demands for concessions by couching them in the terms of the San Francisco Conference, regionalism, and partnership. He agreed with the Commanders in Chief that they should state that troops would be in Egypt not "for purposes of internal security (even in collaboration) and not … for security of Suez Canal but are to be stationed here as part of our mutual contribution to the security of the Middle East stressing the regional aspect but only as a part of the general world scheme of collective security under the United Nations plan."[15]

The Egyptian government officially presented its request for treaty revision on December 20. The note made two main arguments in support of its request, both of which drew heavily on the wartime experience. The first highlighted the changing international environment that resulted from the war. The 1936 treaty had been negotiated in specific circumstances and shaped by the Italian presence in Libya. Egypt had only accepted the treaty out of necessity and had always viewed it as a temporary measure. The postwar world was different from that of 1936: "The international events which have upset the world, the Allied victory which has brought the last war to an end, the agreements destined to maintain the peace and security of the world, render several of the provisions of the Treaty superfluous and without justification." It was now necessary to revise the treaty in light of the changing postwar environment as the continued presence of British troops in Egypt was an insult to national pride.[16]

The second line of argument was Egypt's wartime contribution: "Nothing proves better the loyalty with which Egypt honours her obligations than her assistance to her Ally during the whole of the war, in the course of which she gave the most concrete evidence of her fidelity to her alliances and of her sincerity in her friendship." Egypt had not only fulfilled the commitment of the treaty but exceeded it: Britain had "obtained from their agreement with Egypt more than the text stipulated and much more than the most optimistic British negotiators had certainly been able to contemplate." As a result, treaty revision was necessary "to bring it into harmony with the new international situation; its clauses which detract from the independence and the dignity of Egypt no longer correspond to present conditions." The note called for Britain to set a date to receive an Egyptian delegation in London to negotiate the treaty, and stated that the issue of the Sudan would be included in these discussions.[17]

Egypt asserted that the war had demonstrated that the treaty had served its purpose and was no longer relevant to the postwar environment, but Bevin reached the opposite conclusion, noting in his January 26, 1946, reply that one of the lessons of the war was "the essential soundness of the fundamental principles on which the Anglo-Egyptian Treaty of 1936 was based." However, Britain agreed to enter into talks before the time frame proposed in the treaty and instructed Killearn to hold "preliminary conversations" in Egypt in order to "place it on a footing of full and free partnership, as between equals in the defence of their mutual interests, and with full respect for the independence and sovereignty of Egypt."[18] The British military authorities agreed to this early treaty revision, despite their reservations, because it would allow them to conduct bilateral negotiations with Egypt whereas if they waited they might have to work through the new international organization.[19]

During the war itself, the presence of British troops engaged in the campaigns in the Western Desert acted as a deterrent to large-scale anti-colonial violence. Yet both British officials and Egyptian nationalists commented on the "latent" threat of violence during the war: unrest building underneath the surface of Egyptian society, threatening to break out with great force at any given time. As early as 1941, Laurence Grafftey-Smith, a member of the embassy staff in Cairo, attributed "the ill-will latent and manifest against us in Egypt to-day" to suspicions about Britain's postwar plans for Egypt. He warned that Britain should address these concerns or "we shall have steadily increasing trouble henceforward."[20]

The delay in Britain's response to the Egyptian government's request and Britain's unwillingness to host an Egyptian delegation in London, instead proposing preliminary discussions in Cairo, angered the Egyptian public and sparked the unleashing of the latent violence of which Grafftey-Smith had warned.[21] Amin 'Uthman, who had served as intermediary between the embassy and the Wafd since the negotiations for the Anglo-Egyptian Treaty in 1936, was assassinated while leaving the Old Victorian Club in Cairo and died of his wounds at midnight on the 5th/6th of January. The assassin, Husayn Tewfik Ahmed, was linked to other attacks on British citizens and pro-British officials, including a failed bombing attempt on Nahhas's car. Killearn viewed his death as having a potentially long-term impact on Anglo-Egyptian relations, as Amin 'Uthman was the only person "who was in a position consistently to influence Nahas Pasha in the sense of moderation as regards Great Britain. The Wafd in opposition are henceforth under no such enlightened restraint." The extent of Egyptian resentment of Amin 'Uthman's role as intermediary with the British was demonstrated by the fact that his funeral was the scene of anti-British violence and political demonstrations, with a crowd estimated at 100,000.[22]

The wartime experience had strengthened many of the centers of power that threatened the stability of the three-legged stool. The embassy reported that both the palace and the government were drawing on the support of the Muslim Brotherhood

> whose strength has increased enormously, and who now are stronger in the university and the schools than the Wafd, whose predominance among the uneducated masses still continues ... Strengthened by the folly of successive Governments, who have tried to use them, the Moslem Brethren have now openly become a political body and are not hiding their hope that they will eventually replace the Wafd and become the Government of the country.[23]

The cycle of street protests in February 1946 reflected this new dynamic. After Friday prayers on February 8, a demonstration began at al-Azhar, organized by the Muslim Brotherhood. The Egyptian police peacefully dispersed it, but the protests widened in scope the next day when approximately 1,000 university students marched toward Abdin Palace. The ongoing British military presence was the underlying theme of the protest, with students shouting "To the British Embassy!" as they marched.[24]

As the students crossed the El Gizeh Bridge over the Nile, Selim Pasha Zaki, the Egyptian commandant of the Cairo City Police, who only recently had taken this office from his British predecessor, ordered that the bridge be opened to prevent the students from crossing. According to Major A. W. Sansom, an officer in British security services, the commandant waited until about 500 students were on the bridge before giving the order to open it, resulting in the drowning deaths of about forty of the student protestors.[25] The public outcry against the official response to these events led to the resignation of the Egyptian Prime Minister Mahmud al-Nuqrashi.[26]

Britain's vast troop presence at war's end contributed to escalating tensions between servicemen and the local population.[27] Muhammad Hasanayn, Farouk's long-time chamberlain and an important intermediary between the palace and the embassy, died when his car was accidentally struck by a British army lorry on February 19. As Scrivener observed to an American counterpart, he "particularly deplored loss at this crucial time of Amin Osman and Hassanein and observed that fact that British vehicle was involved in accident causing latter's death was a crowning piece of misfortune."[28]

British lorries also played a role in the violence of the next round of protests on February 21, which had been named "Evacuation Day." Organizers called for general strikes and demonstrations against Britain's presence in Egypt and events turned bloody when British army lorries broke through a crowd of protestors. British troops opened fire on protestors, and British institutions in Cairo, such as the Anglican Cathedral and the Bishop's Residence, were attacked. By the end of the day, twenty-three protestors had been killed and 121 injured.[29]

The new prime minister, Isma'il Sidqi, pointed out that the presence of so many troops in Cairo after the end of the war was partly to blame, and urged Britain to withdraw them. He then returned to the underlying theme of the protests, the call for British evacuation from Egypt, but couched it in terms of Britain's wartime declarations: "Egyptians would consider this as a proof of the genuineness of the principles established by the Atlantic and San Francisco Charters."[30] Further protests occurred on March 4, which was declared "Martyr's Day" in honor of those killed in the February 21 demonstrations. In Alexandria the protests turned violent when symbols of Britain's occupation were attacked and twenty-eight Egyptians and two British soldiers were killed.[31] In his report on the events of 1946, Sansom warned "that Egypt was on the verge of revolution and that we would have either to treat the country as occupied enemy territory—which was almost what we were doing—or take our troops out."[32]

In the midst of this upheaval Ambassador Killearn, the experienced diplomat who oversaw the transition from British high commission to embassy in Egypt and the negotiation of the 1936 Anglo-Egyptian Treaty, left Egypt to take up a position as special commissioner in South East Asia. Before leaving his post Killearn drafted his March 1946 "swan song," which included his own narrative of Egyptian politics and lessons learned during his twelve-year tenure. In 1934 when Killearn arrived in Egypt King Fuad was still on the throne, a monarch who, although often antagonistic to British interests, "in the last resort knew full well on which side his bread was buttered." His untimely death led to the accession of his son Farouk who, unlike his father, "did not even know where the butter came from." The young inexperienced monarch fell under the pernicious influence of 'Ali Mahir, who convinced him to dismiss the Wafd government in 1937 and urged Egypt to pursue a policy of neutrality during the war. After the fall of the Wafd from power in 1944 and the assassination of Ahmad Mahir, Egypt, in Killearn's assessment, "rapidly deteriorated."[33]

This narrative brought Killearn through the end of the war and the postwar negotiations, at which point "British technique had altered—what had been regarded as both legitimate and indeed essential to repel the enemy, was no longer the order of the day." The new British policy was to be one of "nonintervention" in Egyptian affairs: "the role of the British representative was henceforth to remain aloof and let internal bickerings and political squabbles take their course as being no direct concern of ours." Killearn had real reservations about this new policy:

> A convincing and pleasant theory—yet in the long run is it possible? For Egypt continued to occupy the same geographical position as she always has done; she continued to be right athwart the Suez Canal and our imperial communications.

> Furthermore the Middle East has gained greater political and strategical importance than ever before; *and* the Arab League has been born and shows unexpected signs of growth and vigour. To sit back and remain splendidly aloof from Egyptian internal politics sounds extremely attractive in theory; and in normal conditions would be unchallengeable as politically sound. But with Egypt situated as she is, how long will that be possible? Can we allow Egypt to disintegrate and deteriorate at her own sweet will ... Can we in short admit any substantial diminution of our predominance? With all deference I gravely doubt it.[34]

Killearn concluded by warning that Britain should continue to take a real interest in Egyptian internal affairs: "Partnership is splendid but nature has ordered there must be a senior partner." The ambassador had little hope for the future prospects of Egypt on his departure: "in my judgment the internal situation was never worse."[35]

The departure of Lord Killearn signaled a change of policy on the part of the new Labour government as they embarked on discussions regarding treaty revision.[36] Major Sansom observed that the timing of the announcement and replacement of Killearn seemed to send a strong message to the Egyptian public: "It was a pity he could not have made the announcement before the riots, for, rightly or wrongly, everyone in Egypt took it for granted that the British Government had given in to violence."[37] For an ambassador whose closing assessment of Egyptian politics included the conviction that: "with powder in the gun I maintain that in the East it is usually unnecessary to discharge it. The knowledge we mean business is enough," this popular belief that his departure was a British capitulation to violence must have been particularly galling.[38] His collaborative network of intermediaries had collapsed with the assassination of Amin ʿUthman and death of Hasanayn and, despite his long-term commitment to removing Farouk, he never got his not-so-secret wish to see the king unseated while he was still ambassador.[39]

The February–March protests showed the British that their fears of the "spectre of 1919" were well founded, and convinced many officials that Britain would have to choose between large-scale military force and negotiation in Egypt. The participants and their demands reflected the changing political reality in Egypt: the legacy of the British troop presence and the war, the growing power of new actors like the Muslim Brotherhood, and the fact that the British had failed to win over Egyptian youth. Ismaʿil Sidqi, who replaced Nuqrashi as prime minister, warned in a note handed to the British delegation that "a movement of public opinion (stimulated to an equal degree by different causes and currents) may at any moment transform itself into an action which it was possible to repress or contain at the beginning of the present political campaign, but which may subsequently elude all control."[40]

The embassy, now under the leadership of Ambassador Sir Ronald Campbell, urged London to offer "complete evacuation" before beginning negotiations, a position endorsed by the British delegation sent to Egypt in April. Any alternative would provoke unrest, run "the risk of ruining our relations with Egypt," and, if Egypt decided to submit the issue to the Security Council, could cause embarrassment to Britain and provide a precedent for the Soviet Union to press its own claims. The Chiefs of Staff Committee decided to endorse the proposal of "complete evacuation" within a five-year period at the outset of negotiations.[41] Britain's postwar challenges and the transformed international environment, with growing American and Soviet interest in the Middle East, as well as Egyptian expectations of independence based on the formation of the United Nations, all made the cost of outright military confrontation in Egypt too high to pay.

Egypt requested a shorter window of time for evacuation, and the issue of wartime facilities and the Sudan became key obstacles to a settlement. Sidqi traveled to London in October 1946 for direct negotiations with Bevin that resulted in the Bevin-Sidqi Protocol. The Sudan provisions provoked protests in Cairo, the treaty discussions collapsed, and Sidqi resigned in December. Egypt moved to do the very thing Killearn had feared in 1945, attempting to internationalize the Anglo-Egyptian relationship by taking the issue to the United Nations in 1947.

Iraq's Postscript: The Democracy Experiment and Treaty Revision

Throughout the war, embassy officials in Baghdad had decried the weakness of the Iraqi political system, the stubbornness of the old gang of Iraqi politicians, and the apathy of educated youth, which Cornwallis dismissed as "a generation of Hamlets."[42] With the end of the conflict the moment appeared opportune to implement real change. In November 1945 the Iraqi Communist Party circulated a memorandum to the government and the embassies of the great powers calling on them to follow through on wartime promises. The Iraqi government tried to project the image of a democratic, constitutional state to the other Arab states and the world at large in the international conferences. Iraqis supported the Allied war effort in the hopes that they would receive the freedoms promised by Roosevelt and Churchill, as well as the Iraqi government, once the Axis powers were defeated. Yet the war had ended, the emergency laws remained in place, communists were targeted for harassment and imprisonment, and the Iraqi people as a whole were denied basic freedoms such as the right to form political parties and a free press. The memo attacked the British for supporting a repressive government and using the war effort as an excuse to exploit Iraq, in violation of her wartime promises.[43]

Iraqis of various political stripes viewed the British wartime presence as the main culprit behind the country's diseased political system and the clear solution was an end to British intervention. The British agreed that democratic reform was vital but the limitations of their commitment to this cause became increasingly apparent in the immediate postwar period in the midst of the move to reintroduce political parties. In a December 1945 speech the regent asserted Iraq's identity as an independent, democratic monarchy and issued a call for the formation of political parties to pursue an agenda of social reform and justice and ensure equality for all Iraqis. He specifically targeted Iraq's youth, calling on the country's leaders to allow the next generation to bear part of the burden of governance.[44] While skeptical of the effectiveness of political parties, the embassy supported their development as a means of achieving a number of objectives at once. Parties had the potential to bring fresh faces into Iraqi politics, limit the regent's influence, undermine communist critiques of the British-backed system, and open the door for real social reform in line with the priorities of the Labour government.[45]

The new government of Tawfiq al-Suwaydi, formed after the regent's speech, instituted significant reforms, including the release of the Iraqis held in detention, a lifting of martial law, and an end to press censorship. Five political parties were founded in early 1946, the most influential being the National Democratic Party (NDP), the latest manifestation of the Ahali group, and Hizb al-Istiqlal, composed of the pan-Arabists released from detention with the end of the war.[46] The British admitted that there was much to admire in the NDP's platform for internal political and economic reforms but its foreign policy priorities, including complete independence for Iraq and other Arab states and opposition to the establishment of a Jewish state in Palestine, proved problematic. Douglas Busk, an embassy official, observed: "We are thus faced by the alternative between a Conservative Prime Minister indulging in repressive measures of which we heartily disapprove and progressives whose programme, while in some ways admirable, is basically fatal." He suggested that they encourage the formation of a new party to be led by an experienced Iraqi politician who would balance the calls for reform with pro-British sympathies.[47]

Other officials added to the list of desiderata: the ideal candidate would be a "moderate, youngish leader" with administrative experience, perhaps to be found languishing in the provinces as a *mutasarrif*, waiting to be plucked out of obscurity and ensconced in the new Cabinet in Baghdad.[48] Busk optimistically believed that it would be "perfectly easy" to form a new party that would meet Britain's requirements while also attracting the support of "younger Iraqis who are only awaiting a lead."[49] All they needed was a leader who would appeal to the younger generation and advocate for reform at home while maintaining a pro-British attitude in foreign affairs. In the end it proved impossible to find a candidate who met all these criteria and Britain once again reverted to supporting the old gang.

The wartime campaigns for democracy and self-determination proved highly problematic for both the British and the Iraqi government. The opening of Iraqi politics to parties and opposition held promise, and a number of younger politicians were included in Suwaydi's Cabinet. The regent developed cold feet, however, and in May 1946, after only three months in power, Suwaydi's government was replaced by the repressive regime of Arshad al-'Umari. The postwar "democratic moment" in Iraq ended as abruptly as it had started with new restrictions on the press and political parties and a crackdown on political dissent.[50]

The end of the war also saw the closing act of the Mulla Mustafa revolt. In August 1945 the Kurdish leader resumed his attacks on Iraqi interests and the government responded with the imposition of martial law in Kurdish areas. The embassy, in consultation with British military authorities, decided that it could no longer urge restraint on the part of the Iraqi government and when the Barzanis occupied a government building in Bille, the Royal Iraqi Air Force bombed the town. The embassy wanted to ensure that its staff did not get drawn in, so the political advisers were instructed to stay at their headquarters and Major-General Renton, the head of the British Military Mission, made his opposition to the plan clear to the Iraqi government while offering what assistance he could behind the scenes with the planning.[51] The Iraqi army had difficulty defeating Mulla Mustafa until it enlisted the support of other Kurds in return for money and arms, revealing the divisions within the Kurdish leadership and the limitations of the Barzani movement.[52]

Mulla Mustafa, Shaykh Ahmed, and some of their followers escaped over the border to Iran, but it was generally believed that they would renew their efforts in the spring. The Soviets, who were still occupying northern Iran in violation of the terms of the 1942 Tripartite Treaty of Alliance, allowed the Barzani leader to settle in a village in western Azerbaijan, where he established contacts with Iranian Kurdish nationalists. An independent Kurdish state, called the Mahabad Republic, was declared on January 22, 1946, and Mulla Mustafa and his men formed the nucleus of the new republic's military. He conducted numerous raids on its behalf and after the fall of Mahabad at the end of the year sought refuge in the Soviet Union. When he returned to Iraq after the 1958 revolution, his rhetoric reflected larger Kurdish nationalist aims.[53]

In March 1946 Prime Minister Tawfiq al-Suwaydi raised the issue of treaty revision with the British ambassador "so as to make the existing alliance a normal one befitting progress made by Iraq and in harmony with world developments within the spirit of the United Nations Charter."[54] Iraq closely watched the disastrous negotiations taking place in Egypt and, in the longstanding spirit of Egyptian-Iraqi rivalry, having been the first to enter treaty relations with Britain in the 1930s, pushed to be the first to complete the treaty revision process. An Iraqi delegation traveled to Portsmouth in January 1948 to begin negotiations but the talks were accompanied by anti-British riots back at home in the events of the *Wathba*. The violence convinced the Iraqi government to reject the treaty and reflected the ongoing economic difficulties the country was experiencing, anti-British sentiment, and the frustration of young Iraqis with the continued grasp of the old gang on the political system.[55]

The Projection of Power, the Projection of Ideals: A Postscript

In 1946 Muhammad Hadid presented a memo to the British embassy in Iraq in which he asked: "what is the position of Britain in this conflict which is going on in Iraq between the progressive elements composed of the young generation, and the reactionary forces composed of the old generation?"[56] The war had a transformative effect on Iraq as "security laws and regulations limited political activities, but at the same time a great political consciousness was aroused, particularly among young men, by the stream of declarations from the Allied countries about the better life which was to come if democratic forces were to win the war."[57] Britain's influence in Iraq increased during the war and as a result:

> the general opinion is that Britain has something to do with every major event in Iraq. If the country has remained backward, or if its general standard of life is terribly low, or if things were going wrong, the most accepted reason among the public is that British policy positively wants it to be so, or else, because British support of the present regime has negatively prevented matters to be otherwise.

> In the present situation, the British are believed to support the reaction by ruling class against progressive reforms.[58]

A version of this memo was also published in the *New Statesman*, presenting an Iraqi reformist interpretation of the war's impact on Iraqi politics to a British audience. Both documents reflect two recurring themes in Britain's wartime policies in Egypt and Iraq that are so pervasive in British analysis, their discussions with local officials, and the writings of their critics as to become axiomatic, woven through from the prewar period to the end. The first was that, in spite of the terms of the treaties, Britain was still pulling the strings of the Egyptian and Iraqi governments and integrally involved in the internal affairs of both states. The second was that Britain was associated with the forces of conservatism, exacerbating the generational divide. Its interests were closely tied to the preservation in power of reactionary leaders who stifled political and social reform, and as a result the ideals of democracy were repeatedly sacrificed on the altar of Britain's short-term wartime priorities.

A third assumption, the conviction that Britain must "stand by her friends," only reinforced these two trends and provided additional evidence to support critiques of British methods. The failure to do so would undermine the patron-client relations that allowed the embassies to maintain the façade of non-interference. For embassy officials the ability to protect pro-British politicians was vital to preserving British prestige, and was a critical component of the toolbox of informal empire.

A representative for the Ministry of Information warned in 1944 that if they failed to promote "democratic procedure and political growth … we will indeed have won a war for the M. East, but at the same time have deprived ourselves of the fruits of our victory."[59] While it was not immediately apparent in 1945, the postwar history of the region bore out the veracity of this warning. British officials in the realms of diplomacy, propaganda, and intelligence, as well as their American counterparts, repeatedly raised the alarm about the ways in which this reality exacerbated the generational divide in the region and critics just as frequently pointed out their failure to address it.[60]

Perhaps the British should not have been surprised at the outcome. 'Abd al-Rahman 'Azzam, secretary general of the Arab League, shared in a March 1946 lecture that Arab youth ended the war committed to change but not in the British mold, as "For five years they had been brought up to applaud the courage and admire the triumphs of 'resistant groups' struggling with occupying armies."[61] It was surely cold comfort to the British as they watched the application of these wartime lessons at their expense in the tumultuous postwar years, a fulfillment of longstanding warnings raised by British and Arab observers alike of the problems that would develop if they failed to address these issues.

One of the challenges of studying informal empire is to determine when, precisely, it comes to an end, as it is not always as clear as a declaration of independence and a formal ceremony transferring authority.[62] A range of powerful postwar forces contributed to the decline of British imperial power in the Middle East: the crippling postwar British debt, the nascent Cold War rivalry, the transformed global security system, and anti-colonial nationalism driven by the experience of the war. In Egypt, the revolution of 1952, the final withdrawal of British troops from the Canal Zone, and the 1956 Suez Crisis effectively signaled the end of British influence, while the revolution of 1958 swept away British influence in Iraq. The events of the war years were enfolded into the narrative of the revolutions and decolonization, and the disastrous performance of the Arab armies in the 1948 war reinforced the wartime critiques that Britain had deliberately undermined the formation of effective armies, with the complicity of the increasingly corrupt monarchies and pro-British politicians. This was the ultimate indictment of the "three-legged stool" in Egypt and the old gang in Iraq, the backbone of Britain's patron-client networks and empire by treaty in both countries. With the revolutions they were finally removed from power, and British influence fell along with them.

Notes

Introduction

1 Elizabeth Monroe, *Britain's Moment in the Middle East 1914–1971*, new and revised edition (London: Chatto & Windus, 1981), 81.
2 For the long history of this term in the British Empire, see Saliha Belmessous, ed., *Empire by Treaty: Negotiating European Expansion, 1600–1900* (Oxford: Oxford University Press, 2015), and for the use of the term in the Middle Eastern context, see Matthew A. Fitzsimons, *Empire by Treaty: Britain and the Middle East in the Twentieth Century* (Notre Dame: University of Notre Dame Press, 1964).
3 Ashley Jackson, *The British Empire and the Second World War* (New York: Humbledon Continuum, 2006), 112.
4 Minute by Baggallay, 27 May 1940, FO 371/24580, The National Archives, UK [hereafter TNA].
5 Henderson to Secretary of State, 13 March 1944, file 800, Classified General Records, 1936–61, Iraq: U.S. Embassy and Legation, Baghdad, Record Group [RG] 84 Records of the Foreign Service Posts of the Department of State, the National Archives at College Park, College Park, MD [hereafter NACPM].
6 Minute by Baggallay, 16 Jan. 1939, FO371/24570, TNA. In this regard there were important continuities with the interwar period, especially as many of the British officials involved in building these wartime organizations drew on their earlier experiences. For British intelligence in Iraq in the interwar period, see Martin Thomas, *Empires of Intelligence: Security Services and Colonial Disorder after 1914* (Berkeley: University of California Press, 2008) and Priya Satia, *Spies in Arabia: The Great War and the Cultural Foundations of Britain's Covert Empire in the Middle East* (New York: Oxford University Press, 2008).
7 In light of these limitations, extensive endnotes are provided to point to key texts that fill in these gaps.
8 Laurence Grafftey-Smith, *Bright Levant* (London: John Murray, 1970), 223.
9 George Kirk cites Iraqi scholar Majid Khadduri's observation that: "The Iraqi Government seem to have interpreted the minimum provisions of Article 5 as the maximum to which the British were entitled at any time, and to have ignored Article 4." Quoted in George Kirk, *The Middle East in the War* (New York: Oxford University Press, 1953), 69.
10 Speech by the Secretary of State for Foreign Affairs at the Signature of the Anglo-Egyptian Treaty, 26 August 1936, FO371/20118, TNA.
11 Menzies, at the Dominions High Commissioners meeting in London with Eden quoted in Malcolm Yapp, ed., *Politics and Diplomacy in Egypt: The Diaries of Sir Miles Lampson 1935-1937* (Oxford: Oxford University Press for the British Academy, 1997), 592.
12 Huda Sha'rawi, interview in *al-Musawwar* enclosed in Kelly to Eden, 28 September 1936, FO 371/20119, TNA. For a summary of the arguments the Egyptian political parties made in support of or against the treaty in the 1936 debates, see Hoda Gamal

Abdel Nasser, *Britain and the Egyptian Nationalist Movement, 1936–52* (Reading: Ithaca Press, 1994), 20–6.

13 John Darwin, "An Undeclared Empire: The British in the Middle East, 1918–39," *Journal of Imperial and Commonwealth History* 27, no. 2 (1999): 170 provides a valuable overview of the broader regional perspective. For the strategic significance of the region on the eve of the war, see Committee of Imperial Defence, "Strategic Importance of Egypt and the Arab Countries in the Middle East," Report by the Chiefs of Staff Sub-Committee, 14 January 1939, FO 371/23192, TNA; Steven Morewood, *The British Defence of Egypt 1935–1940: Conflict and Crisis in the Eastern Mediterranean* (London and New York: Frank Cass, 2005); Martin Kolinsky, *Britain's War in the Middle East: Strategy and Diplomacy, 1936–42* (New York: St. Martin's Press, 1999); and Lawrence R. Pratt, *East of Malta, West of Suez: Britain's Mediterranean Crisis, 1936-1939* (Cambridge: Cambridge University Press, 1975).

14 For Iraq as an artery of empire, see *PAIFORCE: The Official Story of the Persia and Iraq Command 1941–46* (London: His Majesty's Stationery Office, 1948), 6 [Hereafter *PAIFORCE: The Official Story*]. Ashley Jackson notes: "It might be argued that the focus on the British Empire's defence of Egypt rather misses the point that this was primarily intended to protect what lay beyond it-the oil of Iran and Iraq-as well as the vital Suez Canal, which itself was prized not just as the 'Clapham Junction' of imperial sea communications, but as an artery through which Iranian oil could flow." Ashley Jackson, *Persian Gulf Command: A History of the Second World War in Iran and Iraq* (New Haven: Yale University Press, 2018), 2.

15 For an overview of Britain's oil interests in the early years of the war, see Anand Toprani, *Oil & the Great Powers: Britain & Germany, 1914–1945* (New York: Oxford University Press, 2019), 129–33.

16 For the history of the British Mandate in Iraq, see Peter Sluglett, *Britain in Iraq: Contriving King and Country, 1914–1932*, 2nd edition (New York: Columbia University Press, 2007). Susan Pedersen, "Getting Out of Iraq—in 1932: The League of Nations and the Road to Normative Statehood," *American Historical Review* 115, no. 4 (2010): 975–1000 and Susan Pedersen, *The Guardians: The League of Nations and the Crisis of Empire* (New York: Oxford University Press, 2015), 261–86 are particularly helpful for contextualizing the debate over the end of the Iraq mandate within the internationalist debates of the interwar period.

17 Lampson to Eden, 13 January 1936, quoted in Laila Morsy, "The Military Clauses of the Anglo-Egyptian Treaty of Friendship and Alliance, 1936," *International Journal of Middle East Studies* 16, no. 1 (March 1984): 71.

18 For the strategic considerations behind the negotiations of the Anglo-Egyptian Treaty from the perspective of British defense in light of the Italian threat, see Morewood, *The British Defence of Egypt*, 66–108. For the Egyptian political context, see Malcolm Yapp's introduction to *Politics and Diplomacy in Egypt*, 13–44.

19 Anglo-Iraqi treaty Article 4 and Anglo-Egyptian Treaty Article 7. For the text of the Anglo-Egyptian Treaty, see ibid., Appendix 3, 984–93. For the complete text of the 1930 Anglo-Iraqi Treaty and published notes, see Mohammad A. Tarbush, *The Role of the Military in Politics: A Case Study of Iraq to 1941* (London: Keegan Paul, 1982), Appendix IV, 198–222. For analysis of the treaties, see Majid Khadduri, *Independent Iraq: A Study in Iraqi Politics since 1932* (London, 1951) and Morsy, "The Military Clauses of the Anglo-Egyptian Treaty of Friendship and Alliance." Monroe, *Britain's Moment in the Middle East*, 74–9, provides an interesting comparison of Britain's relations with Egypt and Iraq during the interwar period of treaty negotiation.

20 I.S.O. Playfair, *The Mediterranean and Middle East*, vol. 1, to May 1941 (London: Her Majesty's Stationery Office, 1954), 14–15. For the negotiations surrounding the retention of these air bases and the Iraqi levies, see Daniel Silverfarb, *Britain's Informal Empire in the Middle East* (New York: Oxford University Press, 1986), 23–32 and 47–55.
21 Minute by Baggallay, 3 July 1939, FO 371/23210, TNA.
22 Tarbush, *The Role of the Military in Politics*, 75; Morsy, "The Military Clauses of the Anglo-Egyptian Treaty of Friendship and Alliance," 76–7.
23 See for example Major Hill, 1 October 1940 and comments 14 and 18 February 1941, WO 208/1586, TNA.
24 English translation of Nahhas's speech at the signing of the Anglo-Egyptian Treaty, 26 August 1936, FO 371/20118, TNA.
25 For a biographical sketch of Sir Miles Lampson and details on the residency's structure at the time of the treaty negotiations, see Malcolm Yapp's introduction to *Politics and Diplomacy in Egypt*, 1–13.

Chapter 1

1 For the details of the defense measures undertaken in Egypt in response to Munich, see Playfair, *The Mediterranean and Middle East*, vol. 1, 17–18 and "Political Review of the Year 1938," enclosed in Lampson to Halifax, 15 May 1939, FO 371/23366, TNA.
2 C.H. Bateman's record of conversation with Takla Pasha, 31 January 1939 enclosed in Lampson to Halifax, 10 February 1939, FO 371/23304, TNA. For a deeper assessment of Egyptian press coverage of Munich, see Israel Gershoni and James P. Jankowski, *Confronting Fascism in Egypt: Dictatorship Versus Democracy in the 1930s* (Stanford: Stanford University Press, 2010), 71–6.
3 Minute by R.W.J. Hooper, 23 November 1938, and Lampson to Halifax, 7 November 1938, FO 371/21948, TNA.
4 For the text of the treaty, see Malcolm Yapp, *Politics and Diplomacy in Egypt*, Appendix 3, 984–93.
5 *Egyptian Gazette* cutting, "Sidky Pasha Explains," 2 January 1939, and French text of Debate, enclosed in Lampson to Halifax, 22 December 1938, FO 371/23304, TNA.
6 Lampson to FO, 22 December 1938; "The Treaty with Egypt," *Times* (UK), 31 December 1938; Cartoon in *al-Lata'if al-Musawwara*, enclosed in Lampson to Oliphant, 13 January 1939, FO 371/21949, TNA.
7 Lampson two-month review, 16 January 1939, FO 371/23304, TNA.
8 The extent to which the Arab world embraced fascism and the relationship between Arab leaders and the Nazi regime have been the subject of robust debate. Recent scholarship drawing on Arabic sources has challenged the assumption of widespread Arab support for the Axis powers by focusing on the multi-faceted debates in the public sphere and providing a useful balance to the Foreign Office records: Gershoni and Jankowski, *Confronting Fascism in Egypt*; Peter Wien, *Iraqi Arab Nationalism: Authoritarian, Totalitarian, and Pro-Fascist Inclinations, 1932–1941* (New York: Routledge, 2006); Orit Bashkin, *The Other Iraq: Pluralism and Culture in Hashemite Iraq* (Stanford: Stanford University Press, 2009); Orit Bashkin, "Iraqi Shadows, Iraqi Lights: Anti-Fascist and Anti-Nazi Voices in Monarchic Iraq, 1932–1941," in *Arab Responses to Fascism and Nazism: Attraction and Repulsion*, ed. Israel Gershoni

(Austin: University of Texas Press, 2014), 141–68 and the other essays in that edited volume. For a critique of this approach, see Michael J. Cohen, *Britain's Moment in Palestine: Retrospect and Perspectives, 1917–1948* (New York: Routledge, 2014), 388–94; see also Jeffrey Herf, *Nazi Propaganda for the Arab World* (New Haven: Yale University Press, 2009). For a useful historiographical overview, see Israel Gershoni's "Introduction: An Analysis of Arab Responses to Fascism and Nazism in Middle Eastern Studies," in *Arab Responses to Fascism and Nazism*, 1–31 and Peter Wien, "Coming to Terms with the Past: German Academia and Historical Relations between the Arab Lands and Nazi Germany," *International Journal of Middle East Studies* 42, no. 2 (May 2010): 311–21.

9 Maurice Peterson, "Note on the habitual sequence of political changes in the Government of Egypt," 27 January 1942, FO 371/31566, TNA; Kolinsky, *Britain's War in the Middle East*, 47.

10 French text of Debate, enclosed in Lampson to Halifax, 22 December 1938, FO 371/23304, TNA (my translation).

11 Bateman to Halifax, 25 August 1939, FO 371/23306, TNA.

12 Lampson to Halifax, 23 December 1938; Lampson to FO, 5 January 1939, FO 371/23304, TNA. For Italian propaganda in Egypt, see Manuela A. Williams, *Mussolini's Propaganda Abroad: Subversion in the Mediterranean and the Middle East, 1935–1940* (New York: Routledge, 2006), 36–7.

13 Lampson to Halifax, 3 February 1939, FO371/23304, TNA. Steven Morewood notes that "Of the 70,000 Italians resident in Egypt by the mid-1930s, no less than 25,000 belonged to the local fascist organization." Morewood, *The British Defence of Egypt*, 27.

14 "Political Review of the Year 1938," 15 May 1939, FO 371/23366, TNA.

15 Lampson to FO, 31 March 1939, FO 371/23305, TNA.

16 Hindle James account of conversation with Nahhas, 28 April 1939, FO 371/23305, TNA.

17 Lampson to Halifax, 3 February 1939, FO 371/23304, TNA.

18 Ibid.

19 Lampson to Oliphant, 15 February 1939, FO 371/23304, TNA.

20 Richard Mitchell, *The Society of the Muslim Brothers* (London: Oxford University Press, 1969), 15–30. For the Caliphate campaign and Egyptian views on the Arab revolt and Palestine, see Israel Gershoni and James P. Jankowski, *Redefining the Egyptian Nation, 1930–1945* (Cambridge: Cambridge University Press, 1995), 158–64 and 166–90. For the ways in which the Muslim Brotherhood and Young Egypt engaged with the debates over fascism and democracy, see Gershoni and Jankowski, *Confronting Fascism in Egypt*, 210–65. Kolinsky, *Britain's War in the Middle East: Strategy and Diplomacy, 1936–42*, 43–4, provides a helpful overview of the Palestine issue in Egypt.

21 Cohen, *Britain's Moment in Palestine*, 245–84 and 292–304 provide an assessment of the Arab Revolt and the 1939 St. James Conference and the White Paper in light of British strategic considerations that serves as valuable context for the Egyptian and Iraqi debates over Palestine.

22 "Political Review of the Year 1938," 15 May 1939, FO 371/23366, TNA.

23 Morewood, *The British Defence of Egypt*, 112–19 and 159–62 examine the defense implications of Munich and the British military response in Egypt.

24 Russell Pasha to Kelly, 27 February 1939, FO371/23304, TNA.

25 Harold E. Raugh, Jr., *Wavell in the Middle East, 1939–1941: A Study in Generalship* (Norman: University of Oklahoma Press, 2013), 46.
26 "Political Review of the Year 1938," 15 May 1939, FO 371/23366, TNA.
27 Playfair, *The Mediterranean and Middle East*, vol. 1, 35–6.
28 Minute by Cavendish-Bentinck, 12 January 1939 and Vansittart to Air Ministry, 16 January 1939, FO 371/23304, TNA.
29 Cohen, *Britain's Moment in Palestine*, 263–4; "Political Review of the Year 1938," 15 May 1939, FO 371/23366, TNA.
30 Playfair, *The Mediterranean and Middle East*, vol. 1, 5–38 and 74–80.
31 "Political Review of the Year 1938," 15 May 1939, FO 371/23366, TNA; "Political Review of the Year 1939," enclosure in Lampson to Halifax, 8 February 1940, FO 407/224, TNA.
32 Playfair, *The Mediterranean and Middle East*, vol. 1, 5.
33 "Army Council Instructions to the General Officer Commanding-in-Chief in the Middle East," 24 July 1939, reprinted as Appendix 1, Playfair, *The Mediterranean and Middle East*, vol. 1, 457.
34 "Political Review of the Year 1938," 15 May 1939, FO 371/23366, TNA. Charles Tripp, "Ali Mahir and the Politics of the Egyptian Army, 1936–1942," in *Contemporary Egypt: Through Egyptian Eyes*, ed. Charles Tripp (New York: Routledge, 1993), 45–71 traces the army's politicization in the late 1930s.
35 P.J. Vatikiotis notes: "Of the eleven men who composed the founding committee of the Free Officers group in late 1949, eight entered the Academy in 1936" in *The Egyptian Army in Politics: Pattern for New Nations?* (Bloomington: Indiana University press, 1961), 45.
36 Morewood, *The British Defence of Egypt*, 124–5 and 154–5; Lampson diary, 12 November 1937, in Yapp, ed., *Politics and Diplomacy in Egypt*, 923. For the early years of the military mission, see James Marshall-Cornwall, *Wars and Rumours of Wars: A Memoir* (London: Leo Cooper, 1984), 106–18.
37 "Political Review of the Year 1938," 15 May 1939, FO 371/23366, TNA; Morewood, *The British Defence of Egypt*, 163.
38 "Political Review of the Year 1939," 8 February 1940, FO 407/224, TNA; Maitland Wilson, *Eight Years Overseas* (London: Hutchinson & Co., 1949), 23.
39 Playfair, *The Mediterranean and Middle East*, vol. 1, 31–5.
40 J.C. Walton, India Office to Leeper, 26 May 1939, FO 395/650, TNA.
41 Morewood, *The British Defence of Egypt*, 133–7; Wilson, *Eight Years Overseas*, 24; Playfair, *The Mediterranean and Middle East*, vol. 1, 38.
42 Houstoun-Boswall to Halifax, 4 Oct 1938, FO371/21861, TNA.
43 For interwar Iraq and the politicization of the army: Majid Khadduri, *Independent Iraq*, 20–3; Adeed Dawisha, *Iraq: A Political History from Independence to Occupation* (Princeton: Princeton University Press, 2009), 51–62 and 92–8; Reeva Spector Simon, *Iraq between the Two World Wars: The Militarist Origins of Tyranny*, updated edition (New York: Columbia University Press, 2004), 107–33.
44 Minute by Crosthwaite, 2 October 1939, FO 371/23202, TNA.
45 Michael Eppel, *The Palestine Conflict in the History of Modern Iraq: The Dynamics of Involvement 1928–1948* (Ilford, Essex: Frank Cass, 1994), 41–9 and 86–90.
46 Ministry of Foreign Affairs (Iraq) to Council of Ministers, March 1939, enclosed in Houstoun-Boswall to Halifax, 4 April 1939, FO371/23210, TNA.
47 Houstoun-Boswall to Halifax, 3 April 1939, enclosing text of Nuri's broadcast speech 30 March 1939, FO 371/23210, TNA.

48 RAF monthly intelligence summaries for Iraq, March 1939, FO 371/23213, TNA.
49 RAF monthly intelligence summaries for Iraq, March–July 1939, FO 371/23213, TNA.
50 Baghdad report on "German propaganda activities," 17 June 1939 and Newton to Halifax, 11 July 1939, FO 371/23203; Newton to Halifax, 8 December 1939, FO 371/23202, TNA.
51 RAF monthly Intelligence Summary Iraq August 1939, FO 371/23213, TNA.
52 Minute by Cavendish-Bentinck, 6 July 1939 and Minute by Crosthwaite, 30 June 1939, FO 371/23210, TNA.
53 Edmonds' extensive personal papers, including the diary he kept throughout his service in Iraq, are held at the Middle East Centre Archive, St. Antony's College, Oxford, and provide a wealth of information on his work with the Kurds and an insider's perspective on Iraqi politics.
54 Major Hill, 1 October 1940 and comments 14 and 18 February 1941, WO 208/1586, TNA.
55 Newton to Air Vice-Marshal J.H.S. Tyssen, 12 October 1939, FO 371/23202, TNA.
56 Newton to Halifax, 15 January 1940, FO 371/24557, TNA.
57 RAF Intelligence Summary July and October 1939, FO 371/23213, TNA.
58 Merry (Air Ministry) to Crosthwaite, 24 August 1939, encloses memo, I Branch memorandum, "Tribal situation in Lower and Middle Euphrates Areas," 5 July 1939, FO 371/23202; RAF Intelligence summary August 1939, FO 371/23213, TNA.
59 For Grobba's activities in Iraq, see Simon, *Iraq between the Two World Wars,* 31–40.
60 Peterson to FO, 22 December 1938, FO 371/23202, TNA.
61 J.P. Domvile, Air Liaison Officer, Baghdad report on "German propaganda activities," 17 June 1939, FO 371/23203, TNA.
62 For Axis influence in the Iraqi educational system, see Simon, *Iraq between the Two World Wars,* 69–105. For the Futuwwa Movement, see Wien, *Iraqi Arab Nationalism,* 88–98.
63 Newton to Lloyd, 4 July 1939, FO624/17, TNA.
64 Translation of press statement in *al-Istiqlal,* "Higher Objects of the 'Futua' Organisation" enclosed Newton to Halifax, 5 July 1939; Houstoun-Boswall to Halifax, 20 May 1939, FO 371/23217, TNA.
65 J.P. Domvile, Air Liaison Officer, Baghdad report on "German propaganda activities," 17 June 1939, FO 371/23203, TNA.
66 Newton to Halifax 21 June 1939 and 14 August 1939, FO 371/23217, TNA.
67 Minute by Houstoun-Boswell, 28 September 1939, FO 624/16, TNA.
68 Leaper to Shuckburgh, 13 May 1939, FO 395/650, TNA.
69 Houstoun-Boswall to FO, 6 April 1939 and Minute by Crosthwaite, 11 April 1939, FO 371/23201; Peterson to Oliphant, 31 December 1938, FO 371/23207, TNA.
70 Ogilvie-Forbes (Berlin) to FO, 12 April 1939, FO 371/23201, TNA. Batatu, writing in the 1970s, discussed the "doubts that still surround the incident," in particular focusing on the suspicion that Ghazi's death was plotted by Nuri, the future regent, and his sister, Ghazi's wife. Hanna Batatu, *The Old Social Classes and the Revolutionary Movements of Iraq* (Princeton: Princeton University Press, 1978), 343–4.
71 Translation of *al-Bilad* press extract, 17 May 1939 enclosed in Houstoun-Boswall to Halifax, 18 May 1939, FO 371/23201, TNA.
72 Houstoun-Boswall to FO, 4 April 1939, FO 371/23200, TNA; Simon, *Iraq between the Two World Wars,* 39.
73 RAF Intelligence Summary April 1939, FO 371/23213, TNA.

74 Memorandum by Somers Cocks enclosed in Houstoun-Boswall to FO, 13 April 1939, FO 371/23201, TNA.
75 See Philip Taylor, *The Projection of Britain: British Overseas Publicity and Propaganda 1919–1939* (Cambridge: Cambridge University Press, 1981), 103–114 for the concept of "national projection" in the interwar period.
76 "Meeting in Lord Lloyd's Room to Discuss Possibilities of Propaganda in Moslem Countries," 14 April 1939, FO 395/650, TNA.
77 Quoted in summary of the Egyptian press, 3 May 1939–5 August 1939, FO 371/23364, TNA.

Chapter 2

1 Quoted in Anwar al-Sadat, *In Search of Identity: An Autobiography* (New York: Harper and Row, 1978), 27.
2 *État de siege* was short of martial law, as General Wilson described it: "the Governors of Cairo and Alexandria were appointed to control these areas and a special military governor was appointed to the Canal Zone, while the Prime Minister, who also held the portfolio of Minister of the Interior, became Military Governor over the whole of Egypt." Wilson, *Eight Years Overseas*, 23–4.
3 Newton to FO, 29 August 1939, FO 371/23211, TNA; Khadduri, *Independent Iraq*, 142–3; RAF Monthly Intelligence Summary September 1939, FO 371/23213, TNA.
4 Killearn Diaries, 2, 3, 4, 7, 8, and 9 September 1939, Middle East Centre Archives, St. Antony's College, Oxford [hereafter MECA].
5 Newton to FO, 25 August 1939, FO 371/23211, TNA.
6 Minute by Kelly, 8 September 1939, FO 371/23211; RAF monthly Intelligence Summary Iraq September 1939, FO 371/23213, TNA.
7 'Abd al-Rahman 'Azzam, *Safahat min al-Mudhakkirat al-Sirriya li-Awwal Amin 'Amm lil-Jami'at al-'Arabiyya* (Cairo: al-Maktab al-Misri al-Hadith, 1977), 255.
8 Newton to FO, 7 September 1939, FO 371/23211, TNA; Taha el Hashimi, *Mudhakkirat Taha al-Hashimi, 1919–1943* (Beirut: Dar al-Ta'li'ah, 1967), 315.
9 Killearn Diaries, 7 and 29 September 1939, MECA.
10 Newton to Iraqi Minister Foreign Affairs, 25 September 1939, FO 371/23212, TNA.
11 Minute by Kelly, 4 December 1939, FO 371/23307, TNA.
12 FO to Newton, 9 September 1939, FO 371/23211, TNA.
13 Jean Lugol, *Egypt and World War II: The Anti-Axis Campaigns in the Middle East*, translated by A.G. Mitchell (Cairo: Société Orientale de Publicité, 1945), 18; Raugh, *Wavell in the Middle East*, 47–51.
14 Lampson to Halifax, 8 November 1939, FO 371/23307, TNA.
15 RAF monthly Intelligence Summary Iraq October and November 1939, FO 371/23213, TNA.
16 Ibid.
17 Baggallay to Hammond, 15 December 1939, FO 371/23212, TNA.
18 This section draws on Ronald Robinson's classic article, "Non-European Foundations of European Imperialism: Sketch for a Theory of Collaboration," 1972, reprinted in Wm. Roger Louis, ed., *Imperialism: The Robinson and Gallagher Controversy* (New York: New Viewpoints, 1976) and Colin Newbury, *Patrons, Clients, and Empire: Chieftaincy and Over-rule in Asia, Africa, and the Pacific* (Oxford: Oxford University

Press, 2003), 128–51. Newbury prefers the term "patron-client relationship" to Robinson's "collaboration" because the latter term "misses two essential points inherent in patron-client relations: differences in status and the 'mediating mechanism' common to the brokerage roles of both chiefs and European officials," a distinction that is helpful to keep in mind in the context of Egypt and Iraq (ibid., 262).

19 Minute by Baggallay, 27 May 1940, FO 371/24580, TNA.

20 Lampson to Kelly, 20 September 1939, FO 371/23307, TNA.

21 Bateman to Halifax, 25 August 1939, FO 371/23306, TNA.

22 Lampson to FO, 3 January 1940 and Minute by Thompson, 13 January 1940, FO 371/24622, TNA.

23 Arthur Goldschmidt, Jr., *Biographical Dictionary of Modern Egypt* (Cairo: The American University in Cairo Press, 2000), 220–1. The British documents use the spelling "Amin Osman."

24 Sterndale Bennett to Halifax, 9 August 1939, FO371/23364, TNA.

25 Minute by Kelly, 27 September 1939, FO 371/23307, TNA.

26 Lampson to 'Ali Mahir, 17 January 1940, Lampson to Halifax, 7 February 1940, FO 371/24623; Halifax to Lampson, 17 February 1940, TNA.

27 Tripp, "Ali Mahir and the politics of the Egyptian army," 50–4.

28 "Political Review of the Year 1939," 8 February 1940, FO 407/224, TNA.

29 Lampson to Eden, 28 January 1941, "Political Review of the Year 1940," FO371/27463, TNA. Tripp, "Ali Mahir and the Politics of the Egyptian army," 55–8; Anwar al-Sadat, *Revolt on the Nile* (New York: The John Day Company, 1957), 35.

30 RAF monthly Intelligence Summary December 1938, FO 371/23213, TNA.

31 Comment by the Iraqi Chargé d'Affaires in Egypt, Lampson to Halifax, 16 June 1939, FO 371/23210, TNA; RAF Monthly Intelligence Summary Iraq, November 1939, FO 371/23213, TNA.

32 Simon, *Iraq between the Two World Wars,* 117.

33 Minute by Crosthwaite, 9 February 1940, FO371/24557, TNA.

34 Minute by Seymour, 15 February 1940, FO 371/24557; Newton to Halifax, 27 February 1940, FO 371/24557, TNA.

35 Minute by Baggallay, 13 February 1940, FO 371/24557, TNA.

36 Minute by Thompson, 12 February 1940, FO 371/24623, TNA.

37 Portions of this analysis of British wartime propaganda draw on the author's previously published work, used here by permission of the original publishers: Stefanie Wichhart, "'Innocent Efforts': The Brotherhood of Freedom in the Middle East during World War II," in *Allied Communication during the Second World War: National and Transnational Networks*, ed. Simon Eliot and Marc Wiggam (London: Bloomsbury Academic, 2019), 185–202; and "'What Britain Has Done for Islam': British Propaganda to the Islamic World during World War II, 1939–1942," in *Britain and the Islamic World: Imperial and Post-Imperial Connections*, ed. Justin Quinn Olmstead (Palgrave Macmillan, 2019), 197–223.

38 Minute by Thompson, 24 November 1939, FO 371/23307, TNA.

39 Lampson to FO, 1 September 1939, FO 371/23306, TNA.

40 Killearn Diaries, 21 July 1940, MECA.

41 Killearn Diaries, 14 September 1939, MECA.

42 Minute by Warner, 30 April 1939, FO 395/650, TNA.

43 RAF monthly Intelligence summary, October 1939, FO 371/23213, TNA.

44 Minute by Main to Holt, 17 April 1940, FO 624/20, TNA.

45 Napier, "Memorandum on Press Activities in Cairo," 4 January 1940, FO 371/24619, TNA.
46 Ibid.
47 Lampson to Halifax, 31 March 1939, FO 371/23363, TNA.
48 Sterndale Bennett to Halifax, 9 August 1939, FO 371/23364, TNA.
49 Lampson to Halifax, no. 1506, 7 December 1939, encloses undated "Report on the Staff locally recruited for the Publicity Section, British Embassy, Cairo, and on future publicity expenditure." FO930/123, TNA; Memorandum by Baggallay, "Counter-Espionage in the Middle East," 19 September 1939 and Minute by Kelly, 19 September 1939, FO371/23192, TNA.
50 Lampson to Halifax, 5 April 1939 enclosing Secret Memorandum on Counter-Propaganda by the Oriental Secretariat, FO 371/23342, TNA.
51 Bromilow, Head of the British Military Mission to Iraq, "Morale and Attitude of the Iraqi Army on May 14, 1942" enclosed in Cornwallis to Eden, 21 May 1942, WO208/1586, TNA.
52 Edmonds Diaries, 27 September 1939, MECA.
53 Minute by Main, 9 October 1939, and related correspondence in FO 624/15, TNA.
54 RAF monthly intelligence summary, October 1939, FO 371/23213, TNA.
55 Minute by Crosthwaite, 10 November 1939 and draft letter, 14 November 1939, FO 37/23202, TNA.
56 Minute by Rushbrook Williams, 30 March 1941, FO 371/27101, TNA.
57 Kelly to Major-General Beaumont-Nesbitt, 6 December 1939, FO371/23393, TNA.
58 Cook to Freese-Pennefather, 31 May 1940, FO 371/24548, TNA. This file includes a whole series of correspondence from British officials and civilians living in the region, criticizing the broadcasts.
59 R. Davies, "Report on the Work of the Publicity Section British Embassy, Cairo," 7 March 1941, FO 371/27443, TNA.
60 Wood, "Notes Concerning the Distribution of Propaganda Films," 1939 and Newton to Halifax, 25 September 1939, FO 624/16, TNA.
61 RAF monthly intelligence summary, October 1939, FO 371/23213, TNA.
62 "Note Conditions in Iraq," 24 April 1940, included in Lawrence to Vansittart, 25 April 1940, and Minute by Crosthwaite, 30 April 1940, FO 371/24558, TNA.
63 "Note on the Work of the Brotherhood of the Free (Ikhwan al Hurriya) 1940–1945," 28 November 1945, N. Farquhar Oliver, FO 930/36, TNA.
64 R. Davies, "Report on the Work of the Publicity Section British Embassy, Cairo," September 1939–February 1941, 7 March 1941, FO 371/27443, TNA.
65 Rushbrook Williams memorandum, 6 January 1941, and SOE Middle East and Balkans-Activities of Directorate of Special Propaganda, 10 April 1942, FO898/113, TNA.
66 Edmonds report on "Russia and the Kurds," 15 February 1940 enclosed in Houstoun-Boswall to FO, 12 March 1940, FO 371/24560, TNA.
67 P.R.C. Groves to Brooks, 6 May 1940, FO 898/113, TNA.
68 Grafftey-Smith, *Bright Levant*, 214.
69 R. Davies, 7 March 1941, FO 371/27443, TNA.
70 Adrian O'Sullivan, *The Baghdad Set: Iraq through the Eyes of British Intelligence, 1941–45* (Palgrave Macmillan, 2019), 9–21 and Appendix A, 261–2 provide a useful examination of Stark's career that points to a longer-term relationship with the world of British intelligence.
71 Report by Miss Freya Stark, January 1941, Appendix D in R. Davies, "Report on the Work of the Publicity Section British Embassy, Cairo," 7 March 1941, FO 371/27443, TNA.

72 Dalton to Wavell, 10 June 1941, FO 898/113, TNA. For SOE in the Middle East, see Saul Kelly, "A Succession of Crises: SOE in the Middle East, 1940–45," *Intelligence and National Security* 20, no. 1 (2005): 121–46.
73 "A Report on the Political Tendencies in Egypt Drawn up from Observations Made during the Period December 27th, 1939 to February 3rd, 1940" Dr. Heyworth-Dunne, FO371/24623, and "Propaganda and Intelligence Work Carried Out by Dr. J. Heyworth-Dunne for the Arab-Moslem Area of the Middle East Command during March-May 1941," FO 898/113; Lampson to Hopkinson, 17 October 1940, FO371/24627, TNA.
74 Minute by Rushbrook Williams, 28 November 1940, FO 371/24627, TNA.
75 Donovan to Woodburn, 28 July 1941, FO930/124, TNA.
76 Grafftey-Smith, *Bright Levant*, 215.
77 Minute by Rushbrook Williams, 5 September 1940, INF1/874, TNA.
78 Minute by Bateman, 31 March, 1940, Minute to Jebb, 10 October 1940, FO 898/113, TNA.
79 For the scathing critiques of SOE in the Middle East in this period, see Kelly, "A Succession of Crises," 123–9.
80 R. Davies, "Report on the Work of the Publicity Section British Embassy, Cairo," September 1939–February 1941, 7 March 1941, FO 371/27443, TNA.
81 Mackereth to Rushbrook Williams, 13 December 1939, FO 371/23548, TNA.
82 Lampson to Eden, 28 January 1941, FO 371/27463/J349.
83 Lampson to FO, 1 April 1940, FO 371/24624, TNA.
84 FO to Lampson, 4 April 1940, FO 371/24624, TNA.
85 Lampson to Halifax, 4 May 1940, FO 371/24623, TNA; Abdel Nasser, *Britain and the Egyptian Nationalist Movement,* 54–6.
86 Proceedings of Parliament, Chamber of Deputies, 6 April 1940 enclosed in Newton to Halifax, 20 May 1940, FO371/24558, TNA.
87 Ibid.

Chapter 3

1 Baggallay to Mallaby, 20 June 1940, FO 371/24558, TNA.
2 Killearn Diaries, 17 June 1940, MECA.
3 For the full implications of the fall of France for British strategy in the Mediterranean and Middle East, see Playfair, *The Mediterranean and Middle East,* vol. 1, 125–30. Kolinsky, *Britain's War in the Middle East*, 93–122 provides a helpful overview of the strategic situation in the early months of the war. For a narrative history: Douglas Porch, *The Path to Victory: The Mediterranean Theater in World War II* (New York: Farrar, Straus, and Giroux, 2004). For the implications for the French colonies: Martin Thomas, *The French Empire at War 1940–45* (New York: Manchester University press, 1998), 38–45.
4 War Cabinet "Despatch of Troops to Iraq. Memorandum by the Chiefs of Staff," 29 June 1940, FO 371/24558, TNA.
5 Winston Churchill, *The Second World War*, vol. 2, *Their Finest Hour* (Boston: Houghton Mifflin Company, 1949), 452.
6 Lampson to Halifax, 12 April 1940, FO 371/24624, TNA.
7 Lampson to Eden, 28 January 1941, FO 371/27463, TNA.

8 Newton to FO, 13 June 1940, FO 371/24561, TNA.
9 Edmonds Diaries, 20 and 27 June 1940, MECA; Edmonds to Newton, 1 July 1940, FO 371/24561, TNA.
10 Edmonds to Newton, 1 July 1940, FO 371/24561, TNA.
11 Minute by Kelly, 28 February 1939, FO 371/23304, TNA.
12 Lampson to FO, 13 June 1940, FO 371/24625, TNA.
13 Lampson to Seymour, 29 January 1940, FO 371/24623, TNA.
14 Lampson to Halifax, 4 May 1940, FO 371/24623, TNA; Abdel Nasser, *Britain and the Egyptian Nationalist Movement,* 56.
15 Killearn Diaries, 6 June 1940, MECA.
16 Translation of King Farouk's message, 19 June 1940, and Aide Memoire presented by the Egyptian Ambassador, 18 June 1940, FO 371/24625, TNA.
17 FO to Lampson, 20 June 1940, Lampson to FO, 21 June 1940, and Lampson to FO, 23 June 1940, FO 371/24625, TNA; Killearn Diaries, 23 and 24 June 1940, MECA.
18 Lampson to Halifax, 8 October 1940, FO 371/24627, TNA.
19 Killearn Diaries, 28 June 1940, MECA.
20 Minute by Thompson, 13 December 1940, FO 371/24634, TNA.
21 Lampson to FO, 29 June 1940 and Minute by Norton, 1 July 1940, FO 371/24625, TNA.
22 Raugh, *Wavell in the Middle East,* 64–5.
23 Wilson, *Eight Years Overseas,* 38–40.
24 Lugol, *Egypt and World War II,* 110.
25 Shone to Halifax, 21 September 1940 enclosing Ahmad Husayn, "Statement by the Young Egypt Party on the Present situation," FO 371/24634, TNA. See also Kirk, *The Middle East in the War,* 194–5.
26 Lampson to Eden, 28 January 1941, FO 371/27463, TNA.
27 Lampson to FO, 21 September 1940, FO 371/24626, TNA.
28 Churchill to Halifax, 24 September 1940; Halifax to Churchill, 25 September 1940, G.H. Thompson, "Note on the Egyptian attitude towards war with Italy," 30 September 1940, FO 371/24634, TNA.
29 Parliamentary question, 6 November 1940; FO to Lampson, 10 and 12 December 1940; Lampson to FO, 13 and 14 December 1940; C in C Mediterranean Station to Lampson, 14 December 1940; Minute by Thompson, 13 December 1940 for Seymour, FO 371/24634, TNA.
30 Lampson to FO, 30 November 1940, FO 371/24627, TNA.
31 Playfair, *The Mediterranean and Middle East,* vol. 1, 42.
32 Wavell, "Operations in the Middle East from August, 1939 to November, 1940" published in the Third *Supplement to the London Gazette,* 13 June 1946.
33 Wilson, *Eight Years Overseas,* 24.
34 Ibid., 45; Tripp, "Ali Mahir and the Politics of the Egyptian Army, 1936–1942," 58–9.
35 Lampson to FO, 25 October 1940, FO 371/24626, TNA. Morewood, *The British Defence of Egypt,* 179.
36 Sadat, *Revolt on the Nile,* 24–5. Major A.W. Sansom, who served as Chief Field Security Officer in Cairo during the war, recounts his efforts in tracking anti-British sentiment in the Egyptian army in his memoir *I Spied Spies* (London: George G. Harrap, 1965).
37 Abdel Nasser, *Britain and the Egyptian Nationalist Movement,* 50–1.
38 Lampson to Seymour, 18 May 1940, and Newton to Seymour, 3 June 1940, FO371/24549, TNA.
39 Minute by Crosthwaite, 28 May 1940, FO371/24549, TNA.

40 Letter to Holt from Wing Commander, Air Staff Intelligence, dated 23 May 1940 enclosing report by Squadron Leader Marsack, Air Liaison Officer at Mosul, on "Enemy and Allied Publicity and Propaganda," 13 May 1940, FO 624/18; Newton to FO, 5 June 1940, FO 371/24558, TNA.
41 For an assessment of the Golden Square and the mufti and their role in Iraqi politics in 1940, see Simon, *Iraq between Two World Wars,* 121–31; Eppel, *The Palestine Conflict in the History of Modern Iraq,* 104–8.
42 Eastern Department Memo, April 3, 1940, FO 371/24548, TNA. For an overview of Iraqi weapons requests, see Silverfarb, *Britain's Informal Empire in the Middle East,* 74–86 and Simon, *Iraq between the Two World Wars,* 127–8.
43 Memo, Eastern Department, April 3, 1940, FO 371/24548, TNA.
44 War Cabinet Chiefs of Staff Committee, Minutes of Meeting, 15 October 1940, FO 371/24558, TNA.
45 Crosthwaite, FO Memo "The Despatch of British Troops to Iraq," 6 May 1941, FO 371/27068, TNA.
46 "War Cabinet. Internal Security in Iraq. Memorandum by the Chiefs of Staff Committee." 14 June 1940, and Seymour to Barlow, 21 June 1940, and FO to Newton, 21 June 1940, FO 371/24558, TNA. For an overview of the multiple plans considered for opening the lines of communication in Iraq, as well as the logistical arrangements, see Jackson, *Persian Gulf Command: A History of the Second World War in Iran and Iraq,* 29–37.
47 For the debates on bribery: Lampson to FO, 12 April 1940 and Minute by Crosthwaite, 13 April 1940, FO371/24546; Minute by Baggallay, 14 June 1940, FO 371/24558; Minute by Crosthwaite, 1 October 1940 FO371/24549, TNA.
48 War Office to GHQ ME, 24 June 1940, and FO to Newton, 5 July 1940, FO 371/24558, TNA.
49 Minute by Coverley Price, 18 June 1940 and Minute by Crosthwaite, 18 June 1940, FO 371/24558, TNA.
50 Mallaby, War Office to Baggallay, 8 July 1940, FO 371/24558, TNA.
51 Commander-in-chief, Middle East (C-in-C ME) to War Office, 9 July 1940, FO 371/24558, TNA. For background on this crisis, see Jackson, *Persian Gulf Command,* 15–16.
52 Governor General India to Sec. of State for India, 9 July 1940, FO371/24558, TNA.
53 Minute by Baggallay, 11 July 1940, FO 371/24558, TNA.
54 Crosthwaite, FO Memo "The Despatch of British Troops to Iraq," 6 May 1941, FO 371/27068, TNA.
55 FO to Newton, 12 August 1940, FO 371/24558, TNA.
56 Mallaby to Baggallay, 6 August 1940, FO 371/24558, TNA.
57 Silverfarb, *Britain's Informal Empire in the Middle East,* 103–5.
58 Minute by Baggallay, 12 July 1940, FO 371/24558, TNA.
59 Articles in *al-Istiqlal,* Newton to FO, 7 July 1940, and Edmonds to Newton, 10 October 1940, FO 371/24561, TNA.
60 War Cabinet "Despatch of Troops to Iraq. Memorandum by the Chiefs of Staff." 29 June 1940, FO 371/24558, TNA.
61 High Commissioner, Palestine to Sec. of State for Colonies, 7 August 1940, and 12 September 1940, FO 371/24569, TNA.
62 Royal Saudi Legation, 29 July 1940 and letter from *al-Ahram* journalist to Prince Feisal of Saudi Arabia, 29 July 1940, quoted in censorship summary, Michael Wright to Clifford Norton, 23 August 1940, FO 371/24634, TNA.
63 Edmonds to Newton, 10 October 1940, FO 371/24561, TNA.

64 The question of Nuri's talks with the Germans in 1940 has been the subject of much debate. The classic source is Majid Khadduri, "General Nuri's Flirtations with the Axis Powers," *Middle East Journal* 16, no. 3 (Summer 1962): 328–36 but for an overview of the larger debate, see also Simon, *Iraq between the Two World Wars*, 131–2. On the Newcombe mission and events of summer 1940: Eppel, *The Palestine Conflict in the History of Modern Iraq*, 97–100.
65 Minute by Coverley Price, 30 September 1940, FO371/24558, TNA.
66 Axis Declaration, 21 October 1940, FO 371/24549, TNA. The background to this declaration is discussed in detail in Geoffrey Warner, *Iraq and Syria 1941* (London: Davis-Poynter, 1974), 43–66.
67 Eastern Dept. 30 October 1940, WO208/1215, TNA.
68 Newton to FO, 26 and 27 November 1940 and FO to Newton 9 December 1940, FO 371/24559; Newton to OS, 29 September 1940, Edmonds to Holt, 5 September 1940 and Minute from Main to oriental secretary, 11 September 1940, FO 624/18, TNA.
69 Telegram from Commander-in-Chief, Middle East, to the War Office, 1 October 1940, annex to "War Cabinet. Chiefs of Staff Committee. Situation in Iraq. Memorandum by the Chief of the Imperial General Staff." 9 October 1940, FO 371/24558, TNA.
70 War Cabinet Chiefs of Staff Committee, Draft report on the situation in Iraq, 24 October 1940, and associated minutes, FO 371/24558, TNA.
71 War Cabinet, "An Advance by the Enemy through the Balkans and Syria to the Middle East," report by Chiefs of Staff, 1 November 1940, FO371/24549, TNA.
72 FO to Newton, 14 November 1940 and Newton to FO, 26 and 27 November 1940, FO 371/24559, TNA.
73 Newton to FO, 2 December 1940, FO 371/24559, TNA.
74 FO to Newton, 14 November 1940, FO 371/24558, TNA.
75 Minute by Seymour, 20 November 1940, FO 371/24626; Cawthorn for Mackenzie, from MICE to War Office, 3 December 1940, FO 371/24559, TNA.
76 Wavell, "Operations in the Western Desert from December 7, 1940, to February 7, 1941," 21 June 1941, reprinted in the *Supplement to the London Gazette*, 26 June 1946; Wilson, *Eight Years Overseas*, 50–64.
77 Lampson to Eden, 28 January 1941, FO371/27463, TNA.
78 Newton to FO, 14 December 1940, FO 371/24559, TNA.
79 Newton to Eden, 30 December 1940, FO 624/18, TNA.
80 Crosthwaite Foreign Office Memorandum, 6 May 1941, "The Despatch of British Troops to Iraq," FO 371/27068, TNA.
81 War Cabinet Chiefs of Staff Committee, Iraq: Note by Secretary, 30 January 1941 and War Cabinet, Chiefs of Staff Committee, "Extract from Minutes of Meeting held on 31st January, 1941, at 10.30 a.m." 371/27061, TNA. Newton to FO, 7 February 1941 and Seymour to Newton, 11 February 1941, FO 371/27062/E822.
82 Newton to FO, 30 January 1941, FO 371/27061 and Air Officer Commanding (AOC) to HQ RAF ME, 31 January 1941, FO 371/27061, Edmonds to Newton, 3 February 1941 enclosed in Newton to Baxter, 10 February 1941, FO 371/27062, TNA.

Chapter 4

1 Enclosure "Our Main Requirements from the Iraqi Government" in Newton to Eden, 17 February 1941, FO 371/27062, TNA.
2 Edmonds report, 1 April 1941, enclosed in Cornwallis to Eden, 6 April 1941, FO 371/27067, TNA.

3 Newton to FO, 2/7/1941 enclosing "Translation of Prime Minister's statement in the Chamber of Deputies, Bagdad, on February 6th 1941," FO 371/27062, and Newton to FO, 6 February 1941, FO 371/27061/E405.
4 Lt. Col. G.S. MO4, February 1941 and unnamed official, M.I.2(a), 18 February 1941, WO208/1586, TNA.
5 Baxter to Waterfield, 22 March 1941, FO 371/27062, TNA. For the pros and cons of the different types of financial pressure considered, including the impact on Iraq's oil industry, see Silverfarb, *Britain's Informal Empire in the Middle East,* 118–20.
6 FO to Newton, 9 January 1941, FO 624/22, TNA; David Dilks, ed., *The Diaries of Sir Alexander Cadogan, 1938–1945* (New York: G.P. Putnam's Sons, 1972), 355 (17 February 1941).
7 Newton to FO, 21 March 1941, FO 371/27062, TNA. For a detailed account of the 1941 Rashid 'Ali coup, see Silverfarb, *Britain's Informal Empire in the Middle East,* 123–41; Geoffrey Warner, *Iraq and Syria 1941* (London: Davis-Poynter, 1974). The official Iraqi assessment of the 1941 Rashid 'Ali coup can be found in the report of the Government of Iraq's investigating committee into the events of 1941, reprinted in 'Abd al-Razzaq al-Hasani, *Tarikh al-Wizarat al-'Iraqiyya*, vol. 5 (Sayda: Matba'at al-'Irfan, 1965), 272–82. For the British assessment, see Kirk, *The Middle East in the War*, 56–78.
8 Cornwallis to Seymour, 3 June 1941, FO 371/27076, and Cornwallis to Eden, Annual Review for 1941, 8 March 1942, FO 371/31371, TNA.
9 Statement of Chief of Staff of the Iraqi Army, published in *al-Zaman*, 4 April 1941, press extract enclosed in Embassy Bagdad to FO, 8 April 1941, FO 371/27069, TNA.
10 For translations of both speeches, see Cornwallis to Eden, 14 April 1941, FO 371/27069; Edmonds Diaries, 9 April 1941 and Cornwallis to FO, 10 April 1941, FO 371/27063, TNA.
11 Minute by Seymour, 7 January 1941, FO371/24626, TNA.
12 Leeper to Newton, 14 November 1939, FO 371/23202, TNA.
13 Leslie McLoughlin, *In a Sea of Knowledge: British Arabists in the Twentieth Century* (Reading: Ithaca Press, 2002), 51–2 and Martin Burton, "Cornwallis, Sir Kinahan," *Oxford Dictionary of National Biography*, vol. 13 (Oxford: Oxford University Press, 2004), 485–6.
14 Minute by Seymour to Cadogan, 21 November 1940, FO 371/24549, TNA.
15 Foreign Office Memorandum (Crosthwaite), "The Despatch of British Troops to Iraq," 6 May 1941, FO 371/27068, TNA.
16 Minutes by Crosthwaite and Butler, 1 April 1941, FO 371/27062, TNA.
17 Report by Edmonds, 1 April 1941 enclosed in Cornwallis to Eden, 6 April 1941, FO 371/27067, TNA.
18 Edmonds Diaries, 9 April 1941, MECA.
19 Cornwallis to FO, 3 April and 4 April 1941, Minute by Crosthwaite, 7 April 1941, FO 371/27062; Cornwallis to FO, 7 April 1941, FO 371/27063, TNA.
20 Memo for Cornwallis, from C.G. Hope Gill, 23 April 1941, Minute by Cornwallis, April 1941, FO 624/26, On Gill's appointment: FO to Newton, 28 February 1941, FO371/27049, TNA.
21 Cornwallis to FO, 9 April 1941, FO 371/27063, TNA.
22 Governor General to Sec of State for India, 13 April 1941, FO 371/27064, TNA.
23 Harold E. Raugh, Jr., *Wavell in the Middle East,* 1. Wavell's decision-making at this critical juncture in the war has been the subject significant analysis. For an overview of the debate sympathetic to Wavell, see ibid., 211–16. For Churchill's criticism, see

Churchill, *The Second World War*, vol. 3, *The Grand Alliance* (Boston: Houghton Mifflin Company, 1950), 256–8.

24 Cornwallis to FO, 11 April 1941, FO 371/27064, TNA.

25 FO to Baghdad, 13 April 1941, and FO to Cairo, 15 April 1941, FO 371/27064, TNA.

26 *PAIFORCE: The Official Story,* 20.

27 FO to Baghdad, 14 April 1941, FO 371/27064; Cornwallis to FO, 18 April 1941, FO 371/27065, TNA.

28 Cornwallis to FO, 21 April 1941, FO 371/27066, TNA.

29 FO to Baghdad, 22 April 1941, FO 371/27066, TNA.

30 Foreign Office Note, "Iraq. Note on the Treaty Position," 6 May 1941, FO 371/27068, TNA.

31 Minute by Baxter, 5 May 1941, FO 371/27092, TNA. For analysis of this point, see Daniel Silverfarb, *The Twilight of British Ascendancy in the Middle East: A Case Study of Iraq, 1941–50* (New York: St. Martin's Press, 1994), 4.

32 Cornwallis to FO, 25 April 1941, FO 371/27067; AHQ Iraq to MICE repeat Air Ministry, for Cawthorn from Jope, 23 April 1941, FO 371/27066, TNA.

33 Cornwallis to Eden, 6 June 1941, FO 371/27077 and Cornwallis to FO, 28 April 1941, FO 371/27067, TNA.

34 Air Vice Marshal Smart to Air Marshal Tedder, 5 March 1941, AIR23/1349, TNA.

35 *PAIFORCE: The Official Story,* 21–2; For an assessment of the status of Habbaniya on the eve of the 1941 operations, see Jackson, *Persian Gulf Command,* 66–8; British Military Mission, Report no. 35 on the Iraqi Army and Royal Iraqi Air Force for the period ending 31st July 1941, WO208/1585, TNA.

36 Air Vice Marshal Smart to Air Marshal Tedder, 5 March 1941, AIR23/1349, TNA.

37 Personal for AOC from AOC-in-C, 7 April 1941, AIR23/1349, TNA.

38 RAF HQ Iraq to Cornwallis, 30 April 1941, FO 371/27067, TNA.

39 Cornwallis to FO, 30 April 1941, FO 371/27067, TNA; For Churchill's comment, see Killearn Diaries, 2 May 1941, MECA.

40 Playfair, *The Mediterranean and Middle East,* vol. 2, 184–6.

41 War Office to C in C ME, 4 May 1941, FO 371/27069, TNA.

42 Killearn Diaries, 34, and 5 May 1941, MECA.

43 Wavell to War Office, 3 May 1941, FO 371/27069, TNA.

44 C in C ME to War Office, 8 May 1941, and C in C India to War Office, 12 May 1941, FO 371/27069, TNA.

45 For a detailed assessment of the military operations, see Playfair, *The Mediterranean and Middle East,* vol. 2, 177–97; Robert Lyman, *First Victory: Britain's Forgotten Struggle in the Middle East, 1941* (London: Constable, 2006); Jackson, *Persian Gulf Command,* 66–107; John Broich, *Blood, Oil and the Axis: The Allied Resistance Against a Fascist State in Iraq and the Levant, 1941* (New York: Abrams Press, 2019), 41–180. For an English-language account that incorporates the analysis of Iraqi historians, see Youssef Aboul-Enein and Basil Aboul-Enein, *The Secret War for the Middle East: The Influence of Axis and Allied Intelligence Operations during World War II* (Annapolis: Naval Institute Press, 2013), 39–84. General Sir Maitland Wilson, who took over command of British Troops in Palestine and Transjordan in May 1941, provides his account in Wilson, *Eight Years Overseas,* 105–8.

46 "PAIFORCE Notes on the History of the Command from the Operational Aspect," 1945, WO201/3815, TNA [Hereafter PAIFORCE Notes WO201/3815]; *PAIFORCE: The Official Story,* 39–43.

47 Jackson, *Persian Gulf Command,* 67–79.

48 John Bagot Glubb, *Britain and the Arabs: A Study of Fifty Years, 1908 to 1958* (London: Hodder and Stoughton, 1959), Chapter 17 and Glubb Pasha, "A Report on the Role Played by the Arab Legion in Connection with the Recent Operations in Iraq," 10 June 1941, FO624/26, TNA.
49 British Military Mission, Report no. 35 on the Iraqi Army and Royal Iraqi Air Force for the period ending 31st July 1941, WO208/1585, TNA; PAIFORCE Notes WO201/3815.
50 Playfair, *The Mediterranean and Middle East*, vol. 2, 189; Jackson, *Persian Gulf Command*, 96.
51 "Despatch on Operations in Iraq, East Syria and Iran, from 10th April, 1941 to 12th January, 1942," Despatch by General Wavell, 18 October, 1942, reprinted in *Supplement to the London Gazette*, 14 August 1946.
52 Jackson, *Persian Gulf Command*, 64, 72, and 96.
53 Cornwallis's letter of protest to the Minister for Foreign Affairs, 15 July 1941, FO 371/27079, TNA.
54 Freya Stark, *Dust in the Lion's Paw: Autobiography 1939–1946* (New York: Harcourt, Brace & World, 1961), 88–116 and in a series of articles that appeared in the *Times*, 27, 28, and 30 June 1941, included in FO371/27079. Cornwallis's account can be found in Cornwallis to Eden, 6 June 1941, FO371/27077, TNA.
55 Fisher to Bowker, 7 August 1941, FO371/27079, TNA.
56 Bagdad to Basra, 4 May 1941, FO 371/27068; British Military Mission, Report no. 35 on the Iraqi Army and Royal Iraqi Air Force for the period ending 31st July 1941, WO208/1585, TNA; Stark, *Dust in the Lion's Paw*, 90–101.
57 Freya Stark. "In Iraq during the Crisis." *Times* [London, England] 30 June 1941: 5. *The Times Digital Archive*. Web. 6 June 2017.
58 Stark, *Dust in the Lion's Paw*, 100.
59 Freya Stark. "In Iraq during the Crisis." *Times* [London, England] 27 June 1941: 5. *The Times Digital Archive*. Web. 6 June 2017.
60 Cornwallis to Eden, 6 June 1941, FO 371/27077, TNA.
61 Stark, *Dust in the Lion's Paw*, 95–6.
62 Chancery, Tehran to Eastern Department, 17 May 1941, enclosing Memorandum, Iraqi Ministry of Foreign Affairs to the Belgian Legation, Baghdad dated 2 May 1941, FO 371/27076, TNA.
63 Eden statement in the House of Commons, 6 May 1941, FO 371/27068, TNA.
64 C in C and AOC Middle East to General Basra AOC Habbaniya, 11 May 1941, FO 371/27069; FO to Angora, 17 May 1941, FO 371/27069, TNA.
65 Mideast (MICE) to AOC Habbaniya, for Jope from Cawthorn, 4/27/1941, AIR23/5933, TNA. MacMichael to S of S for Colonies, 9 May 1941, FO 371/27068, TNA.
66 Gardener to FO, 9 May 1941; Knatchbull-Hugessen to FO, 13 May 1941, FO371/27345, TNA.
67 Halifax to FO, 10 May 1941, C in C India to C in C ME, 8 May 1941, Stonehewer-Bird to FO, 8 May 1941 and Knatchbull-Hugessen to FO, 10 May and 12 May 1941, FO 371/27069, TNA.
68 MacMichael to Secretary of State for Colonies, 5 May 1941, Tweedy for Rushbrook Williams, FO 371/27068, TNA.
69 C in C ME to War Office, 8 May 1941, MacMichael to S of S for Colonies, 9 May 1941 and C in C ME to War Office 8 May 1941, FO 371/27068; SOE Executive Committee Weekly Progress Report for weeks ending 7 July and 28 May 1941, HS8/217, TNA.

70 Military Attaché Ankara to C in C ME, 5 May 1941, FO 371/27068, TNA; For the context, see Silverfarb, *Britain's Informal Empire in the Middle East*, 131.
71 Stonehewer-Bird to FO, 15 May 1941, FO 371/27070, TNA.
72 MICE to Prodrome Baghdad, 11 June 1941, FO 371/27075, TNA.
73 Knatchbull-Hugessen, 25 May 1941, FO 371/27072, TNA.
74 Wavell to War Office, 14 May 1941, FO 371/27070, TNA.
75 C in C and AOC in C ME to General Basra Air Officer Commanding Habbaniya, 11 May 1941, FO 371/27069; De Gaury to FO, 22 May 1941, FO 371/27071, TNA.
76 Cornwallis to Eden, Annual Review for 1941, 8 March 1942 and Chargé Iraq to FO, 26 May 1941, FO 371/27072, TNA.
77 Cornwallis to General Basra, 30 May 1941, FO 371/27073 and Cornwallis to Eden, 6 June 1941, FO 371/27077, TNA.
78 De Gaury to FO, 31 May 1941, FO 371/27073, TNA.
79 FO to Baghdad, 31 May 1941, FO 371/27073, TNA.
80 Armistice, 31 May 1941, FO 371/27077; Cornwallis to FO, 6 June 1941, FO 371/27074, TNA.
81 Cornwallis to FO, 8 June 1941, FO371/27074, TNA.
82 Cornwallis to FO, 2 June 1941, FO 371/27074, TNA.
83 ALO Baghdad Domvile to AHQ Iraq Slade, 29 April 1941, AIR23/5933, TNA. Orit Bashkin, *New Babylonians: A History of Jews in Modern Iraq* (Palo Alto, US: Stanford University Press, 2012), 101–30.
84 Warner, *Iraq and Syria 1941*, 117.
85 Cornwallis to Eden, 11 July 1941, FO 371/27078, TNA.
86 Extract from House of Commons debate, 7 May 1941, FO 371/27068, TNA.
87 Ibid.
88 War Office to C in C ME, 6 May 1941, FO 371/27068, TNA.
89 Wavell to Dill, quoted in Ashley Jackson, *Persian Gulf Command*, 106. For an assessment of the factors contributing to the successful outcome for Britain, see ibid., 99–106 and Silverfarb, *Britain's Informal Empire in the Middle East*, 131–41.
90 Annual Review for Iraq 1941, 8 March 1942, FO 371/31371, TNA.
91 Al-Durra titles one section of his work "The Iraqi-British War: War Not Revolution" in order to make this point: Mahmud al-Durra, *Al Harb al-'Iraqiyya al-Britaniyya* (Beirut: Dar al-Tali'ah, 1969), 241–242. Al-Durra served in the Iraqi army during the coup, giving his account special interest. For a useful review of this work and other Iraqi sources on the coup, see Ayad al-Qazzaz, "The Iraqi-British War of 1941: A Review Article," *International Journal of Middle East Studies* 7 (1976): 591–6. For an accessible English-language summary of al-Durra's work, see Aboul-Enein and Aboul-Enein, *The Secret War for the Middle East*, Appendix 2.
92 Khaldun Sati'al-Husri, introduction to Taha al-Hashimi, *Mudhakkirat,* 39. My translation.
93 Al-Durra, *Al Harb al-'Iraqiyya al-Britaniyya*, 12. My translation.

Chapter 5

1 Tedder to d'Albiac, 4 July 1941, AIR23/1349, TNA.
2 A number of works examine the intersection of these critical events from 1941: Warner, *Iraq and Syria 1941;* Jackson, *Persian Gulf Command;* Lyman, *First Victory;* and Broich, *Blood, Oil and the Axis.*

3 Killearn Diaries, 1 January 1941, MECA.
4 War Cabinet Joint Planning Staff, "the Strategic Necessity for Holding Our Present Middle East Position," 23 July 1941, FO371/27081, TNA.
5 Churchill to Cornwallis, 11 March 1941, FO 371/27061, TNA. For background, see Warner, *Iraq and Syria 1941*, 33–4; Thomas, *The French Empire at War*, 100–7.
6 On Vichy aid during the Rashid 'Ali coup, see: Playfair, *The Mediterranean and Middle East*, vol. 2, 195.
7 Tedder to CAS, 19 May 1941 and Smart to Tedder, 3 June 1941, AIR23/1349, TNA.
8 Warner, *Iraq and Syria 1941*, 122–58.
9 War Cabinet, "Our Arab Policy. Memorandum by the Secretary of State for Foreign Affairs." 27 May 1941, FO 371/27043, TNA.
10 Quoted in Kirk, *The Middle East in the War*, 334.
11 Lampson to FO, 3 June 1941, FO371/27043, TNA.
12 Lord Hood, 2 December 1940 and 18 February 1941, INF1/874; C in C ME to War Office, 19 May 1941, FO371/27552, TNA.
13 FO to Cairo, 28 June 1941, FO371/27579, TNA.
14 Minister of State to Ministry of Information, 13 August 1941, INF1/875, TNA. For Lyttelton's own account of setting up the Minister of State's office: Oliver Lyttelton, Viscount Chandos, *The Memoirs of Lord Chandos* (London: The Bodley Head, 1962), 223–36.
15 Minister of Information to Minister of State, 9 August 1941 and 19 November 1941, Minister of State for M of I, 7 December 1941, INF1/875, TNA.
16 "Operations in the Middle East, 5 July 1941–31 October 1941," Despatch by General Auchinleck, 8 March 1942, reprinted in *Supplement to the London Gazette*, 20 August 1946.
17 PAIFORCE Notes, WO201/3815, TNA.
18 E.M.H. Lloyd, *Food and Inflation in the Middle East 1940–1945* (Stanford: Stanford University Press, 1956), 74–5. Lloyd's account of the supply crisis is of particular interest as he served as economic adviser to the British minister of state in the Middle East in 1943–4.
19 For the MESC, see ibid. and Martin Wilmington (Laurence Evans, ed.), *The Middle East Supply Centre* (Albany: State University of New York Press, 1971).
20 Rushbrook Williams, 5 March 1941, Duff Cooper to Dalton, 1 March 1941, INF 1/874, TNA.
21 Lloyd, *Food and Inflation*, 80–1 and 100.
22 Minute by Bateman, 3 June 9141, FO 371/27431, TNA.
23 Lampson to FO, 6 April 1941, FO371/27429, TNA.
24 Lampson to Eden, 29 April 1941, FO 371/27430, TNA.
25 Artemis Cooper provides a vivid account of the personalities who flocked to Cairo in *Cairo in the War 1939–1945* (London: Hamish Hamilton, 1989), 75–82.
26 Lampson to FO, 6 April 1941, FO371/27429; Lampson to FO, 3 May 1941, FO 371/27068, TNA.
27 Thornhill to Brigadier Brooks, 1 October 1941, FO 898/113, TNA. For a summary of events, see Saul Kelly, "A Succession of Crises: SOE in the Middle East, 1940–45," 145 footnote 42.
28 Thornhill to Brigadier Brooks, 1 October 1941, FO 898/113, TNA. Lampson to FO, 9 August 1941, FO 371/27431, TNA. The Egyptian prime minister decided to go ahead with the trial, and Thornhill was sent back to England. Lampson to FO, 28 August 1941, FO 371/27432, TNA.

29 Sansom, *I Spied Spies*, 69.
30 Sadat, *Revolt on the Nile*, 35. The 'Aziz al-Masri affair is recounted in both of Anwar al-Sadat's memoirs: ibid., 35–8 and Anwar al-Sadat, *In Search of Identity*, 28–31 and Sansom, *I Spied Spies*, 70–6. Both Sansom and Sadat's accounts of the actions of the young Egyptian officers were written after the 1952 revolution, and Gershoni and Jankowski, *Confronting Fascism in Egypt*, 5–6 provides a useful historiographical note on using these sources.
31 Lampson to Eden, 12 February 1942, FO371/31569, TNA; Kirk, *The Middle East in the War*, 200; Joel Beinin and Zachary Lockman, *Workers on the Nile: Nationalism, Communism, Islam, and the Egyptian Working Class, 1882–1854* (Cairo: American University in Cairo Press, 1998), 248.
32 Minute by Bateman, 3 June 9141, FO 371/27431, TNA.
33 Killearn Diaries, 14 April 1941, MECA and Lampson to FO, 10 August 1941, FO 371/27431, TNA.
34 Lampson to FO, 22 May 1941, FO to Lampson, 25 May 1941, FO 371/27430, TNA.
35 Lampson to FO, 6 April 1941, Lampson to FO, 12 April 1941, and Lampson to FO, 31 March 1941, FO 371/27429, TNA.
36 Lampson to FO, 4 May 1941, FO 371/27430 and Lampson to FO, 14 November 1941, FO 371/27434, TNA.
37 Kirk, *The Middle East in the War*, 201–2.
38 Lugol, *Egypt and World War II*, 163–4.
39 Lampson to FO, 10 August 1941, FO 371/27431; Lampson to Eden, 26 September 1941 and Aide Memoire, British Embassy, Cairo 8 September 1941, Lampson to FO, 1 October 1941, memorandum on Prince Abbas Halim by Bateman, 2 October 1941, FO 371/27433, TNA. For the tramway strike and labor unrest in the early war years, see Beinin and Lockman, *Workers on the Nile*, 241–54.
40 Cyril Radcliffe, M of I to Bruce Lockhart, Political Intelligence Dept., 19 August 1942, enclosure "Ministry of Information. Overseas Planning Committee. Plan of Propaganda for Egypt. Appreciation," FO371/31579, TNA.
41 Lampson to FO, 1 September 1941 and 14 September 1941, Minute by Bateman, 2 September 1941, FO 371/27432; Lampson to Eden, 23 September 1941, FO 371/27433; Lampson to Eden, 12 February 1942, FO371/31569, TNA.
42 Eden to Lampson, 24 October 1941, FO 371/27432; Lampson to FO, 30 October 1941, FO 371/27434, TNA.
43 Cornwallis to FO, 14 June 1941, FO 371/27103, TNA.
44 D'Albiac, Habbaniya to Tedder, 11 June 1941, AIR23/1349, TNA.
45 Iraqi historian Mahmud al-Durra, who participated in the 1941 coup, used the term "Second British Occupation" to describe Britain's presence in Iraq after 1941 because it draws attention to the earlier occupation during the First World War and the mandate and reflects the way in which Iraqi historians have drawn comparisons between these two periods in Anglo-Iraqi relations: al-Durra, *Al Harb al-'Iraqiyya al-Britaniyya*, 11. Matthew Elliot notes that the term was widely used by Iraqi nationalists: "The phrase implies that Iraq was not at the time independent and that the Mandate—the first occupation—was likewise illegal and based simply on force." *"Independent Iraq": The Monarchy and British Influence, 1941–1958* (London: Tauris Academic Studies, 1996), 14.
46 Cornwallis to FO, 13 June 1941, FO 371/27075, TNA.
47 Edmonds to Holt, 6 August 1941, FO624/60, TNA.
48 Cornwallis to FO, 4 June 1941, FO 371/27101, TNA.

49 O'Sullivan, *The Baghdad Set*, 67–71; for the early SOE presence in Iraq in 1941, see ibid., 96–9.
50 Minute by Perowne, 1 December 1941 and Cornwallis to FO, 16 December 1941, FO624/26/834, TNA.
51 Cornwallis to FO, 21 August 1941 [Perowne to Rushbrook Williams], Savidge to Perowne, 15 October 1941, FO624/26, TNA.
52 Cornwallis to Eden, 30 March 1945, FO371/45302, TNA.
53 Freya Stark, "In Iraq during the Crisis." *Times* [London, England] 27 June 1941: 5. *The Times Digital Archive*. Web. 6 June 2017.
54 Bishop and Stark, "Oral Propaganda in Iraq," 4 June 1941 and Lampson to Eden, 17 June 1941, enclosing the above, FO 371/27101, TNA.
55 Stark, *Dust in the Lion's Paw*, 111.
56 Cornwallis to FO, 2 June and 5 June 1941, FO 371/27074 TNA.
57 Holman to FO, 12 September 1941, FO 371/27080, TNA.
58 Khadduri, *Independent Iraq*, 210–11.
59 Batatu, *The Old Social Classes*, 30–2.
60 Silverfarb's statistics on the Iraqi population during this period are useful: "In 1941 Iraq had about 5 million inhabitants. The population was divided into various groups of which, roughly, Shiite Arabs constituted 51 percent; Sunni Arabs 20 percent; Kurds, nearly all of whom were Sunni, 19 percent; and Turks, Iranians, Christians, Jews, and Yazidis 10 percent. About one-third of the population lived in urban areas, primarily in Baghdad, Basra, and Mosul, the three largest cities." Silverfarb, *The Twilight of British Ascendancy*, 1.
61 Cornwallis to FO, 8 June 1941, FO 371/27075; Cornwallis to FO, 28 June 1941, FO 371/27077, TNA.
62 Edmonds to Cornwallis, 7 September 1941, FO 624/24, and Edmonds to Cornwallis, 2 September 1941, FO 624/60, TNA.
63 Ibid.
64 Cornwallis to Eden, 11 July 1941, FO 371/27078, TNA.
65 Cornwallis to FO, 5 June 1941, FO 371/27074; Cornwallis to Eden, 8 March 1942, FO 371/31371, TNA.
66 Lyon to Cornwallis, 1 September 1941 and Minute by Holt, 6 September 1941, FO624/60, TNA.
67 Dawisha, *Iraq: A Political History*, 100.
68 British Military Mission, Report no. 35 on the Iraqi Army and Royal Iraqi Air Force for the period ending 31 July 1941, and quarterly report ending 30 November 1941, WO208/1585, TNA.
69 Minute by Chaplin, 25 September 1941, FO 624/26, TNA.
70 Cornwallis to FO, 29 September 1941, FO 371/27080/, TNA.
71 Rushbrook Williams to Pearson, 1 April 1941, FO898/113, TNA. For Nuri's role in the Rashid 'Ali government, see Chapter 3. The debate between the embassy and Foreign Office as to what to do with Nuri revealed that he had been receiving regular payments from Britain. In June 1941 Crosthwaite suggested that "it would be well worth our while to add a little to his allowances…to keep him quiet." The Foreign Office instructed the embassy that if Nuri was given a post they "would be prepared to arrange for some addition to his emoluments." Minute by Crosthwaite, 9 June 1941 and FO to Baghdad, 10 June 1941. FO 371/27075, TNA.
72 Cornwallis to Eden, 11 November 1941, FO 371/27082; Cornwallis to Eden, 8 March 1942, FO 371/31371; Cornwallis to FO, 8 October 1941, FO 371/27081, TNA.

73 C in C and AOC in C ME to C in C India, 24 June 1941, and C in C ME to War Office, 24 June 1941, FO 371/27076, TNA. For an overview of CICI and the ALOs, see O'Sullivan, *The Baghdad Set*, 114–44.
74 Cornwallis to FO, 25 July 1941, FO 371/27078; Cornwallis to FO, 20 June 1941, FO 624/25, TNA.
75 Cornwallis to FO, 29 November 1941, FO 371/27082, TNA. For an overview of the work of the Political Advisory Staff, see Elliot, *"Independent Iraq,"* 142–8.
76 Edmonds letter, undated (post 1941), Edmonds Papers, MECA.
77 For example, Wallace Lyon held this position in Mosul from 1918 until 1932.
78 Cornwallis to FO, 24 June 1941, and ME Cairo to Cornwallis, 24 June 1941, FO 624/25, TNA.
79 For Lyon's firsthand account of his experience as a Political Adviser, see his memoir, ed. D.K. Fieldhouse, *Kurds, Arabs and Britons: The Memoir of Wallace Lyon in Iraq 1918–44*, 219–28. The personal papers of E. Kinch, an Assistant PA, including a manuscript of his unpublished memoirs, are held at MECA.
80 Cornwallis to FO, 20 June 1941, Cornwallis to Air Officer Commanding, Habbaniya, 30 July 1941 and Dowson to Cornwallis, 14 August 1941, FO 624/25; Cornwallis to FO, 3 July 1941, FO 371/27078, TNA.
81 Minute by Holt, 22 September 1941, FO624/25/507, TNA.
82 Cornwallis's directive entitled "The Political Advisory Staff," enclosed in Cornwallis to Aston, Lyon, and Dawson, 19 July 1941, FO 624/25, TNA.
83 Tweedy quoted in a Minute by Caccia, 14 March 1942, FO 371/313349.
84 Cornwallis to FO, 20 June 1941, FO624/25, TNA.
85 Lyon, *Kurds, Arabs and Britons*, 219; O'Sullivan, *The Baghdad Set*, 100.
86 Lampson to Eden from Minister of State, 27 October 1941; Cornwallis to FO 4 December 1941, FO 624/25, TNA.
87 For operations in Iran, see Jackson, *Persian Gulf Command*, 131–207.
88 CICI Baghdad, 2 September 1941, WO208/1215, TNA.
89 Grafftey-Smith, *British Levant*, 227.

Chapter 6

1 Sir Robert Greg, 19 February 1942, FO141/847, TNA.
2 For a detailed assessment: Charles D. Smith, "4 February 1942: Its Causes and Its Influence on Egyptian Politics and on the Future of Anglo-Egyptian Relations, 1937–1945," *International Journal of Middle East Studies* 10 (1979): 453–79.
3 PAIFORCE Notes, WO201/3815, TNA.
4 Killearn Diaries, 1 February 1942, MECA.
5 Letter dated 6 January 1942 from the Government of Egypt presented to Britain by the Egyptian Ambassador to Great Britain, FO 371/31553, TNA.
6 Lampson to Eden, 20 January 1942, FO141/837; Lampson to FO, 26 January 1942, FO 371/31566, TNA.
7 Killearn Diaries, 22 January 1942, MECA.
8 Lampson to Eden, 21 January 1942, FO141/837; Minute by Scrivener, 22 January 1942, FO 371/31566, TNA.
9 "The Anglo-Egyptian Treaty of 1936," Appendix 3 in Yapp, ed., *Politics and Diplomacy in Egypt*, 984.

10 Lampson to FO, 26 January 1942, FO 371/31566; Draft Minutes for Meeting held at the Embassy on the 28th January 1942, FO141/837, TNA.
11 Lampson to FO, 1 February 1942, FO 371/31566, TNA.
12 Lampson to FO, 18 January, 26 January, and 2 February, 1942, FO 371/31566, TNA; Artemis Cooper, *Cairo in the War 1939–1945* (London: Hamish Hamilton, 1989), 167; Smart memo, 7 February 1942, Memorandum by Grafftey-Smith, 12 February 1942, FO 141/829, TNA.
13 Weekly Political Report, Cairo, 4 February 1942, FO 371/31567, TNA.
14 Lampson to FO, 2 February 1942, FO 371/31566, TNA.
15 Killearn Diaries, 1 February 1942, MECA.
16 Eden to Lampson, 2 February 1942, FO 141/829, TNA.
17 Ibid.
18 Eden to Lampson, 4 February 1942, Lampson to FO, 2 February 1942, FO 371/31566, TNA.
19 Killearn Diaries, 3 February 1942. MECA. For Amin ʿUthman's earlier role, see Chapter 2.
20 Lampson to Eden, 2 February 1942, FO 141/837; Minute by Peterson, 4 February 1942, FO 371/31566, TNA.
21 Killearn Diaries, 18 May 1941, MECA.
22 Lampson to FO, 4 October 1941, FO 371/27433; Lampson to FO, 21 January 1942, FO 371/31566, TNA.
23 Multiple telegrams from Lampson to FO, 2 February 1942, FO 371/31566, TNA.
24 Killearn Diaries, 4 February 1942, MECA.
25 Ibid.
26 Lampson to FO, 5 February 1942, FO 371/31567, TNA.
27 Ibid.
28 Minute by Peterson, 5 February 1942, FO 371/31567, TNA.
29 Eden to Lampson, 13 March 1942, FO 141/837, TNA. For the revelations surrounding these events at the end of the war, see Ch. 12.
30 Lampson to FO, 10 February 1942, FO 371/31567, TNA.
31 Lampson to FO, 19 February 1942, FO 371/31568, TNA.
32 Address to the Ambassador, 19 February 1942, FO141/829, TNA.
33 Saʿdist Party protest addressed to Lampson, 10 February 1942, FO141/829, TNA. My translation.
34 Minute by Shone, 5 February 1942, Lampson to Eden, 11 February 1942, FO141/829, TNA.
35 Killearn to Eden, 22 December 1943, 1942 Annual Report, FO 371/41326, TNA.
36 Wilson, *Eight Years Overseas,* 129.
37 Jenkins of Defence Security Office to Tomlyn, 9 February 1942, FO 141/841, TNA. The reports in FO141/841 on the Egyptian military in 1942 after the Abdin Palace incident are of interest when read with the accounts of Sadat and Naguib.
38 Naguib identified the Abdin Palace incident as his "own breaking point," leading him to resign his commission, which the King refused to accept. Mohammed Naguib, *Egypt's Destiny: A Personal Statement* (Garden City, NY: Doubleday & Company, 1955), 16.
39 Lampson to Eden, 18 August 1942, FO921/113, TNA.
40 G.J. Jenkins, Defence Security Office to Tomlyn, 2 August 1942, FO141/852, TNA. Anwar al-Sadat was among those arrested. For his account: Sadat, *In Search of Identity,* 33–40.
41 Killearn Diaries, 10 February 1942, MECA.
42 Minute by Peterson, 9 February 1942, FO 371/31567, TNA.

43 For the details, see Lampson to FO, 10 February 1942, FO 371/31567; Lampson to FO, 23 February 1942 and Lampson to FO, 28 February 1942, FO 371/31568, TNA.
44 Minute by Scrivener, 24 February 1942, FO 371/31568, TNA.
45 Minute by Grafftey-Smith, 19 and 22 February 1942, FO141/842, TNA.
46 Lampson to FO, 8 April 1940, Lampson to FO, 9 April 1942, Lampson to FO, 10 April 1942, FO371/31570, TNA.
47 GHQ summary history of the Muslim Brotherhood included in Security Summary Middle East no. 103 on December 10, 1942-Appendix A, "The Ikhwan al Muslimin Reconsidered," FO141/838, TNA.
48 Maunsell, GHQ ME to Smart, 10 October 1942, FO141/838; Killearn to Eden, 22 December 1943, FO 371/41326, TNA.
49 Mitchell, *The Society of the Muslim Brothers*, 27.
50 Lampson to FO, 13 March 1942, FO371/31569, TNA.
51 Killearn to Eden, 22 December 1943, 1942 Annual Report, FO 371/41326, TNA.
52 Lampson to FO, 21 February 1942, FO 371/31568; Lampson to FO, 25 March 1942, FO 371/31569, TNA.
53 'Abd al-Rahman al-Rafi'i, *Fi A'qab al-Thawra al-Misriyya Thawrat 1919* (Cairo, 1951), III: 108 My translation.
54 Lampson to FO, 7 February 1942, FO 371/31567; Lampson to FO, 26 March 1942, FO 371/31570, TNA.
55 Minute by Scrivener, 24 February 1942, FO 371/31568; Minute by Peterson, 26 March 1942, FO 371/31570, TNA.
56 Killearn to FO, 28 September 1942, FO 371/31574, TNA.
57 Consular Agent, Sohag, report to GOC in C, BTE, 14 February 1942, Minute by Smart, 20 April 1942, and Minute by Smart, 4 May 1942, FO 141/829; Lampson to FO, 31 May 1942, FO 371/31572, TNA.
58 Minutes by Smart, 3 June, 5 June, and October 1942, FO 141/829, TNA.
59 Killearn to FO, 11 June 1942, and Killearn to FO, 1 August 1942, FO 371/31573; Killearn to FO, 27 December 1942, FO 371/31565; Killearn to FO, 18 August 1942, FO 371/31574, TNA.
60 Quoted in Lloyd, *Food and Inflation in the Middle East*, 129.
61 Ibid., 130–135.
62 Lugol, *Egypt and World War II*, 330.
63 Grafftey-Smith, *Bright Levant*, 240.
64 Killearn Diaries, 1 July and 5 July 1942, MECA. For a colorful account of "the Flap," see Cooper, *Cairo in the War*, 194–201.
65 Lampson conversation with Amin 'Uthman, 4 July 1942, FO 141/837; Lampson to FO, 1 July 1942 and Lampson to FO, 1 August 1942, FO371/31573, TNA.
66 Lampson to FO, 28 June 1942 and Lampson to FO, 29 June 1942, FO371/31573, TNA.
67 Lampson to FO, 28 September 1942, FO 371/31574, TNA.
68 C in C ME to War Office, 6 July 1942, FO371/31573, TNA.
69 For the debates surrounding the Northern Front, see Nicholas Tamkin, "Britain, the Middle East, and the 'Northern Front', 1941–1942," *War in History* 15, no. 3 (2008): 314–36.
70 Minute by Crosthwaite, 16 March 1942, FO 371/31362, TNA.
71 Bromilow, Head of the British Military Mission to Iraq, "Morale and Attitude of the Iraqi Army on May 14, 1942" enclosed in Cornwallis to Eden, 21 May 1942, WO208/1586, TNA.
72 CICI Tribal and Political Weekly Intelligence Summaries, June and July 1942, WO208/1567, TNA.

73 Cornwallis to Foreign Office, 2 August 1942, FO 371/31371, TNA.
74 PAIFORCE Notes, WO201/3815, TNA.
75 Jackson, *Persian Gulf Command,* 277–80; Silverfarb, *The Twilight of British Ascendency,* 23–9.
76 For the creation of the new command, see Jackson, *Persian Gulf Command,* 260–7.
77 Thompson to Peterson, 17 September 1942, Thompson to FO for Peterson, 18 September 1942, FO624/30, TNA.
78 CICI Tribal and Political Weekly Intelligence Summary, weeks ending September 14, 1942 WO 208/1567, TNA.
79 CICI Tribal and Political Weekly Intelligence Summary, weeks ending August 24 and August 31, 1942 WO 208/1567, TNA.
80 British Military Mission, Report no. 35 on the Iraqi Army and Royal Iraqi Air Force for the period ending 30th November 1942, WO208/1585, TNA.
81 Aston to Cornwallis, Memorandum "Report for Week ending 7/12/41," FO 624/25, TNA.
82 CICI Tribal and Political Weekly Intelligence Summary, week ending November 9, 1942, WO 208/1567, TNA.
83 Wilkes to Holt, 14 March 1942, quoting from personal letter from Corry in Mosul, FO624/29, TNA.
84 Yapp Introduction, *Politics and Diplomacy in Egypt,* 5–6; Lampson to FO, 9 January 1943, FO371/35528, TNA.

Chapter 7

1 CICI Tribal and Political Weekly Intelligence Summary, weeks ending November 9 and November 16, 1942 WO 208/1567, TNA.
2 Proposal submitted by Thirty-Two Deputies at the Meeting held by the Chamber of Deputies on 12 November 1942, translated and reprinted in "Documents relating to the adherence of Iraq to the declaration of the United Nations signed at Washington on 2nd January, 1942," Baghdad Government Press, 1943, FO 371/34997, TNA.
3 Minute by Eden, 17 November 1942, FO371/31370, TNA.
4 Minister of State to FO, 29 November 1942, Cornwallis to FO, 4 December 1942, US Ambassador to Eden, 16 December 1942, FO to Baghdad, 25 December 1942, Cornwallis to FO, 30 December 1942, FO371/31370, TNA.
5 G.J. Jenkins, Defence Security Office, to Tomlyn Embassy, encloses two political reports from B division for the C.C.F., 2 December 1942, FO 141/829 (minor corrections to original quote for clarity). Lampson to Eden, 14 December 1942, FO 921/133, TNA.
6 Analysis of Arab debates surrounding the internationalist rhetoric of the war in this and subsequent chapters draws on the author's previously published work, used here by permission of the original publishers: Stefanie Wichhart, "Selling Democracy during the Second British Occupation of Iraq, 1941–1945," *Journal of Contemporary History* 48, no. 3 (July 2013): 509–36; and "The Formation of the Arab League and the United Nations, 1944–1945," *The Journal of Contemporary History* 54, no. 2 (April 2019): 328–46.
7 Cornwallis to FO 6, 8, and 13 January 1943, FO371/34996, TNA.
8 *Al-Akhbar,* 18 January 1943.
9 Cornwallis to FO, 7 January 1943, FO 371/34996, TNA.

10 Quoted in Herf, *Nazi Propaganda for the Arab World*, 163.
11 Minute by Peterson, 18 January 1943, FO 371/35528, TNA.
12 Translation of "Jamil Madfai's speech in the senate on the occasion of 'Iraq's adherence to the Atlantic Charter and the declaration of war on the Axis." Appendix to Combined Intelligence Centre Iraq Tribal and Political Weekly Intelligence Summary no. 103 for week ending February 1, 1943, WO208/1568, TNA. For the embassy's response, see Cornwallis to Eden, 22 January 1943, FO 371/35010, TNA.
13 Nuri to Churchill, 17 January 1943, enclosed in FO 371/34996, TNA.
14 Albert Hourani, "Great Britain and Arab Nationalism," June 1943, FO371/34958, TNA.
15 Cornwallis to FO, 21 January 1943, FO 371/34997, TNA; Cornwallis to Eden, Annual Review for 1943, 8 February 1944, FO 371/40041, TNA.
16 Nuri to Casey, 14 January 1943, Office of Minister of State to FO, 11 February 1943, FO 371/34955, TNA.
17 Nuri's cover letter to his note sent to Sir Cosmo Parkinson, Permanent Under Secretary of the CO, 15 February 1943, FO371/34956 in Anita L. P. Burdett, ed., *The Arab League: British Documentary Sources* (Great Britain: Archive Editions, 1995), vol. 2.
18 Nuri, "Note on the Arab Cause, with Suggestion for the Solution of Its Problem," enclosed in Nuri to Casey, 14 January 1943, FO371/34955, TNA.
19 Taha al-Hashimi to Nuri, 12 August 1942, quoted in Yehoshua Porath, *In Search of Arab Unity 1930–1945* (London: Frank Cass, 1986), 49–50.
20 Nuri, "Note on the Arab Cause, with Suggestion for the Solution of Its Problem," enclosed in Nuri to Casey, 14 January 1943, FO371/34955, TNA.
21 Cornwallis to Eden, 28 March 1943, FO 371/35010, TNA. British Military Mission, half yearly report on the Iraqi Army and Royal Iraqi Air Force for the period ending 30 September 1943 and 31 March 1944, WO208/1585, TNA.
22 Cornwallis to Eden, 8 March 1943, FO371/34956, TNA.
23 Quoted in Political Intelligence Committee (PIC) Paper No. 30, "Arab Unity" 18 November 1943 in Burdett, ed., *The Arab League: British Documentary Sources 1943–1963*, 2: 379.
24 Killearn to Eden, draft dispatch, 31 January 1943, FO 141/855; Killearn to FO, 22 January 1943, FO 371/35528, TNA.
25 For the multiple motives behind growing Egyptian interest in regional issues and Arab unity, see Gershoni and Jankowski, *Redefining the Egyptian Nation*, 192–211.
26 Minute by Smart, 10 June 1942, FO 141/840, TNA.
27 MI6 report, "Iraqi feeling and morale. An appreciation by our representative" 25 May 1942 and Cornwallis to Eden, 4 June 1942, WO208/1586, TNA.
28 Minute by Peterson, 30 January 1942, FO 371/31337, TNA.
29 Minister of State Cairo to FO, 25 March 1943, FO371/34956, TNA.
30 FO to Jedda, 4 May 1943, FO371/34957, TNA.
31 CO Memorandum on Arab Unity, 1 October 1943, reprinted in Burdett, *The Arab League,* vol. 2.
32 Procès-Verbale of the fourth meeting between Nuri and Nahhas at Alexandria, 3 August 1943 and Procès-Verbale of the fifth meeting between Nuri and Nahhas at Alexandria, 5 August 1943, FO371/34961, TNA.
33 Procès verbal of first meeting between Nahhas and Nuri, 31 July 1943, transmitted by Amin 'Uthman to Killearn, 19 August 1943, enclosed in Lampson to Eden, 29 August 1943, FO 371/34961, TNA.
34 Cornwallis to Eden, 28 March 1943, FO 371/35010, TNA.

35 Killearn to Eden, 16 June 1943, FO 371/35536; Political Intelligence Committee (PIC) Paper No. 30, "Arab Unity," 18 November 1943, reprinted in Burdett, *The Arab League,* 2: 373–92.
36 CO Memorandum on Arab Unity, 1 October 1943, reprinted in Burdett, *The Arab League,* vol. 2.
37 For a detailed account of each of these meetings, see Ahmed M. Gomaa, *The Foundation of the League of Arab States: Wartime Diplomacy and Inter-Arab Politics 1941 to 1945* (London: Longman, 1977). Gomaa's account is based on both the official British and Arab League documents. See also Porath, *In Search of Arab Unity,* 257–277.
38 Minute by Perowne, 18 January 1943, reprinted in Burdett, *The Arab League,* 4: 530–1.
39 Ministry of Information, "Overseas Planning Committee. Plan of Propaganda to Iraq. Draft. First revision of Policy Plan." 24 February 1943, FO 371/35014, TNA.
40 Ministry of Information, "Overseas Planning Committee Plan of Propaganda for Egypt," 1942, FO 371/31579, TNA.
41 Cairo to Ministry of Information, 12 February 1943, FO930/208, TNA.
42 Lampson to FO, 10 April 1943, FO 371/35531, TNA.
43 "Overseas Planning Committee. Plan of Propaganda for Iraq." 25 February 1943, FO 371/35014, TNA.
44 Ibid. Numerous examples of the various forms of print publicity created for distribution in Iraq and other parts of the Arab world, along with distribution figures, can be found in the sample books in INF 2/34 and 2/35, TNA. David Welch, *Persuading the People: British Propaganda in World War II* (London: British Library, 2016), 178–86 includes examples of propaganda materials for the Middle East.
45 Bowen M of I to Scrivener, 8 December 1942, FO 371/31579, TNA.
46 "Overseas Planning Committee. Plan of Propaganda for Iraq." 25 February 1943, FO 371/35014, TNA.
47 "Overseas Planning committee Plan of Propaganda for Egypt," Second Revision of Channels, 11 November 1944, FO 371/41368, TNA.
48 P. Thompson, M of I to Crosthwaite, 12 February 1943, encloses Baghdad Progress report for July–December 1942, FO 371/35014, TNA. For the report on the river boat: 21 January 1944 "Strictly Confidential Memorandum—January 21, 1944 British residents-Basra Area," Classified General Records, 1942–1957, Iraq: U.S. Consulate, Basra, 1942–1944, Record Group [RG] 84 Records of the Foreign Service Posts of the Department of State, the National Archives at College Park, College Park, MD (hereafter RG 84 NACPM).
49 FO 371/41368 "Overseas Planning committee Plan of Propaganda for Egypt," Second Revision of Channels, 11 November 1944, FO 371/41368, TNA.
50 P. Thompson, M of I to Crosthwaite, 12 February 1943, encloses Bagdad Progress report for July–December 1942, FO 371/35014, TNA.
51 Khadduri, *Independent Iraq*, 264.
52 "Overseas Planning Committee. Plan of Propaganda for Iraq," 25 February 1943, FO 371/35014, and "Overseas Planning Committee Plan of Propaganda for Iraq," Second Revision of Channels, paper no. 539, 10 October 1944, FO 371/40042, TNA.
53 P. Thompson, M of I to Crosthwaite, 12 February 1943, encloses Bagdad Progress report for July–December 1942, FO 371/35014, TNA.
54 Draft despatch from Lampson to Eden, 31 August 1943, FO 141/868; "Report by Sir Malcolm Robertson on his Tour through the Middle East and Turkey as Chairman of the British Council, January to April, 1943," 28 June 1943, FO 141/868 and FO 624/32, TNA.
55 F. Mason, "A Report on Mosul: The General Situation," 1 July 1942, FO624/27, TNA.

56 Ibid.; "Overseas Planning Committee. Plan of Propaganda for Iraq." 25 February 1943, FO 371/35014, TNA.
57 Minute by Smart, 3 January 1943, FO 141/904, TNA.
58 "Report of Vice-Consul Bagley on visit to Karbala and Najaf with Khan Sahib Tahir Hussain Quraishi, British (Indian) Vice-Consul at Bagdad, in November 1942," FO 624/33, TNA.
59 Wiltshire, Consul Mosul to Thompson, 26 December 1942, Knight, Consul Basra to Thompson, 28 December 1942, Minute by Pott, 15 January 1943, FO624/30, TNA.
60 "Overseas Planning Committee. Plan of Propaganda for Iraq." 25 February 1943, FO 371/35014, TNA.
61 January 1, 1944 Weekly Propaganda Directive, Middle East Office of War Information Overseas Operations Branch, Classified General Records, 1936–1961, Iraq: U.S. Embassy and Legation, Baghdad, RG 84, NACPM.
62 Shone to Peterson, 13 February 1943, FO141/892, TNA. Scholarship on the new *effendiyya* is particularly helpful for contextualizing the British and American emphasis on youth in their publicity efforts. For the *effendiyya* in Egypt: Lucie Ryzova, "Egyptianizing Modernity through the 'New *Effendiya*,'" in *Re-Envisioning Egypt 1919–1952*, ed. A. Goldschmidt, A. Johnson, and B. Salmoni (Cairo: The American University in Cairo Press, 2005), 124–63; Lucie Ryzova, *The Age of the Efendiyya: Passages to Modernity in National-Colonial Egypt* (New York: Oxford University Press, 2014). For Iraq, see: Michael Eppel, "The Elite, the Effendiyya, and the Growth of Nationalism and Pan-Arabism in Hashemite Iraq, 1921–1958," *International Journal of Middle East Studies* 30, no. 2 (May 1998): 227–50, and on the "Young Effendiyya," Wien, *Iraqi Arab Nationalism,* 14–42.
63 Minute by Rushbrook Williams, n.d, on "Overseas Planning Committee. Plan of Propaganda for Iraq, Draft First Revision of Channels," 25 February 1943, FO 371/35014, TNA.
64 Minute by Smart, 7 July 1943, FO141/855, TNA.
65 Ryzova, *The Age of the Efendiyya*, 254–6.
66 Bashkin, *Jews in Babylon*, 130.
67 Edmonds to Cornwallis, 25 June 1942, FO624/30, TNA.
68 P. Thompson, M of I to Crosthwaite, 12 February 1943, encloses Baghdad Progress report for July–December 1942, FO 371/35014; "Overseas Planning committee Plan of Propaganda for Egypt," Second Revision of Channels, 11 November 1944, FO 371/41368, TNA.
69 Dowson, weekly report week ending 2 December 1941, FO624/25, TNA.
70 Excerpts from Brotherhood of Freedom report, Freya Stark, November 1942, FO624/32, TNA.
71 Scaife's CV, n.d. (fall 1944), FO 624/37, TNA.
72 Freya Stark, *East Is West,* 1945; reprint (London: Century, 1986), 55.
73 Minute by Perowne, 6 September 1942 and note by Holt, 6 September 1942, FO 624/29, TNA.
74 For an overview of US wartime policy in the Middle East, see Christopher O'Sullivan, *FDR and the End of Empire: The Origins of American Power in the Middle East* (New York: Palgrave Macmillan, 2012), 18–26.
75 Killearn to Eden, 10 April 1943, FO371/35597, TNA.
76 David Levering Lewis, *The Improbable Wendell Willkie: The Businessman Who Saved the Republican Party and His Country, and Conceived a New World Order* (NY: Liveright Publishing Corp., 2018), 225–42.
77 Lampson to Baghdad for Information Officer, 6 September 1942, FO624/27, TNA.

78 Cornwallis to FO, 14 September 1942, FO624/27, TNA.
79 Minute by Peterson, 14 October 1942, FO 371/31574, TNA.
80 Wendell Willkie, *One World* (New York: Simon and Schuster, 1943), 14–15; 34.
81 Lewis, *The Improbable Wendell Willkie,* 281.
82 Willkie, *One World,* 15; G. J. Jenkins, Defence Security Office, Egypt to Tomlyn, 25 September 1943, FO141/926, TNA; Killearn Diaries, 31 August 1944, MECA.
83 Cornwallis, "The Present Situation in Iraq. Memorandum by Sir Kinahan Cornwallis for the Middle East War Council," enclosed in Cornwallis to Eden, 26 April 1943, FO 371/35010, TNA.
84 Cornwallis to Eden, 5 June 1943, FO 371/35010, TNA.
85 Thompson to FO, 8 May 1943, FO371/34998, TNA.
86 PAIFORCE Notes WO201/3815, TNA.
87 *PAIFORCE: The official story,* 131.
88 Thompson to Eden, 26 July 1943, FO 371/35011.
89 Text of Killearn's Broadcast Speech, 26 August 1943, FO 141/870, TNA.

Chapter 8

1 Jackson, *Persian Gulf Command,* 288.
2 Minute by Chapman-Andrews, 2 April 1943, FO 371/35530, TNA.
3 Jenkins, Defence Security Office to Smart and Minute by Smart, 26 March 1943, FO141/855, TNA. For a concise summary of the Black Book charges, see Kirk, *The Middle East in the War,* 269–72.
4 Minute by Smart, 1 April 1943, FO141/855, TNA.
5 H.B.M. Crown Advocate in Egypt, W.R. Fanner, analysis of the Black Book, 14 April 1943, FO141/855, TNA.
6 Killearn to Eden, 29 November 1943, FO371/35541, TNA.
7 Minute by Smart on conversation with Ahmed Seddik, May 1944, FO141/937, TNA.
8 Minute by Peterson, 14 April 1943, FO371/35531; Killearn to Eden, 16 June 1943, FO 371/35536, TNA.
9 Killearn to FO, 10 April 1943, FO371/35531, TNA.
10 Minute by Eden on Killearn to FO, 12 April 1943, FO371/35531, TNA.
11 FO to Killearn, 21 April 1943, FO141/855; FO to Lampson, 21 April 1943 and Minute by Scrivener, 17 April 1943, FO 371/35531, TNA.
12 Memorandum by Smart, 22 April 1943, FO141/855, TNA.
13 Tomlyn, 23 May 1943, FO 141/855; Note Verbale presented to Killearn, 17 April 1943, FO371/35533, TNA.
14 Memorandum by Smart, 22 April 1943, FO141/855, TNA.
15 Personal Minute by Churchill for Eden, 25 April 1943, FO371/35534, TNA.
16 Minute by Scrivener, 27 April 1943, FO371/35534, TNA.
17 Report by Tomlyn, 4 May 1943 and Minute by Smart, 5 May 1943, and Major C.A. Lea, Publicity Section, Political Note, 7 May 1943 and Lampson to FO, 15 April 1943, FO 141/855, TNA.
18 Killearn Diaries, 23 April and 7 May 1943, MECA; Killearn to FO, 14 April 1943, FO371/35531; Killearn to FO, 7 May 1943, FO371/35533, Killearn to Foreign Office, 24 April 1943, FO141/855, TNA.
19 Killearn to Eden, 16 June 1943, FO 371/35536, TNA.
20 Memorandum from Farouk, 17 May 1943 and Killearn to FO, 18 May 1943, FO141/855, TNA.

21 Minute by Chapman-Andrews, 23 May 1943, FO371/35534, TNA.
22 Embassy meeting minutes, 26 May 1942, FO141/837, TNA.
23 General Stone, "Some Military Considerations in Connection with the Present Political Situation," 26 April 1943, FO141/855, TNA.
24 Memorandum by Peterson for Eden, 5 May 1943 and Casey to FO for Eden, 4 May 1943, FO371/35533, TNA.
25 Killearn to FO, 29 April 1943, FO371/35532, TNA. Killearn Diaries, 2 May 1943, MECA.
26 Churchill to Wilson, forwarded by the Foreign Office to Killearn, 1 May 1943, FO371/35532, TNA.
27 Killearn to Eden, 16 June 1943, FO371/35536, TNA.
28 Killearn to FO, 22 May 1943, FO371/35534; Minute by Chapman-Andrews, 23 May 1943, FO371/35534, TNA.
29 Killearn to Eden, 26 May 1943, FO371/35535, TNA.
30 Killearn to Eden, June 16, 1943, and Killearn to FO, 13 July 1943, FO 371/35536, TNA.
31 Memorandum, Smart, 4 October 1943, on "Egyptian Xenophobia," and Scrivener to Shone, 21 October 1943, FO 141/917, TNA.
32 Killearn to FO, 18 April 1943, FO 141/855, TNA.
33 Killearn to Eden, 16 June 1943, FO 371/35536, TNA.
34 Translated report of speeches made by Opposition leaders at Menufia, 1 June 1943, submitted to the embassy by Ghazali, 3 June 1943, FO141/855, TNA.
35 Killearn to Eden, 26 May 1943, and Killearn to FO, 12 June 1943, FO 371/35535, Minute by Smart, 3 June 1943, FO 141/855, TNA.
36 Minute, 4 June 1943, FO 141/096, TNA.
37 Minute by Scrivener, 25 October 1943, FO 371/35539, TNA.
38 Killearn to Eden no. 207, 25 February 1944, FO 371/41327, TNA.
39 "Weekly Political and Economic Report from October 14th to October 20th, 1943," FO 371/35539, TNA.
40 Killearn to Eden, 25 February 1944, FO371/41327, TNA.
41 Ghazali, report of speeches, 3 June 1943, FO 141/855, TNA.
42 Memorandum by Scrivener, 21 March 1944, FO 371/41404, TNA.
43 Cornwallis to Eden, 8 February 1944, FO 371/40041, TNA.
44 Cornwallis to Eden, 21 February 1943, FO 371/35010, Thompson to Minister of State, Cairo, 2 August 1943, FO 371/35011, TNA.
45 Cornwallis to Foreign Office, 16 March 1942, FO 371/31371; Cornwallis to Eden, 21 February 1943, FO 371/35010, TNA. For an assessment of internal Iraqi politics under Nuri, see Elliot, *"Independent" Iraq* 44–51.
46 Memorandum by Chaplin, "The Situation in Iraq," 12 January 1944, FO371/40041, TNA.
47 Ibid.
48 Cornwallis to Eden, 28 March 1943, FO 371/35010, TNA.
49 Cornwallis to Eden, 5 June 1943, FO 371/35010, TNA.
50 Thompson to Eden, 26 July 1943, FO 371/35011, TNA; Cornwallis to Eden, 5 June 1943, FO 371/35010, Cornwallis to Eden, 6 November 1943, FO 371/35013, TNA.
51 Cornwallis to Eden, 22 January 1943, FO 371/35010, TNA.
52 Albert Hourani's report, "Great Britain and Arab Nationalism" June 1943, FO 371/45958, TNA.
53 Cornwallis to Eden, 6 November 1943, FO 371/35013, TNA.
54 Thompson to Eden, 12 September 1943, FO 371/35012, TNA.

55 Cornwallis to Eden, 8 February 1944, and Cornwallis to Eden, 23 January 1944, FO 371/40041, TNA.
56 Security Intelligence Summary no. 48 from Defence Security Office, CICI, Iraq, 21 December 1942 and Cornwallis to Gen. Wilson, 28 December 1942, FO371/35010, TNA.
57 Fieldhouse, *Kurds, Arabs and Britons*, 221–3.
58 GSI GHQ Persia and Iraq Force Special Intelligence Review, 25 June 1943; GSI GHQ Persia and Iraq Force, Special Sitrep, 5 July 1943; and Directorate-General of Police, Political and Criminal Investigation branch, Baghdad, 15 August 1943, FO 624/34, TNA. For details on the German Operation Mammut, see O'Sullivan, *The Baghdad Set*, 186–90.
59 Jwaideh confirmed the rumors of famine in Kurdish areas based on his travels to the region in 1943–4 through his position as an inspector of supply for the Iraqi Ministry of the Interior. Wadie Jwaideh, *The Kurdish National Movement: Its Origins and Development* (Syracuse: Syracuse University Press, 2006), 231, 364 n. 10. For the economic situation: Cornwallis to Eden, 5 June 1943, FO 371/35010, TNA.
60 For the revolt itself from the Kurdish perspective, see Massoud Barzani's memoir of his father's early career, *Mustafa Barzani and the Kurdish Liberation Movement (1931–1961)*, ed. Ahmed Ferhadi (New York: Palgrave Macmillan, 2006). The Government of Iraq position is reflected in the documents included in 'Abd al-Razzaq al-Hasani, *Tarikh al-Wizarat al-'Iraqiyah*, vol. 6, 272–82. For the Mulla Mustafa revolt within its wartime context, see David McDowall, *A Modern History of the Kurds* (London: I.B. Tauris, 2005), 290–3; Silverfarb, *The Twilight of British Ascendancy*, 39–53; and Jwaideh, *The Kurdish National Movement*, 230–242.
61 Cornwallis to Eden, 8 February 1944, FO371/40041, TNA.
62 Silverfarb, *The Twilight of British Ascendency*, 92–7.
63 British Military Mission, Half-Yearly report on the Iraqi Army and Royal Iraqi Air Force for the period ending 30 September 1943 and March 31, 1944, WO208/1585, TNA.
64 Cornwallis to FO, 13 December 1943, FO 371/35013, TNA.
65 Edmonds Diaries, 4 and 14 October 1941, MECA and Edmonds to Embassy, 8 June 1942, FO 624/25; Kinch to Thompson, 28 July 1944 and Edmonds to Cornwallis, 23 December 1944, FO 624/66, TNA.
66 Lyon's memoir, *Kurds, Arabs and Britons*, demonstrates how the attitudes of the political advisers were shaped by their experiences in Iraq during the mandate.
67 Cornwallis to FO, 31 December 1943, FO 371/40038/E26 and Chaplin, FO Memorandum "The Situation in Iraq," 12 January 1944, FO 371/40041, TNA.
68 Cornwallis to Eden, 8 February 1944, FO 371/40041, TNA.
69 Minute by Chaplin, Foreign Office, 18 October 1943, FO 371/35012, TNA.
70 Thompson to FO, 7 September 1943, FO 371/35011, TNA.
71 Cornwallis to Eden, 12 October 1943, FO 371/35012, TNA.
72 Cornwallis to Eden, 6 November 1943, FO 371/35013, TNA.
73 Edmonds to Cornwallis, 23 December 1943, FO 624/34; Cornwallis to FO, 30 December 1943, FO 371/35013; Memorandum by Chaplin, 12 January 1944, and Minute by Peterson, 12 January 1944, FO371/40041, TNA.
74 Cornwallis to FO, 6 January 1944, FO624/35, TNA.
75 Cornwallis to Cadogan, 19 February 1944, FO 371/40041, TNA.
76 Edmonds Diaries, 25 March 1944, MECA. The political advisers themselves were divided as to the benefits of the proposed change. For the debates about these plans, see FO 624/35 and FO 624/66, TNA.

77 See for example the exposé of Britain's publicity machine in the newspaper *al-Zaman*, 31 October 1942, reprinted in al-Hasani, *Tarikh al-Wizarat al-'Iraqiyya*, V: 110–11. The underground communist party frequently mentioned names of specific British officials viewed as agents of imperialism. See for example CICI Iraq [Combined Intelligence Centre Iraq] Security Intelligence Summary 1 November 1945–1 December 1945 which describes a communist memorandum that named individual members of the Political Advisory Staff and a CICI officer as "enemies." WO 208/3089, TNA.
78 Henderson to Sec. of State, "Machinery by which Great Britain Maintains Control over, or Exerts Influence in, Various Phases of Iraqi National Life," 13 March 1944 and enclosed memorandum, "British Controls in Iraq," Richard E. Gnade, 25 February 1944, file 800, Classified General Records, 1936–1961, Iraq: U.S. Embassy and Legation, Baghdad, RG 84 NACPM. For an overview of the various publicity and intelligence organizations, see O'Sullivan, *The Baghdad Set*, especially Appendix E, a map that indicates the location of the various British intelligence personnel in Iraq in 1944.
79 Gnade, "British Controls in Iraq," 25 February 1944, Classified General Records, 1936–1961, Iraq: U.S. Embassy and Legation, Baghdad, RG 84 NACPM.
80 Henderson, "Machinery by Which Great Britain Maintains Control," 13 March 1944, Iraq: U.S. Embassy and Legation, Baghdad, RG 84 NACPM.
81 Ibid.
82 Henderson to Wallace Murray, 20 January 1944, "Certain First Impressions Regarding Baghdad and Iraq," Classified General Records, 1936–1961, Iraq: U.S. Embassy and Legation, Baghdad, RG 84 NACPM.
83 Minute by Peterson, 18 January 1944, FO371/40041, TNA.
84 Cornwallis to FO, 3 December 1943, FO 371/35013, TNA.
85 Killearn to Eden, 25 November and 29 November 1943, FO371/35541; Killearn to Eden, 25 February 1944, FO 371/41327, TNA.
86 A copy was forwarded to Killearn and they planned to submit it to the Allied leaders at the Cairo Conference. "Note addressée aux représentants de Grande bretagne, Etats-Unis, Russie et Chine Reunis En Conference Au Caire," 29 November 1943, FO141/910, TNA.
87 Killearn to FO, 28 November 1943, FO371/35540, TNA.
88 For accounts of these protests, see FO141/855, TNA.
89 Minute by Smart, 21 December 1943, FO141/855, TNA.

Chapter 9

1 Cornwallis to Eden, 2 February 1944, FO 624/35, TNA.
2 Cornwallis's speech for the Nasiriya Tea Party, 16 January 1944, FO 624/35, TNA.
3 Cornwallis's speech for the 'Amara Tea Party, 22 January 1944, FO 624/35, TNA.
4 Edmonds to Cornwallis, 14 March 1944, FO624/67, TNA.
5 Cornwallis to Eden, 13 January 1944, FO 371/40041, TNA.
6 Cornwallis to Eden, 23 March 1944, FO 371/40041, TNA.
7 Brotherhood of Freedom Bulletin no. 117, 12 February 1944, FO 371/40078, TNA.
8 Cornwallis to Eden, 23 January 1944, FO 371/40041, TNA.
9 Cornwallis to Eden, 23 March 1944, FO 371/40041; Cornwallis to Eden, 8 June 1944, FO 371/40042, TNA.
10 Cornwallis to Eden, 13 January 1944, FO 371/40041, and Cornwallis to Eden, 8 June 1944, FO 371/40042, TNA.

11 Cornwallis to Eden, 8 February and 23 March 1944, FO 371/40041, TNA. Portions of this discussion of Britain's Kurdish policy are drawn from Stefanie Wichhart, "A 'New Deal' for the Kurds: Britain's Kurdish Policy in Iraq, 1941–1945" *Journal of Imperial and Commonwealth History* 39, no. 5 (December 2011): 815–31, used by permission of the publisher (Taylor & Francis Ltd, http://www.tandfonline.com).
12 Col. Wood, (CICI), 23 October 1944, FO 624/66, TNA. For a list of Mulla Mustafa's demands, and the agreement negotiated with Majid Mustafa, see Jwaideh, *The Kurdish National Movement*, 232–3.
13 Translation of letter from Majid Mustafa to the Council of Ministers, 18 January 1944, FO 624/66, TNA.
14 This term is used in Thompson to Consul Mosul, 22 July 1944; Edmonds to Cornwallis, 6 October 1944; Cornwallis to Eden, 10 December 1944, FO 624/66, TNA.
15 Unsigned, undated Embassy report presented to the Regent by Cornwallis on 30 May 1944, FO 624/66, TNA. Edmonds diaries, 10 June 1944, MECA.
16 Thompson to FO, 30 July 1944, FO371/40038, TNA.
17 Silverfarb, *The Twilight of British*, 98–109.
18 Lyon to Holt, 12 February 1943, FO 624/33, TNA.
19 Edmonds diary, 4 December 1943, MECA.
20 Minute by Thompson, 4 September 1944, Col. Wood to all CICI officers, "Policy-Iraq," undated (received in Embassy 15 June 1944), FO 624/66, TNA.
21 Michael Eppel, *Iraq from Monarchy to Tyranny: From the Hashemites to the Rise of Saddam* (Gainesville: University of Florida Press, 2004), 54.
22 Cornwallis to FO, 6 March 1944, and Cornwallis to FO, 11 March 1944, FO 371/40041, TNA.
23 Edmonds to Cornwallis, 14 March 1944, FO624/67, TNA.
24 Cornwallis to Eden, 9 January 1944, FO371/45302.
25 Edmonds to Cornwallis, 14 March 1944, FO624/67, TNA.
26 Cornwallis to Eden, 23 March 1944, FO 371/40041; Minute by Thompson, 17 February 1944, FO 624/67, TNA.
27 Edmonds to Cornwallis, 14 March 1944, FO624/67, TNA.
28 Cornwallis to FO, 22 May 1944, FO 371/40041; Cornwallis to FO, 26 May 1944, FO371/40042, TNA.
29 Memorandum by Chaplin, 12 January 1944, FO371/40041, TNA.
30 Cornwallis to Eden, 9 January 1944, FO371/45302, TNA.
31 Cornwallis to FO, 26 May 1944, FO 371/40042, TNA.
32 "Subject: Political Crisis Tapers Off," J.E. Jacobs, US Legation Baghdad, to Sec. of State, 2 June 1944, file 800, Classified and Unclassified General Records, 1936–1955, Egypt, U.S. Embassy and Legation, Cairo, RG84, NACPM.
33 Minute by Scrivener, 25 October 1943, FO371/35539, TNA.
34 Minute by Killearn 17 January 1944 and Killearn to Eden, 30 January 1944, FO 141/962, TNA. For the long-term factors behind the malaria crisis, see Timothy Mitchell, *Rule of Experts: Egypt, Techo-Politics, Modernity* (Berkeley and Los Angeles: University of California Press, 2002), 22. For the British response, see also Abdel Nasser, *Britain and the Egyptian Nationalist Movement,* Appendix 2, 287–8.
35 Killearn to FO, 24 February 1944, FO371/41326, TNA.
36 Press cuttings: "Fight against Malaria in Egypt," in the *Times*, 28 February 1944, and "Egypt Has Enough Food, Says Britain," in the *Egyptian Gazette*, 20 February 1944, FO371/41327, TNA.
37 Cutting from *Egyptian Gazette*, 21 February 1944, FO 371/41327, TNA.
38 Note from Nahhas and Killearn to FO, 27 February 1944, FO 371/41327, TNA.

39 Overseas Planning Committee Plan of Propaganda for Egypt 2nd Supplement to Appreciation, paper no. 534A, 11 November 1944, FO 371/41368, TNA.
40 Appreciation of Egyptian Politics by Scrivener, 26 March 1944, FO371/41327, TNA.
41 Killearn to FO, 1 March 1944, FO141/937, TNA.
42 Memorandums by Smart, 1 March and 17 April 1944, FO141/937 and 4 May 1944, FO 141/951, TNA.
43 Memorandum by Smart, 5 March 1944, and Minute by Shone, 10 March 1944, FO141/937; Minute by Peterson, 29 March 1944 and Minute by Scrivener, 29 March 1944, FO371/41327, TNA.
44 Killearn to Eden, 27 June 1944, FO371/41329, TNA.
45 Minute by Peterson, 14 April 1944, FO371/41327; Killearn to FO, 12 April 1944, FO141/937, TNA.
46 Lord Moyne to FO, 18 April 1944, FO371/41327, TNA.
47 Memorandum by Killearn, 17 April 1944, FO141/937, TNA.
48 Minute by Peterson, 14 April 1944, FO371/41327; Churchill to Cadogan, 16 April 1944, FO371/41328, TNA.
49 Churchill to Cadogan, 16 April 1944, and FO to Cairo, 20 April 1944, FO371/41328, TNA.
50 Killearn to FO, 24 April 1944, FO141/937; Killearn to Eden, 4 May 1944, FO371/41329, TNA.
51 Minute by Smart, 11 February 1944, FO141/937, TNA.
52 Kirk to Sec. of State, 15 February 1944, file 800, Classified and Unclassified General Records, 1936–55, Egypt, U.S. Embassy and Legation, Cairo, RG84, NACPM.
53 Translation of pamphlet "The Second Call Issued by the National Front on Thursday, 23rd March 1944," FO141/937, TNA.
54 Translation of "The Third Call Issued by the National Front on Monday 1st May, 1944," FO 141/951, TNA.
55 Minute by Smart, 11 February 1944, FO141/937, TNA.
56 Translation of "Fifth call of national front, June 1944," enclosed in Killearn to Eden, 29 June 1944, FO 371/41329, TNA.
57 Killearn to Eden, 27 June 1944, FO371/41329; Killearn to FO, 29 August 1944, FO 141/987, TNA.
58 Killearn to FO, 6 September 1944, and Shone to FO, 15 September 1944, FO141/937, TNA.
59 Minute by Scrivener, 17 September 1944, FO 371/41332, TNA.
60 FO to Cairo, 23 September 1944, Minute by Eden and Minute by Scrivener, 27 September 1944, FO371/41333; Cairo to FO, 8 October 1944, FO141/937, TNA.
61 Killearn Diaries, 1 January 1945, MECA.
62 Killearn to FO, 5 January 1944, FO 141/937, TNA.
63 Killearn to Eden, 14 July 1944, Minute by Scrivener 29 July 1944, Eden to Lampson, 9 August 1944, Killern to Eden, 17 August 1944, FO 371/41331, TNA.
64 Shone to FO, 17 September 1944, FO 371/41332, TNA.
65 Kirk to Sec. of State, 15 February 1944, file 800, Classified and Unclassified General Records, 1936–1955, Egypt, U.S. Embassy and Legation, Cairo, RG84, NACPM.
66 Translation of pamphlet "The Second Call issued by the National Front on Thursday, 23rd March 1944," FO141/937, TNA.
67 Majid Khadduri, *The Government of Iraq* (Jerusalem: New Publishers Iraq, 1944), 22–4.
68 M.H. Hadid, "Conditions in Iraq," *The New Statesman and Nation*, 14 September 1946.
69 Albert Hourani, "Great Britain and Arab Nationalism," June 1943, FO371/34958, TNA.

70 Major Scaife, "Memorandum on the Ikhwan al-Hurriya by the Area Officer," 17 December 1943, FO930/278, TNA.
71 Overseas Planning committee Plan of Propaganda for Egypt Second Revision of channels, 11 November 1944, FO 371/41368, TNA.
72 Scaife Speech at the opening of the Ikhwan al Hurriya Club Baghdad, April 18, 1944, FO930/248, TNA.
73 Minute by Hankey, 28 May 1944, FO 371/41379, TNA.
74 Directive on Propaganda to Trade Unionists in Egypt enclosed in Killearn to Eden, 15 January 1944, FO 371/41368, TNA.
75 Minute by G.A.W. Lawrence, 24 May 1944, FO 371/41379, TNA.
76 Thompson to Eden, no. 401, 18 August 1944, FO 371/40098, TNA.
77 Scaife, Memorandum, 17 December 1943, FO930/278, TNA.
78 Grubb to Elizabeth Monroe, 5 January 1944, FO930/278, TNA.
79 For the negotiations surrounding the opening of diplomatic relations with Egypt: Rami Ginat, "British Concoction or Bilateral Decision? Revisiting the Genesis of Soviet-Egyptian Diplomatic Relations," *International Journal of Middle East Studies* 31, no. 1 (1999): 39–60.
80 Cornwallis to Eden, 8 February 1944, FO 371/40041; Cornwallis to Eden, 31 October 1944, FO 371/40042, TNA.
81 Jwaideh, *The Kurdish Nationalist Movement,* 246.
82 For a complete run of these reports from the later war years, see WO208/3089, TNA. A number of the most important wartime statements of Fahd are included in Fahd, *Kitabat al-Rafiq Fahd,* ed. Z. Khayri (Baghdad: al-Tariq al-Jadid, 1976). For Fahd's background and role in the party, see Book two, part IV of Hanna Batatu's still definitive work on Iraqi communism, *The Old Social Classes and the Revolutionary Movements of Iraq*, 485–656. For an analysis of Fahd's writings, see Bashkin, *The Other Iraq,* 76–9.
83 For background on the Ahali group, see ibid., 61–73; Batatu, *The Old Social Classes,* 293–306; and Charles Tripp, *A History of Iraq* (New York: Cambridge University Press, 2007), 84–97.
84 Archie Roosevelt, American Military Attaché, Baghdad, "An Outline of the Press in Iraq," report no. 337, 17 August 1944, file 891, Classified General Records, 1936–61, Iraq: U.S. Embassy and Legation, Baghdad, RG 84, NACPM.
85 *Sawt al-Ahali*, 18 August 1944.
86 Minute by Mayer, 29 April 1944 and Cornwallis to FO, 26 April 1944, FO371/40082, TNA.
87 Killearn to FO, 11 March 1944, a point originally made in a Minute by Smart, 8 March 1944, FO 141/978, TNA.
88 Kirk to Sec. of State, 28 April 1944, file 800.2, Classified and Unclassified General Records, 1936–1955, Egypt, U.S. Embassy and Legation, Cairo, RG84, NACPM.
89 Killearn to Peterson, 18 February 1944 FO371/41397, TNA. On Landis, see Wilmington, *The Middle East Supply Centre,* 64–7; on American development as a tactic, see O'Sullivan, *FDR and the End of Empire,* 61–7. For Anglo-American economic rivalry and investment in development in Egypt: Robert Vitalis, "The 'New Deal' in Egypt: The Rise of Anglo-American Commercial Competition in World War II and the Fall of Neocolonialism," *Diplomatic History* 20, no. 2 (Spring 1996): 211–39.
90 Killearn to Peterson, 18 February 1944 FO371/41397, TNA.
91 Weekly Political and Economic Report, 27 July–2 August, 1944, FO 371/41318, TNA.

Chapter 10

1 Description of a *Ruz al-Yusuf* cartoon from cover, Weekly Political and Economic report, September 21–27, 1944, FO 371/41318, TNA.
2 Arab appropriation of internationalist themes was a vital part of the transition to postwar decolonization and reflected a deliberate fusion of the internationalist rhetoric of the Second World War to that of the earlier period after the First World War. This chapter builds on works that span this time period: Erez Manela, *The Wilsonian Moment: Self-Determination and the International Origins of Anticolonial Nationalism* (New York: Oxford University Press, 2007); Pedersen, *The Guardians;* Elizabeth Borgwardt, *A New Deal for the World: America's Vision for Human Rights* (Cambridge, MA: Belknap Press of Harvard University Press, 2005); Mark Mazower, *No Enchanted Palace: The End of Empire and the Ideological Origins of the United Nations* (Princeton: Princeton University Press, 2009).
3 Dr. Fadhil Jamali, undated, "A Personal Note on the History of Popular Feeling in Iraq towards the Allies with Constructive Suggestions," enclosed in Henderson to State, 4 October 1944, file 800, Classified General Records, 1936–1961, Iraq: U.S. Embassy and Legation, Baghdad, RG 84 NACPM.
4 Albert Hourani, "Great Britain and Arab Nationalism," June 1943, FO371/34958, TNA.
5 Scrivener to Shone, 21 October 1943, FO 371/35538, TNA. For a similar message from the US legation: Tuck to Sec. of State, 6 September 1944, file 800, Classified and Unclassified General Records, 1936–1955, Egypt, U.S. Embassy and Legation, Cairo, RG84, NACPM.
6 Peterson to Cornwallis, 19 February 1944, FO371/40079, TNA.
7 Cornwallis to Peterson, 19 March 1944, FO371/40079, TNA.
8 Minute by Smart, 20 January 1944, Minute by Killearn, 18 January 1944, and Cairo to FO, 18 January 1944, FO 141/937, TNA.
9 Shone to Scrivener, 19 January 1944, FO 141/873; Shone to Scrivener, 20 January 1944, FO 141/965, TNA.
10 Ibid.
11 Makram Ebeid, President of the Independent Wafdist Block, to Killearn 1 May 1944 enclosing text of decisions of the General Assembly of the Independent Wafdist Block on 28 April 1944, FO 141/937, TNA.
12 Ibid.
13 Translation of National Front Opposition Manifesto, 11 February 1944, FO141/937, TNA.
14 Draft telegram Killearn to FO, 26 June 1944, FO 141/967; Killearn to Eden, 27 June 1944, FO 371/41329, TNA.
15 *Al-Ahram*, 23 June 1944, translation enclosed in Killearn to Eden, 26 June 1944, FO 371/41329, TNA.
16 Ibid.
17 Memorandum by Smart, 4 July 1944, FO 141/937, TNA.
18 Minute by Smart, 11 May 1944, FO 141/1043, TNA. Two works that are helpful for navigating the complexities of the preliminary conversations, the Alexandria Conference, and the formation of the Arab League: Gomaa, *The Foundation of the League of Arab* and Porath, *In Search of Arab Unity.*
19 Summary of draft letter from Nahhas to Arab leaders, included in Killearn to FO, 14 June 1944, FO371/39988, TNA.

20 Killearn to FO, 26 July 1944, FO371/39989, TNA.
21 PICME 27 August 1944: "Summary of Telegrams Relating to Arab Unity from 31 January 1944 to 12 August 44," FO 624/35, TNA.
22 FO to Killearn, 2 March 1944, Cornwallis to FO, 5 July 1944, FO 624/35.
23 Thompson to Eden, 17 July 1944, encloses "translation of a statement which the Iraqi Prime Minister made to Reuter's representative on July 13th on Arab Unity," FO 624/35, TNA.
24 PICME 27 August 1944: "Summary of Telegrams Relating to Arab Unity from 31 January 1944 to 12 August 44," FO 624/35, TNA.
25 Cornwallis to FO, 21 March 1944, FO371/39987, TNA.
26 Minute by Smart, 25 July 1944, FO 141/949, TNA.
27 Killearn to FO, 5 June 1944, FO371/39988, TNA.
28 PICME 27 August 1944: "Summary of Telegrams Relating to Arab Unity from 31 January 1944 to 12 August 44," FO 624/35, TNA.
29 *Al-Ahram*, 25 September 1944.
30 A complete English translation of the procès verbaux for the Preparatory Committee meetings in included in Killearn to Eden, 22 December 1944, FO371/45235, TNA. These detailed written accounts of the meetings reveal the lines of debate and are a useful source for studying the founding of the Arab League.
31 Shone to FO, 8 October 1944, FO371/39990, TNA.
32 Appendix I, "Text of the Alexandria Protocol, 7 October 1944," in Gomaa, *The Foundation of the League of Arab States*, 272–4.
33 Account by "an unofficial observer" of the Alexandria meeting submitted to PICME, undated, FO624/35, TNA.
34 Cornwallis to FO, 25 September 1944, FO 624/35; Cornwallis to Eden, 31 October 1944, FO 371/40042, TNA.
35 Moyne to Eden, 19 October 1944, FO371/39991, TNA.
36 Cornwallis to Eden, 5 November 1944, Moyne to Eden, 19 October 1944, Shone to Eden, 10 October 1944, FO371/39991, TNA.
37 G. J. Jenkins, GHQ ME Cairo to F.H. Tomlyn, Embassy, "The attached copy of a 'note' received from the Political Section of the Cairo City Police" in Burdett, *The Arab League,* vol. 2.
38 Cornwallis to Peterson, 11 January 1944, FO371/39987; Cornwallis to Eden, 5 November 1944, FO371/39991, TNA.
39 Killearn to Eden, 29 August 1943, FO 371/34961, TNA.
40 Cornwallis to Eden, 18 November 1944, FO 371/40042, TNA. For an overview of the Palestine issue in the 1944 US election and the various proposed resolutions on Palestine and Jewish immigration, see Richard Breitman and Allan J. Lichtman, *FDR and the Jews* (Harvard University Press, 2013) 255–61.
41 Michael J. Cohen, "The Moyne Assassination, November, 1944: A Political Analysis." *Middle Eastern Studies* 15, no. 3 (Oct. 1979): 358–73.
42 Moyne to Eden, 19 October 1944, FO371/39991, TNA.
43 Account by "an unofficial observer" of the Alexandria meeting submitted to PICME, undated, FO624/35, TNA.
44 Sir Lee Stack Pasha was the Sirdar and Governor-General of the Sudan and he was assassinated in 1924.
45 Shone to FO, 23 October 1944, FO141/937, TNA.

46 Memorandum by Smart, 30 October 1944 and 17 November 1944, FO141/937, TNA.
47 Shone to FO, 8 November 1944, FO371/41335; Memorandum by Smart, 11 November 1944, FO141/971, TNA.
48 Killearn to FO, 23 December 1944, FO371/41335, TNA.
49 Killearn to FO, 29 December 1944, FO371/45916, TNA.
50 Overseas Planning Committee Plan of Propaganda for Egypt 2nd Supplement to Appreciation, paper no. 534A 11 November 1944, FO 371/41368; Killearn to Eden, 3 March 1945, FO 371/45930, TNA.
51 Killearn to Eden, 4 May 1945, FO371/45921, TNA.
52 FO to Beirut, 18 March 1945, FO 371/50683, TNA. The eligible states were: Chile, Peru Ecuador, Paraguay, Uruguay, Venezuela, Egypt, Iceland, and Turkey.
53 Cairo Conversations, 17 February 1945, and Killearn to FO, 18 February 1945, FO 371/45918, TNA.
54 Killearn to Eden, 10 February 1945, encloses translation of Ahmad Mahir interview with *New York Times* and *Daily Sketch* correspondents on Egyptian foreign policy, *al-Dustur*, 8 February 1945, FO 371/45918, TNA.
55 Killearn to FO, 25 February 1945, FO 371/45918, TNA.
56 Weekly Political Summary, 22–28 February 1945, FO 371/45930, TNA.
57 Killearn to FO, 26 February 1945, FO 371/45918; Killearn to Campbell, 14 April 1945, FO 371/45920, TNA.
58 Bowker to Bevin, Annual Review for 1945, 5 March 1946, FO403/469, TNA.
59 Ibid.; Killearn to FO, 24 February 1945, FO141/1051; Killearn to Eden, 23 February 1945, 3 March 1945, and 10 March 1945, FO 371/45930, TNA.
60 Palestine would have an observer to participate in the meetings but not an official representative. The Yemeni representatives did not sign the Covenant on site but a copy was sent to the Yemen to be signed there after consultation with the government. Killearn to FO, 19 March 1945, and Killearn to FO, 23 March 1945, FO371/45237, TNA.
61 English translation of the Covenant of the Arab League, enclosed in Killearn to Eden, 12 April 1945, FO371/45238, TNA.
62 Killearn to FO, 19 March 1945, FO371/45237, TNA.
63 Killearn to FO, 3 June 1945, FO371/45921, TNA.
64 Minute by Ward, 19 March 1945, FO to Cairo, 21 March 1945, FO 371/50684, TNA.
65 Monthly Return, R. W. Fey, 30 April 1945, FO 930/248, TNA.
66 Killearn to FO, 2 May 1945, and Minute by Besly, 7 May 1945, FO141/1043, TNA.
67 FO to Cairo, 28 May 1945, FO 141/1043, TNA.
68 Minute by Burrows, 7 July 1945, as part of a broader discussion of issues that Britain wanted to raise with the United States at the Potsdam Conference, FO 141/1059, TNA.
69 Killearn to FO, 11 June 1945, FO371/45921, TNA.
70 *Akhir Sa'a,* March 11, April 29 and May 27, 1945.
71 US Military Attaché Report, Iraq 10 August, 1945 monthly estimate for July 1945, file 800, Classified General Records, 1936–1961, Iraq: U.S. Embassy and Legation, Baghdad, RG 84, NACPM.
72 Ibid.
73 Weekly Political and Economic Report, May 16–23, 1945 and June 21–27, 1945, FO 371/45931, TNA.

Chapter 11

1 Weekly Appreciation, Killearn to FO, 12 May 1945, and Weekly Political and Economic report, May 10–16, 1945 FO 371/45931, TNA.
2 Cornwallis to Eden, 9 January 1945, FO371/45302, TNA.
3 A few of the most useful works from a voluminous body of literature on treaty revision: Wm. Roger Louis, *The British Empire in the Middle East 1945–1951* (New York: Oxford University Press, 1986) remains an indispensable guide to the Labour government's postwar policy in the Middle East; many of the key British documents relating to the postwar defense of Egypt are available in John Kent, ed., *Egypt and the Defence of the Middle East*, Series B Volume 4 Part I *1945–1949*, British Documents on the End of Empire (London: The Stationery Office, 1998 (Hereafter BDEEP B4I). Kent's introduction to that volume and John Kent, "British and the Egyptian problem, 1945–48," in *Demise of the British Empire in the Middle East*, ed. Michael J. Cohen and Martin Kolinsky (London: Frank Cass, 1998), 142–61 provide a useful guide to navigating the complex waters of this issue. Hoda Gamal Abdel Nasser provides insight into the Egyptian position on postwar Anglo-Egyptian relations in *Britain and the Egyptian Nationalist Movement*, 113–79. For the debate over treaty revision in Iraq, see Silverfarb, *The Twilight of British Ascendency*, 125–55.
4 Louis, *The British Empire in the Middle East*, 9.
5 "British policy and organisation in the Middle East": memorandum by Lord Altrincham, 2 September 1945, CO732/88, in BDEEP B4I, 41–2.
6 War Cabinet Memorandum, 13 April 1945, CAB66/65, in BDEEP B4I, 7.
7 "Imperial security in the Middle East": War Cabinet memorandum by Sir E Grigg, 2 July 1945, CAB 66/67, BDEEP B4I, 25 and 30.
8 Nahhas to Killearn, 23 July 1945, FO141/1043, TNA.
9 Extract from *Le Journal d'Egypte*, 24 September 1945, FO371/45926, TNA.
10 Killearn to FO, 12 July 1945, FO371/45922, TNA.
11 Memorandum by Smart, "Anglo-Egyptian Treaty," 29 August 1945, FO141/1043, TNA.
12 Bowker to Bevin, Annual Review for 1945, 5 March 1946, FO403/469, TNA.
13 FO to Cairo, 28 May 1945, FO141/1043, TNA.
14 Memorandum by R. Howe for Cadogan, 10 September 1945, FO371/45925, TNA.
15 Minute by Smart, 23 August 1945, FO141/1059, TNA.
16 Minute by Smart, 11 May 1945, FO141/1043, TNA.
17 Killearn Diaries, 11 May 1945, MECA.
18 Translation of article, March 23, 1945 *An-Nida* enclosed in William Moreland to Sec. of State, 27 March 1945, file 710 and translation enclosed in Robert Meminger, Chargé, to Sec. of State, June 14, 1945, file 710, Classified General Records, 1936–1961, Iraq: U.S. Embassy and Legation, Baghdad, RG 84, NACPM.
19 Minute by Baxter, 25 July 1945, FO 371/45303, TNA.
20 Minute by Holt, "Revision of the Anglo-Iraqi Treaty," 9 August 1945, FO371/45303, TNA.
21 Stonehewer-Bird to Eden, 7 May 1945, and Minute by Campbell, 15 June 1945, Minute by Baxter, 14 June 1945, FO371/45302, TNA; Silverfarb, *The Twilight of British Ascendancy*, 127–8.
22 Minute by Holt, "Revision of the Anglo-Iraqi Treaty," 9 August 1945, FO371/45303, TNA.
23 Killearn to FO, 20 April 1945, FO 371/45930, Weekly Political and Economic Appreciation, April 12–18, 1945, FO 371/45931, TNA.

24 Minute by Smart, 17 April 1945, FO141/1011, TNA.
25 Memorandum by Scrivener, 3 August 1945, FO371/45923, TNA.
26 Cornwallis to Eden, 9 January 1945, FO371/45302, TNA.
27 Edmonds Diary, 30 April and 11 May, 1945, MECA. The Edmonds papers also include a number of press clippings recognizing his retirement that provide useful details about his career and the popular perception of his pervasive influence in Iraqi internal affairs.
28 Cornwallis to Eden, 31 October 1944, FO371/40042, TNA; Fieldhouse, *Kurds, Arabs and Britons*, 227.
29 Capt. F. Stoakes, Deputy Assistant Political Adviser, Erbil to Political Adviser, Northern Area, Kirkuk on "The Confederacy of Barzan," 17 March 1945 and Major R. Wilson, 8 March 1945, FO 624/71, TNA.
30 Memo by Peterson, 10 November 1943, FO 371/34992, TNA.
31 Report from Henderson, 3 November 1944, file 800, Classified General Records, 1936–1961, Iraq: U.S. Embassy and Legation, Baghdad, RG 84 NACPM.
32 Minute by Baxter, 19 April 1945, FO371/45343, TNA.
33 Cornwallis to Eden, Cornwallis's Valedictory, 30 March 1945, FO 371/45302, TNA.
34 Ibid.
35 Tuck to Sec. of State, from American Legation Cairo, August 1, 1945, file 800, Classified General Records, 1936–1961, Iraq: U.S. Embassy and Legation, Baghdad, RG 84 NACPM.
36 CICI Security Intelligence Summary no. 78, 1 August 1945–1 September 1945, and no. 79, 1 September 1945–1 October 1945, WO208/3089, TNA.
37 Baxter (for Bevin) to Bowker, 18 October 1945, FO141/1059, TNA.
38 Ministry of War Transport, quoted in Appendix B, "Provision of Experts," Baxter (for Bevin) to Bowker, 18 October 1945, FO141/1059, TNA.
39 Minute by Bowker, 19 November 1945, FO141/1059, TNA.
40 FO memorandum on the Arab Centre, unsigned, undated [September 1944], FO371/40024. TNA. For the history of the center, see Sir James Craig, *Shemlan: A History of the Middle East Centre for Arab Studies* (London: Macmillan Press, in association with St. Antony's College, Oxford, 1998) and McLoughlin, *In a Sea of Knowledge*.
41 Thompson to Bevin, 26 September 1945, FO371/45295, TNA.
42 Stonehewer-Bird to Bevin, 1945 Annual Review, 4 March 1946, FO406/84, TNA.
43 Killearn to Bevin, quoting an article in the Egyptian newspaper *Ruz al-Yusuf*, 17 December 1945, FO371/45929, TNA.
44 Fahd (Yusuf Salman Yusuf) speech to the first party congress, 1944, "Our National Cause," published in Fahd, *Kitabat al-Rafiq Fahd*, 101–31.
45 Cornwallis to Eden, 2 December 1944, FO 371/40042, TNA.
46 Muhammad Hadid, *Mudhakkirati: al-Sira' min ajli al-Dimuqratiyya fi al-'Iraq* (Beirut: Dar al-Saqi, 2006), 177–8. Muhammad Mahdi Kubba, a former leader of the Muthanna Club, complained that the Brotherhood of Freedom's appropriation of the former Muthanna Club building had turned it into "a center for the Britsh intelligence service." Wien, *Iraqi Arab Nationalism*, 34.
47 Iraq Bulletin no. 171, 21 February 1945, FO 930/278, TNA.
48 Ibid.
49 Iraq Bulletin no. 176, March 26/28, 1945, FO 930/278, TNA.
50 Iraq Bulletin no. 177, 4 April 1945, FO 930/278, TNA.
51 Ibid.
52 The Brotherhood of Freedom, in adopting the format of an inter-generational debate for these articles, reflects a hallmark of the *effendiyya* literature of the period: Ryzova, *The Age of the Efendiya*, 228–36.

53 Stark provided an extensive discussion of this reporting mechanism in "A Pamphlet in Defence of Propaganda," (undated, 1943), FO930/278, TNA.
54 John Kent, Introduction to BDEEP B4I, xxxix. For the challenges the BMEO faced in implementing its agenda: Paul W. T. Kingston, *Britain and the Politics of Modernization in the Middle East, 1945–1958* (New York: Cambridge University Press, 1996), 10–28.
55 Robert Vitalis and Steven Heydemann, "War, Keynesianism, and Colonialism: Explaining State-Market Relations in the Postwar Middle East," in *War, Institutions, and Social Change in the Middle East*, ed. Steven Heydemann (Berkeley: University of California Press, 2000), 132–6.
56 Thompson to FO, 28 September 1945, FO371/45347, TNA.
57 For the debates over the postwar status of the PAs and ALOs, see Minute by Chapman-Andrews, 16 May 1945, Stonehewer-Bird to Eden, 9 June 1945, and Stonehewer-Bird to Bevin, 25 October 1945, and Baxter to Secretary to the Treasury, 11 January 1946, FO 371/45347, TNA. H.K. Dawson-Shepherd, "An Appreciation of the Security Situation in Iraq in the Near Future and in the Post-War Period," CIC Baghdad, 14 July 1945 enclosed in Stonehewer-Bird to Eden, 16 July 1945, FO 371/45350, TNA provides a useful overview of postwar internal security concerns and an assessment of the Political Advisory System and the role of the ALOs.
58 Silverfarb, *The Twilight of British Ascendancy in the Middle East,* 77 and 107–9; Elliot, *"Independent Iraq,"* 153–4.
59 Minute by Perowne, 2 December 1944, FO624/37, TNA.
60 Ryan, "Future of the Ikhwan al Hurriyah in Iraq," 18 September 1945, and O'Malley to Becher, 14 June 1946, FO930/36, TNA.
61 James Vaughan, *The Failure of American and British Propaganda in the Arab Middle East, 1945–1957* (London: Palgrave Macmillan, 2005), 27–8.
62 See Fay's monthly returns 1947, FO 371/63033, TNA.
63 Kelly to Eden, 9 September 1936, FO 371/20119, TNA.
64 For example, in a 1981 interview Anwar al-Sadat described the oriental secretary at the embassy as "the real ruler of Egypt," quoted in Louis, *The British Empire in the Middle East,* 228–9, footnote 5.

Chapter 12

1 For the original text: Lugol, *Egypt and World War II,* 150.
2 Emad Ahmed Helal, "Egypt's Overlooked Contribution to World War II," in *World in World Wars: Experiences, Perceptions and Perspectives from Africa and Asia*, ed. Heike Liebau, Katrin Bromber, Katharina Lange, Dyala Hamzah, and Ravi Ahuja (Leiden: Brill, 2010), 217–47 draws on the reports compiled toward the end of the war and housed in the Egyptian archives. Two examples of postwar pamphlets: The Egyptian-government publication "The Contribution of Egypt in World War II" (Cairo: Government Press, 1947) and Young Egypt's publication "Egypt's War Effort: A Reply to the Charges of the American Christian Palestine Committee" (New York: 1947).
3 Louis, *The British Empire in the Middle East,* 13.
4 Cutting from the *Egyptian Gazette*, 17 December 1945, FO371/45929, TNA.
5 Cornwallis to Eden, Cornwallis's Valedictory, 30 March 1945, FO 371/45302, TNA.
6 Stonehewer-Bird to Bevin, 1945 Annual Review for Iraq, 4 March 1946, FO406/84, TNA.

7 Monroe, *Britain's Moment in the Middle East*, 90–1.

8 "Nahhas Pasha Says 'No Reason to Blush over Feb. 4,'" article in the *Egyptian Gazette*, 14 November 1945, FO371/45929. Translation of "What Happened on February 4th, 1942," article published in *al-Doustour*, 15 November 1945, FO371/45929. This newspaper was considered to be the Sa'dist party organ. For the debate over whether or not Nahhas was aware of British plans in advance, see Smith, "4 February 1942," 470–1, especially footnote 55.

9 English translation of "Text of the British ultimatum to the King—momentous secret published for the first time," by Mustafa Amin, *Akhbar al-Yom*, 17 November 1945, FO 371/45929, TNA.

10 Translation of "What Happened on February 4th, 1942," article published in *al-Doustour*, 15 November 1945, FO371/45929, TNA.

11 Aly el Khochkhani quoted in "Les debats à la Chambre sur les aspirations nationals," *Le Journal d'Egypte*, 16 October 1945, FO371/45927, TNA.

12 "Le Senat appuie les revendications nationales…" *Le Journal d'Egypte* 17 October 1945, FO371/45927, TNA.

13 Minute by Coverley Price, 1 January 1946, FO371/45929, TNA.

14 Howe to Sir Alan Brooke, 5 October 1945, FO141/1053, TNA. See Chapter 11, endnote 3 for some of the most useful works on Britain's postwar strategic requirements and treaty revision.

15 Killearn to FO, 6 December 1945, FO371/46028, TNA.

16 "Translation of the Note communicated by the Egyptian Ambassador to the Foreign Office," 20 December 1945, FO371/45929, TNA.

17 Ibid.

18 Bevin, British reply presented to the Egyptian Ambassador to London on 26 January 1946 (dated 25 January 1946), FO371/45929, TNA.

19 Memorandum by the Chiefs of Staff Committee, 28 December 1945, FO371/46028, TNA.

20 Memo to Smart from Grafftey-Smith, 17 December 1941, FO141/843, TNA. See also Sadat, *Revolt on the Nile*, 38.

21 Al-Rafi'i, *Fi A'qab al-Thawra al-Misriyya*, 180. For an assessment of this postwar violence, see Jacques Berque, *Egypt: Imperialism and Revolution*, trans. Jean Stewart (NewYork: Praeger, 1972), 568.

22 Killearn to Bevin, 6 January 1946, 8 January 1946 and 12 January 1946, FO403/469; Killearn Diaries, 6 January 1946.

23 Bowker to Bevin, 15 March 1946, enclosed annual review for 1945, FO 403/469, TNA.

24 Sansom, *I Spied Spies*, 196.

25 Ibid., 197.

26 Charles Tripp, "Egypt 1945–52: The Uses of Disorder," in *Demise of the British Empire in the Middle East: Britain's Response to Nationalist Movements 1943–55*, ed. M. Cohen and M. Kolinsky (London: Frank Cass, 1998), 116–17.

27 Louis, *The British Empire in the Middle East*, 125.

28 London to Sec. of State DC, 20 February 1946, file 883.00/2-2046 Central Decimal File, RG 59: General Records of the Department of State, [hereafter RG59], NACPM.

29 Al-Rafi'i, *Fi A'qab al-Thawra al-Misriyya*, 185.

30 Sidqi's reply to the British protest, 26 February 1946, enclosed in S. Pinkney Tuck (Cairo) to DC, 28 February 1946, file 883.00/2-2846, Central Decimal File, RG 59, NACPM.

31 Al-Rafi'i, *Fi A'qab al-Thawra al-Misriyya,* 186.
32 Sansom, *I Spied Spies,* 198.
33 Cairo to FO, 6 March 1946, FO371/53288, TNA.
34 Ibid.
35 Ibid.
36 Louis, *The British Empire in the Middle East,* 49 and 125.
37 Sansom, *I Spied Spies,* 199.
38 Cairo to FO, 6 March 1946, FO371/53288, TNA. Killearn Diaries, 4 February 1946, MECA.
39 Killearn to Eden, 17 August 1944, FO371/41331, TNA. Killearn agonized over whether the new appointment was a promotion or "a kick upstairs": Trevor Roper, ed., *The Killearn Diaries, 1934–1946* (London: Sidgwick & Jackson, 1972), 372–5.
40 "'Revision of the Anglo-Egyptian treaty': note for the Cabinet by Mr. Bevin circulating a note presented to the British delegation by Sidky," 24 April 1946, CAB 129/9, reprinted in BDEEP B4I, 120.
41 "'Revision of the Anglo-Egyptian treaty': COS Committee minutes on the offer of complete evacuation," 24 April 1946, CAB79/47, reprinted in BDEEP B4I, 113–16; "'Revision of the Anglo-Egyptian treaty': Cabinet Defence Committee minutes on the offer of complete evacuation," 24 April 1946, CAB131/1, reprinted in BDEEP B4I, 116–18. For an overview of the 1946 negotiations, see Louis, *The British Empire in the Middle East,* 232–53.
42 Cornwallis to Eden, Cornwallis's Valedictory, 30 March 1945, FO 371/45302, TNA.
43 Memorandum of the Iraqi Communist Party, 21 November 1945, reprinted in Fahd, *Kitabat al-Rafiq Fahd,* 309–23.
44 For the complete text, see al-Hasani, *Tarikh al-Wizarat al-'Iraqiyya,* VI: 293–6; Stonehewer-Bird to Bevin, 31 December 1945, FO 371/52401, TNA.
45 Edmonds to Cornwallis, 23 December 1944, FO624/67, TNA.
46 For the new parties, see Eppel, *Iraq from Monarchy to Tyranny,* 62–6.
47 Busk to Bevin, 19 September 1946, FO 371/52402, TNA.
48 Minute from the Foreign Office Research Department, 2 November 1946, FO 371/52402, TNA.
49 Busk to Bevin, 19 September 1946, FO 371/52402, TNA.
50 Busk to Bevin, 6 September 1946, FO 371/52402, TNA. The complexities of this period are perhaps best summed up by Dawisha's heading for the events of 1946: "The anti-liberal state in the (relatively) liberal era." Dawisha, *Iraq: A Political History from Independence to Occupation,* 105–12.
51 Thompson to Foreign Office, 1 August 1945, Thompson to Mead, 20 August 1945, Stonehewer- Bird to Bevin, 10 October 1945, FO 624/71, TNA.
52 Thompson to FO, 22 September 1945 and Stonehewer-Bird to FO, 6 October 1945, FO 624/71, TNA; For British accounts of the military action taken against the Barzanis, see FO 624/71, TNA.
53 See McDowall, *Modern History of the Kurds,* 231–48.
54 Stonehewer-Bird to FO, 1 March 1946, FO 371/52401, TNA.
55 For an account of the treaty revision talks and the *Wathba,* see Eppel, *Iraq from Monarchy to Tyranny,* 73–81; Silverfarb, *The Twilight of British Ascendancy,* 125–55.
56 Busk to Bevin, 19 September 1946, FO 371/52402; Stonehewer-Bird to Bevin, 26 November 1946, FO 371/52405, TNA.
57 M. H. Hadid, "Conditions in Iraq," *The New Statesman and Nation,* 14 September 1946.
58 NDP memo enclosed in Busk to Bevin, 19 September 1946, FO 371/52402, TNA.

59 Grubb to Monroe, 1 May 1944, FO930/278, TNA.
60 See for example the robust postwar debate regarding British policy toward the *effendiyya,* including Bevin to Eyres (Damascus), 15 January 1947, FO 371/52365, and Minute by K.C. Buss, 17 April 1947, FO 371/61538, TNA.
61 Clayton to Smart, 26 March 1946 in Anita L.P. Burdett, ed., *The Arab League,* 4: 621.
62 Kent, “Introduction” to BDEEP B4I, xxxvi.

Bibliography

Arabic Newspapers (Library of Congress and British Library):

al-Ahram, Cairo
Akhir Sa'a, Cairo
al-Akhbar, Baghdad
Sawt al-Ahali, Baghdad

British Newspapers

New Statesman and Nation
Supplement to the London Gazette
Times

Archival Sources

Middle East Centre Archive, St. Antony's College, Oxford (MECA)

Diaries and papers of C.J. Edmonds
Diaries and papers of Miles Lampson, Lord Killearn
Kinch Papers

The National Archives, Kew, UK (TNA)

AIR 23 Air Ministry and Ministry of Defence: RAF Overseas Commands
FO 141 Embassy and Consulates, Egypt: General Correspondence
FO 371 Political Departments: General Correspondence
FO 395 News Department: General Correspondence from 1906
FO 624 Embassy, High Commission and Consulate, Iraq: General Correspondence
FO 898 Political Warfare Executive and Foreign Office, Political Intelligence Department
FO 921 War Cabinet: Office of the Minister of State Resident in the Middle East
FO 930 Ministry of Information and Foreign Office: Foreign Publicity Files
HS 3 Special Operations Executive: Africa and Middle East Group: Registered Files
HS 8 Ministry of Economic Warfare, Special Operations Executive and Successors
INF 1-6 Ministry of Information
WO 193 War Office: Directorate of Military Operations and Plans

WO 208 War Office: Directorate of Military Operations and Intelligence, and Directorate of Military Intelligence

The National Archives and Records Administration (NACPM), College Park, MD

RG 59 Central Decimal File: General Records of the Department of State
RG 84 Egypt, U.S. Embassy and Legation, Cairo, Classified and Unclassified General Records, 1936–1955
RG 84 Iraq: U.S. Embassy and Legation, Baghdad, Classified General Records, 1936–61

Published document collections

Burdett, Anita L. P., ed. *The Arab League: British Documentary Sources*, 8 vols. Great Britain: Archive Editions, 1995.
Hasani, 'Abd al-Razzaq al-. *Tarikh al-Wizarat al-'Iraqiyya*, vol. 5 and 6. Sayda: Matba'at al -'Irfan, 1965.
Kent, John, ed. *Egypt and the Defence of the Middle East*, Series B Volume 4 Part I *1945-1949*, British Documents on the End of Empire. London: the Stationery Office, 1998.

Published Sources

Abdel Nasser, Hoda Gamal. *Britain and the Egyptian Nationalist Movement, 1936–52*. Reading: Ithaca Press, 1994.
Aboul-Enein, Youssef and Basil Aboul-Enein. *The Secret War for the Middle East: The Influence of Axis and Allied Intelligence Operations during World War II*. Annapolis: Naval Institute Press, 2013.
'Azzam, 'Abd al-Rahman. *Safahat min al-Mudhakkirat al-Sirriya li-Awwal Amin 'Amm lil-Jami'at al-'Arabiyya*. Cairo: al-Maktab al-Misri al-Hadith, 1977.
Barzani, Massoud. *Mustafa Barzani and the Kurdish Liberation Movement (1931–1961)*, ed. Ahmed Ferhadi. New York: Palgrave Macmillan, 2006.
Bashkin, Orit. *New Babylonians: A History of Jews in Modern Iraq*. Stanford: Stanford University Press, 2012.
Bashkin, Orit. *The Other Iraq: Pluralism and Culture in Hashemite Iraq*. Stanford: Stanford University Press, 2009.
Batatu, Hanna. *The Old Social Classes and the Revolutionary Movements of Iraq*. Princeton: Princeton University Press, 1978.
Beinin, Joel and Zachary Lockman. *Workers on the Nile: Nationalism, Communism, Islam, and the Egyptian Working Class, 1882–1854*. Cairo: American University in Cairo Press, 1998.
Belmessous, Saliha, ed. *Empire by Treaty: Negotiating European Expansion, 1600–1900*. New York: Oxford University Press, 2015.
Berque, Jacques. *Egypt: Imperialism and Revolution*, trans. Jean Stewart. New York: Praeger, 1972.
Borgwardt, Elizabeth. *A New Deal for the World: America's Vision for Human Rights*. Cambridge, MA: Belknap Press of Harvard University Press, 2005.

Breitman, Richard and Allan J. Lichtman. *FDR and the Jews*. Cambridge: Harvard University Press, 2013.

Broich, John. *Blood, Oil and the Axis: The Allied Resistance against a Fascist State in Iraq and the Levant, 1941*. New York: Abrams Press, 2019.

Churchill, Winston. *The Second World War*, 6 vols. Boston: Houghton Mifflin Company, 1948–53.

Cohen, Michael J. *Britain's Moment in Palestine: Retrospect and Perspectives, 1917–1948*. New York: Routledge, 2014.

Cohen, Michael J. "The Moyne Assassination, November, 1944: A Political Analysis." *Middle Eastern Studies* 15, no. 3 (Oct. 1979): 358–73.

Cooper, Artemis. *Cairo in the War*. London: Hamish Hamilton, 1989.

Craig, James. *Shemlan: A History of the Middle East Centre for Arab Studies*. London: Macmillan Press, in association with St. Antony's College, Oxford, 1998.

Darwin, John. "An Undeclared Empire: The British in the Middle East, 1918–39." *Journal of Imperial and Commonwealth History* 27, no. 2 (1999): 159–76.

Dawisha, Adeed. *Iraq: A Political History from Independence to Occupation*. Princeton: Princeton University Press, 2009.

Dilks, David, ed. *The Diaries of Sir Alexander Cadogan, 1938–1945*. New York: G.P. Putnam's Sons, 1972.

Durra, Mahmud al-. *Al Harb al-'Iraqiyya al-Britaniyya*. Beirut: Dar al-Tali'ah, 1969.

Elliot, Matthew. *"Independent" Iraq: The Monarchy and British Influence, 1941–1958*. London: Tauris Academic Studies, 1996.

Eppel. Michael. "The Elite, the Effendiyya, and the Growth of Nationalism and Pan-Arabism in Hashemite Iraq, 1921–1958." *International Journal of Middle East Studies* 30 no. 2 (May 1998): 227–50.

Eppel, Michael. *Iraq from Monarchy to Tyranny: From the Hashemites to the Rise of Saddam*. Gainesville: University of Florida Press, 2004.

Eppel, Michael. *The Palestine Conflict in the History of Modern Iraq: The Dynamics of Involvement 1928–1948*. Ilford, Essex: Frank Cass, 1994.

Fahd (Yusuf Salman Yusuf). *Kitabat al-Rafiq Fahd,* edited by Z. Khayri. Baghdad: al-Tariq al-Jadid, 1976.

Fieldhouse, D.K., ed. *Kurds, Arabs and Britons: The Memoir of Wallace Lyon in Iraq 1918–44*. London: I.B. Tauris, 2001.

Fitzsimons, M.A. *Empire by Treaty: Britain and the Middle East in the Twentieth Century*. Notre Dame: University of Notre Dame Press, 1964.

Gershoni, Israel, ed. *Arab Responses to Fascism and Nazism: Attraction and Repulsion*. Austin: University of Texas Press, 2014.

Gershoni, Israel and James P. Jankowski. *Confronting Fascism in Egypt: Dictatorship versus Democracy in the 1930s*. Stanford: Stanford University Press, 2010.

Gershoni, Israel and James P. Jankowski. *Redefining the Egyptian Nation, 1930–1945*. Cambridge: Cambridge University Press, 1995.

Ginat, Rami. "British Concoction or Bilateral Decision? Revisiting the Genesis of Soviet-Egyptian Diplomatic Relations." *International Journal of Middle East Studies* 31, no. 1 (1999): 39–60.

Glubb, John Bagot. *Britain and the Arabs: A Study of Fifty Years, 1908 to 1958*. London: Hodder and Stoughton, 1959.

Goldschmidt, Arthur Jr. *Biographical Dictionary of Modern Egypt*. Cairo: The American University in Cairo Press, 2000.

Gomaa, Ahmed M. *The Foundation of the League of Arab States: Wartime Diplomacy and Inter-Arab Politics 1941 to 1945*. London: Longman, 1977.
Grafftey-Smith, Laurence. *Bright Levant*. London: J. Murray, 1970.
Hadid, Muhammad. *Mudhakkirati: al-Sira' min ajli al-Dimuqratiyya fi al-'Iraq*. Beirut: Dar a-Saqi, 2006.
Hashimi, Taha al-. *Mudhakkirat Taha al-Hashimi, 1919*-1943. Beirut: Dar al-Ta'li'ah, 1967.
Helal, Ahmed. "Egypt's Overlooked Contribution to World War II." In *World in World Wars: Experiences, Perceptions and Perspectives from Africa and Asia*, edited by Heike Liebau, Katrin Bromber, Katharina Lange, Dyala Hamzah, and Ravi Ahuja, 217–47. Leiden: Brill, 2010.
Herf, Jeffrey. *Nazi Propaganda for the Arab World*. New Haven: Yale University Press, 2009.
Jackson, Ashley. *The British Empire and the Second World War*. New York: Humbledon Continuum, 2006.
Jackson, Ashley. *Persian Gulf Command: A History of the Second World War in Iran and Iraq*. New Haven: Yale University Press, 2018.
Jwaideh, Wadie. *The Kurdish National Movement: Its Origins and Development*. Syracuse: Syracuse University Press, 2006.
Kelly, Saul. "A Succession of Crises: SOE in the Middle East, 1940-45." *Intelligence and National Security* 20, no. 1 (2005): 121–46.
Kent, John. "British and the Egyptian problem, 1945-48." In *Demise of the British Empire in the Middle East*, edited by Michael J. Cohen and Martin Kolinsky, 142–161. London: Frank Cass, 1998.
Khadduri, Majid. "General Nuri's Flirtations with the Axis Powers." *Middle East Journal* 16, no.3 (Summer 1962): 328–36.
Khadduri, Majid. *The Government of Iraq*. Jerusalem: New Publishers Iraq, 1944, pamphlet.
Khadduri, Majid. *Independent Iraq: A Study in Iraqi Politics since* 1932. London: Oxford University Press, 1951.
Kingston, Paul W. T. *Britain and the Politics of Modernization in the Middle East, 1945–1958*. New York: Cambridge University Press, 1996.
Kirk, George. *The Middle East in the War*, part of the *Survey of International Affairs 1939–1946* produced by the Royal Institute of International Affairs (Chatham House). New York: Oxford University Press, 1953.
Kolinsky, Martin. *Britain's War in the Middle East: Strategy and Diplomacy,* 1936-42. New York: Palgrave Macmillan, 1999.
Lewis, David Levering. *The Improbable Wendell Willkie: The Businessman Who Saved the Republican Party and His Country, and Conceived a New World Order*. New York: Liveright Publishing Corp., 2018.
Lloyd, E.M.H. *Food and Inflation in the Middle East 1940–1945*. Stanford: Stanford University Press, 1956.
Louis, Wm. Roger. *The British Empire in the Middle East*. New York: Oxford University Press, 1986.
Lugol, Jean. *Egypt and World War II: The Anti-Axis Campaigns in the Middle East*. Translated by A.G. Mitchell. Cairo: Société Orientale de Publicité, 1945.
Lyman, Robert. *First Victory: Britain's Forgotten Struggle in the Middle East, 1941*. London: Constable, 2006.
Lyttelton, Oliver, Viscount Chandos. *The Memoirs of Lord Chandos*. London: The Bodley Head, 1962.

Manela, Erez. *The Wilsonian Moment: Self-Determination and the International Origins of Anticolonial Nationalism*. New York: Oxford University Press, 2007.
Marshall-Cornwall, James. *Wars and Rumours of Wars: A Memoir*. London: Leo Cooper, 1984.
Mazower, Mark. *No Enchanted Palace: The End of Empire and the Ideological Origins of the United Nations*. Princeton: Princeton University Press, 2009.
McDowall, David. *A Modern History of the Kurds*. London: I.B. Tauris, 2005.
McLoughlin, Leslie. *In a Sea of Knowledge: British Arabists in the Twentieth Century*. Reading: Ithaca Press, 2002.
Mitchell, Richard. *The Society of the Muslim Brothers*. London: Oxford University Press, 1969.
Mitchell, Timothy. *Rule of Experts: Egypt, Techo-Politics, Modernity*. Berkeley and Los Angeles: University of California Press, 2002.
Monroe, Elizabeth. *Britain's Moment in the Middle East 1914–1971*, new and revised edition. London: Chatto & Windus, 1981.
Morewood, Steven. *The British Defence of Egypt 1935–1940: Conflict and Crisis in the Eastern Mediterranean*. London and New York: Frank Cass, 2005.
Morsy, Laila. "The Military Clauses of the Anglo-Egyptian Treaty of Friendship and Alliance, 1936." *International Journal of Middle East Studies* 16, no. 1 (March 1984): 67–97.
Naguib, Mohammed. *Egypt's Destiny: A Personal Statement*. Garden City, NY: Doubleday & Company, 1955.
Newbury, Colin. *Patrons, Clients, and Empire: Chieftaincy and Over-rule in Asia, Africa, and the Pacific*. New York: Oxford University Press, 2003.
O'Sullivan, Adrian. *The Baghdad Set: Iraq through the Eyes of British Intelligence, 1941–45*. Palgrave Macmillan, 2019.
O'Sullivan, Christopher. *FDR and the End of Empire: The Origins of American Power in the Middle East*. New York: Palgrave Macmillan, 2012.
PAIFORCE: The Official Story of the Persia and Iraq Command 1941–1946. London: His Majesty's Stationery Office, 1948.
Pedersen, Susan. "Getting Out of Iraq—in 1932: The League of Nations and the Road to Normative Statehood." *American Historical Review* 115, no. 4 (2010): 975–1000.
Pedersen, Susan. *The Guardians: The League of Nations and the Crisis of Empire*. New York: Oxford University Press, 2015.
Playfair, I.S.O. *The Mediterranean and Middle East*, vols. 1–4. London: Her Majesty's Stationery Office, 1954.
Porath, Yehoshua. *In Search of Arab Unity 1930–1945*. London: Frank Cass, 1986.
Pratt, Lawrence R. *East of Malta, West of Suez: Britain's Mediterranean Crisis, 1936–1939*. Cambridge: Cambridge University Press, 1975.
Qazzaz, Ayad al-. "The Iraqi-British War of 1941: A Review Article." *International Journal of Middle East Studies* 7 (1976): 591–6.
Rafi'i, 'Abd al-Rahman al-. *Fi A'qab al-Thawra al-Misriyya Thawrat 1919*. Cairo, 1951.
Raugh, Harold E., Jr. *Wavell in the Middle East, 1939–1941: A Study in Generalship*. Norman: University of Oklahoma Press, 2013.
Robinson, Ronald. "Non-European Foundations of European Imperialism: Sketch for a Theory of Collaboration." 1972, reprinted in *Imperialism: The Robinson and Gallagher Controversy*, edited by Wm. Roger Louis, 128–51. New York: New Viewpoints, 1976.
Roper, Trevor, ed. *The Killearn Diaries, 1934–1946*. London: Sidgwick & Jackson, 1972.
Ryzova, Lucie. *The Age of the Efendiyya: Passages to Modernity in National-Colonial Egypt*. New York: Oxford University Press, 2014.

Ryzova, Lucie. "Egyptianizing Modernity through the 'New *Effendiya*.'" In *Re-Envisioning Egypt 1919-1952*, edited by Arthur Goldschmidt, Amy Johnson, and Barak A. Salmoni, 124–63. Cairo: The American University in Cairo Press, 2005.
Sadat, Anwar al-. *In Search of Identity: An Autobiography*. New York: Harper and Row, 1978.
Sadat, Anwar al-. *Revolt on the Nile*. New York: The John Day Company, 1957.
Sansom, A.W. *I Spied Spies*. London: George G. Harrap, 1965.
Satia, Priya. *Spies in Arabia: The Great War and the Cultural Foundations of Britain's Covert Empire in the Middle East*. New York: Oxford University Press, 2008.
Silverfarb, Daniel. *Britain's Informal Empire in the Middle East: A Case Study of Iraq 1929–1941*. Oxford: Oxford University Press, 1986.
Silverfarb, Daniel. *The Twilight of British Ascendancy in the Middle East: A Case Study of Iraq, 1941–1950*. New York: St. Martin's Press, 1994.
Simon, Reeva Spector. *Iraq between the Two World Wars: The Militarist Origins of Tyranny*, updated edn. New York: Columbia University Press, 2004.
Sluglett, Peter. *Britain in Iraq: Contriving King and Country, 1914–1932*. 2nd ed. New York: Columbia University Press, 2007.
Smith, Charles D. "4 February 1942: Its Causes and Its Influence on Egyptian Politics and on the Future of Anglo-Egyptian Relations, 1937-1945." *International Journal of Middle East Studies* 10 (1979): 453–79.
Stark, Freya. *Dust in the Lion's Paw: Autobiography 1939–1946*. New York: Harcourt Brace and World, 1961.
Stark, Freya. *East Is West*. 1945. Reprint, London: Century, 1986.
Tamkin, Nicholas. "Britain, the Middle East, and the 'Northern Front', 1941-1942." *War in History* 15, no. 3 (2008): 314–36.
Tarbush, Mohammad A. *The Role of the Military in Politics: A Case Study of Iraq to 1941*. London: Keegan Paul, 1982.
Taylor, Philip. *British Propaganda in the Twentieth Century: Selling Democracy*. Edinburgh: Edinburgh University Press, 1999.
Taylor, Philip. *The Projection of Britain: British Overseas Publicity and Propaganda 1919–1939*. Cambridge: Cambridge University Press, 1981.
Thomas, Martin. *Empires of Intelligence: Security Services and Colonial Disorder after 1914*. Berkeley: University of California Press, 2008.
Thomas, Martin. *The French Empire at War 1940–45*. New York: Manchester University Press, 1998.
Toprani, Anand. *Oil & the Great Powers: Britain & Germany, 1914–1945*. New York: Oxford University Press, 2019.
Tripp, Charles. "Ali Maher and the Politics of the Egyptian Army." In *Contemporary Egypt: through Egyptian Eyes*, edited by Charles Tripp, 45–71. New York: Routledge, 1993.
Tripp, Charles. "Egypt 1945-52: The Uses of Disorder." In *Demise of the British Empire in the Middle East: Britain's Response to Nationalist Movements 1943–55*, edited by M. Cohen and M. Kolinsky, 112–141. London: Frank Cass, 2010.
Tripp, Charles. *A History of Iraq*. New York: Cambridge University Press, 2007.
Vatikiotis, P.J. *The Egyptian Army in Politics: Pattern for New Nations?* Bloomington: Indiana University Press, 1961.
Vaughan, James. *The Failure of American and British Propaganda in the Arab Middle East, 1945–1957*. London: Palgrave Macmillan, 2005.
Vitalis, Robert. "The 'New Deal' in Egypt: The Rise of Anglo-American Commercial Competition in World War II and the Fall of Neocolonialism." *Diplomatic History* 20, no. 2 (Spring 1996): 211–39.

Vitalis, Robert and Steven Heydemann. "War, Keynesianism, and Colonialism: Explaining State-Market Relations in the Postwar Middle East." In *War, Institutions, and Social Change in the Middle East*, edited by Steven Heydemann, 100–45. Berkeley: University of California Press, 2000.

Warner, Geoffrey. *Iraq and Syria 1941*. London: Davis-Poynter, 1974.

Welch, David. *Persuading the People: British Propaganda in World War II*. London: The British Library, 2016.

Wichhart, Stefanie. "The Formation of the Arab League and the United Nations, 1944–1945." *The Journal of Contemporary History* 54, no. 2 (April 2019): 328–46.

Wichhart, Stefanie. "'Innocent Efforts': The Brotherhood of Freedom in the Middle East during World War II." In *Allied Communication during the Second World War: National and Transnational Networks*, edited by Simon Eliot and Marc Wiggam, 185–202. London: Bloomsbury Academic, 2019.

Wichhart, Stefanie. "A 'New Deal' for the Kurds: Britain's Kurdish Policy in Iraq, 1941–1945." *Journal of Imperial and Commonwealth History* 39, no. 5 (December 2011): 815–31.

Wichhart, Stefanie. "Selling Democracy during the Second British Occupation of Iraq, 1941–1945." *Journal of Contemporary History* 48, no. 3 (July 2013): 509–36.

Wichhart, Stefanie. "'What Britain Has Done for Islam': British Propaganda to the Islamic World During World War II, 1939–1942." In *Britain and the Islamic World: Imperial and Post-Imperial Connections*, edited by Justin Quinn Olmstead, 197–223. Palgrave Macmillan, 2019.

Wien, Peter. "Coming to Terms with the Past: German Academia and Historical Relations Between the Arab Lands and Nazi Germany." *International Journal of Middle East Studies* 42, no. 2 (May 2010): 311–21.

Wien, Peter. *Iraqi Arab Nationalism: Authoritarian, Totalitarian, and Pro-fascist Inclinations, 1932–1941*. New York: Routledge, 2006.

Williams, Manuela A. *Mussolini's Propaganda Abroad: Subversion in the Mediterranean and the Middle East, 1935–1940*. New York: Routledge, 2006.

Willkie, Wendell. *One World*. New York: Simon and Schuster, 1943.

Wilmington, Martin. *The Middle East Supply Centre*. Edited by Laurence Evans. Albany: State University of New York Press, 1971.

Wilson, Maitland. *Eight Years Overseas*. London: Hutchinson & Co., 1949.

Yapp, Malcolm. *Politics and Diplomacy in Egypt: The Diaries of Sir Miles Lampson 1935–1937*. New York: Oxford University Press, 1997.

Index

'Abd al-Ilah, Regent 19
Abdin Palace 3, 75, 79, 82–5, 89, 96, 110, 130, 137, 162, 165, 194 n.38
Ahali group 132–3, 169
Alexandria Conference 140–2
Alexandria Protocol 140–2
'Ali, Prince Muhammad 75, 78, 81
'Ali, Rashid 3, 27, 36, 40–6, 49, 58, 69, 93
 government 44, 49, 52, 55–7, 62, 71
 military crisis 52–5
 propaganda 70
 Wafd Declaration response 33
Allies 4, 33, 34
 and Iraqi declaration of war 91–3, 97–8
 Middle East 107
 military spending 112–13
Anglo-Egyptian Supplies Committee 85
Anglo-Egyptian Treaty 4–7, 9–11, 13, 37, 76, 79, 81, 105, 138, 142, 146, 160, 161, 164–6
Anglo-Iraqi Treaty 2, 4, 5, 16, 17, 41, 47, 48, 50, 51, 67, 71, 87, 174 n.19
Arab League 145, 152, 167, 171
Arab unity 3–4, 19, 22, 62, 92, 94–7, 108, 113, 138–42
Area Liaison Officer (ALO) 17, 71, 72, 154
Atlantic Charter 3, 91, 93, 94, 97, 104, 108, 133, 135, 138, 147
Auchinleck, General Claude 50, 63, 67
Axis. *See also* fascism; Germany; Italy
 broadcasts 56
 declaration of Arab policy 43–4
 influence 1, 19, 40, 41, 44, 67, 68, 82, 87, 88, 101, 116
 powers 20, 28, 43, 44, 48, 76, 86, 93, 94, 105, 143, 168
 propaganda 13, 31, 68, 94, 131, 142, 157
 Rashid 'Ali's advances to 43
 threat 2, 111, 134
'Azzam, 'Abd al-Rahman 22, 25, 95, 145, 171

Badawi, 'Abd al-Hamid 146
Banna, Hassan al-. *See* Muslim Brotherhood (Hassan al-Banna)
Basra 5, 17, 42, 45, 48–54, 57, 58, 68, 72, 87, 88, 94, 98, 100–2, 105, 107, 113, 117, 121
Bateman, C. H. 66–7
Bayliss, Colonel 115, 117, 123
Bevin, Ernest 156, 157, 164, 168
Black Book affair 108–12, 126–8, 136, 140
British
 bayonets 3, 75, 80, 83, 163
 control apparatus 3, 107, 116–18, 133, 159–60
 and Egypt 2–7, 9–11, 13, 14, 22, 25, 28, 37, 39–40, 66–7, 119, 143, 149, 150, 152, 153, 163, 164, 171
 and Iraq 2–7, 19, 26–7, 30, 41–3, 51–9, 67–73, 87–9, 116–18, 130–1, 136, 153–5
 publicity 29–30, 93, 97–100, 107–8, 134
British Council 29, 98, 100, 158
British embassy
 Baghdad 19, 47, 103, 118
 Cairo 13, 15, 28–9, 31–4, 68, 73, 151, 159
British Military Mission
 in Egypt 6, 14–15, 17, 26, 40
 in Iraq 6, 17, 29, 88, 118, 124, 154, 160, 169
Brotherhood of Freedom 32, 68, 102, 121, 122, 131–3, 146, 157–60
Busk, Douglas 169

Campbell, Ronald 167
Casey, Richard 96, 110
Chaplin, J. 70–1
Churchill, Winston 36, 39, 40, 53, 58, 62, 89, 91, 92, 94, 109, 110, 128, 136, 143, 144, 161, 168
Clayton, Brigadier Iltyd 30, 32, 65

Cold War 1, 171
Combined Intelligence Center Iraq (CICI), Col. Wood 71, 118, 124, 132
Cornwallis, Kinahan 48–53, 55, 58, 69, 72, 104, 115, 116, 121–2, 154–5
  Baghdad 57
  departure from Iraq 154–5
  Foreign Office 67–8
  Nuri's administration 114, 125
  optimism 87, 93
  treaty revision 152

D'Albiac (Air Vice-Marshal) 67
democracy
  Egypt 130–4
  Iraq 102, 130–4, 168–70
  liberal 11, 20
Durra, Mahmud al- 59, 189 n.91, 191 n.45

Eden, Anthony 40, 46, 48, 55–6, 77–9, 91, 101, 109, 150
  Mansion House speech 62, 95
Edmonds, C. J. 17, 29, 31, 36, 43, 47, 49, 51, 70, 72, 117, 122, 124, 125, 153, 154, 178 n.53
effendiyya 101, 133, 159, 199 n.62
Egypt
  Abdin Palace incident 3, 75, 79, 82–5, 89, 96, 110, 130, 137, 162, 165, 194 n.38
  agriculture 112
  army 6, 14, 22, 26, 39, 40, 65, 81, 82, 109, 110
  cotton 24, 33, 66, 85, 86, 112
  declaration of war 21, 23, 26, 28, 31, 35, 36, 39, 66, 92, 95, 143–5
  democracy 130–4
  economic challenges 66–7, 111–16
  Flap, the 75, 85–7, 108
  foreign policy 95–7
  inflation 66, 112–14
  and Italy 9, 11, 23, 32, 36–40, 107
  malaria crisis 126–8, 136, 140
  opposition parties 37, 82, 83, 108, 109, 128, 130, 133, 141, 143, 150
  politics 82–5
  postwar violence 162–8
  protectorate 5, 27, 39, 92, 113, 128, 137, 138
  three-legged stool 10–12, 83, 149, 165, 172
  treaty revision 39, 136–8, 145, 150–3, 155, 161, 162–8
empire by treaty 4–7

Farhud 57, 101
Farouk, King 10–12, 37, 38, 75–80, 82, 83, 85, 86, 108–11, 119–20, 127–30, 142, 151
fascism 1, 10, 11, 20, 102, 132, 175 n.8
Faysal, King 15, 69
First World War 5, 16, 21, 27, 41, 48, 53, 88, 94, 95, 116, 129, 150, 154, 163
Flap, the 75, 85–7, 108
FORCE IRAQ 63
Foreign Office 19, 33, 39
  and Kurdish revolt 116
  and Lampson 67, 77–9, 110
  and Nahhas 33, 67, 77–8
  and Rashid 'Ali 44
France
  and Lebanon 20, 24, 62, 92–6, 119
  and Syria 41, 62, 76, 96, 152
  Vichy 35, 62, 76, 77, 96
Futuwwa movement 18

Germany 10, 15, 18, 19, 21–5, 41, 43, 44, 56, 58, 61, 62, 68, 77, 87, 93, 146, 150
Ghazali 129
Ghazi, King 15, 19, 20, 120, 178 n.70
Grafftey-Smith, Laurence 31, 32, 73, 85, 164
Grice, C. R. 101–2
Grigg, Edward (Lord Altrincham) 150
Grobba, Fritz 18, 30, 56

Habbaniya 5, 48, 49, 52–5, 65
Habforce 53, 54
Hadid, Muhammad 157, 158, 170
Hasanayn, Muhammad 78–80, 83, 109, 127, 143, 165, 167
Hashimi, Taha al- 17, 23, 46–8, 94–5, 125
Henderson, Loy 118
Holt, Vyvyan 54–5, 102, 103, 154
Hourani, Albert 94, 131, 135
Husayn, Ahmad. *See* Young Egypt (Ahmad Husayn)
Husayni, al-Hajj Amin al- (the mufti of Jerusalem) 24, 41, 44

India 1, 2, 9, 13, 15, 28, 35, 42, 50–4, 56, 63, 68, 89, 107, 109, 114, 123
Iran
Abadan 5, 42
1941 invasion 73
Iraq
army 16, 17, 27, 40, 41, 48, 49, 52–4, 57, 70, 87, 96, 113, 115, 124
British control apparatus 116–18
British personnel 153–5
declaration of war 21, 23–4, 26, 92–5, 97, 113, 133
democracy 130–4, 168–70
economic challenges of war 88, 95, 111–16, 123
executive control 116–18
Golden Square 40, 48, 57, 58, 184 n.41
inflation 88, 98, 112–14
Kurds (*See* Kurds)
mandate 4, 5, 15, 17, 67, 72, 117, 124, 130, 154
and Northern Front 87–9
population 40, 125, 192 n.60
Rashid Ali coup 3, 27, 33, 36, 40–52, 55–9, 61, 62, 68–72, 77, 78, 87, 93, 101, 117, 119, 123, 162
second British occupation 191 n.45
treaty revision 3, 4, 23, 39, 136, 145, 150, 152–3, 161, 168–70
Iraqi Communist Party/communism 132, 133, 157, 168
Italy 5, 9, 11, 23, 32, 36–44, 47, 48, 57, 107

Jabr, Saleh 114, 115
Jamali, Fadhil al- 135, 147
Jwaideh, Wadie 132, 202 n.59

Kaylani, Rashid ʿAli al-. *See* ʿAli, Rashid
Khadduri, Majid 100, 130
Killearn, Lord (Miles Lampson) 10–12, 23–6, 28, 29, 35, 37–9, 45, 53, 61, 64–7, 89, 91, 95, 102–3, 119, 133, 145–6
Abdin Palace incident 75–80
and Anglo-Egyptian treaty 6–7, 105, 137, 151–2, 163–4
departure from Egypt 166–7
and Wafd 33, 66–7, 75–87, 108–12, 126–30, 143, 144, 151, 165
Kinch, E. 72
Kirk, Alexander 133
Knatchbull-Hugessen, Hughe 56
Kurds 69–70, 73, 88, 115–17, 122–6, 132, 154, 169, 170
Mulla Mustafa revolt 115, 116, 123, 169, 170, 202 n.60, 204 n.12

Lampson. *See* Killearn, Lord (Miles Lampson)
Landis, James 133
Lebanon 3, 20, 24, 34, 62, 92, 94–7, 119, 140, 145
liberal democracy 11, 20
Lugol, Jean 85
Lyon, Wallace 72, 73, 124, 154, 193 n.79
Lyttelton, Oliver 63, 78, 79

Mahir, Ahmad 10, 39, 111, 129, 142–5, 166
Mahir, ʿAli 22, 23, 25–7, 36–8, 58, 65, 66, 76, 81–3, 107, 119, 143, 166
Mahmoud, Muhammad 9, 10, 12, 22
Masri, ʿAziz al- 25, 26, 40, 65, 82
Middle East Command (MEC) 2, 38, 42, 50, 53, 61, 63, 87, 107
Middle East Intelligence Centre (MEIC) 15
Middle East Supply Center (MESC) 64, 85, 115, 123, 133, 134, 159
Midfaʿi, Jamil al- 69–71, 93
Ministry of Information 1, 28–32, 49, 56, 63, 64, 98, 100–3, 132, 160, 171
Monck-Mason 19
Monckton, Walter 78
Monroe, Elizabeth 1, 3, 162
Moyne, Lord 141, 142, 144
Mufti of Jerusalem. *See* Husayni, al-Hajj Amin al- (Mufti of Jerusalem)
Munich crisis 1, 9, 11, 13, 15
Muslim Brotherhood (Hassan al-Banna) 12, 66, 82, 83, 101, 127, 130, 145, 165, 167
Mustafa, Majid 123–5
Mustafa, Mulla. *See* Kurds

Nahhas, Mustafa al- 11, 84
and Abdin Palace 3, 82–5, 162
Arab unity 96–7, 139–42
and Black Book affair 108–12
fall of government, 1944 129, 142

Foreign Office 33, 77–8
Nuri and 97
patronage 108, 113, 138
Wafd government 84, 126–9, 142
National Democratic Party (NDP) 169
Newton, Basil 17, 23, 29–31, 36, 40–2, 44, 45, 47–50
Nuqrashi, Mahmud al- 145, 151, 163, 165, 167

oil 1, 3, 5, 24, 42–4, 50, 53–6, 61, 72, 86–8, 101, 105, 115, 116, 136, 156
One World (Willkie) 104
Operation Trout 42
Osman, Amin. *See* ʻUthman, Amin

Pachachi, Hamdi 125–6, 139, 154
PAIFORCE 51, 105, 118
Palestine
Arab revolt 13, 15, 16
and Egypt 12, 13, 92, 108
and Iraq 67
and Syria 16, 17, 21, 24, 36, 43, 65, 68, 71, 81, 88, 101, 104
Palestine Defence Society (PDS) 17, 47, 68
pan-Arabism 17, 96
patronage
Nahhas, Mustafa al- 108, 113, 138
patron-client relations 125, 128, 171, 172, 179 n.18
Saʻid, Nuri al- 26–7, 113, 114, 116, 125
wartime 25–7
Perowne, Stewart 68, 97, 98, 102, 103, 154, 159
Persia and Iraq Command (PAIC) 2, 87, 88, 104, 105, 118
Persian Corridor 1, 73, 92, 102, 107
Peterson, Maurice 79, 93, 96, 119, 136
Political Advisory System/Political Advisers (PAs) 72–3, 116, 117, 124, 155, 159, 169
propaganda
Axis 13, 31, 68, 94, 131, 142, 157
British 27–31, 97–104 (*See also* British, publicity; Ministry of Information)
German 17, 18, 25, 52, 101
Italian 10–11

Quinan, Lieutenant-General Edward 53, 63

Renton, General 124, 160, 169
Roosevelt, Franklin 94, 103, 143, 147, 157, 168
Rushbrook Williams, Laurence 28, 30–2, 64, 101
Russell Pasha, Thomas 13

Sabri, Hassan 37–9, 67, 81
Sadat, Anwar al- 40, 65, 191 n.30
Saʻdist Party 10, 39, 80, 109, 142
Sadr, Sayyid Muhammad al- 70
Saʻid, Nuri al- 3, 16, 22, 26, 71, 73, 103, 114
Arab unity 96–7
Blue Book 94–5
declaration of war 92–5
government 27, 101, 122, 125
politics 113, 114, 116, 125, 141
San Francisco Conference 144–7, 154, 163
Sansom, A. W. 65, 165, 166, 183 n.36, 191 n.30
Saudi Arabia 12, 56, 97, 140, 145
Scaife, Christopher 102, 131, 132, 160
Second World War. *See also* Iraq, and Northern Front; Persian Corridor
Arabs and 135, 161
El Alamein 85–7
end of war 149–50, 161–2
fall of France 35–6
Italian declaration of war 35–6
in Middle East 1, 4
Operation Compass 44–5, 50
Western Desert campaign 38–9, 50, 63, 65, 67, 73, 85–7, 104, 107
Shaʻrawi, Huda 4, 80
Shawkat, Sami 17, 18
Shiʻi/Shiʻa/Shiʻism 18, 46, 50, 69–71, 100, 101, 114, 125, 141
Sidqi, Ismaʻil 9–10, 161, 166–8
Sirri, Husayn 39, 66, 67, 70, 76, 77, 81
Smart, Air Vice-Marshal H. G. 52–3, 62
Smart, Walter (Oriental Counsellor) 29, 81, 83, 84, 96, 101, 108, 109, 127, 137, 138, 151–3

Soviet Union 56, 61, 67, 77, 86, 92, 93, 105, 121, 122, 132, 133, 138, 151, 155, 167, 170
Special Operations Executive (SOE) 32, 47, 49, 55, 56, 63, 65, 68, 71, 98
Stark, Freya 32, 54–5, 68–9, 102, 131, 158, 159
status quo policy 12, 22–5, 27, 35, 62, 68, 75, 162
Stone, General R. G. W. H. 79, 81–2, 110
Stonehewer-Bird, Hugh 157, 159, 162
Sudan 5, 22, 29, 33, 83, 107, 119, 143, 163, 164, 168
Suez Canal and Suez Canal Zone Base 2, 4–6, 13, 14, 119, 137, 150, 163, 166, 172
Suwaydi, Tawfiq al- 169, 170
Syria 15–17, 19–21, 24, 53, 61–3, 65, 68, 71, 73, 92, 94–7, 152

Tedder, Air Marshal A. W. 52, 61
Thompson, G. 25, 27, 104, 105, 115, 125, 156
Thornhill, Colonel 65
Transjordan 12, 43, 63, 73, 94, 97, 140, 142, 145, 150, 152

'Ubayd, Makram 84, 143, 144, 155
United Kingdom Commercial Corporation (UKCC) 114
United Nations. *See* Allies
United Nations Declaration (January 1942) 3, 92, 97
United Nations Organization 146, 152, 163, 168
United States 1, 32, 64, 92–4, 97, 102, 103, 118, 122, 127, 133, 134, 136, 139, 152, 156, 161
  economic interests 133
  in Egypt 32, 64, 134, 136, 152, 161
  in Iraq 93, 102, 118, 133, 136, 161
  presidential election (1944) 139, 142
'Uthman, Amin 25, 77–8, 83, 112–13, 129, 143, 145, 164–5, 167

Wafd Party 14
  anti-British press campaign 12
  declaration 33–4, 37, 144
  Egypt and 142–3
  fall of the 142–3, 166
  government 78, 84–7, 92, 96, 98, 110, 112, 130, 142
War Office 24, 42, 58
Wavell, General Archibald 15, 30, 32, 37, 38, 40, 42–5, 50, 53, 54, 56–8, 63, 66, 78, 161
Willkie, Wendell 103–4
Wilson, General Henry Maitland 15, 28, 38–40, 63, 81, 87, 104, 110, 179 n.2

Young Egypt (Ahmad Husayn) 12, 14, 26, 29, 39, 66, 82, 83, 101, 127, 145

Zaghlul, Sa'd 150, 163
Zionism 12, 94, 139, 142

Ingram Content Group UK Ltd.
Milton Keynes UK
UKHW022337270323
419281UK00004B/73